WRITING IN THE DARK

Will Loxley was born in London and brought up on the Suffolk coast. He studied at Newcastle University before joining the creative writing course at University of Oxford. He now writes about the strange and wonderful worlds of modern British literature, and lives in Sheffield.

WRITING IN THE DARK

Bloomsbury, the Blitz and Horizon Magazine

WILL LOXLEY

WEIDENFELD & NICOLSON

First published in Great Britain in 2021 by Weidenfeld & Nicolson
an imprint of The Orion Publishing Group Ltd
Carmelite House, 50 Victoria Embankment
London EC4Y 0DZ

An Hachette UK Company

1 3 5 7 9 10 8 6 4 2

FSC
MIX
Paper from
responsible sources
FSC® C104740
www.fsc.org

www.weidenfeldandnicolson.co.uk
www.orionbooks.co.uk

For my parents, for Meg

'*Experience?*' *said Iles. He waved experience aside.* '*My dear man, that's the great illusion. Experience of the last war's worse than useless. War's been revolutionised.*'

Nigel Balchin, *The Small Back Room*

'*One is ridiculous to be still alive and the best thing is to keep one's mouth shut.*'

V. S. Pritchett, *Midnight Oil*

'*The belief in literature as part of life, the belief in the power of the creative imagination to give meaning to life; these were surely going to be as important as ever in the times we were about to enter.*'

John Lehmann, *I Am My Brother*

Contents

CONTENTS

Cast of Characters

Characters, as they appear at the declaration of war

Virginia Woolf – now aged fifty-seven. Internationally famous novelist and essayist, associated in the public imagination with the original 'Bloomsbury Group' of her sister Vanessa Bell, Vanessa's husband Clive Bell, Roger Fry, Duncan Grant, John Maynard Keynes, E. M. Forster, Lytton Strachey and Desmond MacCarthy. Co-founder of the Hogarth Press. Author of *Mrs Dalloway*, *To the Lighthouse*, *A Room of One's Own* and *The Years*. Living in the village of Rodmell in Sussex.

Leonard Woolf – Virginia's husband since 1912; also an original member of the Bloomsbury Group. Author, Fabian Society member, editor of the *Political Quarterly* and co-founder of the Hogarth Press. About to turn fifty-nine. Known for the novel *The Village in the Jungle* and various political pamphlets.

Christopher Isherwood – thirty-five. 'Holds the future of the English novel in his hands' (W. Somerset Maugham). Popular among the young for his Berlin stories and one novel, *Mr Norris Changes Trains*. Screenwriter and playwright, working in collaboration with his best friend W. H. Auden.

W. H. Auden – thirty-two. A poet and the leading influence among the young writers of the day. Bound inextricably in the public mind with two other poets, Cecil Day-Lewis and Stephen Spender, the 'Oxford Group'. Best known for the poems 'Spain', 'Musée des Beaux Arts' and 'To a Writer on His Birthday'.

John Lehmann - poet and editor, also aged thirty-two. Younger brother of Rosamond Lehmann, who wrote the *succès de scandale*, *Dusty Answer*, and the actress Beatrix Lehmann. Founder of the popular literary periodical *New Writing* in 1936. Managing director of the Hogarth Press since 1938. Author of *A Garden Revisited* and co-editor of *Poems for Spain*.

Stephen Spender - poet, thirty years old. The most overtly political of the Auden-Spender-Day-Lewis triumvirate, enjoying a semi-deified status among the young. Journalist during the Spanish Civil War, briefly the poster boy for the British Communist Party. Author of *Poems 1933*, *Vienna*, *Forward from Liberalism* and *Trial of a Judge*.

Peter Watson - about to turn thirty-one. Living on a trust fund of £1,000,000 from the estate of his father's Maypole Dairy Company, whose shops were then ubiquitous in Britain. Has recently fled Paris from the invading Wehrmacht, leaving his self-destructive boyfriend, Denham Fouts, and a valuable collection of paintings.

Cyril Connolly - literary critic, previously of the *New Statesman*. About to turn thirty-six. Self-proclaimed laziest man in west London and obsessed with his own failure as a novelist. 'Smarty boots' (Evelyn Waugh and Nancy Mitford). Wrote *Enemies of Promise* which reshaped the ambitions of young writers and one relatively unsuccessful novel, *The Rock Pool*. Feared by older novelists, that he would deem them *passé*.

George Orwell - thirty-six-year-old author of *Down and Out in Paris and London*, *The Road to Wigan Pier* and *Homage to Catalonia*, also a minor novelist. A political firebrand, adrift between the organised Right and Left. Veteran of the Workers' Party of Marxist Unification (POUM) and the Spanish Civil War. Recently returned from a convalescent trip to Morocco. Living in a ramshackle cottage in Hertfordshire and running a small shop.

Dylan Thomas - poet, twenty-four years old. Currently residing on the Welsh coast, where he is notorious for drunken pub antics. Poem 'And Death Shall Have No Dominion' published in the *New English Weekly* in May 1933.

Julian Maclaren-Ross – aged twenty-seven. Soon-to-be novelist, short-story writer and screenwriter, but currently working as a door-to-door vacuum-cleaner salesman. The most audacious dresser in literary England.

Evelyn Waugh – one of the nation's favourite comic novelists. Famed for bitchiness. Soon to turn thirty-six. Author of *Decline and Fall*, *Vile Bodies* and *A Handful of Dust*.

PART 1

DARKNESS AS THICK AS HELL

(1939–41)

1

Long Goodbye

'If I sent for you, would you come?'

That was how Christopher Isherwood put it, and how it was heard by his lover Jack Hewit. The taxi, which Hewit had brought round to Isherwood's mother's, now picked its way through South Kensington, swinging past St Philip's church onto the long, straight Cromwell Road. Mansion flats, some strapping and red and Victorian, with gold-leaf lettering flashing behind dark glass in their entrance archways, others in the more cerebral modern styling of the last two decades, rose up on either side, settled and stoic in the early evening dark after a Thursday working day. They joined the Brompton Road and then climbed north to where Hyde Park was glimpsed in the interstices between buildings and, finally, shown in full aspect. The warm light of streetlamps shivered on the glistening pavement; black branches stood dormant and dripping.

Isherwood's question was set up, with its sleight of hand placement of the subjunctive, to put the emphasis of decision-making on Hewit. Really, he was asking something different: '*If* I sent for you, would you come?' This was how Isherwood wished to leave things: without ultimatum and, as his friends in England soon came to feel, in active avoidance of clarity, convincing them that they had somewhere missed the point, or been too unworldly to grasp what was going on. It had been much the same with Isherwood's mother, back at Pembroke Gardens. She, too, had been sold a less jarring picture of her son's plans. They would, of course, involve that 'most restless unpeaceful person', the famous poet Wystan Auden, who liked to chain-smoke in her house and drop ash all over the carpet. She had heard all of their arguments but remained unconvinced. Every day of the past week she had watched her son coming and going from innumerable social engagements, their goodbye delayed until the latest possible moment. By that time a certain wistfulness had been allowed to settle over her. Who could say whether they would even see each other again? But such thoughts would have to go unexpressed. Instead, keepsakes were exchanged and great shows of heartiness were made. Travelling towards the river, Isherwood was leaving the territory of his mother, coming as close as he ever had to cutting the cord from the home that they had intermittently shared since 1928, thirteen years after the death of his father in the First World War.

Isherwood and Hewit arrived at Waterloo station having both been in tears during their taxi ride. It was here that they would part, and Hewit handed Isherwood over to Auden, who likely wore his heavy herringbone overcoat over a rumpled work suit with haphazard bow tie. The poet, who stood half a foot over his novelist counterpart, had a long, doughy face, teeth which pushed slightly forward on his lips, and the childlike combination of blond eyebrows and long lashes. His hair was a schoolboy's mouse brown, and uncarefully cropped. On the platform, more familiar faces huddled around to see them off. They were booked on the earliest possible train, set to arrive in Southampton by evening for a preliminary night in their cabin beds, but at least where no further goodbyes would have to be made. 'It was sad, sad as dying, to leave those loved ones behind,' Isherwood reflected later. But both he and Auden were determined to feel optimistic. As the train was about to depart, E. M. Forster had asked 'Shall I join the communist party?' 'No,' Isherwood had answered.

As the train pulled out, there was a nasty sharp wrench, and then the familiar trundling motion as they sank into their seats. Silently, Isherwood experienced a surge of guilty relief at the thought of the insuperable distance that now divided them from the waving, well-wishing friends on the platform. He looked at Auden and both grinned, 'grins which took us back, in an instant, to the earliest days of our friendship'. Suddenly, they were twelve and nine years old again, with all their lives ahead of them. 'Well,' Isherwood said, 'we're off again.'

'Goody,' said Auden.

The two-hour train journey down to Southampton, for the 19 January departure of the French liner *Champlain*, bound for New York, afforded an opportunity for reflection. During the past year, various solutions had been offered to Isherwood to answer the question of what he would do when the war came. The best, and most plausible, had come from the poet and editor John Lehmann, who had a spare room that Isherwood could move in to. But even while expressing interest in this course of action, Isherwood had privately been holding out, like an auctioneer, for the more coveted offer from Auden. If Auden suggested some other course of action, then he would probably go along with Auden. Being with Auden meant 'an unaccustomed freedom' which was the ability 'to speak his mind - to say things which he hadn't known were in it, until the moment of speaking'. Isherwood could think of no one else who understood him nearly as well. So here they were.

Privately, both held very similar reasons for wanting to make the journey, though whether these had been voiced is unknown. For

Isherwood, the principal factor was that he couldn't stop travelling. The mechanism had been set going, he felt, during those years
of wandering around Europe with his German boyfriend Heinz
Neddermeyer. But he was also, as he had, when he thought about
it, always been, running away from himself. Life was okay so long
as his own affectations and neuroses, the encumbrance of his own
personality and the behaviour which he loathed in himself, were
not given time to establish themselves, or to be acknowledged. 'I
could remain in Portugal, for example, as long as I could believe in
an objective Portugal. But, sooner or later, Portugal would dissolve
and reveal itself as the all-too-familiar, subjective "Isherwood Portugal". Then I fled in disgust.' This provided, perhaps, an answer to
the question that was then very much on Isherwood's mind: 'Am
I a deserter?' As his friends and family would agree, it was difficult
to be a deserter of a country where one had spent as little time in
recent years as he.

He had caught a brief glimpse of New York the previous summer,
under the guidance of a friend, George Davis. They had peered
down upon the island from the viewing platforms of art deco skyscrapers, buildings which, in Auden's words, 'proclaim the strength
of Collective Man'. They went to parties and brothels, witnessed a
fight in a dive bar in the Bowery, heard Maxine Sullivan sing in
Harlem, went to Coney Island for the Fourth of July, and met and
chatted to, among others, the great Orson Welles. We 'drank all
day long and took Seconal every night to make us sleep', Isherwood remembered. In that summer of 1938, America had remained
objective, sparkling and brilliant, like a whole different planet to
the England that had raised him. In America, Isherwood could be
someone else entirely. He could bury his own heel-dragging, self-
doubting personality behind layers of showmanship. In the land
of go-getters, he could talk faster and louder and more brilliantly
than anyone else in the room. A life-dream could be realised in the
writers' rooms and studio sets of Hollywood.

As a vignette, however, that summer was 'false, hysterical', and he had returned to England raving about Manhattan and convinced, like every tourist, that New York is the United States. Such a demeanour was typical of Isherwood's 'vulgarity' of the year before, a period which, in remembering, now made him squirm. He had just finished the Chinese travel book *Journey to a War*, co-authored with the man now sitting beside him, and was enjoying his enormous success and celebrity status in London during that 'post-Munich winter'. Isherwood and Auden were arriving, in public view, as a package, with their careers hitched together, having known each other since childhood. Although it probably did not register with the British public that Auden had become a Faber poet at the age of twenty-three, or that the magazine *New Verse* had just run an 'Auden Double Number', it had not escaped their notice that within these two young writers there seemed to be contained the ethos of an entire generation. It was a generation, as Auden wrote, which came to replace another which 'has had its day'.

That message had an extraordinary resonance. For the teenagers and young adults of the day, writes Richard Davenport-Hines, Auden was a 'meeting-ground . . . enthusiasm for his work seemed a measure of intelligence as well as an indicator of literary or sociopolitical seriousness'. For their elders, to understand Auden and Isherwood was to finally decipher the strange habits and lifestyles of a whole population, separated from them by the First World War. The press latched on to Auden and Isherwood as that generation's ringleaders. Isherwood's individual success so far was limited to one full novel and a novella which built on established themes. The novella was *Sally Bowles*, later to form a segment of the episodic *Goodbye to Berlin*, offering Isherwood's most notorious character, the young Englishwoman who has run away from home to exist more irreverently in pre-Hitler Berlin. Sally winds up having an abortion in a scene which Isherwood had to fight against publishers to keep; it did not, of course, seem so shocking to this unshockable generation.

The novella had begun to boom, noted Virginia Woolf, whose Hogarth Press had published the book, in November 1937. The prose was accessible, and while the average reader might not have gone to Auden's poetry, they could through Isherwood find a window into this new mentality. Isherwood's brand of writing was easily identified, and his now trademark use of his own name for the protagonist's ('[a] convenient ventriloquist's dummy', as he explained it) had an unintended self-mythologising effect which said that the author was really living all of the things he was writing about. If fiction had provided the Auden-Isherwood partnership with a more direct link to the public, their recent collaborative success in arguably the nation's favourite form of literature, theatre, had sealed the deal for them as notable public figures. *The Ascent of F6* had filled every seat when it debuted at the Birmingham Repertory Theatre. Then, as Isherwood's biographer Peter Parker points out, *On the Frontier*, which opened in Cambridge in October 1938, even received a favourable review from *Horse and Hound*. Together, they were Britain's 'unofficial poet laureate' and its most prized young novelist.

While Auden remained suspicious of public attention, as a result remaining more fastidious, Isherwood had been intent on cultivating the 'public lives' of himself and Auden as a duo, the *enfants terribles* now mingling in society and at a high point in their collaborative endeavours. Out in public, as soon as cameras appeared, Isherwood would throw a chummy arm around his writing partner. Surrounded by strangers, they were 'as polite as mere acquaintances'; Isherwood, in particular, knew all the 'tricks of modesty'. It mattered little that Auden would afterwards have to reproach his friend for some foolish comment; in the moment, he would allow Isherwood his spotlight, his disapproval betrayed only by a slightly furrowed brow and a twitch at his mouth. The same restraint was displayed when, at parties with friends, Isherwood would begin to boast about this new-fangled lifestyle and exuberant sex life. It was an attitude that Auden was regularly moved to condemn, and Isherwood was charged with being the cruellest and most unscrupulous person Auden had ever met. Other friends seemed lately almost embarrassed in his company, Isherwood in his new persona a volatile element which few could match up to. He knew this as well as anyone. Social life was a game which Isherwood played at expert level, pushing away those who saw through him and performing his most enthusiastic self around those only just met; only he - in the mirror, perhaps, shaving - saw who he really was. To understand Isherwood's writing, one must accept the narrator and namesake protagonists to be different beings, one floating above the other, separated by self-loathing. This was lying awake at night, face crushed into the pillow, torturing oneself for one's past indiscretions, but done for a public audience.

Then there was the war. It was 28 September 1938 when Isherwood, like so many others, had finally conceded his hopes of a shift in the political direction. Horace Wilson had now returned to England having failed to deliver the letter to Hitler that detailed Chamberlain's proposed settlement between Germany and Czechoslovakia. Hitler had been in a bad mood, and refused to listen; as the British media picked up the story, the resounding feeling across the nation was that the final shreds of hope were vanishing down the drain. It was that afternoon that the German army had begun to mobilise, and Parliament had met to introduce conscription. 'London is all gas masks and children screaming when they're fitted on,' Isherwood wrote in his diary. He had been fitted for one himself and found that 'you can hardly breathe through them at all'. The smiles of the officials at the fitting stations were a veneer that only went so deep; everyone else, it seemed, was either enlisting or running away from town. There were trenches being dug in Hyde Park, and the ubiquitous slogan, 'Keep calm - and dig.'

Air Raid Precaution (ARP) notices went up all over town, on the railings of the squares and in windows. Two days later, when the prime minister himself travelled to Germany to make amends, Isherwood would feel an unutterable sense of relief at the knowledge of the Germans having been paid off and, temporarily, appeased. This was the Munich Agreement, which allowed Hitler his way with the German-speaking Sudetenland region of Czechoslovakia in exchange for his word that no further claims would be made on European territory, but which was celebrated, including by the prime minister, as a perfect success, without injury to any party. Isherwood would declare to his friends, in an attitude of 'high-minded disgust', that England had helped betray the Czechs, but privately savour this moment of relaxation. A war had been postponed, he thought, and a war postponed is a war which may never happen. The newsboys cried 'No war! No war!' and a country which was primed to mobilise now seemed slumped and flat, as if the wind had gone out of it. Deeper down, below even Isherwood's private jubilation, was the truth: it was humiliation for Britain. 'It was not', T. S. Eliot wrote, 'a criticism of the government, but a doubt of the validity of a civilization.'

Unlike others, perhaps, for whom the announcement of war would represent a total and unprecedented change of circumstances, Isherwood did not experience any disproportionate alarm from its developments. The build-up had been so gradual, since Isherwood's own time in Berlin when stormtroopers had blocked the entrances to department stores, and now, with diplomatic interference from all sides, the Nazi wave seemed less implacable. For one who had been so close to the stories at the time when National Socialism began to assert itself as an electoral force, the war was 'that familiar, six-year-old shadow in the background' and little more. He even found himself assuring his friends that they would 'probably have lots of excitement and even fun - including shelter parties and sex pickups in the blackout.' It was no use running away, he had initially thought, because he had already known the madness of London in wartime, and would only take that madness with him. The actual prospect of attack figured surprisingly little in his mind, and, Isherwood insisted, had less to do with his emigration than anyone would believe.

Though their fellow train passengers might not have thought it to look at them, Isherwood and Auden were veterans of the proto-war, having travelled towards the site of danger and the battlegrounds of the Sino-Japanese conflict. As Isherwood wrote in his diary, he was 'one of the relatively few people in [London] who have been in a modern air raid'. It was not war itself that frightened him, any more than it did anyone else. It was war in a country with which he already had such a fragile, even antipathetic, relationship. 'I fear the atmosphere of the war, the power which it gives to all the things I hate - the newspapers, the politicians, the puritans, the scoutmasters, the middle-aged merciless spinsters,' he wrote. It was English authority which he dreaded, and which he felt now to be closing in. He read multiple newspapers each day and hated Chamberlain and his colleagues as much as he hated Hitler. The past - his adolescence in England - held him by the throat and choked him. Yes, there were the Nazis, but would he ever be able to take them half as seriously as he took his first headmaster?

When Isherwood wrote that he had a 'terror of uniform and all it implies' he was including the entire infrastructure of British exceptionalism - the obscene cult of antiquity, systems which took pleasure in belittlement, hegemonic masculinity - which refused modernity and revelled in a dull status quo. He remembered a childhood lived in the shadow of his father's soldiering, of the supposed virtues of the fighting man's way of life. Despite being subjected, as every child of his era was, to a 'falsified and sentimentalized view' of the 1914 war, Isherwood's father would in due course reveal a private abhorrence of the institution to which he belonged. 'I remember his telling me, before he left for France, that an officer's sword is useless except for toasting bread, and that he never fired his revolver because he couldn't hit anything with it, and hated the bang.' Devoid even of his father's superficial sense of duty, Isherwood could only feel that he lacked the necessary conviction for war. On top of this, like much of his nomadic, Germanophile cohort, Isherwood had a conflict of interest in the form of friends who would, in theory, soon wear the colours of the Wehrmacht. This was, principally, Heinz, the boy he had met in Berlin in 1932 and who had been his companion until they parted, finally, in Luxembourg in 1937. As they chugged their way through the Home Counties and South Downs, the figure of Heinz now loomed large in his mind, and was accompanied by a familiar hypothetical question. If Isherwood had in his hand a button, which, on pressing, would decimate an entire Nazi army, including, of course, Heinz, then would he do so? And what if Heinz was there not out of cowardice or moral infection but because he wanted to be? The answer was still no, as it always was. Isherwood would call himself a pacifist, but he knew that pacifism had positive obligations – 'you had to do something instead of fighting'. All he had was a negative decision: if war came, he wouldn't fight.

It was a crushing feeling to lose his political faith at a time like this. Even nationalism, with its reactionary sense of purpose, was preferable to this lead-heavy emptiness and disgust. The belief, prevalent in the 1930s, that wholesale political change was imminent had become foundational to so many lives, a kind of God substitute. But more than not getting better, the world had actually become worse than it was before. Christopher's conviction that he must stay in England and face the war with his family and friends had lasted as long as his spirit could take it. He was now quite far along into a personal crisis which would eventually culminate in his conversion to Vedanta, a school of Hindu philosophy. He had urgently needed to make a change in his life and was, one suspects, happy to defer the question of his future to Auden.

For Auden, it was also a question of place. Theirs was a peripatetic generation, not only for the innate pleasure of movement, as Christopher had felt, but for the way that life in different countries was lived with varying degrees of interference and expectation from external influences. The aim always was to find a place where social values reflected internal ones. England was dull and settled in its ways; it had long since decided that its own way of life was superior to all others ('So utterly self-satisfied,' as Christopher put it). Oxford had offered a brief respite, but away from its punts and quads and dreaming spires, England remained the small-minded and insular community that had birthed the pecuniary public school and other Mrs Grundys of Auden's childhood. It was 'terribly provincial', Auden later wrote. 'It's all this family business. I know exactly why Guy Burgess went to Moscow. It wasn't enough to be a queer and a drunk. He had to revolt still more to break away from it all.' In his plan to become an American citizen, Auden felt confident that he would achieve this final transcendence. 'Become an American citizen and you've crossed to the wrong side of the tracks,' he teased.

Auden believed in travel as a kind of spiritual inquiry. It was something he had realised three years before, during the impromptu trip to Iceland that would inspire his brilliant *Letters from Iceland*. It came to him one day, while exploring the alien terrain of what was then a seldom-visited country, that 'an effect of travelling in distant places is to make one reflect on one's past and one's culture from the outside'. He could, in theory, write even in exile or isolation. As Richard Davenport-Hines has written, in travel, Auden was deliberately unsettling himself; he was 'inspired by an intellectual masochist's need of the neurosis of estrangement'. About the war, and the potential for America to be entirely a new start, he was perhaps more realistic than Isherwood. Even in Iceland, edging towards the Arctic circle, Auden had known that whatever happened in Europe, he and everyone he knew was implicated irreparably. It was already too late, he decided: 'We are all too deeply involved with Europe to be able, or even to wish to escape.' But taking a direct part in politics, Auden felt, had the consequence of falsifying a writer's work. In truth, Auden was less committedly anti-fascist than were many of his friends. He wasn't a pacifist and would never become one – unlike many others, he had actually gone to Spain to fight against Franco – but Auden's left-wing convictions had always been determined somewhat by a desire to conform. As would become clear, there was gap of comprehension between the political persona Auden presented as in his poetry and the more forlorn, less decisive character behind the pen, as if in his innocent brain he could not quite believe that 'now matters are settled with gas and with bomb' ('Danse Macabre' (1938)). He had gone off to Spain knowing, with bashful self-awareness, that he would be 'a bloody bad soldier' (not least because of his absolute horror of seeing people in pain) but wanting to follow in the footsteps of his hero Wilfred Owen. Auden's actual, personal beliefs were concerned more with the religious feeling he had inherited from his mother. It was to these that he returned again and again as the war in Spain raged on, and he was deeply wounded by the idea of churches being razed or anti-religious propaganda being put out by the government. Though he retained a clear allegiance with that side, there were now two competing worldviews which he wanted nothing more to do with.

It was not until they were safely aboard the boat and really alone together that Christopher and Auden could stop 'playing parts'. For years, they had been performing for friends, comrades and the media, repeating slogans created for them by others. Now they wanted to stop. They stood on the deck of the *Champlain* the following day as two men abandoned by the causes they had put their energy and support behind, Auden as a Christian and both passionate about their identities as gay men. This, for Isherwood in particular, had been the deciding factor. Despite the Soviet Union's

1917 pronouncement on the rights of the individual in private, Stalin was now intent on locking up homosexuals for heavy prison sentences. In this respect, there was little that distinguished the great liberators in Russia from the bogeyman Nazis. At some point, Isherwood had made the firm resolution to always refer to the treatment of homosexuals as the test by which every political party and government must be judged. Despite having tried his hardest to minimise the Soviet betrayal - 'After all, anti-homosexual laws existed in most countries' - it was this incursion that hurt the most. 'If the Communists claim that their system is juster than capitalism,' he wrote in *Christopher and His Kind*, 'doesn't that make their injustice to homosexuals less excusable and their hypocrisy even viler?' Isherwood had always felt somewhat embarrassed that he could only muster a romantic approval of communism, where others were totally pragmatic, but now his indifference offered him a route out. What he had accepted glibly could also be dismissed glibly. He resolved to extricate himself from the communists. Turning to Auden on the deck of the ship that day, he had declared, 'You know, it just doesn't mean anything to me anymore - the Popular Front, the party line, the anti-fascist struggle . . . I simply cannot swallow another mouthful.' 'Neither can I,' Auden had replied.

Something changed the moment those two men stepped across the gangway of the *Champlain*. On an extant passenger list, their ticket numbers, 30542 and 30543; ages, thirty-four for Christopher and thirty-one for Auden; and occupations, both 'Author', betray little of either their celebrity or the significance of their passage. While other passengers, like nineteen-year-old Violet Finn, a nurse previously of Kent, are noted as intending to settle in the USA, Isherwood and Auden's 'country of intended future permanent residence' remains 'England NI'. Neither, however, had plans to return. They kept this fact from their families and friends. What was quickly publicised as a national betrayal was really a personal betrayal felt by many separate individuals in their long list of acquaintances. Each, in some way, had bought into the new philosophy of life which was communicated in the trilogy of Auden-Isherwood plays, or sent packaged as novels or poems from the continent. It had offered them hope. As passengers 30542 and 30543 boarded the boat, an era was concluded, a 'literary-political movement' yanked close to extinction. For the community of writers, artists and readers they were leaving behind, this was the gust of wind that swept away the final, guttering flames of optimism around which they had huddled. Even more than the lousy diplomatic capitulations of four months before, the exodus of a generation's ringleaders inspired a deep, existential fear of what was to come, and whether or not they now had the wisdom, or equipment, to face it.

Across London, friends and rivals alike were united in vitriol towards the famous duo. Virginia Woolf sat down with T. S. Eliot, whose face was 'sallow and shadowed', and listened to him speak of his disappointment in the whole affair. 'Tom said the young don't take art or politics seriously enough,' she recorded. Three decades later, more extreme opinions – of duplicity and betrayal in the eleventh hour – were still keenly felt. Devouring Auden's obituary in the *New Statesman* in 1973, Anthony Powell was vindicated. 'I'm delighted that shit has gone,' he announced. 'It should have happened years ago . . . scuttling off to America in 1939 with his boyfriend like a . . . like a . . .' There was no description strong enough.

John Lehmann, on the other hand, could only regret that they had not remained in the country to stand by his side and ease his burden. 'How often I was to think in the coming years of all that had been lost by their not sharing what the rest of us were experiencing in Britain under siege,' he wrote later in life, adding 'what treasure there would have been for us to lighten the darkest days.'

2

Dishonourable Gentlemen

The question was addressed to the House of Commons by Major Sir Jocelyn Lucas, a Conservative who in a by-election of 1939 had been elected Member of Parliament for Portsmouth South. He had previously held the office of Portsmouth District Officer for Sir Oswald Mosley's British Union of Fascists. He was fifty-one years old, grey-haired and with a faint moustache, and outside of Parliament would typically be found in country tweeds and wellington boots, accompanied by his eponymous crossbreed 'Lucas Terriers', 'the gent of the working-terrier world'. Sir Lucas was a product of Sandhurst and had risen to the rank of major during his service in the 4th Battalion, Royal Warwickshire Regiment in the First World War. He was the author of two books: *Pedigree Dog Breeding: For Pleasure or Profit* (1925) and *Hunt and Working Terriers* (1931).

Sir Lucas wished to know whether the Member for Rushcliffe, Ralph Assheton, 1st Baron Clitheroe, Winston Churchill's Minister of Labour, would see to it that British citizens of military age, such as Mr W. H. Auden and Mr Christopher Isherwood, who had gone to the United States and expressed their determination not to return to this country until war was over, would be summoned back for registration and calling up, in view of the fact that they were seeking refuge abroad?

The young, narrow-featured baron stood up to answer: 'I have no information with regard to Mr Isherwood,' he said. 'Mr Austin gave an undertaking before leaving the country that he would return if called upon to do so; he is outside the age groups so far required to register under the National Service (Armed Forces) Act.'

George Mathers, Scottish Labour Whip, interjected: 'On a point of Order. There is no mention of Mr Austin in this Question.' Assheton had confused Auden, whom he clearly hadn't heard of, with the tennis star Henry Wilfred 'Bunny' Austin, a conscientious objector. Assheton's mistake proved too much for some fast-working journalists to disentangle, so that in certain parts of the country it was reported that Christopher Isherwood and a W. H. Austin had escaped to America together.

Sir Lucas continued: 'Is my honourable friend aware of the indignation caused by young men leaving the country and saying that they will not fight? If they are not registered as conscientious objectors will he see that they lose their citizenship?' Sir Lucas was referring to the flurry of indignant letters sent to magazines like the *Spectator*, which had begun off the back of reviews of Auden and Isherwood's rather ironically titled *Journey to a War.* According to the poet and editor John Lehmann, this hostility had been brewing for some time. 'The intellectuals of the 'thirties were by no means popular at that time with Members of Parliament, influential Civil Servants and Generals in authority,' he wrote. It was too easy for those in power to point out that, at every stage in the long escalation to war, the writers had been loudly proposing a radically different strategy, fraying public opinion and curtailing their more nuanced diplomatic approaches. They had, after all, been harping on about Russia since the late twenties; they had opposed the government's appeasement measures. Actually, wrote Lehmann, 'all our miserable efforts had been directed towards preventing the mess.' But their association, in particular, with international communism and the war in Spain, would hang over them. Gallons of fuel were now being gleefully drained over this fire by the writer Wyndham Lewis, who was pushing the British public's buttons when, in the *Bystander*, he demanded that Auden return the King's Gold Medal for Poetry which he had been awarded a couple of years before. Even better, Lewis wrote, it should be 'publicly detached from the poet's bosom by the Poet Laureate, standing in a hollow of Foot Guards, after which the poet's fountain pen is formally broken across his knee by a sergeant-major amid the rolling of drums . . . A little job in the frontline could then probably be found for all the returned prodigals of good health and military age.' The ensuing comparison to the front-line poets of 1914 does not need to be spelled out.

'No exit permits would be issued by the Home Office now,' was the Minister of Labour's only reply.

Seymour Cocks, Member for Broxtowe, then joined in to drive the point home: 'Will the honourable gentleman take steps to deprive these people of British nationality?'

3

Two Bloomsburys

For much of her lifetime, London had been illuminated by gas lamps. The lamplighter, with his pole on his shoulder, would, if you happened to be standing at the window at the right time in the evening, be seen to emerge into the dusk from behind the right-hand pane, leaving little stars and pools of yellow light in his wake. Stopping at each lamp along Hyde Park Gate, a trail which led to the dead-end of the cul-de-sac, he would lift the thin pole, eyes crossed on its point, as if disturbing a wasp's nest; shortly, to a keen ear, would be heard the click of the gas-chain, and then a plop as the flame burst in the mantle, a green flower exploding against the quiescent blue of evening. As the flame settled, it became 'shaped like the eyes in peacocks' feathers'. These men had made up the silent brigade of the gloaming, like folkloric guardians of dreams, bringing a moment of focus and serenity after the flurry of another day in the capital. To a child, recalled one writer, the memory of that little pool of colour had been infinitely consoling before sleep. And, in the stillness of a night of ugly dreams, what could have been more comforting than to hop out of bed and see the lamp burning there, so still and calm, so brave in the dark?

That was the time of landaus, victorias and hansom cabs. In 1939, as Virginia Woolf worked in her study, quite a different figure was doing the rounds, perhaps not so different in age or appearance, but irreconcilable in his intentions, like a fidgeting navvy arriving to do the job of a man on strike, or the young postman who has replaced a village stalwart. These men were coming to take away the light, to ensure the unobstructed passage of an approaching, menacing darkness around the labyrinth of the city. The lowering of the lights signalled the start of a hushed suspense, and then, perhaps, the violent crash of the orchestra. The trick then was to hide, to anticipate the man's return by some other circadian inflexion, and to bolt the windows and cover them up, board oneself in. Fortunately, the warmest days had now passed, the draught through a jarred window becoming less indispensable, but this meant also that the sun would be setting earlier and earlier. Come winter, the average Londoner would have to subsist on the meagrest ration of natural light.

'So with the lamps all put out, the moon sunk, and a thin rain drumming on the roof a downpouring of immense darkness began,' Woolf wrote in *To the Lighthouse*, of a different situation. 'Nothing, it seemed, could survive the flood, the profusion of darkness which, creeping in at keyholes and crevices, stole round window blinds, came into bedrooms, swallowed up here a jug and basin, there a bowl of red and yellow dahlias, there the sharp edges and firm bulk of a chest of drawers.' This was the Isle of Skye, along a coastline so remote that 'there was not a house scarcely, not a single village for miles on end'; only sandhills dwindled away into darkness. The setting now was central London, just a klick north of Lincoln's Inn Fields, or south of St Pancras station, amid the interlocking residential squares of Bloomsbury. The three-sided Mecklenburgh Square - on its west side it erupted into the foliage of the square garden, and then Coram's Fields behind – was a repeating pattern of stucco ground floors, wrought-iron balconies, and three featureless upper storeys of golden brick, now smoke-stained black. All were tall, boxy, and clumsily narrow – some so much so that they might be deemed worthy only of half numbers. The effect of these buildings, when compared against their showier architectural cousins, the sugar sculpture John Nash Regency terraces, or the more Palladian homes of nearby Bedford Square, was a kind of hesitant grandeur, placing privacy above all else.

Even though this was central London, the dark was 'thick as Hell', and, Virginia wrote in her diary, 'one seemed cut off'. Those early days of the war, she kept her ears pricked, unable to suppress the feeling of having entered 'open-eyed into a trap' and anticipating danger at every moment. Because she could not see what was going on outside (the blackout curtains by now fastened in place), she had to listen. What did she hear? The occasional whistle sounded, a call for assistance (Where? To whom?), and then died away. Stammered footfall meandered across the square as people 'grope[d] their way to each other's lairs'. The wind, faint but detectable, bristled through the trees of the park.

Outside, on these nights, one felt that time had wound back to the Middle Ages, and that the spot where one was standing, previously a co-ordinate corresponding to a populous, modern city, was now the territory of dark, silent, ominous countryside. It was a 'forest of black houses', and one expected 'a badger or a fox to prowl along the pavement'. Any light was delivered directly from the firmament, which on calm nights presented itself vast and highly polished to Londoners for the first time. Now and then, some residue of modern life would manage to cross over into this wild, sequestered place. 'A torch blinks. An old gentleman revealed. He vanishes. That red light may be a taxi or lamppost.'

Such was Virginia Woolf's way of seeing the world, with what her husband, Leonard Woolf, called 'an almost terrifying profundity and beauty'. It began with objects, or other signifiers - the long, black cigarette holder, the rosewood and satinwood secretaire, the loose, curlicued strokes of one of her sister's still lifes on the wall - which are swept up into a vast and kaleidoscopic sensory experience. These objects present themselves to the observer with the full weight of their solidity and provenance, as when, in *The Years*, Eleanor Pargiter sits at her desk. Her particular set of objects, arranged before her, include a silver candlestick, a miniature of her grandfather, a set of tradesman's books and a spotted walrus with a brush on its back given to her by her brother:

> It's awfully queer, she thought, touching the ink-corroded patch of bristle on the back of Martin's walrus with the point of her pen, that *that* should have gone on all these years. That solid object might survive them all. If she threw it away it would still exist somewhere or other. But she never had thrown it away because it was part of other things - her mother for example . . .

Each object presents itself quizzically. It presses the observer for an answer to the question, asked by so many of Virginia's characters, 'What is the meaning of life?' Within that were other related problems: 'Am I that, or am I this? Are we one, or are we separate[?]' At this point the unconscious is set going, searching through its library of impressions for others which seem fit. But, again, the question finds no satisfactory answer. The blinking torches and spectral figures and hovering red lights begged the same question now.

There is a dependence on these landmarks of normalcy - of domestic life - as if contained within each thing was a fragment of one's identity, or evidence of one's reality, and that if they were found to be not in place, or were unable to be called upon, then all might suddenly fall apart. In this communion with the inanimate, or unconscious, was the foundation of intense solitude. This attachment to one's surroundings becomes so intense – so desperate – that even the slightest disturbance in their order could expose one's fragility. This was the threat presented by the war; the threat of interruption or distortion. In *To the Lighthouse*, the anxious but resolute matriarch Mrs Ramsey becomes fixated on the composition of the fruit in a fruit bowl. Throughout dinner, she has been keeping guard over it, 'jealously, hoping that nobody would touch it'. Her eyes go 'in and out among the curves and shadows of the fruit', and this action soothes and reassures her. But then, alas, a hand reaches out to take a pear, and the whole thing is spoiled. 'No happiness lasted; she knew that.' Or, later on in the novel, as Lily Briscoe watches Mr Ramsey and his children move out to sea on a boat, she notices a sudden change in the sea and clouds and boats and 'the view, which a moment before had seemed miraculously fixed, was now unsatisfactory. The disproportion there seemed to upset some harmony in her own mind. She felt an obscure distress.' Revelations in fundamental physics, appearing in the newspapers with increasing frequency since Virginia's adolescence, seemed to suggest the fixed and inanimate actually to be something constantly in motion – particles swimming and swirling on every surface. 'What was it made of?' asks Eleanor Pargiter, 'Atoms? And what were atoms, and how did they stick together?'

Despite her strong and self-sufficient nature, it was nonetheless a fragile world that Virginia inhabited, a world poised on a knife's edge due to her intense receptiveness and sensitivity to change. The building in whose study she now sat was the recently acquired new home of the Hogarth Press, the small publishing outfit she had started with her husband in 1917 with a small press they bought on the Farringdon Road and which was now run from their basement, and consequently the Woolfs' temporary lodgings for their trips up to London.

They had left their previous premises, no more than a ten-minute walk away in Tavistock Square, because of ongoing building work in the two plots next door. In May 1939, a large portion of Tavistock Square was being turned into offices. It had been rumoured as early as 1931 - an entire row of houses, including number 52, which was the Woolfs', to be pulled down - then postponed, and now was finally happening, with a few exceptions including the Woolfs' property. Virginia and Leonard's writing - Leonard was at that time making the final revisions to *Barbarians at the Gate* - as well as general life had had to go on against the persistent and intrusive soundtrack of destruction and construction. 'My head is a tight wound ball of string,' Virginia had written, at the end of her tether. 'To unwind it, I lie on my Heal's chair bed and doze of an evening.' The noise unsettled her. It was an additional attack on her nerves even more disturbing than her previous grievance, the traffic on the arterial Southampton Row which ran up from the Strand, through Holborn, and cut around the square garden which, she confessed, 'gets at me'. 'I long for 37 Mecklenburgh Square,' she had written, thinking presumably of how those higher numbers were tucked away behind tall trees in a miniature cul-de-sac created by the perimeter of the park, '[it] will be heavenly quiet'. At that point, it seemed unlikely that they would be successful. One of their tenants at 52 Tavistock Square, a Mr Pritchard, was by occupation a solicitor, and had agreed to do the negotiating on their behalf; he would, however, be coming up against the Duke of Bedford Estates, needing to convince them to surrender the current lease long before it was due to end. The Woolfs had not initially been able to set up the Press at number 52 because of the belief of the Bedford Estate that housing a publisher would create a precedent regarding commercial opportunities in the square, and 'vans would stop at the door'.

Virginia and Leonard went over to Mecklenburgh Square on 13 July. The first challenge was furnishing its rooms. Virginia decided she would want to have electric lighting fitted in the kitchen. Other questions, such as how they would move all of their books, carpets and furniture, only deflated her. 'The practical difficulty appals,' she wrote.

It was 24 August by the time they moved in. Rather than heavenly quiet, those first days in the house were 'complete chaos'. The upstairs flat, where she and Leonard would sleep, was 'in such a mess - very small, very crowded'. There were as yet no beds or carpets, nowhere they could sit down and rest, only the 'perpetual need for clearing drawers, arranging furniture'. The stairs creaked exasperatedly as they went up and down with big bits of furniture often found to be too large for the rooms. The kitchen was very small. The Hogarth Press clerks, assisting with the move, began to bicker and 'scream[ed] like parrots'. In the end a Miss Woodward left in floods of tears. Virginia's temper continued to rise throughout the ordeal; all they had set out to do was to make the flat liveable - they would only be there for two or three days each fortnight - but even that was proving impossible in the current circumstances. No doubt she was wishing to be back in Rodmell in the South Downs, clearing her head with a turn on the terrace or pulling on her wellington boots to 'flounder over the marsh'. On top of the confusion of the house was the fact that there was nowhere in London where the war could be escaped. 'Very few buses. Tubes closed. No children. No loitering. Everyone humped with a gas mask. Strain and grimness.' What upset Virginia most was the way that all the magic seemed to have been rendered out of her beloved city. No longer, it seemed, would its streets and alleys spark in her flights of fancy, and bring peace to a troubled mind; now, the city had become 'merely congeries of houses lived in by people who work'. All was 'serious and concentrated' when she required it to be free and malleable, an extension of her imaginative world.

'Virginia Woolf,' recorded John Lehmann, now a partner at the Press, 'was one of the writers who felt that the only thing that made sense was to devote oneself to one's work, to the inner world of order as the outer world collapsed in disorder.' This was her biography of Roger Fry, a close friend and former member of the Bloomsbury circle who had died unexpectedly in 1934 after a fall at his home in Surrey. It was at this time that Virginia had reluctantly agreed to write his biography; she had been asked to do so on multiple occasions by both Fry's partner, Helen Anrep, and his sister Margery. But had she not been too close to the subject? 'One cannot escape the impression that, though she was keen to try her hand at a real biography, a "solid" book, she regretted her promise before the work was done,' wrote Lehmann. Virginia had been half in love with Fry for his immensely lively mind, the fresh bubble of his ideas in many long discussions they would have on painting and the art of writing. After Fry, Virginia confirmed, there was 'such a blank wall. Such a silence. Such a poverty. How he reverberated!' Writing about Fry could have been, but was not, a labour of love. Aside from the painstaking nature of the biography process was the constant awareness that she was trying to capture - must, for her own happiness and sense of accomplishment, capture - something which was incompatible with any 'summing up'. Fry was 'a saint who laughed', a man who 'made goodness seem desirable'. But how, she asked, could she describe 'the pure delight "of watching a flower unfold its immense cup of red"?' Those who knew him best would not even attempt to do so. And yet this was what she had been tasked with, and what the subject's relations evidently expected from her.

She had started writing about Fry in April 1938 - a rather morbid landmark in her career (Virginia was then fifty-six; it was twenty-three years since her debut, *The Voyage Out*) in that she had reached the point when a writer is required to become retrospective. Then, after eight novels, she had craved its solid, dependable ground, the practical rather than creative difficulty of fact-finding - perhaps too the chance to look outside of herself, to not have to give so much of herself to the world. Few, if any, gave as much of themselves to their writing as Virginia. The process of turning herself inside-out, for her novels, was so violent that on more than one occasion, overwhelmed with exhaustion and depression on the completion of a project, it had come close to killing her. It was impossible to know how tumultuous the effect on Virginia's mind would be when, in Leonard's words, 'the umbilical cord was severed and the MS sent to the printer'; she would torture herself imagining bad reviews. This time she was determined to anticipate the 'horrible anticlimax' of finishing a book, and to already have the next one under way. So she began *Roger Fry* as she was 'drowsing away' the final revisions of her essay-book *Three Guineas*. 'I must ward off the old depression,' she wrote in her diary, 'the book finished, what's the use of it, feeling.' Her doubts about *Three Guineas* were too severe, and she fully expected its publication to 'excite nothing but mild sneers'. People would say 'How very inconsequent and egotistical Virginia Woolf is!' and the falling star of her career would finally burn out. She would be 'no longer famous, no longer on a pedestal, no longer hawked in by societies'. Virginia pictured herself like George Eliot, who in later life 'became one of the butts for youth to laugh at, the convenient symbol of a group of serious people who were all guilty of the same idolatry and could be dismissed with the same scorn.'

What Virginia perceived as her fall from favour had begun when she was 'decapitated' by Wyndham Lewis and 'Miss Stein'. In his essay 'Virginia Woolf: "Mind" and "Matter" on the Plane of Literary Controversy', Lewis had held Woolf up as the paradigm of militant feminism or 'sex-nationalism', even going so far as to offer a mock apology to those critics who would think him fatuous for even mentioning a name that was 'taken seriously by no one any longer today'. Rather exasperatingly, Lewis's indignation was directed at a paper Virginia had read no less than fifteen years ago to the Heretics Society in Cambridge, back when the 'Edwardian' giants of H. G. Wells, John Galsworthy and Arnold Bennett were threatened by the Joyces, Forsters and Eliots. Virginia had argued then that the real fracture was in the understanding or presentation of human character, which she felt had fundamentally changed 'in or about December, 1910'. Lewis could affect no pity for Virginia's complaint that the Edwardian novelists had equipped readers poorly with any tools for understanding the subtleties of the human spirit, most catastrophically the female one. He argued instead that she was merely interpreting a great societal shift from the perspective of her feminised 'Bloomsbury' world. The Bloomsbury Group were 'minor personalities, who were impelled to arrange a sort of bogus "time" to take the place of the real "time"'. In Woolf's method there was entirely lacking the 'realistic vigour' of a James Joyce, for example, and therefore, in the eyes of most readers, her insistence on prioritising the spiritual over the material world would be self-defeating. 'It's true that after *The Waves*, or *Flush*, scrutiny I think found me out,' Woolf fatalistically reflected; 'I was aware of an active opposition.' 'Bloomsbury is ridiculed; and I am dismissed with it.'

It is easy to be made to feel frivolous for one's past behaviour, as Lewis would have wished Virginia to feel, but this does not prove that such behaviour was wrong. Grinding along with her biography of Roger Fry, thoughts of Old Bloomsbury were at the front of Virginia's mind. Central to any retrospective criticism of that cohort was its perceived exclusivity and snobbishness, as if the sole purpose of its London gatherings was to continue the hijinks of Cambridge. If this was true of some of the group, it did not apply to Virginia. To her, it had been an incredibly necessary turning point in her young life, more so than Lewis could possibly have imagined.

'Bloomsbury is ever so much more interesting than Kensington,' Virginia had remarked after arriving in Gordon Square with her sister, Vanessa. This move took place upon the death of their father, and the point at which they began their independent life as adults.

The death of Sir Leslie Stephen was, inevitably, a moment of liberation from the long nineteenth century, for which others would
yet have to wait another ten or fifteen years. Sir Leslie had never
been tyrannical, but during his lifetime it was a given that the girls
would be only appendages to his lifestyle and household. Now,
it seemed, anything was possible. As Rosamond Lehmann would
write in *Invitation to the Waltz*, 'What happens to the descendants
of those Victorian grandees?' To which Virginia might have said,
as she did in one *Common Reader* essay, 'Money is no longer going
to do our thinking for us.'

Life in this broad square suited Virginia. In 1904 it was 'the most
beautiful, the most exciting, the most romantic place in the world':

> It was astonishing to stand at the drawing room window and look
> into all those trees . . . The light and the air after the rich red gloom
> of Hyde Park Gate were a revelation. Things one had never seen in
> the darkness there – Watts pictures, Dutch cabinets, blue china –
> shone out for the first time in the drawing room at Gordon Square.

Having ascended from the cul-de-sac of Hyde Park Gate, where
sympathetic neighbours had daily stopped the girls on the pavement to talk local affairs, Virginia and Vanessa now felt themselves
to be unleashed on the real London. The 'muffled silence' of their
Kensington nook became a 'roar of traffic'. And then a sea of new
faces, sinister and strange, who 'prowled and slunk' past their
windows.

Inside the house, they exploded out of the late Victorian, upper-
middle-class bubble that had carried them through to adulthood.
Red plush, black paint and William Morris wallpaper transmog-
rified into white and green chintzes and, on the walls, 'washes of
plain distemper' – the curtains had been thrown open and a new
age ushered in. 'We were full of experiments and reforms,' wrote
Virginia for a short vignette she read aloud to her friends. To an

audience in 1928, these revisions might have appeared trifling; but after the glacial and systematised Victorian years, their significance could not be underestimated. They were going to do without table napkins, have coffee after dinner instead of the Stephens' customary tea at nine o'clock. 'Everything was going to be new,' Virginia read, 'everything was going to be different.'

Even greater shifts forward - paradigm shifts - were to take place in due course, when the young men began to amble in, among them the 'astonishing fellow' Clive Bell, the 'essence of culture' Lytton Strachey, and 'that violent trembling misanthropic Jew' Leonard Woolf 'who had already shaken his fist at civilization'. These men, the two sisters would immediately have noticed, had no manners 'in the Hyde Park Gate sense', and soon all barriers of reticence and reserve had come down between the sexes. Conversation was no longer the 'light, ceremonious' confection of those evenings with family friends when 'at seven thirty dress and hair overcame paint and Greek grammar'; instead it fizzed and ricocheted, and nothing was off limits, not even that great taboo sex itself. No longer were they only asked to admire and applaud when their male relations played the intellectual game. It was a revolution.

To Virginia, even in 1928, this earlier period had represented 'a great advance in civilization'. Were they allowed to be as exalted as their continental counterparts, they would have made the point that 'Bloomsbury' stood not only for a social circle but for an artistic sensibility that was the passion of some of the nation's foremost artists and critics. They lived, at first, in the 'variegated lights' cast by the post-impressionist movement in France and now in Britain with the artist Augustus John. They put these paintings in the galleries of London for all to see. At this early juncture, the movement represented an explicit and very necessary reaction against bourgeois Victorianism. Lytton Strachey, in his *Eminent Victorians*, made to look foolish some principal nineteenth-century 'heroes', and Roger Fry rattled the cage of a stagnant and insular Royal

Academy. Suddenly, as happens sometimes, the questions of art - abstract issues of form and symbol - seemed again matters of great urgency. Fry especially saw in the London of the 1910s the potential for a 'real society', arising spontaneously out of a period of nationwide philistinism: 'It was to be a society of people of moderate means, a society based upon the old Cambridge ideal of truth and free speaking, but alive, as Cambridge had never been, to the importance of the arts. It was possible in France; why not in England?'

Fry knew that without such a group formation where ideas could be discussed in common, 'the young English artist tended to become illiterate, narrow-minded and self-centred with disastrous effects upon his work'. And then there were further permutations of Bloomsbury. Despite the intellectual predominance of Strachey, Bell and Fry in the 1910s, it was Virginia and E. M. Forster's novels of the twenties that best justified the group's cultural seniority. It was the genius of these two novelists that sealed the legacy of the group, with Virginia's output of 1925 to 1931 among the high-water marks of modern literature.

But had that Bloomsbury time been a real 'time', of the kind that they were always having in France? Or was it, in fact, only the aftermath of more seismic developments in Paris, with London being sucked along in the wake of that titanic vessel of art production? The very concept of a group, an enthusiastically shared and altruistic identity, as Fry had conceived it, seemed un-English. Fry was 'always hoping that he had discovered some such centre', Virginia wrote in his biography, and 'naturally, he was often disillusioned'. Public notoriety, moreover, has never been an accurate reflection of achievement. But it had been Virginia's life; the Bloomsbury 'friends' were her real friends, its activities her activities. Perhaps its significance was less dramatic than Lewis had implied it needed to be. Certainly, as young women without a formal education, Virginia and Vanessa had got from it an invaluable experience; but it was 'probably much the same pleasure that undergraduates get when they meet friends of their own for the first time'. Virginia tended to object to the collective noun 'Bloomsbury', as if the term embarrassed her. Indeed, after the poet Stephen Spender published a book in which Bloomsbury was a point of discussion, Virginia had told him 'rather sharply' that if he insisted on referring to her as belonging to Bloomsbury then she would refer to him and his neighbour William Plomer as 'Maida Vale'. And yet Spender's supposed *faux pas* reveals an important fact: if 'Bloomsbury' as a single creative unit now seemed little more than a construction to Woolf and Lewis, then it was definitely still perceived that way by younger generations, for whom it had represented an undeniable and major influence. 'The label "Bloomsbury",' Spender conceded, 'was applied to people more by others than by themselves.' Alix Strachey, ten years younger, remembered Virginia as being 'so much part of the Bloomsbury scene when I was living in Blooms-bury - indeed, one felt she was the centre of it'. Strachey contrasted the 'extremely highbrow Bloomsbury Group' against 'other per-haps more friendly people whom I knew', and hardly a day went by in which she did not hear Virginia talked about 'by my friends and by almost everyone I met'. John Lehmann's relationship with Virginia 'began with an ardent youthful hero-worship': 'She was irradiated in my eyes with the halo of having written *Jacob's Room*, *To the Lighthouse* and *Mrs Dalloway*. No other books seemed to me to express with anything like the same penetration and beauty the sensibility of our age.'

She was the 'sacred centre' of the adored, and oftentimes feared, Bloomsbury circle. For Christopher Isherwood, Bloomsbury mem-bership guaranteed an indelible and unmistakable watermark on all of its creative output. One need only open *To the Lighthouse*, *The Common Reader* or *The Waves* and read a couple of pages, he said, to become immediately 'a distant relative of the Bloomsbury fam-ily' in 'the inner sanctum, the Woolf drawing-room'. More likely,

Virginia merely resisted the idea of Bloomsbury as a kind of insti-tution, or bearing any discernible structure; for her that would be to drain it of its spontaneous and explorative beauty.

Wyndham Lewis's attack on Virginia was as bitter and deceit-ful as they come. It was, in actual fact, an attack on Roger Fry, with whom Lewis had been affiliated at Fry's Omega Workshop in Fitzroy Square. It had been Fry's greatest idea, to establish a work-shop where, during the working day, fine artists could apply their skills to artisanal projects, namely furniture-making, and so gener-ate a steady income which in turn would allow them to continue as painters. It was to be a new economic model for artists' lives. By doing this they would assert the freedom of art 'from all tram-mels and tyrannies', and, to judge by the popularity of the Omega products, it had so far been a success. But by 1914 a sort of splin-ter group had emerged with Wyndham Lewis at its helm, and Fry was reporting to Duncan Grant that 'the Lewis group do nothing even now but abuse me'. They sent round a circular to all prospec-tive customers of the workshop claiming that inside the operation there was much less 'generosity of dealing and care for art' than had been advertised. Fry, as leader, they said, was a 'Pecksniff-shark, a timid but voracious journalistic monster, unscrupulous, smooth-tongued and, owing chiefly to its weakness, mischievous.' As one of Fry's most famous affiliates, Virginia could hardly avoid the blast of anger Lewis sent their way.

Lewis's essay on mind and matter was published in 1934, in his book *Men Without Art*. Virginia had seen it announced in the *Times Literary Supplement*. 'Chapters on Eliot, Faulkner, Hemingway, Vir-ginia Woolf,' she recorded in her diary, 'now I know by reason and instinct that this is an attack.' Although there were more influ-ential writers than Lewis, none was at that point making such a concerted attempt to kill her off as in Lewis's claim that she was responsible for the feminisation of white Europe. Virginia imagined he still had influence in the more masculine intellectual centres of the universities. 'I am publicly demolished,' she concluded, 'nothing is left of me in Oxford and Cambridge and places where the young read Wyndham Lewis.'

In writing about Roger Fry, Virginia was conjuring up a time of great excitement in her life, in which the most exciting factor was inclusivity. By 1939, however, she felt herself to have been shunned by what comparable groupings there were. Most recently there was the dissenting, iconoclastic voice of Cyril Connolly, who in his book *Enemies of Promise* had lumped Virginia in with the 'Ivory Tower' old guard. He, too, pitted her against more sincere writers, in this case not realists per se but the less mannerist, more content-heavy 'vernacular', thus defining Woolf as an obstacle to literary progress. Consequently, in Virginia's diaries, Connolly mutated into 'baboon Connolly' with his 'cocktail criticism' who '[brought in] the roar of the Chelsea omnibus', spoiling the intimacy of Bloomsbury. Unfortunately for Virginia, unlike Lewis who was now seen as what Auden called 'that lonely old volcano of the Right', Connolly had the ears of the young. Her outlook was grim: '[I] am now, I think – let me see – out of date, of course, not a patch, with the young, on [E.] Morgan [Forster]; yet wrote *The Waves*, yet am unlikely to write anything good again; am a second-rate, and likely, I think, to be discarded altogether.' By 1938 she had believed her fate to have been sealed; for the rest of her life her territory would be obscurity, her art the displeasure of critics. The question was whether this mattered to her or not. After sending off the final draft of *Three Guineas*, she was euphoric. 'I now feel entirely free,' she wrote. 'Why? Have committed myself, am afraid of nothing. Can do anything I like.' A month later the feeling still held: 'I am an outsider. I can make my way: experiment with my own imagination in my own way. The pack may howl, but it shall never catch me.' She was like Septimus Smith in *Mrs Dalloway*, 'who gazed back on the inhabited regions ... a drowned sailor, on the shore of the world', and felt 'an isolation full of sublimity; a freedom which the attached can never know'.

This was what Virginia called a 'mountain summit moment' - the sensation of 'looking out at peace from a height'.

At other times, however, the voices of her detractors got inside her head to chip away at her resolve. The slurs she anticipated - 'charm and emptiness' played on her mind most often - would be all the more hurtful because, for perhaps the first time, she had bent to the will of public opinion. They had called her writing dec-orative and inconsequential and so in response, in *Three Guineas*, she had given them her truest and most violent feelings, the anger of the highly educated woman who is permitted no influence in public life. To have attempted to placate her critics in this way would be revealed as all the more shameful when - Virginia knew what was coming - their grievances only shifted to new issues. She was angry because she felt betrayed. Just as in her personal life she seemed to be 'forever climbing the endless stair; forced; unhelped; unthanked; a mere slave to some harsh . . . destiny', she was upset to have received no thanks or enthusiasm from the young, for whose benefit she had 'toiled'.

BRACING FOR IMPACT

Virginia liked to fill every waking moment with questions of her writing. Any chance of happiness or well-being depended on the unobstructed release of the deep reserves of creative energy which fidgeted inside her. When her writing was going well it 'whirled [her] like a top miles upon miles over the downs'. Looking back on her fifty-seven years she felt that her art was no less absorb-ing then than when she was 'a little creature, scribbling a story in the manner of Hawthorne on the green plush sofa in the drawing room at St Ives while the grown-ups dined'. In fact, writing about Jane Austen, who died at forty-two, 'at the height of her powers', Virginia expressed her belief that the changes that take place from middle age onwards 'often make the final period of a writer's career the most interesting of all'. If writing upset her moods by putting her in mind of cruel fluctuations of public opinion, then the joy she took from it was also the antibody for the angst and depression that rose up periodically inside her. By 1939, however, it had become quite clear that the mental strain of writing the biography was outweighing the uplifting effect of its creation.

Wednesday, 6 September 1939, was the day that Virginia first heard an air-raid alarm. She was awoken at 8.30 by its warbling, and the sound grew louder and more oppressive as she lay in bed and listened. This was at Monk's House in Rodmell, the old village cottage she and Leonard had bought just after the First World War and 'rebuilt to make an ideal home for two authors to live and work in'. An occasional visitor, John Lehmann loved 'the untidy, warm, informal atmosphere of the house, with books and magazines littered about the rooms, logs piled up by the fireplaces, painted furniture and low tables of tiles designed by the Bloomsbury artists'. It had the same handmade quality – as if each wall and panel were coated with brightly painted papier-mâché – as, a few miles down the road, the famous Charleston Farmhouse owned by Virginia's sister. Monk's House seemed a sort of gatehouse to that larger property, and each seemed to exist in a dreamworld of perpetual artistic creation, not a world where wars were allowed to happen. Its tranquillity was disturbed that morning, but out here, still, the war seemed far away. When Virginia and Leonard got up they walked out onto the terrace to have a look: the morning summer sky was perfectly clear, with no sign of the enemy.

Arriving in London that afternoon, it was with Lehmann that they first touched base. From number 37 they walked up the street to his flat, past the gang of Irish labourers who were digging a bomb shelter in the square, and were shown upstairs to his sitting room. For a couple in their late fifties, living mainly in the heart of the Sussex countryside, thirty-two-year-old John Lehmann with his perpetually furrowed brow and determined eyes seemed to live at the very centre of things. Though in Virginia's eyes Lehmann represented only a middling poet, she could see how his desire to mould and curate his fellow writers – was it a desire to dominate? – had made him an important and redoubtable figure. By what seemed at times to be the sheer force of his will, this fledgling poet 'interested in printing', recommended to the Woolfs by their nephew Julian Bell, had got himself to the top of the Hogarth Press, even convincing Leonard to sponsor *New Writing*, a biannual magazine of Lehmann's own conception. He went about like a Member of Parliament for the Bloomsbury ward, deeply involved in his constituents' affairs and ready always to crack the whip.

Virginia felt a sense of trepidation around Lehmann, as if he was going to ask things of her which she could not deliver, and he in turn found her frustratingly unpredictable. There was an irregularity to her disposition which could be easily explained (these mental troughs, Lehmann observed, always began with acute headaches), but more than that there was a diffuseness, a reverse gravitational force which seemed to pull her brain out of the immediate moment. At any moment, Virginia could withdraw behind a veil, and that veil could conceal any range of things, most commonly the problems of whatever she was writing at the time. 'It was hard,' Lehmann wrote, 'to draw out her interest in the activities of the Press.' On this occasion, however, she had a valid excuse. There was no subject that was not at that moment contaminated by what Virginia liked to call 'our dear old war'. It hung over everything like 'a kind of perceptible but anonymous friction'. By this point, Lehmann had bought Virginia out of the Press, but still she was to be found at all of its meetings, sitting on an armchair smoking hand-rolled cigarettes from her long holder while Leonard sucked pensively on his pipe. Lehmann had drawn up a memorandum for them both which outlined the steps he believed they should take under the new conditions of war: 'Essentially, they boiled down to doing nothing in a hurry, except draw in our horns.' The office would remain open, though largely avoided, and they would release those of the staff who wanted to join their families or look for war work. All books currently in the pipeline would be seen through to publication, but nothing new would be accepted for at least a month. The most vital thing was getting in as large a supply of paper as they could (and could afford) before the rationing started.

With these suggestions Leonard was broadly in agreement. He cheered up momentarily to remark what bad luck it was for Lehmann for the war to have come so soon at the start of his new career in publishing. They moved on to lunch, and some cold sandwiches Lehmann had prepared. These were eaten 'despondently'. Afterwards a distraught-looking Virginia got to talking about the progress - or lack of - she was making with *Roger Fry*. 'She confessed that the only way she could find to dispel the restless visions of anxiety that continually oppressed her was to force herself to carry on with [it] . . . and to re-create herself in her diary,' Lehmann recalled.

At the time of this meeting, Leonard felt that life had become 'like one of those terrible nightmares in which one tries to flee from some malignant, nameless and formless horror, and one's legs refuse to work, so that one waits helpless and frozen for inevitable annihilation'. In due course, Leonard would share with Lehmann his and Virginia's plan, in the event of invasion, to poison themselves with car fumes, and later the fact of his having acquired two lethal doses of morphine from Virginia's brother, the psychiatrist Adrian Stephen. This was not uncommon. By the time of the German invasion of Denmark in early April 1940 there was a sense that the war was 'looming large' or 'coming nearer', and people were bracing themselves in strange ways for invasion. Mad rumours were put about of Nazi parachutists landing in the English countryside disguised as nuns or clergymen, and the Home Guard were erecting fake signposts which pointed in different, contradictory directions intended to confuse the invaders. The writer Julia Strachey had devised a plan to make herself look old and ugly so as not to be raped, and madcap letters flooded into *The Times* saying things like 'Just see me die, how dashingly I'll do it' and 'If we must die let's die *gaily*.' The critic Raymond Mortimer's French doctor friend admitted to having been asked 'by almost all his patients' for a safe poison, 'generally by means of hints'. But Leonard was Jewish, and so could not afford to be so ambiguous. Shortly before the war, Adrian had travelled to Berlin to negotiate the release of a friend who had been imprisoned for dissent. Upon his return, having seen first-hand what the Nazis were doing, Adrian insisted that Leonard take no chances. Leonard was almost certainly amongst the latter of the two different kinds of people defined by Frances Partridge in her famous diaries, the first of whom had a horror of suicide, and the second which did not. All his adult life he had been acquainted with the black dog depression, and he had come close to shooting himself in 1906 while stationed in the village of Marichchukkaddi, now part of Sri Lanka. 'If you hear that I have died of sunstroke, you may be the only person to know that I have chosen that method of annihilation,' he had told Lytton Strachey. So, in 1940, 'one continues to cook and eat one's eggs and bacon for breakfast' while 'contemplating suicide by asphyxiation in a damp and dirty garage'.

Leonard did not need to be warned by Adrian; he was already, in his words, 'look[ing] into the abyss'. As early as 1935, he had driven through Germany and seen outside each village he encountered 'gigantic notices . . . informing us the Jews were not wanted'. In a magazine, more recently, he had seen a photograph of 'a Jew being dragged by storm troopers out of a shop in one of the main streets in Berlin'. The victim, in the photo, stared blankly, hopelessly, almost disinterestedly at some far-off point, while his circumcised penis was uncovered from his torn fly-buttons to prove he was a Jew. 'What was even more horrible was the look on the faces of respectable men and women, standing on the pavement, laughing at the victim,' Leonard wrote.

Leonard was deeply shaken. As Virginia's mental stability was always his primary concern, it is likely that he concealed most of these anxieties from his wife, but at the end of 1939 it is likely that his state of mind was worse than hers. Virginia waited until about nine months later to mention the persecution of Jews in her diaries: 'We discussed suicide if Hitler lands,' she wrote on 15 May 1940, 'Jews beaten up. What point in waiting?' Only when the threat of invasion became greater following the Dunkirk evacuation did the danger begin to seem real. Three weeks later, the 'restless visions of anxiety' regarding their being a Jewish socialist and his wife persisted: 'Capitulation will mean all Jews to be given up. Concentration camps. So to our garage,' she wrote.

According to John Lehmann, Virginia did not seem to have any deep interest in politics. He believed that 'she was a socialist basically because Leonard was a socialist'. Indeed, a selection of vignettes - Leonard in 1913 dragging his reluctant wife along on a tour of the industrial northern cities; her dismay at 52 Tavistock Square being made a headquarters of the 1926 General Strike; Virginia's expertise, as secretary of the Rodmell Labour Party, for turning debates about the formation of a united front into gossip about the vicar's wife - seem to bear this out. And yet here they differed on a crucial point: Virginia remained instinctively opposed to the idea of armed resistance. Indeed, she seemed to see no point in fighting whatsoever. She suspected that, either way, things were destined to go badly, noting in her diary, with a kind of masochistic relish, the little snippet of news that 'Poland being conquered, and then - we shall be attended to'. When politicians spoke on the radio, she began to talk of 'us' and 'them'. It was 'they' who made wars, she said to Leonard, who had been anti-appeasement, and now intended to join the Local Defence Volunteers; 'we' as usual remained outside and had no voice in our fate. It was as if she saw

the entire process of war as an inevitability. It was, she felt, 'a per-
functory slaughter, like taking a jar in one hand, a hammer in the
other. Why must this be smashed? Nobody knows.' One suspects
that her mind had been made up after the death of her nephew,
Julian Bell, little more than a month into his voluntary service in
the Spanish Civil War. Virginia had been by her sister's bedside
to witness the first inconceivably, inhumanly painful convulsions
of grief. She herself took some consolation in the 'kind of grandeur' of Julian's sacrifice, but confided to a friend that 'Only to see
what she has to suffer makes one doubt if anything in the world is
worth it.'

'Pacifist' or 'conscientious objector' are not labels Virginia uses
to describe herself. She signed anti-fascist petitions and joined
anti-fascist committees, but her opposition to the war was less
ideological than it was intuitive and individual. From the soul-
searching journeys of mental illness she could pinpoint exactly the
phenomena and characteristics of life most antithetical and incomprehensible to her core being. Bellicose male systems were one,
as was the thought of anyone being uprooted from their home or
forced to grieve a loved one. War was the status quo, but Virginia
would not accept that.

On 6 July 1940 the *New Statesman* ran a piece by Eleanor Rathbone, the independent Member of Parliament and women's rights
campaigner, which argued that the present was 'no time to speak of
women's rights - except one: to give their lives for their country'.
As a blinkered view it was representative of what Virginia called
'the myth making stage of the war we're in', with the papers and
BBC performing the 'dreary false cheery' dance around the icon
of 'the laughing, heroic Tommy', asking 'How can we be worthy
of such men?' But Virginia did not see the war as a separate issue,
nor one that made all previous problems go away. It had been the
subject of *Three Guineas*, her 'war pamphlet', the way in which all
of these systems bolstered and played off each other. Wars could

not, she argued, be prevented as long as oppressive hierarchical structures endured and women had to share the opinions of
their husbands and fathers to ensure their financial security as a
dependant.

Virginia had promised Phyllis Moir, an editor of the New York
review *The Forum*, that at some point she would inevitably 'boil
over' from irritation and would be happy to put down the results
for her magazine. This was as far back as September 1938, and Virginia had seen an opportunity in this 'painted battered professional
journalist' who was desperately seeking 'controversial articles' and
had sought her out as appropriately off-beat. So at the end of 1939
Moir had written to remind Virginia of her promise. Evidently she
had read *Three Guineas*, and wanted more of Virginia's unpopular
'outsider' take on women and peace. For it *had* been unpopular.
Virginia had felt that even her closest female friends wished to
'send her to Coventry' over it, and the instinct of most journalists
had been to mock the author for oversensitivity. The *Sunday Referee*, for instance, carried the banner headline 'WOMAN STARTS
NEW SEX-WAR/Says Men's Clothes are "Barbarous"'. Female critic
Q. D. Leavis wrote in the quarterly journal *Scrutiny* that the book
'contains some dangerous assumptions, some preposterous claims,
and some nasty attitudes'. The book, however, found a receptive
audience with other non-conformists, like the nun who wrote to
ask if Virginia would head a meeting of outsiders in Hyde Park and
the 'middle class provincial lady' who requested the same for the
select few women of Yeovil who were shocked to find much of
their old female society 'in uniform, greedy for honour and office'.
There was also a letter from a soldier in France who said he had
read *Three Guineas*, felt it to be generally true, and was so 'unspeak-
ably bored' that he would be happy to hear any more views on the
same lines.

After receiving the letter from Phyllis Moir, Virginia's mind was
off, 'thinking of a dozen things as usual'. She evidently had more to

say on the subject. It was significant that the commission had come from an American magazine, the country where, as mentioned in *Three Guineas*, there had since 1915 been an explicitly pacifist feminist contingent in the form of the Woman's Peace Party. In Britain, attempts made around the same time to mobilise a faction of women against the violence of the First World War had quickly been swallowed up in larger, more nebulous European projects. The essay that Virginia would eventually deliver to Moir two years after their initial conversation, 'Thoughts on Peace in an Air Raid', made a direct address to the American people from 'the shadowed half of the world'. In it, Virginia would describe the nightly sensation of lying awake in bed as German planes arrived in the sky above the house and began their droning 'like the sawing of a branch overhead'. The correct woman's place, in those moments, was in her bed, while the young man's place was in the aeroplanes. Each was a victim, but because the pilot could not stop to think lest he be killed, it was imperative that women do his thinking for him. Though there was not a single woman in the war cabinet, women still had the ability and freedom for private thinking. In this unmonitored position, they were under no obligation to conformity. 'Mental thinking means thinking against the current, not with it,' Virginia wrote. It was being able to say what others could not – that, for example, Hitler was a symbol for the 'aggressiveness, tyranny, the insane love of power made manifest' that was found in every human culture, baked into the psychology of its men. Virginia's wartime feminist writing was transmitted as if by Morse code to a more sympathetic (she thought) audience in America.

But her anti-war position was entirely her own; she admitted this in a letter to Lady Shena Simon, written after she was contacted by *The Forum*, where she jokes about the 'great danger' of her becoming 'angular and eccentric', living as she does in the country. She asks for Lady Simon's more considered view, as one who operates on a more official level. Virginia was concerned at the way that 'the human race seems to repeat itself insufferably'. There was manliness, and manliness breeds womanliness, 'both so hateful', and so men went off to war while the women gave birth to sons who would also eventually go off to war. Mustn't the next task of the women's movement be the emancipation of man? Virginia asked.

> How can we alter the crest and the spur of the fighting cock? That's the one hope in this war: his soberer hues, and the unreality, (so I feel and I think he feels) of glory. No talk of white feathers anyhow; and the dullness comes through the gilt much more than last time. So it looks as if the sexes can adapt themselves: and here (that's our work) we can, or the young women can, bring immense influence to bear. So many of the young men, could they get prestige and admiration, would give up glory and develop what's now stunted - I mean the life of natural happiness.

Virginia felt she had spotted a crack in the great and deep ideological construction of manliness, which was that if women could be other than dependants then men would also be permitted to flourish on their own terms. They should not have to go to the grave on the battlefield like all of their forebears. It was another of Virginia's 'outsider' theories. 'I tried to put this to our local Labour Party, but was scowled at as a prostitute,' she told Lady Simon. 'They said if women had as much money as men, they'd enjoy themselves: and then what about the children? So they have more children; more wars; and so on.' 'It seems a little futile to boil with rage as I do about twice a week - in these marshes,' Virginia concluded.

But Leonard saw nothing inevitable in this version of events. He believed the recent behaviour of the German nation - 'this crude and savage silliness' - to be an anomaly in modern civilisation. 'The Europe of 1933 was infinitely more barbarous and degraded than that of 1914 or 1919,' he wrote in his memoirs. What was happening now, he felt, was not a historical inevitability but something much more dangerous. As he saw it, 'after 1933 as one crisis followed upon another, engineered by Adolf Hitler, one gradually realized that power to determine history and the fate of Europe and all Europeans had slipped into the hands of a sadistic madman.' Now, all of Germany was infected with his insanity.

4

Memories

'Everything here was motionless, as if under an enchanter's spell,' John Lehmann wrote of the first days of the war in London. For example, the theatres were now all closed (as well as galleries and music venues) for the first time since the English Civil War. Most notably in his own life, the book trade appeared to have ground to a halt. It was, in fact, 'dead to all appearance'. Even before the war, critics and publishers had been calling a moratorium on literature. 'Poetry . . . is dead letters,' Herbert Read wrote in *New Verse*; 'poetry is ceasing to be printed; poetry is no longer read. Nothing can bring it back into circulation.' And according to Geoffrey Faber, president of the Publishers' Association:

For the last year shrewd observers . . . have been noting a progressive decline in the quantity and quality of worthwhile manuscripts. The reason is easy to see. Ever since Munich the atmosphere of Europe has grown more and more unfavourable to creative literary work . . . 'How can I write with the world in this state?' is a cry I have heard more than once in the past few months.

Now, really, *nothing* was being published and, of the books already on shelves, nothing was being bought. To occupy empty afternoons on the 'calm surface' of London, Lehmann used to walk into the West End to find out if any customers were creeping back to the bookshops. There, in the commercial centre of the city, the streets were so still and empty of uniforms; it was only the sandbags, stacked up against shopfronts, that placed the scene after the arrival of war in Europe. Entering the shop of J. G. Wilson, 'genial *maestro* among London's booksellers', on Oxford Street, the little alleys and cul-de-sacs created by the shelving seemed more than usual in darkness, and nothing stirred. Lehmann located Wilson 'in the shadows' and asked him how things had been getting on, to which the veteran bookseller could only reply, 'Terrible blow for an institution like this, the war.'

Little wonder, for the general public was currently busy making preparations for what was to come, namely 'a series of air-raids which would lay the capital in ruins'. London was currently absorbed in a process of regimented upheaval, though doing well to avoid an atmosphere of total hysteria or terror. The same could not be said for the provinces and Home Counties, from where, on 4 September, Leonard Woolf wrote to Lehmann that they had been 'working like coolies' preparing for the arrival of evacuees, of which most were pregnant women. All of the houses in Rodmell, the Woolfs' included, had been expecting to welcome a share of a hundred school children, but these, alas, got lost on the way and never arrived. In this new scenario, it seemed clear to Lehmann that many of the beliefs and interests of the literary world were now impossibly remote. They had been 'overtaken by the roaring express of international events'.

One item of literary interest that Lehmann seemed sure would not make the cut was his own editorial project, the magazine *New Writing*. This had been his main distraction since 1936, and it was strange and upsetting to Lehmann that many of its achievements seemed already to be those of a different, now forgotten world. Everything the publication had stood for – all the energy, anger and optimism that formed its anti-fascist assault – would soon, he felt, 'become no more than a memory'. Now, many of the stories included in the magazine appeared to him in a different light. They were the remnants of a world when, among other things, belief in Soviet Russia as ally to the international masses had been strong. But on 23 August, thirteen days before the declaration of war, a pact was signed in the Kremlin by the Soviet Foreign Minister Vyacheslav Molotov – afterwards sealed with a handshake and a smile from Stalin – agreeing a pact of non-aggression and mutual recognition of annexed territories between Russia and Germany.

It was the dashing, blond Joachim von Ribbentrop who had signed on Hitler's behalf, giving the official photographs an unctu-ous, corporate air despite the enormous and grave repercussions of the moment. Stalin, in his famous beige tunic, smoking a ciga-rette, cut a rather different figure to Ribbentrop, in black suit with pocket handkerchief, but the handshake said it all, that these two administrations – these ideologies – were more similar than they were different. The Nazi-Soviet Pact had an empowering effect on 'the contemptuously told-you-so Right' in Britain, who had always scorned the youthful affiliation to international socialism. It was there, among the group now being ridiculed, that *New Writing* had sat. The magazine was associated with stories of working-class life, of miners, factory workers and the unemployed, and occupied the hinterland between fiction and reportage. The aim of this kind of story had been 'to arouse pity and indignation', but looking back Lehmann saw that they fell victim to 'a certain flatness and too monotonous an insistence on dejection and misery'. In the mat-ter of a few years this form, which had seemed so essential, had become redundant. Even the chasm of unemployment was to be temporarily papered over as the War Office scrambled to fill uniforms and factories. Privately, he was being drawn away from these public duties; 'no more clenched fists raised as one attacked one's typewriter in the morning,' he wrote, 'but the silence of the monk's cell, the quiet.' Was this admitting defeat in the mission of anti-fascism and class struggle? Lehmann seemed to be thinking more of a hiatus, a period of reflection marking the inescapable fact that in 1939 the world, and literature, had been permanently changed.

About eighteen months earlier Lehmann had taken a flat on the north side of Mecklenburgh Square, only a few doors down from the new premises of the Hogarth Press. As with all of the James Burton Bloomsbury terraces, open, high-ceilinged rooms were complimented by large windows and views into the green spaces of corresponding squares. Lehmann had made one of the rooms into a bedroom-office, which he decorated with maps of Vienna and Austria, their sides overlapping and bordered with black like a composition by Mondrian. Working at his desk, Lehmann could look out onto Heathcoate Street, where he had had his first flat in London nine years ago when he started his job at the Hogarth Press. It was the other side of the apartment, however, that was of the most interest to him. From there, the view was over 'the tall, shadily spreading pom-pom-hung plane trees of the Square garden', as well as, to the left, the entrance of the Hogarth Press building and, across Coram's Fields to the right, number 6 Lansdowne Terrace, 'a row of small smoky dun-brick houses' where the poet Stephen Spender had just taken a ground-floor flat.

The maps of Vienna and Austria plastered above Lehmann's desk were symbolic of his dual identity – were, in fact, preserved from the decoration of a flat he had held for many years on the Invalidenstrasse in Vienna, the city he had thought of as home for eight years. Lehmann's German name originated with the marriage of his Scottish grandmother - daughter of one of the founders of the Edinburgh publishing firm W. & R. Chambers - to the merchant Frederick Lehmann, from the Free City of Hamburg, and he wore this identity each day in his severe Germanic - even Aryan - appearance, what Isherwood would call the 'high-cheekboned, Gothic style', its effect rather beautiful. It was the awareness of this preliminary, official self, the German surname that had haunted him through school ('Leh*munn* the *Hun*,' they jeered) and the First World War, that haunted him again now, as did thoughts of the intimate friends in Austria who, up until the previous year, had comprised a large portion of Lehmann's social group. Being in Vienna in those final months was like observing a piece of fruit going brown and then suddenly rotten; the susurration of bustling city crowds rose to a deafening '*Sieg Heil! Sieg Heil! Sieg Heil!*' 'The comparatively mild Austro-Fascism,' Lehmann wrote, 'had been swallowed up in the vaster, more demonic police-state of the Swastika.' He had left Vienna in the week following the *Anschluss* of March 1938, with a parting gesture from the now rampant Nazi bureaucratic machine in the form of a horde of young *Sturmabteilungen* (SA) brownshirts who invaded his train at the border searching for jewels and valuables being smuggled out. Had Lehmann's birth and upbringing been compliant to his genealogy then he would still be there, on the other side of the power dynamic. It was hurrying past the central train stations as he went around conducting his final errands when this fact sunk in most. The newly kitted-out soldiers of the Wehrmacht milling around the station entrances to begin their journey eastward - were those young men, deep down, really so different from himself?

'This was the season of farewells to the young,' Lehmann wrote in *In the Purely Pagan Sense* - a time of heightened emotion when kisses were exchanged with those one would never in normal times have reached the point of kissing. Beneath an oddly calm surface, life was changing very fast, like one shot fading quickly into another in a silent film. As Londoners piled into shops around the city, buying up as much stock as they could without being perceived as hoarding, there was a distinct awareness that what mattered now was the present and future, not the past. Though its images still flashed and ached in the background, there could no longer be time, or room, for it. This did not change the fact, however, that so recently life had been lived so differently. Another world had existed – now unrecognisable. One day, Lehmann was turning out the pockets of a now obsolete summer jacket when he found an old, clipped railway ticket to St Gilgen, a picturesque village on the shores of the Wolfgangsee. 'It brought back with almost unbearable vividness the happiness of summer expeditions among the Austrian mountain lakes and mountain forests,' he wrote. 'Such memories, after a time, began to hurt so much that I found myself trying to avoid them. And yet they refused to be clamped away.' Looking at a photograph of himself, Lehmann asked, incredulously, 'Was it really as amusing, as easy, as good as that?' The only remaining consolation was the knowledge that if he could outlive this war then such a life could be restored to him. Until a finger beckoned from some window-slit in the vast fortress of the war bureaucracy, he would 'try to piece together some of the fragments of one's old hopes and plans, peer into the fog, find long books to absorb one's thoughts, Gibbon or Proust or *Seven Pillars of Wisdom*'.

As he lay in bed that night, he imagined his 'friends-transformed-into-enemies' lying in their beds also. They, too, lay behind blacked-out windows, and under the 'guardian sentinel watch' of nearby anti-aircraft guns. In Vienna, only the moon lit the Danube where it flowed peacefully, perennially through what would soon be thousands of miles of Axis territory. It was only that same moon that now testified to the existence of this vast, modern settlement of the Thames, where millions more Europeans cowered indoors.

On the morning of 1 September, Spender had made the walk across the square as his first call of the day. Echoing Leonard

Woolf's fears, Lehmann had been feeling that morning like he was 'slipping down into a pit, clutching at grass on the ledges but failing to stay the accelerating descent into darkness', and Spender felt much the same. Two days before the declaration of war – the news had just come through of Hitler's attack on Poland – the upper parts of their minds still clutched at straws. Could there, despite all odds, still be a possibility of escape or diversion? We were like prisoners, Lehmann wrote, 'tapping every corner of a cell into which they have been flung in the hope of finding a loose stone'. Such irrational musings soothed them and allowed them to return to their usual jokes and laughter, or sudden bursts of nostalgic recollections, but in silent moments melancholy would enshroud them like a fog.

The greatest blow to Lehmann and Spender's sense of morale wasn't the inevitability of war – 'War be dreaded, but war was better than giving in to Hitler if it came to that,' Lehmann wrote – but what had been revealed as the fraudulence of the communist project in Russia. The endurance of that revolutionary state for over twenty years had been a beacon of hope to so many of the London intelligentsia who were seeking radical change after stagnancy. In the minds of those caught up in this grand paradigm-shifting vision, a wilfully myopic image persisted of Stalin as a 'friendly Uncle Joe' jealously misrepresented in the Western world. Lehmann and Spender were not so zealous or unquestioning, but had for many years still found themselves making excuses for the behaviour of the Soviet Union. Compared to others, like the heretical George Orwell, they were much more accommodating of Stalin's transgressions. But this could not last. 'Disillusionment had set in for most of us many months before the Nazi-Soviet pact . . . had blown a huge hole through the myth of an idealistic revolutionary Russia leading the forces of resistance to Hitler,' Lehmann wrote. This was true of all but the most 'hypnotised', who clung like shipwrecked men to the 'desperate hopes' that occasionally bobbed up to the surface. These comrades believed 'the war against Nazi Germany had suddenly become an imperialist war, with Russia in the role of far-sighted defender of the peace'. That was before the news, on 17 September, that the Red Army had invaded Poland from the east to co-ordinate with the murderous rampage of the Wehrmacht. Then, towards the end of November, Russia launched its attack on neighbouring Finland.

To continue to pledge their support would be unforgivable. But how had they failed to recognise the signs earlier on? Isherwood and Auden, comparatively unmoved by politics, had. 'I discussed it with Stephen Spender again and again during those weeks,' wrote Lehmann.

> Our general position, we still felt, had been right: poets, and other creative artists, cannot, if they are to remain fully living people, if they are to fulfil their function as interpreters of their time to their own generation, fail to interest themselves in the meaning behind political ideas and political power.

Their failure, it was concluded, was in siding with a specific and pre-assembled group of people, the assumption being that every-one within that group had only the group's interests at heart. In the heat of the battle, they had been too eager to give their assent to a particular set of slogans. Yet, it was now clear, it was 'not only politicians of old and conservative parties who are unscrupulous, who in their scramble for power will use all means to gain sym-pathy, kudos, votes', but also the new leaders of revolutions. 'Man may be a political animal,' Lehmann wrote, 'but a politician has to be a particular kind of man.' To believe in communism did not mean to believe in Stalin, or the ever-shifting 'party line'. Nor was the day-to-day programme of a political party - involving increas-ingly dirty, tactical manoeuvres - the equivalent of the idealism it claimed to represent. Lehmann got the chance to publicise his new feelings in a review for the *New Statesman*, published the day before Britain declared war on Germany, of a book about the relationship of poets to society. Firstly, he argued, the failure of the British government to intervene in Spain and in Czechoslovakia had confirmed a doubt in the country's democracy as spineless and unsure of its purpose. Although the sincerity of its contribution has since been brought into question, Russia *had* been there in Spain, or so it seemed, pitting itself against fascism. In an unstable modern world, communism was a sort of religion substitute - quite possibly, as one character in Isherwood's *Down There on a Visit* puts it, the only meaning to life. And it is meaning which holds the atoms of the universe together. Robbed of its ideological direction, Lehmann and Spender were struggling to recalibrate themselves in this post-Russia world. One reaction seemed the most natural of all: there was evident now, Lehmann wrote, 'a revulsion from all political platforms'.

It was over Spain that Lehmann and Spender had bonded most intensely. In 1937, they edited an anthology together of *Poems for Spain*, a publication, among countless others, which took the Spanish conflict to be much more than a domestic struggle between two factions. The Spanish war was all-encompassing; it became, in the minds of many international writers, a kind of Armageddon for the human spirit. It seemed to rip the veil off the world, and human history. As Spender wrote in his introduction to the book, Spain was a challenge which 'aroused hope all over the world', to which Lehmann added, 'All our fears, our confused hopes and beliefs, our half-formulated theories and imaginings, veered and converged [towards Spain], like steel filings that slide towards a magnet suddenly put near them.'

Both writers were political because it provided an outlet for their wilful personalities. In politics their ambition met its greatest provocation, the potential to shape the world to one's own design. It was this stubbornness, this tunnel vision, that stopped them from picking up, as Auden and Isherwood had, on all the ways that the Russian version of communism was antithetical to their beings. On paper, there were other similarities, too. Both were poets as well as editors. They had a best friend in common, in Isherwood. Lehmann and Spender clung to each other through these first weeks of the war; they were slightly frenzied collaborators in the 'great conspiracy of secrecy', as Lehmann put it, which was the new, emptier London. They confronted this uncanny metropolis together. In the blackout, one became indistinct, furtive, anonymous, like the shadowy figures that passed by on the street, or the taxis that trundled eerily along the pavement. Famous landmarks loomed up into an indigo sky, and without the homely golden light typically filling their windows, squares became purely symbolic and 'seemed to take on nightmare proportions'.

In Bloomsbury this was exemplified by the monolithic, almost totalitarian Senate House, now home to the Ministry of Information, rising 210 feet to claim the status of London's first skyscraper. For many writers at the time it had become a sort of beacon representing the possibility of a wartime occupation within their comfort zone and skill set. They were, in fact, falling over each other to get inside. Through those doors, Lehmann wrote, 'many of their kind had already disappeared to pursue impenetrable activities that seemed to have no obvious results.' The supposed fulsomeness of these writers seemed especially dubious against the backdrop of the spreading disillusionment regarding institutions. All that their peers needed to know was that they were now employed in working towards greater censorship. Going into a pub or club ('one felt one had reached some beleaguered subterranean den or cave in the mountains'), mingling with the journalists and poets who were one's neighbours in Bloomsbury, one discovered a sense of camaraderie formed in opposition to the 'Big House' and its workers. 'Making fun of the Ministry of Information became the favourite intellectual pastime of the first year of the war,' Lehmann wrote.

For those who were close to them, however, the differences in Lehmann and Spender's personalities would seem to far outweigh the similarities. Lehmann was Spender but with a sharper edge. He thought his current companion woefully unscrupulous and unserious, and would have agreed with Cyril Connolly, who saw Spender as 'an inspired simpleton, a great big silly goose, a holy Russian idiot' and a wily operator who was 'shrewd, ambitious, aggressive and ruthless'. The former group of traits seemed to be there to mask the less amiable ones. He presented as - in his own words - 'dotty and neurotic', the Stephen Savage of Isherwood's *Lions and Shadows* who bursts into Auden's rooms at Oxford 'blushing, sniggering loudly, contriving to trip over the edge of the carpet - an immensely tall, shambling boy of 19, with a great scarlet poppyface, wild frizzy hair, and eyes the violent colour of bluebells'. To those who knew Spender, his charm was his honesty; he seemed unembarrassable. Lehmann, however, still found this shocking; he found Spender 'the most rapidly self-revealing person' he had ever met. Lehmann went the other way, using his professional persona to obscure the realities of his personal life. This disarmed Spender, who had always been slightly afraid of Lehmann. In a letter to Isherwood in 1933, he described Lehmann as a 'Victorian statesman'. By 1938, Lehmann was prematurely grey, and 'look[ed] distinguished enough for the Cabinet'.

As strange a pairing as in many ways they were, in the autumn of 1939 there really seemed to be no one else around. Finding privacy in these busy pubs, Lehmann and Spender hatched plans for the rebirth of his magazine *New Writing*. Despite all the bookshops being empty, publishers cancelling or postponing their lists, and manuscripts lying on shelves 'like orphans without prospects', it was possible to believe that literature could still arise from the ashes. Thinking about it rationally, ignoring the thudding of enemy boots over the horizon for a moment, society, of course, needed, and had always needed, literature. 'The belief in literature as part of life, the belief in the power of the creative imagination to give meaning to life; these were surely going to be as important as ever in the times we were about to enter,' Lehmann felt. On top of this - though he admits to only making the connection after the event - it was true that the book market had experienced something of a boom period during the First World War.

Lehmann believed that *New Writing* could be made feasible if it avoided the political but emphasised 'the human'. It would

> be committed to the human scene even more completely; it could be a laboratory, an experimental ground for the development of a new consciousness; it would probably find itself moving towards something more lyrical and individual, burlesque and satire too of a kind that represented the revolt of the free human spirit against the prisons of war with its imperatives and its bureaucratic impersonality threatened to build up round us.

Its response to the war would, Lehmann knew, be determined by the practical difficulties posed by the war itself. Previously, *New Writing* had appeared as a hardback volume with a multicoloured dust jacket, but 'packed volumes of 150,000 words each' were now, Lehmann realised, impossible. He admits to the influence of his 'natural obstinacy' on the decision to continue, but there had also recently come a flurry of reviews which helped to rekindle his sense of responsibility. One admiring writer at the *Manchester Guardian* had implored the magazine's staff to persevere: 'Now that the *Criterion* [edited by T. S. Eliot, closed January 1939] and the *London Mercury* [edited by J. C. Squire, closed April 1939] have gone the way of all literary reviews, there is nothing left but *New Writing* to supply the demand for good prose, good verse and good criticism.' This new iteration of the magazine would not need to be extravagant of paper, time and finance; even in a skeleton form it would represent 'welcoming signals to the young men who still believed, who had transferred their fountain-pens and notebooks to the pockets of their battledress'.

THE ISHERWOOD PROBLEM

The dining room at the Athenaeum Club on Pall Mall was one of only a few places in London to be strictly 'no smoking'. The atmosphere, nonetheless, was heavy, both with the surface tension of wartime and the formalised eccentricity of English institutions: members sat under ceilings reinforced with inches of panelling and gilding, and weighty tasselled drape curtains which would have contained satisfactorily the light emission of a supernova. That two poets should be occupying one of the tables was not incongruous. This had been Dickens' club, as well as Thomas Hardy's and Matthew Arnold's. The conversation had been slowly declining in intensity and volume since then and had recently dipped to a low, contained murmur. Consonants made a feeble impression on the air while proceeding vowels sank and were lost. Gloved hands placed cutlery down with bomb-defusing carefulness and plates were whisked away without anything more than a nod in acknowledgement.

If Spender was to be helping Lehmann with *New Writing* then he needed to understand how things stood at that moment. One thing Lehmann had been thinking about a lot was Auden and Isherwood. He felt that he and Spender had been left to deal with the fallout of what he now called their 'abdication' - to field questions and make their excuses. Lehmann's own feelings, which were proving difficult to work out in his mind, found some catharsis in the 'suppressed emotions of hostility' of the nation which 'broke violently into the open over the 'Auden-Isherwood' affair', as if the media were saying what he could not:

Christopher and Wystan were suddenly branded as traitors and cowards in a campaign that was waged with the utmost fury against them in dailies and weeklies, respectable as well as less respectable; questions were asked in Parliament, scathing judgements were passed on them under privilege by people who may never have more than glanced at their works. They had, these accusing voices thundered, called on their contemporaries to fight fascism, and now that we were in fact at war with Hitler they had run away to America and refused to return. Flocks of wish-dream white feathers winged their way across the Atlantic to them.

One of these white feathers was sent by the Dean of St Paul's, Walter Matthews, who submitted a short, four-line diatribe to the *Spectator* titled 'To Certain Intellectuals Safe in America', at the moment when invasion seemed most imminent. The unnamed intellectuals had fled crying 'this Europe stinks', but, the Dean asserts, 'since you have left us, here the stench is less'. Evelyn Waugh summarised the event in a letter to Lady Diana Cooper, who was then in America, saying 'the highbrows have split - half have become U.S. citizens, the other half have grown beards and talk of surviving to salvage European culture'.

In all of Lehmann's plaintive recollections of European living there was the real or symbolic presence of Isherwood. At the beginning of the decade, he had provided the blueprint for Lehmann's wanderlust in the anecdotes, put about in London by Spender, of the novelist's 'stark poverty' in his Berlin garret and his wonderful sexual adventures. Spender's adulation was infectious; he was, Lehmann wrote, 'a great maker of legends, and saw his most intimate friends and fellow-writers as a closely-knit, in fact heroic band who were out to create an entirely new literature'. At the time, Paris as perceived wellspring of the creative world was gradually being superseded in people's minds by the regions 'across the Rhine'. Even to set foot in Germany or Austria at that time was considered a revolutionary, humanist act. Weimar Germany, in particular, had responded to post-war unemployment and disillusionment with what contemporary critic Siegfried Kracauer has called a 'cult of distraction'. With the relaxation of censorship laws came a boom in the entertainment industry, and urban communities were revitalised in the lights and music of their nightlife. Germany became decadent, Isherwood wrote, as a 'commercial line' developed in competition with Paris: 'Paris had long since cornered the straight girl-market, so what was left for Berlin to offer its visitors but a masquerade of perversions?' Surprisingly, as Stephen Spender discovered, Germany did peace like no one else. 'It dripped with peace,' he wrote, 'no one knew what to do with all the German peace.' There was much to be recounted, in particular the horrors of inflation, and of course the Germans were sorry about the war, but one was unable to escape the feeling they had just emerged from some pagan cleansing ritual.

Spender believed that it was directly because of Germany's defeat and ruin that it had been allowed to shake itself free of the shackles of the past and escape from 'the mortal sickness of Western civilization'. Possibly implicit to Spender's description – though in his case more likely graphically expressed – was the characterisation of Germany as a place where one was free to pursue and make love to other men, something which at that point would have seemed tauntingly farfetched to the more repressed Lehmann. On the other side, in England, people 'were chained still by guilt, ossifying bourgeois conventions, and philistinism'; youth and art could not be expected to flower under the shade of such inhibitions. Isherwood, Spender made clear, was the great rebel against England. As was fast becoming the central philosophy of their peer group, guilt had to be resisted at all costs. Isherwood's rejection of his English background had to do with the notion that all English boys, particularly those educated in the public schools, were raised to share in a debilitating stigma regarding the more impulsive aspects of mind and body. English schoolboys were, as Cyril Connolly wrote, 'Created sick, commanded to be sound'. To Connolly's mind, the overall effect was that most, arriving at adulthood, found their individual spirits to be defeated; in their 'permanent adolescence' they were 'school-minded, self-conscious, cowardly, sentimental, and in the last analysis homosexual'. By their early thirties, they were 'haunted ruins'.

Lehmann and Isherwood had first met in Lehmann's little back-room office at the Hogarth Press in Tavistock Square. It was August 1932, six months after the Press - largely by Lehmann forcing the Woolfs to like it - had published its first Isherwood, *The Memorial*, and not too much longer since Lehmann had joined as trainee manager. To get to Lehmann's office, back then, Isherwood would have been led down to the basement level of the house, dodging innumerable trip hazards and sidling through a saturated room of typists who seemed to chatter, much as they took dictation, in shorthand. Lehmann must have apologised for the lack of all but standing room around his desk, and perhaps even the defiance of a restful room temperature. Against this backdrop - the W.C., for example, sans working light, where old galley proofs were provided as lavatory paper - Isherwood seemed, as advertised, an authentically modern figure, who radiated the unbridled spirit of life beyond the Rhine. His deep-set eyes twinkled with tenderness and fun, and the impression which he always gave 'of the total absurdity of everything in the world'. Against Lehmann's six feet, and severe editor's countenance, the much shorter Isherwood, with his full-toothed smile and flashes of boyish charm, still seemed to have command of the room. It was, to Lehmann, that power of dominating 'which smaller people of outstanding intellectual equipment often possess'. In the moments when the shorter man's smile broke, Lehmann had become self-conscious of his entire being, as if, after all, he was part of the absurd, bourgeois thing that Isherwood was revolting against.

Lehmann and Isherwood's relationship had remained a largely formal one – in correspondence, they still addressed each other by title and surname – until the winter of 1932, when Lehmann had stepped down from his role at the Press with the aim of re-immersing himself in poetry. On his way to Vienna, he had stopped in Berlin to spend some time getting to know Isherwood properly. By this point, at least from the vantage of the capital, Germany had been dragged screaming out of the prelapsarian state of Spender's earliest memories. Berlin in winter had a specific quality which Isherwood was currently working to describe. The dead cold smothered the city, forcing it into silent submission; it was a 'skeleton which aches in the cold'. One became painfully aware that 'beyond the last new-built blocks of concrete flats, where the streets end in frozen allotment gardens, are the Prussian plains. You can feel them all around you.'

Walking around the city from his lodgings off the Nollendorfplatz, a precarious layer of ice over everything and his face swaddled against the flaying wind, Lehmann saw too how the city was exposed and terrified, with powerful, capricious forces blowing through it. In the run-up to that crucial July 1932 election, in which the Nazi Party would gain 123 seats, Berlin was 'laid out like a patient about to undergo an operation without any anaesthetic at all'. Nothing which had filtered back into the 'rational, easy-going atmosphere of London' had prepared him for what he saw. It was with disbelief that he had watched a patrol of SA men bursting through the doors of the bar where one night he had been drinking, and seizing all the young Jews, one henchman standing at the door with his pistol aimed at the remaining clientele. Likewise the lorries full of political suspects driving top-speed towards the Alexanderplatz, and the 'Jew-baiting, sabre-rattling, hysterical tone of the press'. This was not a battle between right and left but a sea wall against a tidal wave; Hitler and his party had already assumed their victory. 'All over Berlin, especially in the middle-class shopping and residential districts, huge pictures of Hitler were displayed at night in windows illuminated by devout candles.' A few nights later, another tribute in fire as great flames licked up through the decimated glass dome of the Reichstag. A new Germany had arrived. To have spent time in that country during the first years of the 1930s was to have been forced into the shared knowledge of some horrible secret of incoming catastrophe which could not sufficiently be portrayed in conversation or writing.

It was interesting to reflect, in 1939, how fervently Isherwood had dug his heels in in Germany, through all of those develop-ments, when others had gone elsewhere. The challenge had been: get as close as possible to the wire trap without it snapping down on your finger. Isherwood had embodied the desire of the young British writer to push away from his arch-capitalist homeland and immerse himself in the unfolding mysteries of the Central Euro-pean situation. He was, to John Lehmann, 'one of the first prose artists of his generation to receive the full impact of fascist-menaced Europe'. So how could he no longer be a writer in Europe?

Lehmann evidently had a number of questions to put to Spender. Spender had known Auden and Isherwood since university, and so possessed a fuller cache of observations. Lehmann felt strongly that their friends' departure had affected the credibility of *New Writing*, the success of which had to at least be partly ascribed to the reputations of its most frequent contributors. It was something he had been able to depend on as an editor, those 'long foolscap sheets in Wystan's minute, squashed handwriting, more like the recordings of a highly sensitive seismograph while a road-drill was breaking up the street outside than an attempt at human commu-nication'. For the seventh volume of the magazine he ran a bumper harvest of eight 'Audens'. That same issue listed Isherwood, on the front cover, as a co-editor. The understanding at the time of their going away had been that, though they might be leaving for a while, nothing would substantially change. Lehmann had guarded jealously over a group of contributors that seemed to him a high-water mark in English writing, 'a meeting of young talents at their best under a common impetus'. He had wanted the inevitable declaration of war to be a 'prelude to a long maturity rather than a final curtain-call'. Otherwise, the decade that had just passed, when so many writers had shown so much promise, would still not add up to enough. 'Christopher Isherwood's case was,' he wrote, 'the most spectacular example of an experience that was typical': '*Mr Norris Changes Trains* and the stories of *Goodbye to Berlin* seemed to me far too inadequate an *oeuvre* for someone who had been tipped, for every kind of good reason, as the most promising novelist of his generation.'

Isherwood was 'the most important of the younger non-proletarian novelists whose art has been a mirror of modern social decay' and had the advantage of his Central European experience with which to proffer a greater insight. And yet so far the work had appeared slowly, at times doubtfully. *Mr Norris Changes Trains*, a novel, was published in 1935. Next came *The Nowaks*, a long short story, which appeared in *New Writing* in the autumn of 1936, then *Sally Bowles,* released as a standalone piece in 1937, to be followed two years later by the subsequent sections of *Goodbye to Berlin*. Long forgotten was Isherwood's original idea of 'one long novel of Berlin life during the critical years of 1929-1933, to be called *The Lost*'. Despite comprising some of literature's most humorous, moving and colourful vignettes of that fatal turning point of history, at no point do the character sketches of *Goodbye to Berlin* give any indication of Isherwood fully committing himself to his work. He was brilliant but he was blasé, and that frightened Lehmann.

What Lehmann saw as Isherwood's betrayal actually had more to do with the Hogarth Press than its connected magazine. Two years earlier, after a period of feeling that it had become an intolerable burden, Leonard Woolf had come up with an idea of 'making the young Brainies' - this was Virginia's epithet for

Lehmann, Isherwood, Auden and Spender - buy out the Press as a co-operative company, a move which would allow him and his wife to 'creep out'. Virginia thought it could be advantageous for everyone involved: as she saw it, the young writers were 'bubbling with discontent and ideas' but needed focus and organisation. The Hogarth could be their united front, their flag to wave. Lehmann had liked the suggestion, and Virginia noted that 'I think the young are eager to bite'. But they would have to find £6,000 between them. In the end, only Lehmann had been able to stump up any money (£3,000 - enough to buy out Virginia), which he accomplished by borrowing from his mother. In this new arrangement, he would be taking on a lot of work in order to release the Woolfs to write 'a steady stream of masterpieces'. 'I stand with both hands extended, waiting for them,' Lehmann had told Virginia in a letter.

Lehmann had experienced a 'dizzy sense of promotion' at his 'honourable position in such a distinguished and old established firm', but had been assured that he would be sharing the overwhelming workload with all three of his fellow Brainies. They would be his advisory board, scouting new authors from across the world. 'We are only too glad of any chance to co-operate,' Isherwood had written. Though initially charmed and convinced, however, Lehmann had soon come to feel that Isherwood was 'dreaming and pretending'. Rather than helping the Press, 'he had seemed withdrawn into obscure preoccupations which he only shared with Wystan'. Even before leaving for America, Isherwood was 'rarely to be found'. 'How, may I ask, are you to lighten my work of reading at the Press, if you use England rather as I use my Club?' Lehmann challenged. The original idea of the four of them, Spender's 'heroic band', working together under the illustrious Hogarth banner - taking it forward, together, as the new generation - had seemed the stuff of high reverie to Lehmann. Then Isherwood had said he would move into Lehmann's Mecklenburgh Square flat, before disappearing with Auden instead.

Spender, who had stuck around to help, understood this. As he knew from experience, Auden and Isherwood set their own parameters, made their own rules; they were, he said later, 'a club of two'. Wherever those two were seemed to Spender 'to be the trenches', specifically of the kind imagined by children in a role-playing game that was exclusive of those less intimate. Both felt they were being taunted by Isherwood, who had now settled in California after finding a dislike of New York, where he complained of being homesick. To Lehmann, Isherwood had regularly been sending teasing hints of his return. How much simpler everything would have been, he wrote, if he and Lehmann were living together as they had planned. After being so desperate to get away, he now missed the Hogarth Press office and Spender's 'jokes about his psycho-analysis'. And then there was his writing: he would say things like 'I have been working on something for the autumn number of *New Writing*', before adding 'but I . . . can't publish it as it stands. I doubt if you'd want to print it, either. So once again, I am the criminal, the oath-breaker.' In a coded way, he seemed to be telling Lehmann what to think of him:

> John, I am so utterly sick of being a person - Christopher Isherwood, or Isherwood, or even Chris. Aren't you too? Don't you feel, more and more, that all your achievements, all your sexual triumphs, are just like cheques, which represent money, but have no real value? Aren't you sick to death of your face in the glass, and your business-voice, and your love-voice, and your signature on documents? I know I am.

It is hard to imagine that Lehmann did feel so nihilistically. He had had a plan - ready, waiting - for both of them, and it was Isherwood who had opted for more upheaval and uncertainty.

The letters sent from California show a rare glimpse of a deferential Isherwood, eager to impress and not to offend. There were jokes, made at the expense of New York: 'Oh God, what a city! The nervous breakdown expressed in terms of architecture. The skyscrapers are all Father-fixations. The police-cars are fitted with air-raid sirens, specially designed to promote paranoia.' Lehmann would read these scatty, self-deprecating monologues and feel the same affection for Isherwood he had used to. Then he would go out around Bloomsbury and hear through friends that the memoirist Gerald Hamilton (the model for Arthur Norris in *Mr Norris Changes Trains*) had had a separate correspondence with Isherwood in which the latter admitted 'I have no intention of coming back to England.' Quite apart from how this inconsistency hurt the feelings of his friends, the statement also carried a graver significance. Isherwood had told various officials how he would honour his pre-war commitment to the Foreign Office to work for them if required, or join the Red Cross or a Quaker ambulance unit. He was now breaking the conditions of his bail, so to speak. It was to Lehmann that Isherwood first admitted his burgeoning pacifist feeling, to which Lehmann answered coolly that he was 'puzzled'.

At the Athenaeum Club, Spender explained that Isherwood had always been difficult to pin down. He had always kept one foot in the door. Isherwood's method of writing, for example, involved producing his characters without saying what he thought of them. Christopher Isherwood the narrator was both sexless and egoless, permitted to observe but not to pass judgement, metaphorically a 'camera'. Isherwood was not the saintly 'Isherwood' of his narration, and yet in his mischievous nature found the same capacity not to obstruct the big personalities of those around him, to allow them to be fully what they were, whether benevolent or pernicious. Spender found this trait to be suspect in him. 'He wasn't really political,' he recalled, 'even about the Nazis':

> He was anti-Nazi, of course, and he saw how terribly they behaved
> in Berlin . . . but there was always the feeling underneath it which

is that he might very well have got to know some terrible Nazi. And then he would have written something about him showing how terrible he was and so on, but the real connection was a kind of sympathy, almost love, for the other person, however wicked he may be . . .

After a depression following the recent break-up of his marriage, Spender had refound 'the old spice of affectionate malice' which was so entertaining in him. He would joke about the 'bland over-the-battle tone' of Auden's 'September 1, 1939', first published in the *New Republic* issue of 18 October, arguing that it was all very well to say 'We must love one another or die' from the safe distance of three thousand miles, when soon bombs would be dropping on London. Even more laughable, and irritating, was Isherwood's reported plan to reappear in Europe with an American Ambulance Unit 'to soothe our dying moments among the ruins'. As they pondered this last point, Spender's grin seemed to spread right across the huge dining room: 'Christopher and Stalin,' he declared, 'those great neutrals!'

Isherwood once admitted to Spender that he was unable to imagine how people behaved when he wasn't in the room. This included his friends. 'It was only if he was there, as it were like a sort of controller in a median session, that everything worked, and when it did work it worked as magic, because everything became sort of magnified through his sensibility.' The best example of this had come a year earlier, around the time of the Munich Agreement. Lehmann and Isherwood were alone in the flat in Mecklenburgh Square, going over the newspapers they had picked up on their way home. Lehmann was crestfallen. The Munich Agreement, in his eyes, was a 'tragedy', and represented 'the final sell-out of the Czechs'. 'That's the end of Europe as *we* wanted it,' he had announced, feeling deflated, but also expecting to be able to share his misery with a friend. Instead Isherwood had replied, rather thoughtlessly, 'That's all behind me now, I shall be in America.' Lehmann had spoken of 'we' - the ideals he believed they had shared since they had been living in Berlin and watched the Reichstag burning - whereas Isherwood was only thinking of himself. In his mind, at that moment, the war was not really going to happen because he would not be there to see it. None of this, of course, could take away from his, and Auden's, undeniable brilliance. But Lehmann felt possessive. He was possessive of Isherwood as a friend - feeling 'dismay' at the news that he was getting close to the 'phoney' Gerald Heard who was converting him to Yoga philosophy ('I [felt] that it would draw him away from me') - but also as a writer.

Perhaps the problem with Lehmann and Isherwood was a deeper one. As Lehmann's biographer, Adrian Lewis, has brilliantly observed, 'there is a longing for Isherwood's presence that runs the thread of Lehmann's life, pages of worry, admiration and love.' These feelings do not, however, appear to be reciprocated. Outside the Athenaeum was the point where Pall Mall opened out, around the John Bell statue of the three guards of the Crimean War. Above their bearskin hats, with arms outstretched, stood 'Honour' - the moral value that was most fretted over in those days. Stacked up around it were the administrative buildings of import and export, Empire, and money, all in virginal white. If you squinted you could imagine them all to be one building, snaking on and on in a grid shape like the nerve system of the country; with the war memorial, too, the country that Isherwood had found so suffocating in its insistence on the status quo. It did not seem so poisonous now, with the streets largely deserted and curtains drawn in the panoply of windows - there were, for one thing, no swastikas flying on these classical facades. At six o'clock the sun would begin to set, and even Buckingham Palace, around the corner, would obediently go dark. From the sky, the British Isles would dissolve into its black, watery surrounds. It would seem almost insignificantly small. There was a phone box on the corner of the street where, until September 1939, one could still have reached an operator and be redirected, long-distance, to America. But the first and final stop had been called in the game of musical chairs, and players were forced to bed in at their seats, with all but the least efficient form of communication cut off. Lehmann had to put everything in letters, where, if one felt one had a lot to convey, there was at least the benefit of intermissions in which to gather one's thoughts. A few weeks ago Lehmann had written to Isherwood telling him to stay in America, and he meant it. 'Don't come back now,' he begged, 'across those barbarous seas. I want someone to survive, I want you to survive . . .'

5

Towards the Fire

The light-hearted version of Spender that Lehmann had with him in his club that day in October was a version that Spender himself had not known for months. At the end of summer – he was returning from an afternoon walk with his sister-in-law and brother along the sun-shocked Suffolk lanes when it happened – Spender's wife of three years, Inez Pearn, had left him to move into a worker's cottage in Bolton with Charles Madge of the Mass Observation Project. Spender was informed of this by a note which was left on the bed where they had been sleeping, and which was now decorated with Inez's discarded clothes. She had intended to explain to her husband in person that she was leaving, but in the end had lost her nerve. She would not, she wrote, be coming back.

Part of the trouble had had to do with Spender's ex-boyfriend, a young Welshman called Tony Hyndman whom he had met in Piccadilly Circus tube station back in 1933, who could still claim to be the most important relationship of Spender's life. That entanglement which, three years later, had reached something of an impasse, was of the kind that is most difficult to unpick. It was not until Spender and his future wife had crossed paths at a Spanish Aid Committee meeting at Oxford University in 1936 that Spender had felt he could see a way out of it. Tony had been behaving, throughout the slow denouement of the relationship, like a child refusing to be put to bed. Spender had found him a flat, and a part-time job working on the *Left Review* (Tony had actually got himself a new lover), but still he seemed unable to accept the new distance between them. 'He has just made the most terrific scene,' Spender told Isherwood in a letter, without going into detail. So he had married Inez quickly and without the approval of any of the friends whose opinion mattered to him. They bemoaned the tribulations of 'Poor Tony', and were seriously doubtful of Spender's explanations for his change of heart, which boiled down to - as he put it in a letter to Isherwood, a fan of Tony's - 'I'm just not capable any more of having "affairs" with people. They are simply a part of a general addiction to sexual adventures. She also wants to marry me, and I think that we shall be able to build up a satisfactory life together.' His friends felt the relationship had been doomed from the start. In Isherwood's mind, at least, Spender was homosexual. This was all just part of his 'new image'.

Spender had reservations about homosexual relationships that would stay with him for life. Though they were often more roman-tic - and despite his finding men, or boys, more attractive - in an all-male relationship the threat of 'sterility' loomed large. It was something to do with Spender's complex of needing always to be moving forwards. He was not thinking of the impossibility of mar-riage or children but rather the danger of falling in love with those whose appeal was self-identification. Loving a man was an individ-ual process characterised by the need for a partner to be a mirror to one's own desires and neuroses. Once that obligation had been sat-isfied, Spender soon found his interest waning; the only thing left was to feel content with 'keep[ing] their friendship static'. This was all too apparent during his relationship with Tony. 'We had come up against the difficulty which confronts two men who endeavour to set up house together,' he wrote. 'Because they are of the same sex, they arrive at a point where they know everything about each other and it therefore seems impossible for the relationship to develop beyond this.'

Tony had further excited Spender's hatred of idleness by never being gainfully employed. It was a prejudice Spender had carried since his teenage years:

> It is not only unhappiness that distresses me deeply, but also tiredness, laziness, and other weaknesses in people. I don't mention this, but I freeze with horror. When I was 16 and used to go home on the tube from my grandmother's house on Sunday evenings, a thing that irritated me almost beyond bearing was if my sister or her companion, who were with me, yawned.

Tony had been in the station at Piccadilly that night because he was then 'plying his trade' in the Amusement Park near Marble Arch or in the Haymarket. Spender was 'in the mood when people advertise for a companion in the newspapers', and knew full well what he was taking on when he decided to pursue the connection. He wanted, in fact, to offer Tony a hand up from his uncertain employment, and the pair immediately began to live together, with Tony being brought home to Spender's flat. In a role invented purely to support Tony with the money that would otherwise have been handed over freely, Stephen had appointed his new boyfriend as his secretary.

It was easy for Tony to fall in step with Spender's life. Watching him chatting and laughing with old friends, it was as if Spender had merely discovered him stumbling drunk and aimless around central London and redirected him home, or else gone to collect him in a taxi from the station after a month's holiday. In much the same way, however, it had seemed they could never again be apart. While this was not, romantically, the most disagreeable notion, it did describe a reality with some logistical issues. They seemed too closely joined, and there was little with which Tony could fill his time. 'I really did not need a secretary,' Spender wrote. Besides, Tony was naturally resentful of being treated as an employee, so it was very difficult to make him work. Tony's 'restless desire to amuse himself' distracted Spender from that which was most important to him, his writing, and made him impatient. He began to feel like his own work 'was a kind of disloyalty . . . the exercise of an unfair advantage'. 'The strain on my side,' he wrote later, looking back on the relationship that had defined an era of his life, 'came from the impression of being with someone whose life was empty.' It was during their relationship that Spender had his first sexual encounter with a woman.

Inez, that day in Oxford, had seemed to hold inside her a little unreachable store of mystery. Spender had found being with a woman to be 'much more of an experience'; it was, he told Isherwood, 'more satisfactory, more terrible, more disgusting, and, in fact, more everything'. That it was awkward and alien and confounding was part of its appeal. It broke the repetitive cycle of his previous relationships by introducing this factor of feminine inscrutability. Inez had seemed the most beguiling of all. She had kept her 1920s Eton crop, as if to fix her age within the adolescent range, and pronounced her name as the Iberian 'Inês'. Watching him through brightly shining eyes, she had spoken in a cool, measured way of her work as a scholar of Spain and Spanish poetry, the trips she had taken there and a love affair with one of the country's painters. She had just got back from working as a governess to a family of 'rich Spanish reactionaries'. Spender and Inez's interests - at that time heavily weighted towards Spain - aligned exactly. Spender had returned to his alma mater as a celebrity in the new zeitgeist of Spain hysteria, at the top of the bill for the day's speeches. He was the poster boy of the movement of British intellectuals against European fascism, and, as one friend noted, possessed in Oxford at this time a 'semi-deified' status. According to Lucian Freud, it was a thing you heard all the time: 'We've got so and so on the petition . . . Stephen Spender.'

Despite what seemed to many the blunt and callous rebuff of his hasty marriage to Inez, the question of Tony had not gone away. It all got mixed up in the question of Spain, which, it soon became clear, was much more of an obsession for Spender than it was for Inez. The day of their wedding, at Hammersmith Register Office on 15 December 1936, Tony had begun to speak with casual bravado of his plans to go to Spain to join the fighting. To Spender's surprise, he had followed through; with rather unfortunate timing from Spender's point of view, the International Brigade had just been formed and was advertising for British volunteers. So Tony put his name down; it all happened 'quite suddenly'. Joining the fight in Spain was a step that Spender had been unwilling to take. This was not a shrinking from duties but, as he had protested to Harry Pollitt, secretary of the British Communist Party (who secretly wished, as Virginia Woolf noted, for him to join the International Brigade at Albacete and 'be killed, in order that there might be another Byron'), Spender still regarded himself as a pacifist. This was a test: would the privately educated son of a politician (Harold Spender) and nephew of a newspaper editor (J. A. Spender) be willing to show the same commitment to this 'class war played out on an international scale' as his working-class 'comrades'?

Virginia Woolf's diary entry for a day in February 1937 gives a picture of anxiety and instability during what should have been the 'honeymoon period' of the Spenders' new marriage. Inez had taken her postgraduate research to the Royal Library of Belgium. Meanwhile, back in London, Virginia was interrogating Spender about his motives in what Hugh David calls a 'typically Bloomsbury-ish way':

Stephen Spender came to tea and dinner the other day . . . great enthusiasm, now tempered, and rather metalled because, having married, his friend, the male, joined the F[oreign] Legion, is fighting in Spain; Inez, who is political in the Oxford way only, sits at Brussels studying Spanish [manuscripts]. Stephen finds this intolerable . . . Now [he] is torn two ways: so Inez sits there, in order, should he be killed in Spain - but he's only broadcasting - she may have her job to fall back on. A curious interpretation of marriage: [I] told him not to fight. He said it was the easiest thing to do. I said give up speaking - he said But it brought in money. He argued that we cannot let the Fascists overrun Spain: then it'll be France; then us. L[eonard] said he thought things had gone so far it did not matter. Fighting did no good.

As it turned out, Tony made a rather guileless soldier, constantly getting into trouble. Spender blamed himself. At one point, he became so restless that he decided to get in touch with one of Tony's sisters, who thought it was the fault of his own political coaching that Tony had got himself into the situation he now was in. Spender was beginning to see why this was true. As he reflected in his autobiography, Tony's decision 'confronted me with the consequences of my own actions. Without my influence he would never have become a Communist, and unless I had decided to live apart from him, and had then married, he would certainly not have joined the Brigade.' What seemed clear was that he could not now abandon Tony to his fate.

From the vantage point of late 1939, Spender could see the thread of causality which connected all of these events. As far as Inez was concerned, he could appreciate the symmetry in his having constantly kept one eye on Tony, and she, at some point in 1938, having happened upon Charles Madge standing outside his publisher's office in Red Lion Square and fixed his eye with an 'unforgettable' look. The indecision that had crippled Spender's political life had bled into his relationship. Inez had sought solid ground. There was the occasion, for instance, when Spender had left Inez in Brussels just before his twenty-eighth birthday to travel onwards to Spain. With Tony and the great ideological struggle of Spain on his mind, other responsibilities fell by the wayside. Spender admitted that 'throughout the whole duration of our marriage I was obsessed as I have never been before or since: by hatred of Fascism, by the Spanish war, by the anxiety on [Tony's] account.' As well as seeking Tony, without whose company in London he had been feeling lonely, he had been, he said, drawn towards the site of humanity's potential destruction:

> Somewhere I felt that there was a place which was at the very centre of the world, some terrible place like the core of a raging fire. Perhaps it was in a cell where some helpless old man was being beaten to death, perhaps it was in a café over some frontier where exiled leaders were plotting to return. If I could ever approach it, I felt it would be the centre where the greatest evil of our time was understood and endured.

Inez did not want to live her life in this way. There must, she thought, be some degree of detachment from massacres and schisms. 'I know that she cannot bear being with me when my forehead is split with anxiety,' Spender later wrote of Inez. 'I inhabited a mental world that terrified her.'

When he was not with Lehmann, that autumn of 1939, Spender found himself taking long walks around London, to catch the city in its process of shapeshifting. The pain of his loss was at this moment intense enough to push the war back, and the changes struck him as both superficial and novel. All was observed 'as through a thick pane of glass, seen very clearly, but all sound shut out', like the new aluminium barrage balloons which floated above the city - one over Tower Bridge, another the Tower of London - bobbing and rotating in the wind like yachts in a harbour. Crowds of people waiting for buses on High Holborn and in the West End made the city seem 'interesting and almost gay'. Did it occur to him that many were making preparations to leave? Spender had just got the keys to his Mecklenburgh Square flat, on the ground floor of a narrow Georgian house, which, though comprising only a few compact rooms, had been chosen as a more comfortable space for himself and his wife. Now it seemed the home of some deceased distant relative and filled with their unwanted stuff. When one feels at home somewhere one opens it up to the world. Spender did the opposite. On the rare occasions he was inside the flat, he kept the blinds down. He picked up books and forced himself to 'stare at the letters'; they seemed 'hieroglyphs on sand and as meaningless'.

As Lehmann had detected, Spender had not been at all himself since Inez's elopement. Privately, her departure had made him violent and vindictive in a way that was unnatural both for himself and their relationship. As Inez's daughter, Vicky Randall, later wrote, even decades after their split 'my mother still liked him and I never heard her speak harshly about him.' But Spender was shattered. 'Everything I read in the papers about broken faith, broken pledges, disloyalty, etc seems about her,' he wrote, 'the wireless, the papers, food, my relations [all] gives me a sense of nausea.' He wondered if he would ever write again:

> Words seem to break in my mind like sticks when I put them down on paper. I cannot see how to spell some of them. Sentences are covered with leaves, and I really cannot see the line of the branch that carries the green meaning.

Thoughts of Inez with Charles Madge - 'Are they happy? Perhaps they have the secret of happiness, which I have lost' - squeezed his brain and cut off the supply of creative ideas. Like so many other writers during this period, Spender found himself drawn to his diary, where he could allow his pen to go in circles around Inez and the war and 'write anything, anything at all that comes into your head, until gradually there is a calm and creative day'. Everything was pulled back to her. On the day that the banshee-wail of an air-raid siren was first sounded throughout London, when men and women picked up their children, pets and gas masks and rushed to air-raid shelters with knees knocking and stomachs churning, it was Inez that his mind went to. She seemed so far away. 'I imagine her in her red dressing gown and she looks pale and dazed,' Spender wrote.

The sense that an era of his life was coming to a close was intensified by everything around him. Though the weather was still pleasant and the streets glittered 'biscuit yellow', the blackout time became earlier with each day that the autumn evenings drew in. It was in these circumstances, with his marriage in tatters and Britain and its empire at war with Hitler's Germany, that Spender was approached by his friend Peter Watson regarding the role of assistant editor on *Horizon* magazine, a new monthly magazine of literature and the arts. Watson had been forced to flee Paris after the German army unleashed the brute force of its tank divisions and Luftwaffe on neighbouring Poland, and while living in the French capital had obviously missed out on the latest developments in Spender's personal life. Thus did he imagine that Spender could be the person to provide a certain stability to counterweight the third person involved – the one who had come up with the idea and convinced Watson, a trust-fund millionaire, to fund it – the mercurial Cyril Connolly. Watson was wary of Connolly as a potentially unstable figure who would be unable to keep a tumultuous personal life from affecting his work. Connolly made no secret of his laziness and protracted bouts of melancholy, and recent marital trouble had seen him falling in love with at least one other woman. Any new problems involving either of the two women

might set him off and bring the work of the magazine to a grinding halt. Rich as he was, Watson was cautious about investing his
money in one who potentially lacked follow-through. 'Peter asked
me specifically to help edit *Horizon* because he wasn't absolutely
sure about Cyril,' Spender said. 'He wanted to have three editors,
and then if Cyril didn't work out, I would be there to help Peter
carry on.' Watson, it seems, was not the only one who had doubts
about Connolly's ability to sustain anything serious. Spender was
having to field questions from all sides about the rationality of the
project. 'I say, is Cyril seriously going to call his magazine *Horizon*?' Geoffrey Grigson asked, at the Café Royal. He joked that
'magazines called *Horizon* never last for more than two numbers'.
Grigson had just been at a dinner party, with guests including John
Betjeman, and relayed that 'there was quite a lot of laughter' about
the whole thing.

On 19 October Spender visited the Woolfs at Rodmell, where,
after tea and croquet, he and Virginia walked around the garden
admiring the view across the Downs and talking about Inez and
writing. Spender loved being at Monk's House: the large pond with
water lilies and its shoals of goldfish, the way the house, part of the
village on one side, opened itself to spacious country and the train
line to Newhaven behind. The Woolfs' lawn was a perfect window
to the area's unique topography - the way the Downs slip and carve,
puffing then bunching up. The towns and villages slid down into
these pockets, and in Rodmell - a long, curving street of houses,
cut into two segments by a larger road - one had the impression of
the flint and dark clapboard houses being strategically positioned,
relics of earlier wars fought between royal and baronial forces. The
house's wrought-iron weathervane, dated 1930, the year before the
publication of *The Waves*, took in the entire patchworked bowl of
the surrounding valley like a sentry.

Virginia told Stephen how, with the war unfolding around
her, 'every day an occasion arises in which one sees things in an

entirely new and different way'. He explained that he was keeping a journal, which pleased Virginia 'because she found it was the only thing she could do, too'. T. S. Eliot, as his editor, said something similar: 'just writing every day' was 'a way of keeping the engine running, and then something good may come of it'. What Spender did not tell Virginia was about his involvement in Connolly's new magazine. He knew how close Virginia was to John Lehmann, with whom Spender had not so long ago been discussing the possibility of reviving *New Writing*, and also how she felt about Connolly. One of the conditions of Spender's acceptance of Watson's offer had been that his name be kept off the masthead. 'I am not officially connected with it,' he told a friend, 'as I don't want to start any rivalry with the Vesuvius of 45 Mecklenburgh Square.' This was Lehmann, who, Spender joked, 'casts a red glow across Bloomsbury in the blackout'.

But Spender's involvement in the magazine was unmistakable. He had come up with its name, been present in its formative moments, even arranged with a good friend of his, Tony Witherby, whose family owned a printing firm in High Holborn, that the printing be done at a discount cost. He was also now offering the flat at 6 Lansdowne Terrace that he had intended to share with Inez for use as the magazine's office - with the way his life was up in the air at that moment, it seemed a better use of the space. Spender would live in the small bedroom at the rear of the apartment.

When Lehmann found out, there was an 'explosion' which 'spread over most of our literary world'. 'It must be admitted,' Lehmann has recalled, 'that there were some angry scenes and exchanges of letters between Stephen and myself . . . Sides were taken, and I was encouraged to find how many strong partisans I had.'

He was much less restrained in his unpublished diaries. There, Lehmann scrawled that Spender was a 'natural traitor', one 'pathologically eaten up . . . with jealousy, vanity, egotism, and utterly corrupted by years of extravagant self-deception'. It seemed even more brilliant to everyone else that the two offices should be facing each other across the square, as if the rival editors had snipers' guns trained on one another. Virginia Woolf, caught up in what she saw as little more than a playground spat, noted that 'John gets garrulous after wine. He can't make it up with Stephen. Stephen half lies about *Horizon* and his part in it mostly. Offers to bring it to the Hog[arth]. Steals young writers.' The last time she had seen them both together it had been clear the effect the war was having on people's nerves. Spender had crashed into the Hogarth office having not slept since the 2.30 a.m. false alarm. 'His great joints seemed to crack. Eyes stared. Is writing reams about himself,' she recorded in her diary. 'John had drunk a glass of water and sat in the cellar.' The nature of their dispute – 'a queer little eddy, just below the surface' – reminded Virginia of the various schisms among her own circles, in previous times, despite not being 'so highly organised'. She could be forgiven for not taking them entirely seriously.

BLOOMSBURY'S FIRST MARXIST CRITIC

Virginia's accounts of reading Stephen Spender's work in the 1930s give a picture of one who has stumbled upon something inexplicably new and alien to herself, and which is not immediately palatable. Spender had made contact with Virginia while still an undergraduate at Oxford, sending her several poems and saying, in a letter, that he cared more for her praise than that of any other critic. He had already been in touch with Vita Sackville-West and her husband, Harold Nicolson, who had had him over to their house at Long Barn in Kent and experienced an 'intelligent' young man with 'wild blue eyes and a bad complexion'. Virginia, as she got to know him in the subsequent years, saw the same wild-eyed literary faun, but seems to struggle in describing his personality.

At the least, his very demeanour was perplexing to her. First, he was 'a rattle-headed, bolt-eyed young man, raw-boned, loose-jointed who thinks himself the greatest poet of all time'. Next he was deferential, and yet, as she wrote in a letter to Quentin Bell, 'talks incessantly and will pan out in years to come a prodigious bore. But he's a nice poetic youth; big nosed, bright eyed, like a giant thrush . . . Yeats has praised him; I see being young is hellish. One wants to cut a figure.' She wondered 'by what alchemy you refine these rough youths to gold'. Despite not understanding him, Virginia was always sympathetic and accommodating towards the one who, it has been suggested, saw Woolf as his literary mother figure.

In 1935, she reports having developed a new technique for reading his books. 'At a gulp,' is how she puts it, meaning too quick to stop and think, 'without screwing my wits tight to the argument'. Once she had finished reading, she would consider going back to try and work it out. Her response, in this case, is rather touchingly self-aware; there is no denying that the book is not something she would typically enjoy, or want to write herself, 'but I recognize my own limitations'. 'No creative writer can swallow another contemporary,' she admitted, 'but I admire Stephen for trying to grapple with these problems.' Otherwise, she thought the book, *The Destructive Element*, too arbitrary in its pattern; it tried to hitch its discussion too much to the author's own predicament, and thus could only be fully apprehended by a reader in identical circumstances. Virginia would discuss the young poet with her older friends, particularly T. S. Eliot, who was publishing Spender and his peers at Faber, and thus having to promote them. This he did with complete enthusiasm. In a lecture tour given by Eliot in the United States in the spring of 1933, the famous poet was keen to tell as many people as possible about who he thought were the most promising of the young British poets, and always named Spender. In Virginia's company, however, he could be franker; there was, he thought, some melody or rhythm or emotion lacking in the 'Audens and Spenders'.

It was, nonetheless, a mutually beneficial relationship. Lehmann and his cohort needed Old Bloomsbury, if not for their praise then for their editorships and publishing houses. The elders, in turn, fretted over the youth opinion, and found validation in these friendships. Spender was quick to come forward in Virginia's defence after Wyndham Lewis published *Men Without Art*. He reviewed the book for the *Spectator*, and despite finding 'the burlesque account' of Woolf's essays somewhat amusing, was compelled to highlight all of its contradictions. Like many a bitter critic, Lewis allowed the writers discussed to symbolise things external to their books, and to themselves, while at the same time neglecting 'any serious critical appraisement of any writer'. 'This is a book', Spender writes, 'in which *The Waste Land* is referred to with contempt, as are also the novels of Mr. E. M. Forster, and in which Mrs. Woolf is attacked with a great deal of malice and without any show of evidence that Mr. Lewis has read either of her best works, *The Waves* or *To the Lighthouse*.' It was a neat and sober putdown, cutting right through Lewis's belligerent flailing. 'The moral of the book was that there was no reason for any writer to exist except Wyndham Lewis,' Spender reflected in a letter to Isherwood, adding that he himself would happily trade all of Lewis's works for a book like *Howards End*. Virginia seems to have appreciated his support, mentioning it in her diary, as she does many of his other compliments. In 1935, she refers to a letter from Spender in which he calls *To the Lighthouse* 'the most delightful book I can imagine', adding, 'It is the only novel, apart from *War and Peace*, which I have read four or five times.' Having first spoken to him as an undergraduate, it is clear that Virginia saw Spender as youth incarnate; indeed, something in his spirit seemed to demand it.

Spender, as only a few others, bridged the gap between new and old Bloomsbury. He was, David Leeming suggests, 'adopted' by some of its members (an appropriate term for one who, by now, was an orphan) - most notably the famed hostess Lady Ottoline Morrell. Christopher Isherwood had a similarly filial relationship to E. M. Forster. It began with young men wishing to meet their heroes - there was a sense of fulfilment in it, Spender wrote - and quickly, after about two generations, trying to get the measure of the other, each ultimately finding the other inscrutable. Virginia Woolf wanted to protect the starry-eyed Spender against the pitfalls of certain literary behaviours. 'She talked also about the danger of creating a literary personality for oneself,' Spender recorded after a meeting with Virginia in 1939:

> Her dislike of self-importance links up with her dislike of the egotism of successful men. She said that the mistake of ambitious women was to try to compete with men on their own ground, to become masculine. Women had a life of their own which they could develop without being diminished by men.

Old Bloomsbury cast a long shadow, partly because its most successful literary members were still very much operational, but also because, like any successful group, it was aware, at least subconsciously, that it survived on the perpetuation of its own myth. Certainly the activities of the Memoir Club, the group to whom Virginia had recounted the revelations of Bloomsbury living, could be seen in this light. But there was a sense, when Spender talked with these writers at Lady Ottoline's 'Thursdays', or at parties at Leonard and Virginia's in Tavistock Square, that the younger writer was being encouraged to adopt the values of his elders. 'To them there was something barbarous about our generation,' he reflected - and like missionaries they believed there to be no greater crime. Spender saw Bloomsbury as 'almost a cult' of taste and attitude. 'Not to regard the French impressionist and post-impressionist painters as sacrosanct, not to be an agnostic and in politics a Liberal with socialist leanings, was to put oneself outside Bloomsbury,' he wrote. As in any parent-child relationship, there was an upwards resistance. These parents espoused freedom and experimentation, were tolerant in their attitudes towards sexual morals, and yet were inexorably of the past. Their creations, such as the Hogarth Press, were the subjects of affectionate ridicule. Spender warned Isherwood against calling his novel 'Mr. Norris Changes Trains' because it sounded so 'Hogarth Pressy'. 'It gives one a sense of earrings,' he added. When the book came out, he reports that 'the dear old Hogarth even fluttered out into a tremulous announcement'.

Stephen Spender was Bloomsbury's 'first Marxist critic'. Until Spender, the discerning elders of Bloomsbury had never been judged for their politics. What were their politics? 'Like a watered-down aristocracy they made moderate but distinct claims on society,' Spender wrote: 'They were individualists who asked for themselves . . . the independence in which to do their best work, leisure for reading, and pleasure.' Some, like Leonard Woolf, were fairly proactive in their involvement with the Labour Party and other causes, which usually operated through committees. Spender was present at a meeting in 1934, for example, when E. M. Forster spoke against the Incitement to Disaffection Bill. 'He was beautifully elegant,' Spender reflected; 'It's obviously a sort of example of their Greek spirit coming out - Morgan emerging as a kind of Pericles.' They were teasing, but Spender and his friends had a great respect for Forster, who was a 'wonder' in himself for having written *Maurice*, his novel of unrequited homosexual love (Forster had let Isherwood and his friends see the unpublished manuscript), while 'imprisoned within the jungle of pre-war prejudice'. It was exactly the kind of writing they aspired to - an author giving a frank declaration of their faith.

Among Greater Bloomsbury, or its contemporaries, however, there was Eliot's Anglican conservatism, and, in the case of W. B. Yeats, Ezra Pound and Wyndham Lewis, an idealistic interest in fascism. These men saw fascism as a means of 'rediscovering order in society - recovering old values in a modern context'. What struck Spender was that such contradictory political identities could exist together without politics becoming the main talking point. It seemed to boil down to the assumption, made by these writers and others before them, that 'the purpose of art was not to change the world but to celebrate sensibility, the process of literary creation, and consciousness itself'. Politics cheapened literature, turned it into propaganda. Such beliefs were foundational in high modernism. In a sense, the outer world where politics took place did not exist for these writers. They made the 'exterior world an object of interior sensibility'. The hero of this literature, Spender writes,

> was inevitably the exceptionally sensitive person, that is to say he who was most capable of receiving a wide range of impressions, most conscious of himself as a receiver of impressions, and most likely to make use of his impressions as a means of cultivating himself rather than acting upon the world.

Eliot's heroes, as Woolf's, Joyce's and Proust's, were passive spectators of a civilisation falling into ruins. 'Bloomsbury was felt to be inadequate by the requirements of a social conscience,' Cyril Connolly reflected of Spender's reaction.

As Woolf and Eliot were perplexed by Spender, so Spender was incapable of comprehending the strangely detached process of their writing. Their writing had revealed to him 'areas of sensibility of which I had hardly been conscious before reading them', and yet it was as if they were anonymous penmen through which brilliant language and imagery were transmitted. Virginia told Spender that when she wrote *Orlando* she began writing the first sentences without knowing how the book would continue; Eliot that he wrote the last verses of *The Waste Land* 'in a trance - unconsciously'. The writer sits at their desk and holds a pen, and, wrote

Spender, 'through the veins of the hand there flows the blood which is the whole life of the literary tradition joining the writer, sitting at his desk, with Shakespeare'. For the new generation it seemed incomprehensible - was perceived as a privileged state of ignorance - that writing could happen without a clear sense of purpose, that the exercise could be treated in much the same way as it had three hundred years ago.

Eliot, no doubt, saw himself as being just as political as the younger poets. But, as Spender attests, it was a politics which insisted on 'abstract principles', with all roads leading to a fundamental principle of 'supernatural authority'. Spender goes on:

> Eliot was, in the strictest sense of the term, a 'reactionary'. He reacted against non-conformism, Liberalism, ideas of progress and of the perfectibility of man. Better regard man as wicked and fallen than have him listen to the inner voice of his own conscience and judge himself by his own human standards.

It was George Orwell who wrote, during the 1930s, that the old guard of English letters seemed much more likely to swing towards fascism than any liberal ideology. Indeed, Eliot admitted that there were concepts which might have attracted him in fascism, but he found them, ultimately, to be inferior to his own non-mainstream beliefs of national religious faith and hierarchy. 'He rarely thought about politics in terms of political realities,' Spender reflected, dismissing his editor's politics as not to be taken too seriously. It was the question of 'perfectibility' - of man, of society - which stuck like a wedge in their relationship. Though Eliot would write to Germany, wanting to hear about everything that was going on over there, he shared none of the younger man's desire to affect the course of events. What it came down to, Eliot explained, was that he believed in Original Sin. As much as he agreed that 'there are plenty of material injustices to be set right', the world would always be an unpleasant place. Spender recalls a conversation in which he asked Eliot what he thought was the future of Western civilisation. Eliot – who, Virginia Woolf joked, often resembled in his talk the narrators of his poems – predicted 'internecine conflict . . . people killing one another in the streets'. Watching the great poet as he spoke – 'grave, slightly bowed, aquiline, ceremonious' – he seemed quite as futile as Prufrock. And yet, the vision of the world he had presented to his readers – decaying, disillusioned, without hope – was in practice interpreted as one overdue a radical transformation which would cure its malaise. The poems had, in fact, reinforced the need for protest and action.

Virginia seems to have felt the call of political writing more strongly than most of her contemporaries. She would draft works that combined fiction with the essay form, but never committed herself to the experiment. In 1931 she was reading D. H. Lawrence – a writer who had galvanised the young Spender because he 'turned outwards from himself' and 'challenged the passive sensibility' – and regretting 'that a man of genius wrote in my time and I never read him'. Lawrence, she reported in her diary, had given her a lot to think about – 'about writing for writing's sake'.

There was a view, developed by Spender in *The Destructive Element*, that this previous generation of writers possessed an idiosyncratic and remote kind of genius. They were in the vein of Henry James, who turned away from the modern world and took an interest instead in the past and in his own individuality. Convinced in the decadence of European – particularly English – society, James's subject matter was 'imbibed from history; from the cities of France, and from Venice and Florence in particular'. He had an extreme sensibility, and took pride in seeing life through a lens which distorted its image. The ideas he enjoyed were the impracticable ones: that a modern aristocracy could reverse its decadence; that there should be an aestheticism in human behaviour. James Joyce, W. B. Yeats, Ezra Pound and Eliot could all be considered in the same light. 'These writers,' Spender felt, 'have all fortified their works by creating some legend, or by consciously going back into a tradition that seemed and seems to be dying.' The attitude is explained 'by the consciousness of a void in the present'.

Owing to recent events, however, the moral life of the individual had become comparatively insignificant. 'In revolutionary times,' Spender thought, 'it is questions of social justice, of liberty, or war or peace, of election, that become really important.' The younger, modern writer would look at civilisation and see 'not his own quiet image reflected there' but 'something fierce and threatening, that may destroy him'. Civilisation's destruction is the writer's own destruction, and therefore it must be fought for, and saved, so that the writer may be saved. But what did it mean to fight, politically, through the medium of literature? It meant an awareness, first of all, that writing was always political, in the sense that it was moral. *The Waste Land*, for example, was not a poem without any belief or subject, as many had said, because its 'fragments' were its subject. It was Eliot's vision of the world, as money and Venice and Florence had been James's, and his only responsibility was to communicate it to the best of his understanding. 'I am committed then to a theory of communication,' Spender wrote, 'that the poet is not dealing in purely aesthetic values, but that he is communicating an experience of life.' He would not let the older generation of writers hide behind the assumption that they did not come bearing their own beliefs and moral subjects. 'What a writer writes about is related to what he believes,' Spender summarised; 'What he writes about also implies an attitude to the time in which he was living.'

The danger for contemporary writers was not in 'having a particular moral or political axe to grind'; this would only diminish the art if the writer '(a) suspends his own judgements and substitutes the system of judging established by a political creed; (b) assumes knowledge of men and the future course of history'. It was more important that the writer had a deep and clear sense of what is the modern subject, that is 'a subject large enough to enable the poet to write long poems'. Their greatest danger is with an individualism, or isolationism, which, though full of moral feeling, could not relate to the political life, the morality and manners of the time because it had not properly attempted to understand them. Thus did writers like James eventually make themselves redundant. James's political subject – as those of the Bloomsbury writers – had made sense when 'it seemed primarily the duty of the individual to escape from his environment, and, with a few others who cared about such things, to preserve, in isolation, the values of our civilization'. But the political subject had changed. The writer was required to change their direction and walk back towards the fire. Addressing his contemporaries, Spender argued that what a book is actually about mattered just as much as 'fine technique', and, perhaps more importantly, 'that there are things going on in the world that are worth writing about'. 'It is the business of artists to insist on human values,' he summarised; 'If there is need for a revolution, it is these human values that will make the revolution.'

Spender, born in 1909, was the youngest of his poetic cohort. His first proper collection, *Poems*, was published in January 1933, the same month that Hitler became chancellor of Germany, meaning he – Spender – immediately became a symbol for something. Critics in 1933 wished it to be so, that the twenty-three-year-old poet would arrive in total embodiment of a new political era characterised not only by the rise of Hitler but also by a depression, nascent revolution in Spain and war in Manchuria, and a collapsed Labour government. Herbert Read, in the *Adelphi*, was 'positively ecstatic', though focusing not on technique but on the role Spender was expected to play as a poet. 'Mr. Spender is conscious of his social heritage of chaos and despair,' wrote Read. Interestingly, Spender had anticipated this commendation. He could also, he told Christopher Isherwood in a letter, depend on it being well reviewed by William Plomer in the *Sunday Referee*, Michael Roberts in the

Listener, and 'someone' in the left-wing *Manchester Guardian*, a paper founded in the aftermath of the Peterloo Massacre. Spender, it appears, craved the identity of a political poet. The book, he told Isherwood, was 'selling very well already apparently in the shops in Kensington, Baker Street and Charing Cross Road'; and, he added, 'will sell in the universities'. A political poet in 1933 knew exactly his target audience: he had his friends in the weeklies, all the prominent socialist publications, the flat dwellers of Chelsea, Marylebone and Bloomsbury, and a student population as interested in international politics as they were in the writing of the moment.

Spender was rightly proud of the collection, though abashed by the comparison with Auden in Faber's precis, which, he felt, 'seems to have been written out of pure malice'. It suggested that Spender had achieved something which Auden had been trying and failing to do:

> In his work the experimentalism of the last two decades is beginning to find its reward . . . Technically, these poems appear to make a definite step forward in modern English poetry. Their passionate and obvious sincerity ranks them in a tradition which reaches back to the early Greek lyric poets.

He had written to Faber to challenge its wording, which Isherwood agreed was 'portentous tripe', adding 'What idiot wrote it?' It was a curious incident – Spender being heaped with praise and touted as historically significant but wanting to distance himself from such claims. His public image was already being taken out of his hands: he was already a symbol.

If any poem in the collection seemed to encapsulate Spender's moral vision it was 'The Pylons'. It is an image of a transforming world, seen from hundreds of years into the past through to the future. The ages are layered one on top of the other like rock strata –

stone roads made from the stone of the hills, the hills and roads concreted over. The newly erected pylons seem to patronise the natural landscape of the valley, and prophesise an even greater transformation, of metropolises ascending towards the clouds. The description of technology's overwhelming physical presence in Britain's landscapes was not exactly new to these poets, but the perspective had now shifted. Auden, who in his early poems adopted the stance of D. H. Lawrence towards industry as a blight on nature, had described an old world 'already comatose' and on its way out.

The mood then was sorrowful. Spender had consigned both that world and the mourning of it to the sediment; here, he was saying, is something truly new (the National Grid was completed in September 1933), something forward-thinking. It was a romantic notion, for its implications were revolutionary. As Faber had noted, some anxious, deliberated modern sentiment seemed to have been distilled in Spender's poems - a sentiment which Auden, in his obscurity and mysticism, could only hint at. Spender recognised his own limitations against Auden's '"tour de force" power' and 'fireworks', but could also see how the other lacked the 'strong, lucid, objective, free-verse style' which would give himself the edge in directness of message. Spender, Isherwood points out, was being widely quoted in the same way that the poet Rupert Brooke had been (and in private, sometimes, ridiculed). 'And left the vivid air signed with their honour' was the popular phrase, from the closing line of the heraldic, spirit-affirming 'I think continually of those who were truly great' (Isherwood took pride in having suggested the transposition of 'vivid' from its original penultimate position in the sentence). Isherwood's initial response to the collection appears to be representative. 'I will stick to my favourites,' he wrote, 'The Port. Children who were rough. Oh young men. After they have tired. And, above all, The Pylons. The Pylons is the best thing in the book, I think.' He was, he explained in *Christopher and His Kind*, 'charmed by Stephen's left-wing romanticism, with its accent on Comrades' (later, he would prefer the 'explosive egotistic artlessness' of the love poems). Spender himself later felt he had to justify the artistic decisions of his youth, which, he said, had become 'an embarrassment to my friends' luggage more even than my own'. But the moment was all that mattered. By 1935, in the dust-jacket blurb of *The Destructive Element*, it could meaningfully be said that Spender was 'a representative figure of the youngest generation'.

So Spender's reputation was sealed on the eve of Europe taking its first proper step towards war. 'The news from Germany is awful', Spender wrote to Isherwood in Berlin a month after Hitler's appointment. He deleted the ensuing passage, fearing that it would get his friend into trouble. Soon Isherwood would begin the desperate mission of keeping his boyfriend Heinz out of German conscription, considering various alternatives, including paying for him to be repatriated. Spender suggested that Isherwood, with Heinz, could go to America. 'I somehow feel that you would be able to write there, perhaps even better than in England,' he explained. Instead, Isherwood, like Spender himself, remained intent on seeing everything that this new, schismatic Europe had to offer, things which seemed impossibly remote to those at home in the relatively settled England of the National Government and the burgeoning suburban heartlands.

6

The Pain Two Lovers Inflict

Floorboards squeaked under feet, sometimes accented with the knock of a wooden heel, as post was collected and brought back again, giving a solidity, a tactility, to the hours which peaked around lunchtime and then slid into the afternoon. There were transient figures who kept their long dark coats and scarves on, most of them writers, but also *Horizon*'s business manager, Bill Makins, a 'redoubtable' Scotsman with a fierce, high-boned face. Running along one side of the room was everything that would be needed to throw a party together at a moment's notice - a large gramophone, records lined up in their sleeves, folded trestle tables, all sitting beneath a small Picasso owned by Peter Watson. A look to the clock: a couple of hours yet before the bottles could come out. The typewriters went on perpetually until conversation cut through and prevented fingers from reaching keys. The pools of vague shadow under desks and feet remained static throughout the day as the winter sun abandoned its crescent and deferred its duties to an unbroken screen of white. What would it look like if a plane were to enter Bloomsbury's airspace at that moment? Would it be seen to slip through a cloud, leaving a little tunnel behind it, or just suddenly *be there*?

At the desk in the far corner of the room, Cyril Connolly was reclined deep in thought. One of the liberties he had taken as editor of the magazine was to establish a 'defensive enclosure' keeping him from the outside world. Between himself and the door, where rejected poets and aggrieved novelists might suddenly appear, were three other desks, home to Stephen Spender, Peter Watson, and the office's two secretaries, Lys Lubbock and whomever else was available for temporary work at the time. These made up the first lines of defence. The chair Connolly occupied had been offloaded on him by a friend who found it 'exceptionally ill-proportioned'. With its wide, low seat, however, it suited Connolly, who seldom sat upright while working. Across the huge flat arms he had balanced a wooden board, on top of which was constructed a drystone wall of books, papers and pens. It 'protected him against intrusion'. 'At a distance,' Peter Quennell, a regular *Horizon* contributor, wrote, 'only the crown of his head was visible.'

This was Connolly's first attempt at editing a publication that he started himself. It was a dream he had held on to through over a decade in the trenches of literary journalism at the *New Statesman*, the *Sunday Times* and the *Observer*, and one which multiple people had tried to discourage him from. As an early mentor had put it, there were three illusions that everybody had to survive: falling in love, starting a magazine and thinking they could make money out of keeping chickens. The stakes were particularly high, in this case. In 1938, Connolly had published *Enemies of Promise*, his first piece of book-length criticism, which attempted – successfully, in fact – to reverse the dynamic of British literature away from the 'Mandarin' style of the early twentieth century and towards the new 'vernacular'. Readers had been enchanted by this young critic who, according to Stephen Spender, arrived at literary judgements at lightning speed, and justified each by his unique use of metaphor and wit. Or else they had been offended. Because Connolly had seemed so certain of his judgements, he could not now be seen to fall short of his own high standards. Not to finally put his name on a masthead, however, would be to submit to the abiding sense of personal failure that tormented him. It could not wait any longer; as a friend had observed, Connolly's hairline was already beginning to surrender to middle age, and a 'circumference of double chins' now encompassed his features.

Safely established in his corner, Connolly could follow his train of thoughts 'through landscapes of past and present'. Presently, his mind dwelt on three things. 'As a man, he was suffering from a private grief,' he wrote of himself at this time, 'a separation for which he felt to blame';

> as an editor, he was struggling against propaganda (the genial guidance of thought by the state which undermines the love of truth and beauty); as a Londoner, he was affected by the dirt and weariness, the gradual draining away under war conditions of light and colour from the former capital of the world . . .

The transformation of London in this moment was for Connolly absolute. On top of the exodus of large, panicked swathes of the population, and the general deterioration of hope and happiness under thoughts of what lay ahead, he also found his home life suddenly changed. He had moved into the little red-brick maisonette on Yeoman's Row as a married man, set on finding some peace and harmony in the domestic routine, being monogamous, and getting down to his work. Instead, he and his wife, Jean Bakewell, found themselves slipping back into the old, and now apparently inescapable, routine of fairly constant quarrelling, she drinking heavily and throwing tantrums in the company of friends, and Connolly running back to his mistresses. Now two of those women were working with *Horizon*, and Jean had gone back to her home country of America.

Being a secretary at *Horizon* paid more – albeit only fractionally – than the £2 a week offered by the ARP for patrolling the blackout, and for far more amenable work. Central to being what Peter Quennell called a 'lost girl' – a term encompassing most of *Horizon*'s female employees – was the necessity of 'making one's own way in life'. Lys Lubbock, for instance, had been orphaned as a teenager; Diana Witherby's parents disapproved of her lifestyle and limited her financial support to the occasional ten-pound note surrendered at the price of a pointed remark. *Horizon* was a family in ways which would have been unfamiliar to many of its members. The staff lent each other money, bought each other presents, sent each other postcards from their trips. Wages could be supplemented by the wealthy, paternal Peter Watson, beneficiary of his father's Maypole Dairy Company fortune, but they were also sometimes forgotten altogether. Sonia Brownell, who helped out in her evenings and on weekends after shifts with the Ministry of Transport, remembers having to raid the petty cash tin for her bus fare home. There was no hierarchy (the term 'secretary' cannot really be applied to those who frequently had to pick up the slack on editorial work) and seldom a clear sense of order. Women who were able to understand the mind of Cyril Connolly enough to fall in love with him were deemed to be qualified as his understudies. Somehow, it worked. Diana was a fledgling painter when she and Connolly met before the war; by March 1941, her poetry and short fiction were rubbing shoulders in the magazine's pages with Louis MacNeice and Aldous Huxley. By all accounts, Lys was about the best administrator in London.

One evening at the beginning of October 1939, Diana and Connolly had been taking a taxi back to her flat in Sloane Square when an army lorry, failing to spot them in the moonlight, had gone right into the door on Diana's side. As she lay amid the wreckage,

unable to move her legs, and as it became clear that neither Connolly, the taxi driver, nor any of the soldiers in the lorry had been
hurt, Diana began to curse the noise of the inchoate crowd which,
in 'delighted smugness', drew attention to her compromised state.
'When the ambulance clanged nearer and nearer,' she wrote, 'a
feeling of resignation swept over me; this time it was for me.' Since
the day the blackout regulations had been imposed, posters had
been going up all over London warning against the various ways
that impaired vision could lead to accidents. Cars with blinkered
headlights posed a much greater threat at that point than the Wehrmacht, and as Evelyn Waugh noted in his diary, 'all the gossip is of
traffic casualties'. Now, Diana felt embarrassed to become a number
in these statistics. The crowd seemed almost disappointed to see
her lifted out of the vehicle without any visible marks of injury, as
if the war was somehow failing to deliver on its promise of blood.
From there Diana was taken to a temporary hospital ('carried up
the steps I had seen so often from a bus') and on to an X-ray room,
after which doctors could deliver news of a fractured pelvis and a
fortuitous near miss for her spine.

The couple who were travelling in the taxi that night were more
likely to be arguing than cooing with romantic sentiment. The saga
of Connolly's guttering marriage had rather unfairly imposed itself
on the life of the twenty-five-year-old Diana, who reaped only
intermittent benefit from this ménage à trois. Diana did not dislike
Jean, instead resenting the bitterness that had been allowed to fes-
ter in her as the Connollys' dénouement was endlessly spun out. 'I
see you and Jean maundering on for years,' she told Connolly, adding that she was sick of having the same old conversations wherein
he would contest that 'Of course you're "better" for me but I must
get over being in love with Jean first.'

Now, as Connolly was getting on with the first issues of *Horizon*,
Diana had been transferred to the Cottage Hospital in Chesham,
Buckinghamshire, with a long confinement with which to

contemplate the injustices of her love life. To fill the days more constructively, she had asked Connolly to send her some manuscripts to read and judge for the magazine. In due course, the *Horizon* staff would land on a tentative system for these appraisals, designating submissions, somewhat vaguely, as either 'no good at all', 'doubtful', 'good' and 'outstanding', but at this point there was not even such a crude system as that to aid the process. The doormat at 6 Lansdowne Terrace was subjected to daily landslides of stories and poems, and even Diana, with entire days to fill in her hospital bed, felt a little daunted by the task. 'I did not anticipate quite so many,' she wrote to Connolly, 'will you be able to stand the strain of editor?' Indeed, as D. J. Taylor has noted, Connolly seemed already to be getting cold feet. Possibly, he simply had not anticipated such an enormous workload. Long working days spent yes-ing and no-ing the scribblings of the nation's dilettantes would leave little room for the virtuosic Connolly personality to shine. 'An editor frays away his true personality in the banalities of good mixing,' he later grumbled, 'he washes his mind in other people's bathwater, he sacrifices his inner voice to his engagement book.' Perhaps the greatest shock, however, was regarding the quality of much of the work submitted. In a note sent to Diana to accompany the first batch of manuscripts, Connolly had warned of a scourge of juvenile writing. 'It is terrifying that so few people write poetry after adolescent age,' Diana had replied, 'and any that do remain in that state forever.'

Stephen Spender had arranged with Diana's brother, Tony Witherby, that the first four issues of the magazine were to be printed by the family firm of H. F. and G. Witherby. Diana, who found her brother maddeningly undependable (most recently, he had forgotten a simple promise to send his ailing and downcast sister a copy of the *New Statesman* to alleviate her boredom), ended up having to take charge of these negotiations from her hospital bed. It was an awkward situation all round. As talks progressed, Connolly,

Watson and Spender had begun to feel they had been led on by Tony into thinking they would be dealing with him directly. In reality, Tony had only an informal influence inside the company, and the *Horizon* editors would actually be dealing with Diana's rather dour father. Diana's father was eager to print 'a really good literary magazine' but also, it became clear, fully intended to exercise the right of printers at that time to veto any content that was deemed to reflect badly on themselves. Connolly had been planning to write what Diana calls his 'pacifist article' and it was for this that her father had put his foot down, not on any grounds of illegality but because he didn't agree with it. A 'very ill-worded letter' had been sent to Peter Watson making this absolutely clear, but Watson had already paid a cheque in advance for the printing. Further complicating the situation, Diana's parents were at that time trying to sue the army for damages from their daughter's crash. Again and again the Witherbys were told by their solicitor that this man, Connolly – whom they must have assumed was just a friend to Diana – had failed to respond to another letter requesting a written statement of the incident.

So for five days out of the week ('she comes twice a day and has even begun reading aloud to me') Diana would have her mother by her side, steadfastly defending her husband's principled stand against the younger generation. Then, at the weekends, Connolly would come to visit to argue the opposite view. Diana would take *Horizon*'s side in any dispute but, as a young woman without a husband, was still 'absolutely in Mummy's grip'. As well as laying her up for two months, the 'one-second crash', as Diana despairingly referred to it, had also dragged her away from her life as an adult in London – her modern life – and back into the dominion of her parents. They wanted her to stay away from London, even once she had fully recovered. 'Her will is like a rock,' Diana said of her mother, 'she is trying to make me say I'll live in the country.' Consequently, there seemed to be an implicit threat in the way her mother would suggest going through the clothes in her London flat, or bringing her her letters. The wider family, too, were rallying against her self-determination, including an uncle who 'always assumes I am living in sin and likes to embarrass me in front of my parents by drawing attention to it'. 'What can I do if they say it's impossible for me to live in London yet?' Diana asked. 'That is the unendurable part of having one's parents "responsible" for one if one is ill, as one cannot be responsible for oneself (excuse "ones") and a reason why I wish to God I was married and could escape from the accurate accusation of ingratitude.' As for her father, Diana resented his 'English creepy crawly puritan caution' and could not believe that her brother had not seen this tension coming.

Back in London, the deserted Connolly now claimed to have in his possession only three suitcases. Diana's convalescence had taken a turn for the worse when she developed renal colic, a condition exacerbated by immobility and which manifested in what she calls 'kidney attacks' caused by a build-up of what was then called sediment. Some days she was vomiting every half hour from the pain, and a constant twitch had developed in her mouth. By Christmas, she was able to walk with nurses supporting her on both sides, and was practising standing on 'butter legs'. Her letters from this time are impressively reticent as regards the love triangle with Jean, who at this time seemed comfortably out of the picture, not yet in America but staying with friends in the Worcestershire countryside. Rather, she seems to distrust Connolly's ability to make decisions when he is feeling so lonely, such as finding them a flat to live in together in London, and pleads for him to be patient. Having had time to reflect on it, she decides he would not be happy living with her on the spartan allowance she was receiving from her father. Jean was rich, while she, Diana, was not. They could afford to have fun together, but not to live together. On his part, Connolly would later claim to have been plagued by nightmares in which the two women would take turns to reproach him. He made repeated references to 'the two faces' which played havoc in his imagination and dreamworld, drifting in and out of taunting focus. 'The tyranny of the human face,' he quoted mysteriously, without offering a source.

There was, thankfully, a daily respite from the cycle of thoughts (like 'a worn gramophone record') in the form of the office routine. There was immunity in that diurnal ritual, Connolly said, and in the company of old friends. As soon as he arrived at 6 Lansdowne Terrace - immersing himself in the company of the charming and attentive secretaries, the *click-clack* of typewriters, and the general buzz of interesting conversation - the anxiety of the night-time would have disappeared from his face. He also seemed to be find-ing some enjoyment in 'cheering up Peter', which, he told his mother, took up most of his time. Connolly assumed that he and Watson - who had been brought away from Paris entirely against his will, and consequently separated from his boyfriend, the beau-tiful but tortured Denham Fouts - were in the same boat. Jean had been a great friend of Watson's, and together she and Connolly had often visited him in Paris. Hanging in the corner of one of the rooms there - presumably still - was a piece of mistletoe which Jean and Denham had nailed up the previous Christmas. Spender, who sat opposite him, thought Connolly 'the best living parodist'. To each of his colleagues in the office he 'allotted a character for which, in a brilliant parody, he would invent the dialogue'. Spender became a bishop. 'Bishop Spender will now say a few words,' he would start off, before proceeding to give a full sermon. He might also, as Peter Quennell remembered, 'execute one of his famous knockabout turns'. These included 'a brilliant impersonation of the chimpanzees' tea party he had witnessed at the London Zoo'. His face would contort in those moments and be overcome by the vis-age of the creature he was impersonating.

Connolly's desk looked out on to the knotted, naked grey plane trees and playground of Coram's Fields, where the absence of children was representative of the new uncanny wartime landscape. Connolly's summary of London around this time, given in his foreword to the first issue of *Horizon*, focused on the deceitful and mocking presence of the almond blossom and shining sun. As the natural world continued to manifest its splendour, it was even more shameful that, on the ground, 'the streets look shabbier and the shops emptier, and the war slowly permeates our ways of living'. Later, as the possibility of invasion loomed, Connolly would once again rue the coincidence of renewing spring with an escalation of terror, joking that nature had been mechanised by the Germans to distract its adversaries. 'Green grass, blue sky, white clouds, primroses; everything will be tried that may distract our attention and sap our resolve,' he wrote. 'Don't look at 'em. Wear dark glasses.' The perversion of these warmer and more leisurely months offended the core of Connolly's being:

> We must destroy the day dreamer, the memory hoarder, the escapist, the beauty-wallah, the reading man. Then and then only, bastioned in this island buttress, will we be totally conditioned to total war, and when victory is ours, when the war has swept the world, when nobody gets more to eat than the poorest Spaniard or the most starving Chinese, when nobody can read or write, when nobody has anything, nobody wants anything, nobody does anything except work, work, work - when we've got the race war, the class war, the age war, the sex war, going simultaneously, when you look back at to-day as the happiest period of your life, and when happiness is recognized everywhere as what it is, a dull and dishonest evasion of necessary pain, when we have reduced humanity to its lowest denominator - then the sacrifices we have made in conditioning ourselves against the daffodil and the blackbird will not have been worthless.

This changed London landscape involved a new awareness of and symbolism around the sky, even more so since on bright, clear days one felt that a big and obvious target had been placed over one's head for German bombers. As Connolly sat going over manuscripts in the chair by the window, his concentration would break only for the occasional glance up at London's airspace to check for German planes coming over. Here was the root of the problem.

Art, in Connolly's mind, was something which occurred organically and irreverently like nature. Its worst enemy was any form of distraction - be it 'the clarion call' of profitable journalism, a flippant version of writing; politics, which presented a diversion for a writer's spiritual energies towards what Auden called 'the flat ephemeral pamphlet and the boring meeting'; and escapism, whether in sex, social life or travel. To that list he could also now add the threat of death. He took an idealistic view of the lives of artists in history, writing that, for example, the impressionist painters never had to worry about money and 'believed in devoting a long life to the worship of beauty and the observance of nature'. The artist, in Connolly's mind, needed almost to be bubble-wrapped by society in order, in return, to show it something that had previously been invisible. He needed a stable liberal-bourgeois lifestyle, and time and space for his mind to wander towards eternity. Connolly's philosophy of artistic production could be summarised with the phrase, from a later instalment of the editor's 'Comment' section: 'put them down in the sun and let them be: results will soon follow'.

But was any of that possible in 1940? The coming of spring reminded Connolly of something else, which was that 'the English were once a migrant species, taking wing at Easter for Paris, Rome and Seville'. The pain of being deprived of such opportunities - getting on the boat train at Victoria, crossing to Boulogne - was almost unbearable, and resulted in 'an angry protest against the office walls and street walls against which we knock our heads till they are bald and polished'. Without Paris, Rome and Seville - both in a personal and a symbolic sense – art and culture could not exist. At an earlier point in Connolly's life, perhaps travelling after university in the twenties, it had seemed that Europe was coming close to attaining its final, brilliant form. There was 'a steady humanitarian trend', he writes. Medicine and psychiatry were healing the sick; the problems of crime, poverty and malnutrition were gradually being solved. Now, all this movement towards a better world had been put into reverse by Hitler.

What troubled Connolly at this time was the realisation that it was now up to England to uphold the traditions of the Parisian boulevards and Mediterranean shores. It was fighting not for the political right to its continent but rather its invisible spirit. By the time of the German invasion of France, England was 'the only country in Europe where a man may still paint or write very much what he likes', and thus inherited the task 'of restoring paper and ink and paints and canvases to occupied Europe'. The jury was still out, however, on how much its leaders or wider population cared to save those things. The British character was 'stolid, practical, tolerant, pleasure-loving, responsibility-taking', but it seemed doubtful whether it could see beyond the office walls and street walls of its practical existence. Unlike his historical heroes, Connolly saw another way besides the total isolation of the artist. The artist could be given a place in the conception of the meaning of the State. He should not, however, be 'etiolated by official conformity', as in Russia, but instead would provide a philosophical service, as the scientist would give explanations for human life, for the spiritual benefit of his countrymen.

Connolly's real gripe with propaganda around this time was not how it was imposing on the content of *Horizon*, but rather how much it depended on the time and mental resources of the nation's artists.

The artist-administrator in the Civil Service or the BBC is not only prevented from writing by the pressure of work, but his life offers

him no material for future creation. These artists will emerge from
the war with no artistic achievement and no pent-up artistic energy.
They will have talked or minuted their works away . . .

There was enormous potential in the socialising of art through
institutions like the BBC and Ministry of Information, but also
great dangers. The success, for example, of Penguin Books was
an insight into the developing consciousness of the nation and
the new diffusion of culture. 'The appreciation of art is spreading everywhere,' Connolly writes, 'education has taken wings, we
are at last getting a well-informed inquisitive public.' He also lists
the War Artists' Advisory Committee, the *Brains Trust* radio programme, the Committee for the Encouragement of Music and the
Arts (CEMA) and the Army Bureau of Current Affairs lectures. But
culture diffusion was not automatically art, and it would amount to
nothing 'if we deny independence, leisure and privacy to the artist
himself'.

When Connolly prophesied around this time that 'we are in a
world which may soon become unfit for human beings to live in'
he was thinking not of material dangers like invasion or gas attack
but rather what he saw as a wave of philistinism which threatened culture and the individual soul. Fascism represented not so
much militarism and the iron fist, but more the undermining of the
individual, spiritual existence; it was 'the enemy of art'. It sought
to corrupt human existence by taking it away from its essential
values of beauty, spiritual advancement, and its relationship with
nature. Fascism, in this sense, is any denial of or departure, by way
of strict material-based lifestyles, from basic ontological truths.
Connolly's attitudes on the subject came to be shared by his colleague Stephen Spender, who described the conflict in an essay
titled 'Two Landscapes of the Novel'. There, Spender describes
how the work of E. M. Forster carries within it an awareness of
'life being confronted by death', but that in modern life thoughts

of this kind are treated as being almost superstitious. 'A money-civilisation chooses not to consider this confrontation,' he wrote: 'It is one of our most pertinacious refusals and we support it by calling "mystical" anyone who does consider it.' The 'realities in life such as beauty, personal relationships, sex and death', Spender says, are 'generally ignored by the arrangements of our machine-made society'.

In the early years of the war, he says, Connolly maintained a 'complex attitude of supporting the war, and even the government'. *Horizon* had avoided giving a manifesto for literature in wartime, insisting only that writers should try to find a way of continuing their work and, failing that, be taken under the wing of the state. If a writer felt they needed to turn away from the war entirely, then so be it. Judging from Diana's letters, Connolly had at this time been toying with the idea of pacifism, which was the ultimate way of what he called 'keeping the calendar at 1938', but this did not last long. Looking back at the literature of the 1930s, much of which now '[had] the moth in it', he could see that, however wrong the left-wing writers had got it, the 'literature of appeasement' had turned out to be stupendously ignorant and almost immediately unreadable. Connolly's own politics were self-centred. A government could either support his vision of the world, and allow him the things he wanted, or take from him the luxuries - both material and spiritual - he so depended on. Where Spender and others had dogma and altruism, Connolly had a humanism which had its roots in his love of free and fine living for all, and was no less valid for that. Bourgeois liberal democracy represented for the most part a clear path to Connolly's lifestyle, but there was much more that it could do for him, namely providing him with a comfortable living arrangement in which to think and write and a yearly stipend.

In this first period of the war, between its declaration and Churchill's appointment as prime minister, the question as yet remained unanswered regarding what Britain represented, ideologically, in this conflict. It was to fight against Nazism, true, but did it have courage in the conviction of its own way of life as *ne plus ultra*, to the eradication of all others? Then there was Connolly's fear, really, of himself. He was greatly disturbed by what was happening to France as a centre of the arts, but also as a culture he saw as the antidote to - or which validated - his own personality. French culture was the ideal because it was equal parts romantic and complacent. There, it was believed, the eloquence of the artist alone was enough to influence the destiny of humanity. The artist could survive on reverence and his own mystique, and perhaps it was that which Connolly feared losing most. In France, the great Connolly novel that was always 'coming' - and which Diana was frequently reminding him of - could remain in gestation indefinitely.

One notion that appeared again and again in his writing of this time was of the war as being primitive and regressive. He described it as an event that was 'archaic and unreal' and 'as obsolete as drawing and quartering'. As echoed by Stephen Spender in 'Two Landscapes of the Novel', Connolly would in early 1940 write that the war 'negatives every reasonable conception of what life is for, every ambition of the mind and delight of the senses'. To understand the situation he had turned to Freud's essay *Beyond the Pleasure Principle*, which was written at the end, rather than the beginning, of a world war, after the damage had been surveyed. Vienna in 1919 was facing major problems. These included the financial ruin of the middle classes as a result of hyperinflation, food shortages, overcrowding in the city's apartment buildings, and the spread of diseases such as tuberculosis, Spanish flu and syphilis. In the previous five years, the Austro-Hungarian Empire had lost an estimated 1.8 to 2 million of its people.

At his home at Berggasse 19 in the Alsergrund suburb, Freud had developed his theory of *der Todestrieb*, or death drive, the instinct towards destruction, repetition, aggression, compulsion, and self-destruction which in human beings struggled eternally against the pleasure principle. *Lustprinzip* is the desire for life to continue, to be spent in joy rather than pain, and, as Connolly so often discussed, to search for and create that which is beautiful. Reading *Beyond the Pleasure Principle*, Connolly seemed unsure whether, like Freud, a 'minor pessimist', he believed 'we blindly enjoy destruction and can think of nothing better', or that beauty, knowledge, entertainment and sex were the guiding principles, and violence a vulgar political interjection championed by abnormal minds. One passage of the book in particular stood out for him; it concerned the 'repetition-compulsion' which both makes war a constant reality and, in private life, made humans re-enact 'certain patterns of childhood unhappiness and separation'. Connolly saw himself in the individuals described by Freud for whom

> every relationship ends in the same way: benefactors whose protégés invariably after a time desert them in ill-will, men with whom every friendship ends in the friend's treachery, lovers whose tender relationships with women each and all run through the same phases and come to the same end . . .

With his magazine and in his personal life, Connolly wanted, as he had told Jean, 'to create something permanent in the flux'. For himself, that was 'a foyer, a monogamous marriage, a baby, books', but for literature, it was an editor who chased down the young writers departing on their troop trains, or buttonholed the Ministry of Information employee to ask him to start writing again, and allowed them to say whatever they had been feeling.

The first issue of *Horizon* had appeared on the shelves on 15 January 1940. It had sold out in a week and become 'a collector's rarity'. A star-studded contents list included a new poem, 'Crisis', by W. H. Auden, and one by Walter de la Mare; poems by John Betjeman and Louis MacNeice; and essays about the war from lynchpin figures Herbert Read and J. B. Priestley. Influential critic

Geoffrey Grigson contributed a round-up of the country's up-and-coming poets, including the 'sensual means-fuddled' Dylan Thomas whose poems are 'still very much about himself'.

But the reception had not been entirely positive. In one of his early editorial 'Comments' articles, Connolly responded to various recurrent strands of criticism, which he summarised thus: 'The cover is old-fashioned and Georgian, as are many of the contents; a similar magazine in the last war was the first to print Eliot, Joyce etc, *Horizon* can only discover Bates and Priestley.' He had also - it seemed the readership was able to tell this - failed to deliver on a number of promising leads, having, as he did, close connections to E. M. Forster, Virginia Woolf and T. S. Eliot. Spender's tiff with Lehmann had ruined their chances there. At least one of those writers, Virginia Woolf, had hinted that she did not intend to ever write for the magazine: 'Small, trivial, dull. So I think from not reading it,' she told her diary. Finally, it was seen as par for the course that he should have been able to get his friends, Auden and MacNeice, however fashionable, on board.

That the magazine's cover was 'old-fashioned' was completely intentional. In his foreword to the first issue Connolly had made clear the editors' focus on functionality; *Horizon* would try to be no more than the medium through which the best writing would be communicated to readers. This editorial restraint and emphasis on functionality was embodied in the magazine's no-frills, economical design. The plain cream covers soon followed a single formula through all of the war years and beyond, with just the colour of the logo, in early-nineteenth-century 'fat face' italic lettering, changing with each issue between brilliant greens, blues, pinks and purples. Beneath the title was a list of the contents printed in bold majuscule. Considering the moment, it was important that they refuse mannerism and showmanship. Modesty seemed the proper approach at a time when food, drink and fuel restrictions seemed all-consuming. Like the elegantly functional paperbacks of Allen

Lane's Penguin, the sole purpose was the dissemination of good reading material.

But although he would defend his work, saying 'Horizon . . . makes no apology for Priestley's admirable essay, or Sir Hugh Walpole's revealing glimpse of Henry James', he knew that more had to be done if a crucial statement was to be made for the advancement of literature. It was not enough just to fall back on this old guard of stock celebrity authors and middlebrow darlings, regardless of the increased sales they might bring. After all, it was Connolly who had been the loudest voice in opposition to the lightweight, 'Ivory Tower' stylings of Georgian literature. As D. J. Taylor has written, 'by the mid-1920s – even earlier in sophisticated circles – "Georgian" was a term of abuse.' It stood for the 'fight to preserve the literary standards of the past against the devitalising influences of the post-war era'. Though the contents of the first issue of Horizon could never, realistically, be likened to the heavy symbolism, enumerated descriptions and 'lyrical evocations of landscapes' of Georgian stylisation, the mere mention of the word in relation to his magazine was enough to make Connolly squirm. He knew that it was his duty to find the best new writing, that in which the accuracy and insightfulness of content reigned over the pretty adornments of high style.

Walking home through the 'sad streets and squares' of Bloomsbury, Connolly was stout and heavily overcoated, bearing a load of books and magazines, and with that wide, pale, domed forehead and soft baby face that gruffly nestled itself into heavy jowls. He passed by Brunswick Square, described by the character of Isabella in Jane Austen's Emma as being a 'part of London so superior to many others . . . we are so very airy'. Connolly had felt that way once, touring the Ivy, the Berkeley, Boulestin's, the Tour Eiffel of an evening. 'I get happier and happier,' he wrote in 1927, 'autumn intoxicates me, so does London.' London was the capital of prose, as Paris was to art, and in its prose was torn between dandies, slums and fog. The London of the dandies was the one where Connolly had wished to be - particularly the period of 1760 to 1840 'where it lies embalmed' - but now it seemed one great slum, under one heavy, unabating fog. London was a place for the strong and methodical, for the brute and the bank manager, not the sensitive 'who used to think once of all the fabulous houses that they might be lucky enough to enter'.

In the first few months of 1940, Bloomsbury's green spaces and period buildings seemed to have lost their lustre. Buildings sat to all intents and purposes abandoned, 'To Let' signs mounted over their brickwork and sandbags piled over basement windows. Connolly passed by classical facades of grimy brick and faded stucco mansions long since converted to flats. A major preoccupation of his, through the war years, was of the city itself as a cause of anxiety. London wore him down and was the focus of numerous rants recorded in his journal. Most people in London, he said, 'are run-down, querulous, constipated, soot-ridden, stained with asphalt and nicotine and, as a result of sitting all day on a chair in a box and eating too fast, slightly mad sufferers from indigestion.' Later in life, he would return to these spots from the country and find himself 'doubled up with a nameless and immediate anguish, blackened with fear'. He would dash into a bookshop, or gallery, to efface himself among the antiques. The sight of a young couple greeting each other on a doorstep had a suffocating effect, recalling for him some words of Petronius, 'An old love pinches like a crab.'

Once back in his empty home, he began again the cycle of anxiety and remorse that had been set in motion the day 'Jeannie' had set sail for America, and that was exacerbated with every day that she failed to write. Despite a 'momentary depression at sunset', he was at his best from six o'clock to ten. Then the feelings of anger would creep up on him. The 'two faces' would inevitably return, and through all of this 'a feeling of claustrophobia, of being smothered by my own personality'. After an hour in bed, anger turned to misery, then misery to panic. 'The low tide and nadir of hope about 2 a.m. to 4. Magical euphoria wells from 4 a.m. to 6 – the thalamic "All Clear"; peace and certainty arise through despair.'

This, assuming he was not stood somewhere away from his bed awaiting a real 'All Clear'. Air-raid sirens he referred to as 'the nymphs wail[ing] from the top of the hill'. From the one-month period he had been living on the King's Road while the first alarms, all false, had resounded throughout the city, Connolly had got into the habit of walking up to Sloane Square. There, in the island made by four roads now empty in the blackout, beneath a slight canopy of trees that might perhaps have been a reassurance in their resemblance to a barrier or guard, local residents could hobble down to below the city's surface. On another occasion, Connolly had gone to Markham Square to try out the private shelter of his great Oxford friend Noël Blakiston. Blakiston was immensely proud of the bunker he had installed in his back garden, stocking it with anti-gas blankets, anti-gas suits, tin helmets and mustard gas treatment. In different circumstances, Connolly and Jean might perhaps have created a private sanctuary of their own. As things stood, however, Connolly found Blakiston's stronghold all rather too real and 'couldn't stay in it for a second'. He preferred to be squeezed in among Sloane Square's 'horrible old colonels and stiff upper lips of both sexes'. Disappearing into huddles of bodies in overcoats, among the taciturn upper middle classes, one could experience a pleasant feeling of anonymity.

7

England Their England

Eric and Eileen Blair, the former better known by his pen name, George Orwell, had just finished moving into their cheap top-floor flat at 18 Dorset Chambers, Chagford Street, near Marylebone station. They had brought with them a newly acquired dog, named Marx. They were there for Eileen's work, at the Censorship Department in Whitehall, and to be ready should Orwell's application for war work - he was currently on a waiting list of authors and writers - be successful. The move brought to an end what could reasonably be called Orwell's wilderness years. The phase of his life spent tramping, his stint as a militiaman in the cold, squalid and rat-infested trenches of Spain, and intervening years absorbed by animal husbandry and an unruly vegetable garden at his dilapidated Hertfordshire cottage, were in some respects a deliberate act of protest against London-centrism. The London of Orwell's novels had so far been an outsider's London - sleeping in 'spikes' (the casual wards of workhouses) in *Down and Out in Paris and London*, Gordon Comstock's move south of the river in *Keep the Aspidistra Flying*. 'Insider'

London was the domain of Orwell's now disowned wealthy and carefree Eton classmates, not scholarship boys like himself.

The Orwells had arrived on 1 May, and would still have been orientating themselves to this new area of north-west London when news outlets began delivering the most shocking news of the war since its declaration the previous year. It was the beginning of the course of events that would lead to evacuation from the beaches of Dunkirk and the Fall of France. Though without a radio in the new flat, Orwell followed these events closely, as he was used to doing with any political or military news, through the pages of the *Daily Telegraph* and the London papers the *Star*, *Evening News*, and *Evening Standard*. With the perspective of a war veteran, he observed how the manoeuvres of the German army on land were being supervised by the newly assembled and powerful Luftwaffe, which was making it impossible for its opponents to concentrate an army. Orwell decided passionately that it would be better that the British Expeditionary Force be 'cut to pieces' than capitulate. Everything seemed to hang in the balance; as John Lehmann wrote in his diary at this time, 'The attack on England must come, and soon, and it will be one of the biggest events in history.'

Some nights he and Eileen would go to the pub – likely the Gloucester Arms on Ivor Place – to hear the nine o'clock news over the communal radio. What struck Orwell most about this time was the way in which the British public were avoiding giving the war their full attention. For Orwell, the war was all-consuming; but in his local pub, the radio would sit silent until either he or Eileen could convince the insouciant barmaid to switch it on. Even then the warnings of 'dark and heavy tidings' had fallen largely on deaf ears. As in the years leading up to the war, people adopted a vague and non-committal approach to the sharing of information. Discussions were conducted in hushed tones. 'It is impossible to overhear any comments on it in pubs, etc', Orwell put down in the first entry to his wartime diary.

There was, it seems, a widespread distrust of information caused by the ubiquity of what Orwell calls 'rumours'. Three days after the first regiments had landed, a whole range of different realities were filtering back from overseas. It was discussed how

> Beaverbrook since his appointment has got 2,000 extra aeroplanes into the air by cutting through bottlenecks. That the air raids, possibly on London, are due to begin in 2 days' time. That Hitler's plan for invading England is to use thousands of speed-boats which can ride over the minefields. That there is a terrible shortage of rifles (this from several sources). That the morale of the ordinary German infantry of the line is pitiably low.

There were other whispers – God knows where they came from – which presented a more critical view of the British war effort, such as those which claimed embarrassing mistakes by military command in landing troops in Norway not in the darkness of night but in broad nocturnal daylight. These apocryphal scraps, where they slipped through the grate, must have been of professional interest to Eileen, who spent her days on the trail of potentially disparaging news sources. Orwell, on the other hand, was using this black-market news to inform his political writings. He wrote to the editor of *Time and Tide*, a left-wing and feminist publication for which he was now theatre critic, to insist that the slogan 'Arm the People' be adopted for political dissent. 'When the civil population is unarmed,' he wrote, 'parachutists, motor cyclists and stray tanks can not only work fearful havoc but draw off large bodies of regular troops who should be opposing the main enemy.' Orwell had drawn up a radical plan for national defence. All place names ('shopfronts, tradesmen's vans, etc., bearing the name of their locality') and signposts should be painted out, fields must be blocked to prevent aircraft from landing, while hand-grenades, shotguns and radio sets should be distributed among the general population.

Some events were so big that they were impossible to contain. Eileen was in the pub one night, without her husband,* when she first heard the French city of Dunkirk mentioned in relation to the fighting on the Western Front. This was horrible news: her much loved brother, the chest and heart surgeon Laurence ('Eric') Frederick O'Shaughnessy, was in France with the Royal Army Medical Corps, and would be among the now cornered troops. It was a strange broadcast, a sort of argument in which the broadcaster kept interrupting a recorded speech by a colonel who was returning from Belgium to say that the French were to blame for what was happening, as well as the British military authorities for leaving their men in the lurch.

Orwell had been with Cyril Connolly that day, taking a walk around a park and discussing his current favourite subject, the possibility for the war as first stage in an English revolution. For this to happen, however, the public would have to take an active interest in the war. Connolly had attempted to answer some of Orwell's questions regarding the surprising idleness of Londoners. 'It is seemingly quite impossible for them to grasp that they are in danger,' Orwell had reflected, watching a game of cricket being played. Evidently the reasoning was that 'the air raids didn't happen last time, so they won't happen this time'. Connolly felt that they would grasp nothing until the bombs were dropping, then pandemonium. Orwell spent the first of June at Waterloo and Victoria stations trying to get some news of Eric from the men (reportedly 150,000 of them) now returning from Dunkirk ('Quite impossible, of course.') It would be a few days before they heard of his death, on one of those French beaches. Walking out into London the following day, Orwell saw 'the usual Sunday crowds drifting to and fro, perambulators, cycling clubs, people

---

* Orwell was at the newly opened Torch Theatre on Hyde Park Corner, reviewing a play for *Time and Tide*, when he heard the news, delivered by an usher, in the interval.

exercising dogs, knots of young men loitering at street corners'. There was not the slightest indication 'in any face or in anything' that people had grasped that they were likely to be invaded within a few weeks. He picked up a copy of a popular newspaper, the *People*, to examine how it was treating the situation. Adverts for all kinds of unnecessary luxuries - soap, cosmetics, holiday resorts and fraudulent patent medicines - and only three which even mentioned the war. Britain was doing what Orwell thought it always did: sleepwalking into disaster. A few days later, he passed a bus bearing a huge advert: 'FIRST AID IN WARTIME, FOR HEALTH, STRENGTH AND FORTITUDE. WRIGLEY'S CHEWING GUM.'

FRIENDS IN HIGH PLACES

Orwell and Connolly were quite the unlikely pairing, though they understood each other the way only those who have met in earliest childhood can. They had been together through preparatory years at St Cyprian's School in Eastbourne - they were among a minority of graduates to later claim that they had a disagreeable time - and at Eton, where both had been deposited by academic prizes. At St Cyprian's, they had kept themselves entertained and soothed their woeful victims' hearts by walking over the Downs and discussing literature.

> He liked these very morbid stories about mysterious plagues and illnesses [Connolly remembered]. He liked *The Masque of the Red Death* and he liked all Wells's imaginative stories about people from other worlds causing epidemics and pestilences. He liked these fearful morbid, moral questions like 'Would you drink a pint of blood to save your father?'

Though easily ridiculed as 'one of those boys who seem born old', Orwell had maintained popularity as the voice of cold reason among their teenage cohort. He proved to his fellow students that there was more to life than the values espoused by the pre-1914 English school system, and that true intelligence was a powerful gift which made one in some ways untouchable. At the time, Connolly had felt himself to be a stage rebel, whereas Orwell was a true one. This was still the case thirty or so years on. It seems unlikely that Connolly would have risen to any serious political conviction during the war period had he not, in the latter years of the 1930s, been reunited with Orwell and begun to edit his work. In return, Connolly showed Orwell through the door into literary London. He used his own position to better Orwell's, suggesting publishers for manuscripts and offering entrées around town ('I am sure Secker would jump at you. I know them if you want me to suggest it').

It is unclear exactly when Orwell and Connolly had met again in person, though a line in one of Orwell's letters ('I was sorry I missed seeing you again before leaving London') suggests at least one meeting to have taken place in January of 1936. Orwell had then left to travel to Wigan for his book. Connolly remembers that he had received 'an invitation to dinner with him at his rooms in Islington', where he had had an 'excellent' meal of steak and chips prepared by Orwell himself.* It is an amusing scenario to imagine – a notoriously snobbish gourmand being cooked an 'excellent' meal by a famous ascetic. In the company of Orwell, Connolly became his most compatible and adaptable self; both men were, in a sense, in awe of each other. Meeting each other's eyes on that doorstep, a teasing and unpretentious schoolboy friendship had recommenced

---

* Orwell's final London address of 1936 was, in fact, at South End Road, next to the heath in Hampstead. In remembering this meeting, Connolly seems to have transposed the day's activities on to a later Orwell London residence, 27 Canonbury Square, Islington, where he spent the years 1944 to 1947.

immediately. 'His greeting was typical,' Connolly wrote, 'a long but not unfriendly stare and his characteristic wheezy laugh, "Well, Connolly, I can see that you've worn a good deal better than I have" . . . My fat cigar-smoking persona must have been a surprise to him.' Connolly was unable to speak, so appalled was he by 'the ravaged grooves that ran down from cheek to chin', which he put down to years of suffering and privation, on his old friend's face. In respect of Orwell's personality, which had captivated a young Connolly, much was still the same. 'Anything about Orwell is interesting,' he reflected; 'He was a man, like Lawrence, whose personality shines out in everything he said or wrote.' He said the same to Anthony Powell, when they had dinner together a few weeks later. Powell had just read and enjoyed *Keep the Aspidistra Flying* and was wondering why he could not dredge up any memories of Orwell from Eton. Perhaps because they were a couple of school years apart. 'Connolly, in his own special way, was enthusiastic about Orwell,' Powell wrote. What he seemed to enjoy most was the way that the Connolly and Orwell personas fell on entirely opposite ends of a spectrum. Orwell's 'rigid aestheticism, political intransigence [and] utter horror of social life' must have been quite inconceivable to Connolly.

Returning from the North of England at the end of March, Orwell had then invited Connolly and Jean to come up and visit him at Wallington, in Hertfordshire, where he had now set up. If it is difficult to imagine Connolly enjoying a no-nonsense steak in a no-nonsense London flat, it requires an even greater effort of the imagination to place Connolly and Jean, together, at this small, unheated cottage where the garden was a 'pigsty' and the only toilet at the end of it. There is no record of this visit, if it took place, though Connolly at some point would meet Eileen, whom he described as charming, intelligent and independent.

As courteous and enthusiastic as Orwell, in person and in correspondence, could be, it was not the easiest friendship for Connolly to maintain. Not only was Orwell constantly on the move, but, as Connolly attests, he was also deliberately keeping himself at arm's length. Orwell seems to have felt that, after leaving Eton, that carefree and privileged world had then closed its doors on him. Connolly recalled 'tr[ying] to overcome his prejudice against the left-wing university group of the 'thirties [Auden, Spender, et al.] which I so admired', and would reintroduce him to some of their old schoolmates ('I am not in touch with many of the Etonians of our time,' Orwell explained in a letter reaching out to his former friend Denys King-Farlow, adding, to confirm the picture of himself as an odd man out, 'I have had a bloody life a good deal of the time but in some ways an interesting one'). But his attempts at softening Orwell were slow to bear fruit. In *The Road to Wigan Pier* (1937), Auden and Spender were still the 'fashionable pansies' and the London literary scene 'a sort of poisonous jungle where only weeds can flourish'.

When Orwell wrote to Connolly asking the dates of publication for his novel *The Rock Pool*, he had explained his intention of reviewing the book for the *New English Weekly*. It was a gesture of friendship. 'Not that [the *New English Weekly*] gives one much of a boost,' he wrote, 'but every little helps.' When the review was published, however, it turned out to be filled with puritan indignation towards everything Connolly represented. It is an example of the 1930s Orwell at his most unpleasantly pious. Connolly's desire to write about 'so-called artists who spend on sodomy what they have gained by sponging' suggested 'a kind of spiritual inadequacy'. 'It is clear,' Orwell wrote, 'that Mr Connolly rather admires the disgusting beasts he depicts, and certainly he prefers them to the polite and sheeplike Englishman.' It was disappointing, because the book was otherwise so skilfully composed and Connolly 'almost the only novel reviewer in England' who did not make Orwell sick; Connolly simply had to change his course and write about 'normal' people instead. Orwell's subsequent letters seem sheepishly apologetic; Connolly's, in response, admirably forgiving. With Orwell, of course, he knew who he was dealing with. He had reviewed *Burmese Days* as an 'admirable novel', but one composed from 'efficient indignation . . . and irony tempered with vitriol'; *Keep the Aspidistra Flying* held many truths but was a 'savage and bitter book'.

Orwell and Connolly got back in touch while the former was still away in Spain with the POUM (Workers' Party of Marxist Unification). It was the peak of British left-wing agitation regarding the ongoing conflict. Connolly, an unlikely war correspondent, had recently travelled to Barcelona on the *New Statesman* payroll; he was safely back in character when he wrote home, approvingly, that the city was 'much more social than before'. Otherwise, his report was a gloomy one. Everything - the political, economic and military situations - seemed worse than at the time of his last visit. Official communist backing, Stalin's endorsement of the Popular Front, had blunted the revolutionary vision, giving power to careerist moderates and alienating other factions. 'Left-wing groups [were now] apparently more intent on fighting one another than opposing Franco.' Connolly had returned to England 'with a hopeless premonition of defeat'. It was perhaps because of his unfitness as a political commentator that he was able to give such a frank account; he had not committed himself, emotionally, devoutly, to any mission. In many ways, like Orwell - like Virginia Woolf - he was an outsider. To British fellow travellers who, Connolly wrote, 'could mount a very solid cold shoulder . . . controlling, as they did, so many columns and corners in the Press', these accusations were unthinkable. Stalin was above criticism and there was no way the revolution in Spain, with great traction globally, could fail. Stephen Spender was among those who found Connolly's 'defeatism' unhelpful and felt that he should have kept his mouth shut.

Seemingly the only person who was not offended - who, in fact, agreed with what Connolly had written - was Orwell, who wrote from Sanatori Maurin in Barcelona that he was with the POUM militia and had recently been 'nastily wounded':

> not really a very bad wound, a bullet through the throat which of course ought to have killed me but has merely given me nervous pains in the right arm and robbed me of most of my voice. The doctors here don't seem certain whether I shall get my voice back or not.

Somehow, even while laid up in hospital, Orwell had been keeping a close eye on all the Spain coverage. He praised Connolly's article, which he had just been reading, and the *New Statesman* in general, for presenting other viewpoints besides the communist one. He thanked Connolly for telling the public 'that [he] should probably write a book on Spain'; he did, indeed, intend to. Orwell ended the letter by, quite sweetly, expressing his regret that Connolly had not been able to visit him while he was posted in Aragon. 'I would have enjoyed giving you tea in a dugout,' he wrote. He would be back in England soon, to begin writing about his experiences.

Then came the incident involving Nancy Cunard's 'Authors Take Sides on the Spanish War' questionnaire, a pamphlet produced by the *Left Review*, no doubt one of the publications Orwell had, since his years in Burma, liked to nail to a tree and shoot at. One hundred and forty-eight of the world's best-known writers had responded to the questions 'Are you for, or against, the legal Government and the People of Republican Spain? Are you for, or against, Franco and Fascism?' positioning themselves for, against, or neutral. Orwell, recently returned from Spain and at the height of his paranoid, self-martyring isolation, had spoiled his ballot. 'Will you please stop sending me this bloody rubbish,' he replied.

> This is the second or third time I have had it. I am not one of your fashionable pansies like Auden and Spender, I was six months in

Spain, most of the time fighting, I have a bullet-hole in me at present and I am not going to write blah about defending democracy or gallant little anybody.

He then challenged the editors to have the 'guts' to reproduce his rant. Thankfully for him, they did not. He had ended the letter with a threat spoken directly to his now favourite scapegoat:

By the way, tell your pansy friend Spender that I am preserving specimens of his war-heroics and that when the time comes when he squirms for shame at having written it, as the people who wrote the war-propaganda in the Great War are squirming now, I shall rub it in good and hard.

It is difficult to believe that Spender, as a principal signatory, would not have read these words. As D. J. Taylor rightly puts it, 'Quite why Orwell should have selected Stephen Spender as the luckless victim of his asperity is not immediately obvious.' To Orwell, Spender seemed 'the epitome of the well-intentioned, left-leaning non-combatant' who would have entirely missed the point of the recent events in Spain. It was no longer a question of being simply for or against the Republican government. Since the communists, with Russian backing, had emerged on top in the disputes between the left-wing factions, the jails had begun to bulge with excommunicated revolutionaries of different shades. The Spanish government was far more afraid of a real revolution, of being 'too victorious', than it was of the fascists. It wanted essentially to remain liberal-bourgeois, and the fact that even the intellectuals in Britain had failed to realise this was proof of the success of British propaganda in diverting their attention away from what was really a regression toward a capitalist status quo. Orwell had arrived in Barcelona in December 1936 willing to fall in with any of the pro-government contingents, providing their objective was all-out social revolution.

The POUM was merely the first to be willing to take him. Less than eight months later, however, Orwell and Eileen, for their association with the group, had been flagged as Trotskyist traitors both in official Soviet documents and in a report to the Tribunal for Espionage and High Treason at Republican headquarters in Valencia. Orwell and his wife fled Barcelona knowing that they could be shot for being the wrong kind of revolutionaries.

It was after the manuscript of *Homage to Catalonia* had gone off to the publishers that Orwell wrote to Connolly that he had come down sick and was in bed. 'I've been spitting blood again,' he wrote – he had been through this at least three times before. The entire thing was little more than an inconvenience; he was going to the Preston Hall sanatorium near Aylesford to be X-rayed but had little doubt that he would be found to be perfectly all right. 'It always turns out to be not serious, but it's alarming when it happens,' he explained. More importantly, would Connolly be willing to review the book when it was out? Books about the Spanish conflict were now tediously common, but an endorsement from Connolly could help this one to stand out.

Orwell had many visitors to his bedside at the sanatorium, but one person he had not expected to entertain was Stephen Spender, who wrote to say that he had heard from Connolly that Orwell was unwell and, if the patient was bored, he would like to come and visit him. Though embarrassing for Orwell, particularly in these humbling circumstances, neither man saw this as a confrontation. Surprisingly, Orwell had actually been trying to meet Spender for some time, once asking Connolly whether they might all have lunch together. 'I've often said rude things about him in print, etc., but I daresay he won't know or won't mind,' Orwell had written, making a rather bold assumption of Spender's benevolence. He was right, Spender didn't mind. Ubiquitous in the limelight, Spender was a seasoned professional and used to being the focus of such complaints. If Orwell believed that what was written in criticism should have little bearing on personal relationships, then Spender's policy was even more forgiving. After Orwell had apologised for attacking him, Spender asked how he could feel he had attacked him if they had never actually met and exchanged words. What mattered was how one behaved in person, not what was written down. But Orwell insisted. He had, he said, made offensive remarks 'in passing' about 'parlour Bolsheviks such as Spender and Auden'. These had not, of course, been his exact words.

> I was willing to use you as a symbol of the parlour Bolshie because *a.* your verse, what I had read of it, did not mean very much to me, *b.* I looked upon you as a sort of fashionable successful person, also a Communist or Communist sympathiser, and I have been very hostile to the C.P. since about 1935, and *c.* because not having met you I could regard you as a type and also an abstraction.

The communist movement in Western Europe had begun as a movement for the violent overthrow of capitalism but 'degenerated within a few years into an instrument of Russian foreign policy', as Connolly had noted in his article on Spain. Orwell felt that writers like Spender had been duped into identifying with the Russian bureaucracy; they had needed something to believe in, after disowning the beliefs of their fathers, and communism is the 'patriotism of the deracinated'. Their lives had been too comfortable and they could be orthodox about communism, could toe the party line, only because they had never known the brutality comprised in its mindset. They wrote with a clear sense of purpose, could wing it as poets, but could never write great novels, 'the most anarchical of all forms', because they were too devout. Orwell could, however, acknowledge Spender and Auden's recent shift in tone; neither had lately written about the Spanish war with anything resembling their usual romantic zeal.

Once again Spender brushed this off; Orwell should not feel that

he had to retract his comments just because they were now personally acquainted. He should, of course, be true to his impressions.
The contrast of views here explains more about why Spender was
on the inside of this world and Orwell on the periphery than could
any detail of their backgrounds. Orwell was a man with a mission,
but he was not, like Spender and John Lehmann in particular,
a man of the will. He did not share their adaptability and open-
mindedness, and had no interest in the fate of 'literature' in and of
itself. Spender found all passion, where it related to literature, to
be exhilarating and, indeed, validating. Orwell was quite comfortable with being, as Connolly had written, 'savage and bitter' in his
writing - it suited him, being the curmudgeonly outsider - but this
could not translate to real life:

> Even if when I met you I had not happened to like you, I should still
> have been bound to change my attitude, because when you meet
> anyone in the flesh you realise immediately that he is a human being
> and not a sort of caricature embodying certain ideas. It is partly for
> this reason that I don't mix much in literary circles, because I know
> from experience that once I have met and spoken to anyone I shall
> never again be able to show any intellectual brutality towards him,
> even when I feel that I ought to, like the Labour M.P.s who get
> patted on the back by dukes and are lost forever more.

Connolly believed that Orwell 'suffered from a typically English
form of the Oedipus complex, by which, having dealt his father's
authority a swinging blow he would rush up to say, "Have I hurt
you?"' Nonetheless, seeing Orwell so physically compromised,
hearing him backtrack like this, had left an impression on Spender
that no amount of fist-shaking and foot-stamping could ever change;
Orwell could not write as humanly as he did without being, first and
foremost, a man of great sincerity and principle. Something else
had stuck with Spender, which was the aura of sorrow that seemed

to hang about the patient: 'I remember this rather drizzly voice. Listening to one of Orwell's monologues, with all its rambling speculations, was very English in a way. It was like walking through a drizzly street - hearing his very monotonous voice.'

HOUSES COLLAPSING LIKE PLAYING CARDS

On 10 June, Orwell and Eileen heard the news that Italy had declared war. They shared the same appetite for first-hand experience so, the following night, had walked around Soho to see whether the damage to Italian shops was as had been reported. They saw three shops with smashed windows, leaving Orwell to wonder where this political fervour had been dug up from among a population that for the past months had been struggling to even mention the war. 'The Spanish war simply did not touch the mass of the people,' he reflected. 'The low-down cold-blooded meanness of Mussolini's declaration of war must have made an impression even on people who as a rule barely read the newspapers.' The Italian community appeared to have anticipated this reaction. The majority of its businesses had already relabelled themselves as 'British' - F. Gennari Ltd, the Italian grocers on the corner of Frith Street and Old Compton Street, was now 'entirely British', the Spaghetti House on Goodge Street, selling Italian foodstuffs, a 'British Food Shop' - or had gone neutral and 'Swiss'.

In a sense, Orwell was exactly where he wanted to be. Perhaps the principle conflict of his life was with his nation, which he loved and loathed in equal measure. In London, he felt close to any developments, any word of government failure and dishonesty (particularly with Eileen doing the job she did), and being alive in wartime was a privilege to a documentarian. Auden and Isherwood were equally obsessed by their English identities - were the poets of Englishness in crisis – but also felt they had possessed enough of their country to dismiss its dishonesty and move on. From foolish, ignorant, bigoted England Orwell could never have walked away. In England one breathed a different air to abroad. The grass was greener here, and even the cooking, Orwell felt, deserved to be esteemed among the best in the world. Orwell, as Anthony Powell explained, was a rebel, and like most rebels he was half in love with the thing he was rebelling against.

Orwell and Eileen were watching at the front door of Eileen's family home in Greenwich when the East India docks were hit. It was 24 August, the first real raid on London so far as Orwell was concerned because it was the first in which he could hear the bombs. He recorded 'a loudish bang but not alarming and gave no impression of making the earth tremble, so evidently these are not very large bombs that they are dropping'. This was an 'accidental' attack; on direct instructions from Hitler – or so it was reported – London was off limits, and the bombing crew intended for the Shell Haven oil refinery at Thurrock on the Thames Estuary. Ostensibly, they had become lost due to a mixture of poor navigation and bad weather, and the cargo was released over parts of north-east London and the City. On the other side of the river, the church of St Giles Cripplegate had taken a direct hit. As one journalist reported, describing the aftermath of this proto-raid, the flames had quickly spread over a sizeable territory and 'silhouetted St. Paul's in the glow'. Haphazard though the attack was, the bombs that fell that night were sufficient to turn Churchill's focus towards Berlin. That first impact Orwell heard from the doorstep was of untold significance.

From that moment on, the people of London had – in Stephen Spender's words – 'lived in a trance-like condition'. Orwell stayed at Spender's flat the night of 12 September while a battery gun, firing in the square with only short intervals of respite, kept everyone and their dog awake. But that was later. In the two weeks following the 24 August attacks, it was air-raid warnings that did not culminate in actual bombing - about half a dozen every twenty-four hours - which caused the greatest trouble. The successful advance to Dunkirk had allowed Germany to position its airfields on that northernmost point of France, little more than half an hour's journey from the British capital. This made it possible for the Luftwaffe to orchestrate flyovers for all hours of the night. 'It is perfectly clear that these night raids are intended chiefly as a nuisance,' Orwell wrote after another night of broken sleep back in the Marylebone flat with Eileen. They had been woken around 3 a.m. and had to decide in groggy disorientation whether to dive for a shelter or fall back to sleep, in this case choosing the latter. 'Hitler only needs to send his planes half a dozen at a time to hold up work and rob people of sleep to an indefinite extent.' Of the final three nights of August, Orwell calculated that the noise of the alarms had consumed about sixteen to eighteen hours which could have been spent in sleep. On these occasions, drifting in and out of consciousness 'with a vague impression of anti-aircraft guns firing', he would find himself 'mentally back in the Spanish war, on one of those nights when you had good straw to sleep on, dry feet, several hours' rest ahead of you, and the sound of distant gun-fire'. Not surprisingly, Orwell was also having bad dreams.

Two nights later, the Orwells were awoken by a 'tremendous crash' caused by a bomb about a mile away in Maida Vale. They had quickly returned to sleep, Orwell's attitude at the time - one likely shared by Eileen - being that the British people simply had to learn to ignore the bombs, and go on as normal. But a three-day silence in the pages of his diary, lasting from the daytime of 7 September through to 10 September marks a shift in attitude, an acceleration of fear. Since that first date, the fateful opening night of what the newspapers had coined 'the Blitz', London had been held in the grip of terror. Houses in the East End were now collapsing 'like playing cards', the Docklands had sustained another, this time more deliberate, attack, and there had been significant damage in Holborn and parts of Marylebone. 'Can't write much of the insanities of the last few days,' Orwell had put down when the diary entries restarted. He was already, like everyone else, feeling the exhaustion of war. 'I should think three months of continuous raids at the same intensity as the last four nights would break down everyone's morale,' he wrote. A continuous anti-aircraft barrage was now being kept up through the night, 'apparently firing blind or merely by sound', but this, conversely, was 'well worth it, for the effect on morale'. Orwell continues to record the quality of his sleep: okay, the night at Stephen Spender's, despite the battery gun drilling away in Mecklenburgh Square, but other times the whole house would shake, enough to rattle objects on the Blairs' kitchen table. Almost every night the lights would go out at least once, dimming when a bomb passed close by ('Why . . . nobody seems to know') then coming on again in about five minutes. The dog would become 'subdued and uneasy', but not, thankfully, wild and savage, like some had been reported to do. 'Almost impossible to write in this infernal racket.'

In the morning, 'the streets would have an unreal air,' Spender's friend, the writer and auxiliary fireman William Sansom recorded:

> The City continued about its business, there was an atmosphere of normality in the traffic and the people going to work; but the undertone whispered, the memory of the firebells and the ambulances of the night, the sharp smells of burning and the poison of plaster dust, the knowledge of the stretcher and the shroud.

Orwell noted that for the first time in his life he had heard sleep-deprived bus conductors losing their tempers and shouting at passengers. The burden of exhaustion was made heavier by the understanding that all of the destruction of the past night would have to be cleaned up, a ceaseless war of attrition fought against broken gas and water pipes, mangled electricity lines, expectorated glass, and the debris from crushed buildings - there was a 'miniature pyramid in Hyde Park' - which had to be piled up around London. Getting around the city had also become much more difficult, often impossible. Entire streets in Marylebone were now cordoned off for unexploded bombs, meaning Orwell had been unable to get to a stationer's for a new notebook to continue his diary entries. 'To get home from Baker Street, say 300 yards, is like trying to find your way to the heart of a maze,' he grumbled. He was up on the roof of Cyril Connolly's new flat, in the Athenaeum Court building near Piccadilly, when bombs began to rain down as they had most nights of the past seven months and an enormous fire swelled up from behind St Paul's. 'It's the end of capitalism,' Connolly had declared; 'It's a judgement on us.' The blaze was also watched by Stephen Spender in Bloomsbury, who observed smoke and gigantic flames 'seen against the silhouetted foreground of Bloomsbury's eighteenth-century squares'. 'It recalled Turner's picture of the destruction of the ancient Houses of Parliament,' Peter Quennell, Cyril's great friend, said of the scene; 'and Pepys' record . . . of how he had watched the Great Fire as it rushed up the hill of the city, "a horrid malicious bloody flame, not like the flame of a normal fire"'. But Orwell was far away, in his exhaustion mesmerised 'by the size and beauty of the flames'. Connolly suspected that Orwell 'felt enormously at home in the Blitz, among the bombs, the bravery, the rubble, the shortages, the homeless, the signs of revolutionary temper.'

Orwell was now spending more time at the *Horizon* office in Bloomsbury, as well as seeing John Lehmann across the square. His pre-war publishers, Gollancz, being in Henrietta Street, Covent Garden, with Gerald Duckworth's company and Chapman and Hall, this was the first time he had been inside this world. He was a hit, socially, known for his gentle manners if not his sartorial etiquette. Watching him around these new acquaintances, Connolly saw that Orwell was like a 'John the Baptist figure coming in from the wilderness':

> He came along looking gaunt, shaggy, shabby, aloof, and he had this extraordinary magical effect on these women. They all wanted to meet him and started talking to him and their sort of fur coats shook with pleasure. They were totally unprepared for anyone like that and they responded to something.

Orwell was impressed by *Horizon*, for whom he had now contributed a handful of articles and reviews. The first and most substantial, 'Boys' Weeklies', had appeared in issue 3, of that March 1940. It was a genuine departure from the kind of content typically expected from a publication of high literary aspirations, and another step away from the ivory tower for *Horizon*. By stopping to scrutinise that which was meant to be skim-read, laughed at and then tossed away, Orwell set a new bar in analytical thinking in an age that aspired to meritocracy. He made the most unpretentious and ephemeral of forms seem as legitimate cultural artefacts as the adult literary novel. The article was the product of a truly original mind, and Connolly was a welcome recipient. As D. J. Taylor has written, '*Horizon* provided Orwell with a ready-made medium for his work, administered by an editor who was prepared to sympathise almost indefinitely with what he wanted to say.' Orwell wrote in his 'London Letter' for the US left-wing publication *Partisan Review* that *Horizon* was a 'sort of modern democratised version' of the now infeasible highbrow literary magazine. They kept going only with difficulty, but nonetheless held firm in their literary standards at a time when, despite an increasingly high demand for fiction, hardly any good books were appearing, only those 'of a trashiness that passes belief'. The shorter forms contained in its pages were becoming increasingly indispensable. 'Only the mentally dead are capable of sitting down and writing novels while this nightmare is going on,' Orwell wrote; 'The conditions that made it possible for Joyce and Lawrence to do their best work during the war of 1914-18 (i.e. the consciousness that presently the world would be sane again) no longer exist.'

In Bloomsbury, Orwell would have met many, like Peter Quennell, who were currently residing in the 'Big House', Senate House, in Russell Square. The staff there - perhaps it was the same for Eileen - 'were required to work in shifts - so many hours in a stifling subterranean dormitory under hairy much-used blankets; so many above ground crouched at [their] usual desks or, during a lull, asleep on the floor'. The news came in on pieces of tape, which had to be scrutinised while an assistant barked 'No reference to a certain type of bomb! No mention of the latest raid!' Specific numbers of casualties became 'some casualties'. Though they made up much of this workforce, this was not the job for a writer: 'It went against the grain,' Quennell wrote, 'to pick up my blue pencil, and reduce a dozen ominous sentences to a few mangled and comparatively meaningless lines.' This was not yet what Connolly had described as 'the genial guidance of thought by the state which undermines the love of truth and beauty'. Opinion still remained officially free, the dust had settled over the schismatic Auden-Isherwood affair, and magazines like *Horizon* and what had been relaunched at *Folios of New Writing* were in favour with the leadership, seen as good for morale. Books were not being censored except by conscientious editors on a voluntary pre-publication system. 'No poet,' John Lehmann wrote, 'got into trouble with the civil authorities over the expression of alarming or gloomy sentiments'.

But still that looming tower of 'concentrated purpose' seemed to represent something, not just for the German planes who were nightly taking potshots at it, but for the (Lehmann's words) 'denizens of neighbouring squares creeping beneath its pile'. The stories that leaked out into the pubs from inside its walls - amusing as they were - had to be closely monitored. All kinds of injustices were possible now that the goalposts had started to shift. There was something about that building. Early in 1941, the Orwells moved to a new flat at 111 Langford Court, in St John's Wood, a nondescript interwar apartment building. From the window there, one could make out the chalk pyramid of Senate House on the skyline across Regent's Park. One could stand, then, like Winston Smith, on the seventh floor of Victory Mansions, and from the window look out at the Ministry of Truth 'tower[ing] vast and white above the grimy landscape'.

8

Now We Are in the War

Virginia finished *Roger Fry* in the week beginning 19 February 1940. By the Friday it had been sent to Fry's sister, Margery, for reading, and the following day Virginia came down with bronchitis. It had been a hostile winter at Rodmell, with the snow blowing in drifts across the garden and under the door of the shed she used for writing, and Virginia all the time thinking how fortunate she was not to be on one of the British ships then patrolling the North Sea. That she would fall ill on almost the very day the book had been expelled from her system, having to spend most of the following fortnight in bed, seemed both cruel and humorously opportune. She read Havelock Ellis, who had died the previous year, and listened to the dithering but surprisingly persistent rainfall haunting the valley. By the time she was able to walk out again, spring had appeared in crocuses and snowdrops and Leonard was building a rock garden. Virginia felt cleansed and free.

Writing Fry's biography had been the bane of her existence

for coming up two years, and now it was off her hands. A typical diary entry regarding its progress runs as follows:

> A bad morning, because I'm dried up about Roger. I'm determined though to plod through and make a good job, not a work of art . . . But there's no blinking the fact that it is drudgery and must be; and I must go through with it. My hand, as I see, won't write.

The description of 'drudgery' appears frequently, as well as words like 'churning', 'grinding' and 'chafing'. For the duration of the project Virginia had been forcing herself completely outside of her comfort zone of creative and polemical writing, and the joylessness of the challenge cast a gloom over her general mood. In these circumstances, life could seem empty and endless. 'I seem forever climbing the endless stair,' was the way she expressed it. To keep herself happy, Virginia was having to supplement her groans of non-fiction with brief jolts of secret novel-writing; this was *Pointz Hall*, later renamed *Between the Acts*. This was necessary, for, as Leonard writes in his memoir, though she 'was an intellectual in every sense of the word' and possessed a 'strong, logical, down-to-earth brain' as shown in her essays, she could deal with facts and arguments on the scale of a full-length book 'only by writing against the grain, by continually repressing something which was natural and necessary to her peculiar genius'. The light now showing itself at the end of the tunnel, Virginia heaved a sigh of relief: 'Thank God, this time next week I shall be free,' she noted for 31 March 1940, in between entering Margery's corrections.

But perhaps that drudgery – the burdensome weight of the challenge others had set for her – was an anchor that she did not realise she needed. In the proceeding months, Virginia would begin to feel oddly devoid of context, as if the definitions of her life had been blurred. On 27 June, she visited her sister at Charleston, yet another event which she experienced as slightly unsettling. She thought how, despite her sister and niece, as well as Duncan Grant and Clive Bell, being inside the house, it was only *Pointz Hall* that now kept her from floating away. 'I'm loosely anchored,' she reflected. The confinement of wartime had fostered introspection, and she could now not feel herself in relation to the public or society as a whole. Her actions sank silently down then came dutifully to rest without any commotion. 'No echo comes back.' In this state of mind, the impending publication of *Roger Fry* was imbued with none of the old angst. 'I have so little sense of public that I forget about Roger coming or not coming out.' At any other time, circumventing these dark feelings would have been a cause for celebration. Now, the absence of any strong feelings either way seemed symptomatic of the deadening effect of wartime, and the growing sense of unreality. 'Those familiar circumvolutions,' though insidious, had 'given back an echo and so thickened my identity'. What lay beyond these new feelings, this deadness? Virginia wondered.

Adding to this, everything at Rodmell was now up in the air. Some of the changes seemed less important than others, like how the Woolfs had given away all of their saucepans to a neighbour, Mrs Ebbs, 'to make aeroplanes with', or the fact that there was now a large hare hanging in the kitchen, the basis of their meals for the week. But even Rodmell, with its population in the low hundreds, seemed to have been swept along in the militarisation efforts of the country. In the early mornings, from the window, the 'broad stalks' of the searchlights still rose off the meadows, making their final checks on the sky before locking up for the night. In the daytime, men would come to excavate along the river for fitting gun emplacements - to Virginia, they looked like little swarms of busy ants. Then there were the lorries carrying materials that thundered along the Roman Road. What might have once seemed impossible had also come true: a shortage of visitors, the phone sleeping silently on the hook, and totally free time. She was similarly intrigued by what she called 'the effect of the war on weather', a capricious, extreme climate that sent strong gales battering on her window from the direction of Europe.

In due course, German bombs aimed at Rodmell cement works would miss their target and land with the dull thuds of explosions on the banks of the River Ouse, some way behind Leonard and Virginia's house. 'There happened to be quite a high tide at the time and the river poured through the gap and flooded the fields,' Leonard reported. 'Then some days later there was an abnormally high tide with a strong wind, and a great stretch of riverbank gave way. The whole Ouse Valley was flooded and a great lake of water now stretched from the bottom of my garden to Lewes on the north and almost to Newhaven on the south.' Virginia was made gleeful by this mutation in the topography; it meant a new stimulus for her mind, a new prompt for writing while tramping about the nearby countryside of an afternoon. 'The sea comes almost to our gate,' she wrote to a friend. 'The gardener has just called me to come and look at a swan.' Through all the novelty of these conditions, however, came the occasional sudden realisation of being 'remote in this waterlogged country', and the practical restrictions of wartime – prices rising by first tuppence and then thruppence – all amounting to the gradual tightening of the screw. Virginia lived closer to boredom than before, and news over the radio illustrated a more widespread stagnation: 'Now and then the wireless reports a ship sunk in the North Sea,' she noted on a slow day snowed in at the house. Life was so much changed by the war that Virginia couldn't now imagine London in peacetime, 'the lit nights, the buses roaring past Tavistock Square, the telephone ringing'. Tied up with the changes imposed by wartime was the fact that her existence was now predominantly a rural one. When the fire at Monk's House set her dreaming, she would often return in her thoughts to the little alleys of London, the smell of the Thames, and her walks up to the Tower. 'That is my England,' she always concluded. When this boredom was disturbed, it was usually to be supplanted by much more ominous moods, as on one night, sat by the wireless with Leonard, listening to the villainous Nazi propagandist William Joyce, 'Lord Haw-Haw', teasing and snickering about the inevitable British capitulation. Afterwards, the radio was switched off, and 'we sat silent in the 9 o'clock dusk'. This was the moment when invasion was felt to be coming 'any day now'.

Virginia had started out the year with positive resolutions, something only possible once *Roger Fry* was in its final stages. Her ambition was, in her words, to always be enlarging the circumference of her ideas, giving her brain an ever-wider scope. By doing this she would guarantee that she was always moving forwards, and thus defeat the 'shrinkage of age'. She would be objective, detached, and cut herself adrift from fussy, cyclical personal feelings. 'One has no real identity there,' she believed, perhaps responding to the conditions of war where the 'I' was so much diminished, and yet ideas and values seemed more important than ever. Personal feelings were by definition excitable and inconstant, uncertain ground for this next, important phase of her life. Only by shedding them could she gain, finally, the kind of happiness that's secure. Like Connolly, Virginia had been rereading the late Sigmund Freud. Freud, she felt, could provide the model for this new objectivity, could help to centre her. The Romantic poets offered a similar service. In comparison to the contemporary poets, they seemed pure and uncorrupt. They clarified the relationship of the individual to his surroundings, rather than muddying it: they reminded one of how to feel. 'How lightly and firmly they put down their feet, and how they sing and how they compact, and fuse, and deepen,' Virginia reflected, reassured.

Next, it was important that she avoided any and all controversy; no more being 'stung' by the pugnacious literary world. This was not, however, a mode of living which she had ever sustained for long. Virginia was not sensitive per se, but by her own admission she could be 'snobbish' about good or bad reviews because they seemed a social embarrassment as much as anything else. Like-wise, she claimed that the only criticisms of her books that 'drew blood' were 'those that are unprinted; those that are private'. Peo-ple could be saying all kinds of things about her, and she would never know. In 1931, after a downbeat review from Hugh Walpole for *The Waves*, Virginia had been horrified at the thought that he 'should be running about London saying the new Virginia Woolf is a disappointment - all about nothing - exquisitely written of course'. A self-protective streak made her quick to fight back, or even to pick fights. Frances Partridge described how, in Virgin-ia's company, 'there was always electricity in the air, and though enthralled by the display of lightning, few people were entirely at their ease there, or could fail to wonder where the next flash would strike.' Partridge had been there, on one occasion, to witness Alix Strachey zapped by this lightning god. That evening, after dinner, Virginia was not in the most genial mood and had launched one of her 'frequent' attacks on 'the younger generation'. She targeted Strachey, saying 'And I know all about you, Alix. You simply spend your whole time dancing, and sink further into imbecility every moment.' Later, as Leonard led his wife out of the door, he had said, 'Come on, Virginia, don't disgrace the older generation.'

Avoiding controversy for Virginia meant staying well clear of the recent fracas surrounding *Horizon*. She knew Lehmann better than she did Spender, had been working closely with him at the Press for almost nine years, but as fate would have it both were her closest companions in the world of young Bloomsbury. The whole affair further complicated what was an already ambivalent relationship she shared with the younger generation. Publicly, she was eager to maintain an air of stateswomanly impartiality. When she received a letter from Spender which asked her to contribute for *Horizon* an article 'on the young', she responded carefully that she thought his invitation 'very nice' but 'I don't much want to do articles for anybody.' It was not, she said, a question of hurting

John's feelings, though it was true that *Folios of New Writing* was to be a Hogarth Press venture and Virginia would offer it any help she could. The primary reason for her refusal was that, after offending some critics in November with her article 'Reviewing' published in the *Times Literary Supplement*, she did not want to set all the young against her too.* It was not in her nature to hold back her true feelings, and everything she said now seemed to cause offense.

It is difficult to understand why Virginia made these statements when, for a full five months leading up to the end of April, she had been preparing her most extensive statement about the young writers of the day, to be given as a lecture in Brighton for the Workers' Educational Association (WEA), with whom she and Leonard had close ties. It is perhaps telling that, after announcing this intention in her diary on a Saturday in December, she returned the following day to mention that she had been thinking about her status as 'an outsider' and reflecting on her 'defiance of professional decency'. It is too much of a coincidence, otherwise, that the first day she mentions the talk she will give for the WEA is the same day she had refused Spender's appeal to discuss 'the young'. In all likelihood, it was Spender who gave her the idea; and Virginia's mind was like a wheel which, once set in motion, could not be stopped. She could never resist what she called 'the tug of vision'.

Walking from Rodmell up to Telscombe one mild day in February, Virginia had invented pages and pages of her lecture, which she had already worked out was to be titled 'The Leaning Tower', based on a metaphor she had constructed early on. She had been thinking a lot around that time about the younger writers, a

---

* One commentator, Robert Lynd of the *Political Quarterly*, who wrote under the pseudonym Y.Y., called Virginia's stance on reviewers 'surely the most contemptuous yet uttered: she tells them that they have ceased to be of any use to the world'. Another 'letter of abuse' was printed in the *TLS* on 11 November, after which Virginia wrote in her diary, 'Never again shall I be asked to write for the *TLS*: that's a gain.'

fact not unrelated to all the fuss and bother she had been party to surrounding Lehmann and Spender's falling-out. She had also been reading Spender's autobiographical novel *The Backward Son*, recently delivered in proof to the Hogarth Press, which would publish it. If Virginia mapped in her own recent works a gradual decline of something - authority, perhaps - then in Spender she sensed something in the ascendancy, his youthful and vigorous spirit. It gave her 'a pang of envy', no doubt reminding her, though the contexts could not be more different, of her earlier self. 'Some good novelist's touches,' she added, 'I could pick holes though.'

Spender was not a natural fiction writer, but he had a certain genius for self-examination and exposure, by turns serious and silly, always totally truthful, of the Pepysian variety. He describes in his diaries, for instance, the instance of letting out a long fart while walking down the street and the consequent hysterical laughter of a group of children positioned nearby. Despite the breakthroughs of the Bloomsbury cohort in regard to prudishness, Virginia had always had an uncertain relationship with self-revelation. It is true, as Hermione Lee has pointed out, that in her most substantial auto- biographical effort Virginia had begun 'to speak openly about her own sexual history'; courageously, too, in the sense that both of her abusers were only recently dead and the memoir clearly intended for publication. But more commonly she writes about herself 'in a deliberately self-restrained, jocular way', 'meant for suppressing sentiment'. This is because, as a woman, she feared the 'vision- ary figures' of the censors, who might admonish her. What Lee writes about Virginia's performances at the Memoir Club is also true of her feelings in the weeks leading up to the publication of *Three Guineas*, which could be broken down to 'her fear of expos- ing the "soul", her self-denigration, her horror of being laughed at, her turning of that male laughter and boredom on to herself, her determination to wear a mask rather than humiliate herself again'.

Virginia's fiction was at home with the steady and inanimate and flourished deep in the subconscious, whereas Spender's interest was in the finite, depraved and tumultuous centres of anatomy and emotion. A strong sense of the male form as both a focus point of carnality and something which is imperilled still lingered from a youth tainted by the negative augury of the first war and exalted by sexual exploration among the preened and athletic boys of Weimar Germany. The body fascinated Spender the way it fascinated Auden; it represented, paradoxically, the liberation of the laboriously constructed young English mind. Integral to this idea was the notion, made a mantra by Auden at Oxford, that all efforts must be made to do away with guilt and self-conscious shame. 'Now I am beginning to feel that I may soon come to regard my body as a source of joy . . . Perhaps, after all, I may become a complete human being,' reflects Paul, the narrator of Spender's *The Temple*, while experiencing the delights of Hamburg.

Fiction had become so direct in the course of the thirties that it now seemed an entirely different language to the one that Virginia had been working in. Post-impressionism (what Connolly calls 'the supreme flowering of bourgeois society') and its lightness of touch had gone. Lines hardened, serene streets were populated, and buildings and pylons cluttered the landscapes. John Lehmann had John Banting decorate a wall of his flat with a surrealist nightmare-vision. Peter Watson gifted his lover Denham Fouts with Pavel Tchelitchew's *Bathers*, an erotic painting with a distorted, *enlarging* perspective. But Virginia still believed, for example, that the best writing, the best art, was that which was suggestive, for 'it is made of the fusion of many different ideas, so that it says more than is explicable'. Writing now, she thought while on her walk to Telscombe, was not unconscious 'but stirred by surface irritation, to which the alien matter of politics, that can't be fused, contributes'.

Virginia's lecture fell on a Saturday, 27 April, a couple of weeks before the Germans launched their tripartite invasion of the Low Countries and just a few days before Orwell's arrival in London.

Roughly two hundred of Brighton's 'working classes' came to watch her speak for about an hour on the subject of the latest great revolution in British literature. She opened the talk by asking the question of why writers are so common sometimes, and other times so rare; and, by extension, 'Why do they sometimes write nothing but masterpieces, then nothing but trash?' To answer the question, Virginia took her audience on a whistle-stop tour of the century of writing which preceded the First World War. In 1815, she said, England had been at war, just as it was now. But the Napoleonic Wars 'did not affect the great majority of . . . writers at all'. Neither Jane Austen nor Walter Scott, both of whom were publishing books through this period, even mentioned the war in their novels. 'It is easy to see why that was so,' Virginia explained. 'Wars were then remote; wars were carried on by soldiers and sailors, not by private people.' And news of battles took a long time to reach those at home. There was no wireless. Jane Austen 'never heard the cannon roar at Waterloo' as today they might hear the gunfire across the Channel. Neither Austen nor Scott ever heard Napoleon's voice as every member of that audience would have heard Hitler's. After the Napoleonic Wars 'there was the Crimean War; the Indian Mutiny; all the little Indian frontier wars, and at the end of the century the Boer War. Keats, Shelley, Byron, Dickens, Thackeray, Carlyle, Ruskin, the Brontës, George Eliot, Trollope, the Brownings – all lived through all those wars. But did they ever mention them?' The Battle of Waterloo, she concedes, is described in *Vanity Fair*, 'but only as an illustration, as a scene. It did not change [Thackeray's] characters' lives; it merely killed one of his heroes.'

Another thing that the writers of the nineteenth century had in common was their status as 'fairly well-to-do middle-class people'. Most were educated at either Oxford or Cambridge, some were civil servants or professors, and all brought in 'considerable fortunes' from their work. The contrast here with the present day was less explicit. Indeed, Britain's most successful writers were still, overwhelmingly, sourced from its public schools and ancient universities. Of the names closest associated with the current movement, all had enjoyed the privileges of one or both of these kinds of institutions. Orwell had attended a preparatory school in Sussex with Cyril Connolly and Cecil Beaton as classmates; afterwards, Orwell and Connolly had gone off to Eton on scholarships, and Beaton went to Harrow. At Eton, Cyril Connolly had known John Lehmann. Stephen Spender went to Gresham's School in Norfolk, where Auden had enrolled a couple of years before him. Both, like Connolly, went on to study at Oxford. Christopher Isherwood met Edward Upward at his boarding school in Derbyshire; both went up to Cambridge, as did Lehmann. It had been a similar story with Virginia's male friends. Then what had changed since the last century? Only that, to the nineteenth-century writer, the upper-middle-class identity was a very clearly defined one. 'To the nineteenth-century writer,' Virginia explained, 'human life must have looked like a landscape cut up into separate fields. In each field was gathered a different group of people. Each to some extent had its own traditions; its own manners; its own speech; its own dress; its own occupation.' This, she argued, was the status quo, and as it generally went unchallenged, writers when they talked about members of other classes, or, more likely, of their own, could treat them as 'individuals' rather than the embodiments of political tension, or 'types'. They constructed their characters out of familiarity and a generally convivial sense of the worthiness and interest of others – but also while safe in the knowledge that life was not suddenly going to change. They, the writers, 'had leisure; they had security', as did the people they wrote about, of a different sort. They wrote without urgency. Because they only wrote about what they knew then they could work from the unconscious part of the brain, what Virginia calls the 'under-mind', the place where all true art is born.

Such easy-going types lasted 'roughly speaking, till the year 1914'. Before 1914, Desmond MacCarthy could write how, at Cambridge, 'We were not very much interested in politics. Abstract speculation was much more absorbing; philosophy was more interesting to us than public causes.' They, like the nineteenth-century writer, could go about their leisure studying Latin and Greek and rambling happily in the long summer holidays through England, France, Italy. Now and then they published books, but all in their good time. 'It seemed to them that they were to go on living like that, and writing like that, for ever and ever,' Virginia said. 'Then suddenly, like a chasm in a smooth road, the war came.'

The concept of the leaning tower seems in many ways to be a response to Connolly's *Enemies of Promise*, which two years before had named and populated the category of its opposite, the ivory tower. Connolly, in the twenties, was a member of the last Oxford generation which retained any sense of themselves as non-political beings. He insists they were still aesthetic beings, and grotesquely materialistic. As Connolly tells it, there was a watershed between his own 'unconscious political generation' and those who would come of age in the engaging thirties' struggle.

Stephen Spender, who left Oxford in 1929, was conscious of a 'generalised rebelliousness' filtered down from young dons who had been through the first war, and remembered with resentment how their fighting compatriots had been promised 'a land fit for heroes to live in'; but politics mixed with university life at a fairly weak dilution. In 1929, while Julian Bell was an undergraduate at Cambridge, 'the central subject of ordinary intelligent conversation was poetry'. Returning in 1933 as a research student, however, he found himself immersed in impassioned communist cells, and joined hunger marchers on stomps to London and in clashes with police. Overtly political or not, no one who came of age after 1914 was immune to the sense of injustice, unacknowledged and thus unresolved, which seemed to expose the greater evils of the class system. The young learnt 'from Noël Coward, from Wilfred Owen and Siegfried Sassoon . . . to loathe the old men who had made the war'. Their socialism was based on hatred for senior figures, conservative or liberal, who they believed to have sent the young to their deaths, and on sympathy for the men they had fought alongside - or commanded - at the front. Flags, memorials and uniforms made Isherwood 'tremble with rage'. The development of leftism at universities would culminate in a passionate response from the undergraduate community to the Spanish Civil War. This was the period which began with the readoption of the gold standard in 1925, was punctuated by the General Strike and Great Depression, and ended with the creation of the National Government as an emergency measure in 1931. The luxuries enjoyed by the pre-1914 writers were thus denied to writers like Connolly who otherwise fitted the mould, and he would spend a lifetime bitter about this age-old, implicit agreement which had not been upheld. The 'representative names' mentioned in Virginia's lecture - G. K. Chesterton, T. S. Eliot, Somerset Maugham, Hugh Walpole, Rupert Brooke, E. M. Forster, Aldous Huxley, the Sitwells - were the scorned denizens of Connolly's ivory tower. They had sat upon a tower 'raised above the rest of us; a tower built first on [their] parents' station, then on [their] parents' gold', and it had been a steady tower.

The post-1914 writers, Virginia explained, had also been raised up above others on a tower built for them by their parents. 'At first sight,' she said, 'there seems little difference, in station, in education.' But what did they see from up there? The same which everyone else saw - 'everywhere change; everywhere revolution. In Germany, in Russia, in Italy, in Spain, all the old hedges were being rooted up; all the old towers were being thrown to the ground.' New towers were raised which flew the flags of communism and fascism, and a sense of urgency ran through everything. The towers in England 'built of stucco and gold' could no longer be steady towers, for they stood on shifting ground. They were, therefore, 'leaning towers'. From now on all books written inside these towers 'were written under the influence of change, under the threat of war'.

Virginia went on to accuse the younger generation of a terrible hypocrisy. Though sympathetic to their predicament, she disliked the cynicism that arose as a response. The impact of being inside the leaning tower, she said, was 'first discomfort; next self-pity for that discomfort; which pity soon turns to anger'. From here they began to lash out. 'The bleat of the scapegoat sounds loud in their work, and the whimper of the schoolboy crying "Please, sir, it was the other fellow, not me",' Virginia told the audience at the WEA. She was referring to the criticism or caricature of such figures as the 'retired admiral or spinster or armament manufacturer', but it is tempting to hear this as her conviction that she herself had become a scapegoat for the paranoia of literary elitism and whingeing schoolboys such as Connolly. Such whingeing was distasteful, regardless of whom it targeted, for it railed against the exact people who had given them, after all, 'a very fine view and some sort of security'.

Less applicable to the only temperamentally political Connolly was Virginia's description of the huge currents of class guilt which ran through these stripling writers. 'In 1930,' she explains, 'young men at college were forced to be aware of what was happening in Russia; in Germany; in Italy; in Spain.' That they should not was out of the question. And they could not, like Desmond MacCarthy and his entourage, sit around discussing aesthetic emotions and personal relations. They had to read Marx, and become communists and anti-fascists. In doing so, they began to resent their status and the identities that had already established inside of them, and yet, however much they wished to, they could not throw away their educations or their upbringings. Whether they liked it or not, they were stuck with the Chestertons and Eliots and Maughams and

Woolfs. Their sense of guilt regarding their backgrounds trapped them and destroyed their abilities to write from the more neutral, less contextualised subconscious. Their poems and plays and novels - she names Cecil Day-Lewis, Auden, Spender and Louis Mac-Neice - were 'full of discord and bitterness, full of confusion and of compromise'.

The crux of Virginia's argument was her belief that politics and literature could not be fused, just as the upper and lower parts of the brain would always operate at different levels of intensity. 'The poet in the thirties was forced to be a politician,' she said. This explained 'the pedagogic, the didactic, the loudspeaker strain that dominates their poetry'. To Spender's memory, though representing 'an under-lying left-wing orthodoxy', the well-known writers of the twenties, including Virginia herself, had always dissociated themselves from politics in their literary work. In their political writing, too - they wrote for the *Daily Herald* and the weekly *New Statesman and Nation* - they believed that their own creativity had nothing to do with their political opinions. Spender and his friends had made a con-scious decision to introduce political thought to their creative work, despite being aware of renouncing 'values which we contin-ued nevertheless to consider aesthetically superior, in Joyce, Yeats, Eliot, Lawrence and Virginia Woolf'. He would have agreed with Virginia that much of his generation's political poetry had a 'tem-porary "for the duration" look' - it was oratory, not poetry, she felt - and would never experience the million afterlives of the passages of Wordsworth she quoted for the WEA. But then, Wordsworth was not facing the Nazi SS. More offensive to Spender was the view of the poet 'as detached, clinical and never expressing his own opin-ions or personality'; by their reckoning, the 'impersonality of Eliot' was as unhelpful as the 'passive, receptive, analytic' but personal poetry of Keats. It did nothing to hold politicians to account, allow-ing them to go on acting out of self-interest.

Such feelings had arisen organically among a disaffected youth.

They came less from an attitude of abrogation – they did not, like Julian Bell, take to politics to shake off the aestheticism of Blooms-bury – than from a clear comprehension of the new world they lived in. What they were writing, Spender felt, was 'a variety of war poetry', and he could accept the jokes published in Geoffrey Grigson's *New Verse* which called him 'the Rupert Brooke of the Depression'. Both he and Auden, for instance, were 'profoundly influenced' by the diction and attitudes of Wilfred Owen – 'a kind of anti-fascist pacifist poetry'. Everything in Spender's life so far had made him more politically anxious and self-assertive than Virginia could ever be, and, consequently, the two writers were viewing the matter from entirely opposite vantages. To Spender, Louis MacNeice's *Autumn Journal* was 'the best political commen-tary of the decade', whereas Virginia in 'The Leaning Tower' would call it 'feeble'.

She believed that they had been influenced too much by 'the films' ('explains the lack of transitions in their work and the vio-lently opposed contrasts') and were too eager to ape the gradually developed styles of Yeats and Eliot (they did so 'clumsily and often inappropriately'). Though vocally unimpressed with their writing, Virginia was in awe of their personalities. In a sense, they were everything she was not. They shared Leonard's dogged altruism, which Virginia so admired, and were anti-bourgeois to a degree that her Bloomsbury set had never achieved. It was an enormous challenge that they were taking on, being a voice for all and writing their experience when they 'had nothing settled to look at; nothing peaceful to remember; nothing certain to come'. In their 'curious, bastard language' – somewhere between the aristocrat and the peasant – they longed to be closer to all. Most admirable was the way in which, in writing about their 'petty, vain, mean, frustrated, tortured, unfaithful and successful' selves, they were telling the unpleasant rather than flattering truths. 'By analysing themselves honestly . . . these writers have done a great deal to free us from nineteenth-century suppressions,' Virginia told her audience, who were much closer to peasants than aristocracy, and would have seen themselves more in the new kind of literature. These developments were, she said, germane to a moment in history when, as politicians were so fond of saying, a war was being fought 'to bring about a new order in Europe'. This was a good and necessary thing, for Virginia had felt herself an outsider just like the writers of the day and everyone in the audience. Evoking her earlier metaphor of the fields neatly contained and protected by their hedges, she ended by saying 'Let us trespass at once. Literature is no one's private ground; literature is common ground.'

A week later Stephen came around to number 37 for tea and a chat. He was upset because *The Backward Son*, now published by the Hogarth Press, had been 'sneered at'. 'I praised it,' Virginia wrote in her diary. And it was sincere praise. Stephen was yet to find out what Virginia had said in her lecture, for it would not be published (in *Folios of New Writing*) until the autumn.

AN UNUSUAL OUTING

'The real air war began for us in August 1940,' Leonard wrote in his memoir. The first sight of German planes over Rodmell was, he felt, 'very odd'. It was a Sunday afternoon, and he and Virginia had just sat down to eat their lunch when they heard 'a tremendous roar' and rushed over to the window. 'Right on top of us they came,' recorded Virginia the following day, 'three, I think'; there were two planes, remembered Leonard, and they flew 'a few feet above the church spire, over the garden, and over our roof'. His eyes were fixed on the black crosses which flashed on the underside of the planes' wings, and swastikas on the tails. Virginia recalled feeling like 'a minnow [staring] at a roaring shark', and noted the colour of the aircraft as olive green. 'Then pop pop pop' (Virginia): the

German planes fired and hit a cottage in the village, and then again unleashed a volley of bullets on a house in the neighbouring hamlet of Northease. Virginia heard later that day that the planes they had encountered had been five bombers 'hedge hopping on their way to London'. Leonard could add in retrospect that, of all the hundreds of German planes he saw during the war, except in this incident he never experienced any of them firing bullets at people or buildings on the ground. For most others it was the bombs that came first.

On 31 August they got a phone call from Vita Sackville-West, who had planned to arrive that evening for her visit to Monk's House but instead found herself trapped by falling bombs in her Sissinghurst home in Kent. 'Can you hear that?' she said down the line to Virginia. No, Virginia couldn't. Then a pause. 'That's another . . . That's another.' Quoting her friend in her diary, Virginia could not bring herself to describe the feeling 'of talking to someone who might be killed any moment'. 'Now we are in the war. England is being attacked,' was all she could muster by way of a vignette.

Three weeks later Virginia and Leonard had their 'strangest visit' to London. It came just three days after the entry in her diary for Saturday, 7 September, where Virginia reported seeing more planes over the house 'going I suppose to London'; the capital, she reflects, was being raided every night. But though it may have seemed that way to a frightened onlooker, the attacks on London prior to 7 September were in fact only sporadic, with all efforts focused on specific targets – thirty bombers targeted RAF Croydon aerodrome on 15 August, and on subsequent occasions suburbs in the south-west and north-west of the city. According to William Sansom, who served as a firefighter for the duration of the war, the first bombs to strike the city's metropolitan area 'fell just before eleven o'clock on the night of the 30th of August, 1940. They fell in Belgravia – four one kilo incendiaries . . . each a foot-length candle of smooth silver magnesium fused and fired by a dark pith of thermite.' It was on 6 September that Hitler and Reichsmarschall Hermann Göring, commander-in-chief of the Luftwaffe, had agreed the new strategy of daily, widespread and indiscriminate attack. The raids had begun in earnest the following night. If, like Virginia, the population of London had believed that the bombing would continue at the pre-7 September rate, then the reality of the following weeks was more horrible than anything they could ever have conceived.

The seventh of September was one of the fairest days of the century, a day of clear warm air and high blue skies. It continued the trend of what had so far been a vintage summer; Virginia had written in her diary just two days before that it was 'hot, hot, hot. Record heatwave, record summer if we keep records this summer.' It was that same cloudless sky and glorious sun that back in May had been getting on Frances Partridge's nerves. 'It's impossible not to remember that it is ideal weather for air-raids,' she wrote. The seventh was such a pleasant day that, Sansom says, 'in many men's troubled, taut minds there was yet an appreciation of that queer lullaby of peace brought with the weather, an evocation of London summers of the past'. But by 6 p.m., with the sun still lingering in the sky, this spell was abruptly broken. True, air-raid sirens sounded distantly, where they could be heard, from the city's East End, but more alarming were the reports, passed on informally by neighbours and pedestrians, that something more significant was taking place. 'Report Centres and other official quarters knew that at last the Luftwaffe had struck hard, there and then, that after-noon, at London proper,' writes Sansom:

The docks were ablaze. And as the sun set, those in the West End streets grew conscious of the unbelievable, for the sunset occurred not only in the accustomed West near Putney and Willesden, but also incredibly in the East over St. Paul's and where the City of London was held to lie.

By eleven o'clock high explosives were being dropped on the main pedestrian streets of central London, including five bombs in the vicinity of Victoria station, an 'unlucky time', Sansom writes, due to the fact that the pubs had just closed and punters had made their way up to the end of Vauxhall Bridge Road to where they would board their night trams and buses. Many people were killed and many were wounded; many also experienced for the first time 'the powdered smell of smashed plaster and brick' which 'poisoned the air'. The bombing continued in this manner for the remaining hours of the night. It was the perpetrators of this deadly, personal attack, as opposed to the usual strategic or warning shots, that Virginia had witnessed en route to London that day.

Leonard and Virginia approached Bloomsbury in their car from the direction of Tottenham Court Road, but were presently met with a cordon at the bottom of Gower Street. There were no visible signs of damage, but traffic was being directed east into Holborn. When they arrived at Doughty Street they found a crowd blocking their entrance. There was, they saw, another cordon, this time around Mecklenburgh Square, and they were told by some wardens that they would not be allowed to enter. Virginia spotted the Hogarth Press clerk Miss Perkins at the window of number 37. What they found was that the house 'about 30 yards' from theirs, just opposite across the road, one of the numbers 26 to 34 in the white building 'Byron Court', had been struck at one that morning and completely ruined:

We walked round the back. Stood by Jane Harrison's house [at 11 Mecklenburgh Street, the street which, from the Heathcote Street entrance, flanked Virginia and Leonard's row of houses from the left]. The house was still smouldering. That is a great pile of bricks. Underneath all the people who had gone down to their shelter. Scraps of cloth hanging to the bare walls at the side still standing. A looking glass I think swinging. Like a tooth knocked out - a clean cut.

One of their neighbours, J. D. ('Sage') Bernal, Professor of Physics at Birkbeck College, was wearing an ARP armband and stepping precariously across the rubble. 'Who lived there?' Virginia found herself wondering. 'I suppose the casual young men and women I used to see, from my window; the flat dwellers who used to have flowerpots and sit on the balcony.' They had, she presumed, been 'blown to bits'. Their own house, they saw, was as yet undamaged, with not even the windows broken. Word among the onlookers was that 'the Jerrys had been over for three nights trying to bomb King's Cross'. Privately, Virginia had already decided that she did not want to spend the two nights in London that they had planned.

It was the right decision. The following day Lehmann rang them up at home; he sounded flustered. He had been in the Square overnight and the bombs had come perilously close. He was adamant that Virginia and Leonard come up as soon as possible to move the Press. The windows at 37 were all broken, and Mecklenburgh Square had once again been evacuated, on this occasion for the quite obvious fact of the great time bomb which had buried itself in the Square garden, not far from where Dorothy L. Sayers' Harriet Vane, in the opening pages of *Gaudy Night*, hears men playing tennis. Lehmann was now staying with his mother at her home in Bourne End, Buckinghamshire, after 'three of the most extraordinary days of [his] life'. 'Mecklenburgh Square was a pretty sight when I left it,' he joked.

Broken glass everywhere, half the garden scorched with incendiary bombs, and two houses of Byron Court on the east side nothing but a pile of rubble. Clouds of steam were pouring out of one side, firemen still clambering over it and ambulances and blood-transfusion units standing by with ARP workers and police. The road was filled with a mess of rubble muddied by the firemen's hoses, but the light-grey powder that had covered the bushes at dawn had been washed off by the drizzle. The time bomb in the

Square garden sat in its earth crater, coyly waiting. The tabby Persian cat from no. 40 picked her way daintily and dishevelledly among the splinters of glass on her favourite porch.

It was agreed that the Woolfs would come up the following day, Friday the twelfth, and meet Lehmann in the bar of the Russell Hotel in Russell Square to discuss the removal of the Press. While in London, they would also patch up the windows at 37, collect their post, and salvage any valuables. This, of course, was assuming they were allowed into the Square.

When they met Lehmann the following day they heard that the Square was in fact still closed. It was clear that they would not be able to carry out the various tasks they had wanted to, and so sat down in the hotel with Lehmann for a slow lunch. Within twenty minutes it was decided that, if business were to continue, all the work of the Hogarth - publishing, typesetting and printing - would have to be done under the roof of the Garden City Press in Letchworth, an unlikely hub of English printing where could also be found J. M. Dent, of Temple Classics and Everyman Classics, W. H. Smith & Sons, and the Arden Printing and Bookbinding works. It was an idea they had had in mind for some time. The Hogarth Press had been offered the use of two rooms, at a cost of £150 - a nuisance, Virginia felt, considering they were still paying the rent on two London properties. 'Never mind.'

It was only a day later that the time bomb exploded. The Woolfs heard about it on Wednesday, phoning ahead to Miss Perkins before setting off on another trip to London. Consequently, Virginia spent that morning with the phrase 'We have need of all our courage' going around in her head. She had of late been trying to visualise the experience of being killed by a bomb. It was an unpleasant notion, naturally, for Virginia had it in mind that she should like to live another ten years, and to write some more books. But she was more prepared than most. 'I've got it fairly vivid - the sensation,' she wrote in her diary, 'but can't see anything but suffocating non-entity following after.' Death would, she knew, and had said in a letter to Vita Sackville-West, be the one experience she would not get to describe. But more than death itself, she was picturing

> the scrunching and scrambling, the crushing of my bone shade in on my very active eye and brain: the process of putting out the light - painful? Yes. Terrifying. I suppose so - Then a swoon; a drum; two or three gulps attempting consciousness - and then, dot dot dot.

The windows that remained had now been finished off. 'Why did we ever leave Tavistock?' Virginia asked herself, in the pages of her diary. But, 'What's the good of thinking that?' More painful was the thought of her own, personal version of London - the London that had appealed to every happy, simple impulse in an otherwise complicated mind - being overwritten. 'Another bad raid,' she noted the following day. 'Oxford Street now smashed. John Lewis, Selfridge, Bourne & Hollingsworth, all my old haunts.' And then 46 Gordon Square, that first, most magical Bloomsbury address - the place where it had all begun - was collateral damage to a bomb landing elsewhere in the quadrangle.

It made sense now that they should sever all ties with the capital. The easiest way that this could happen would be if both properties were finally expunged. The tricky contract with the Duke of Bedford estate, landlords for an area of the West End and Bloomsbury containing Tavistock Square, was a tipping point, but one that could easily be circumvented were their former residence to be crushed by a German bomb. Already they were becoming more cut off. By the second month of bombing, the Lewes train would travel only as far as Peckham. Virginia heard stories from friends in the village of people who, leaving work in London at six o'clock, would not arrive home in Rodmell until two in the morning.

Leonard had now made contact with the Bedfords regarding their tenancy of 52 Tavistock Square. They were not going to take no for an answer. 'If refused,' Virginia wrote, 'we mean to tackle the Duke, and ventilate in the papers.' Despite the years of prosperity granted by the Hogarth Press - £1,000 annually for Leonard between 1935 and 1938 - as well as the surprise success of *Roger Fry*, it was inconceivable that they should be paying the costs of three separate properties, at least one of which was completely unoccupied, during the years of wartime austerity. Mecklenburgh Square in particular represented a substantial financial responsibility; the rent was 'so high', Virginia wrote, about £250 a year. The latest news from that house was that the servants had now nailed carpets over the broken windows. Virginia and Leonard were to make another attempt to get into the building, to salvage some belongings, that following Monday, 23 September.

The flat was dark, even on that 'lovely September day . . . of tender weather', with the heavy rugs plugging up the window voids, and yet the extent of the damage was perfectly obvious. The ceilings were down in patches and heaped everywhere was grey plaster dust and shattered china. It was the day that Lehmann was coming to initiate the transfer of materials to Letchworth. He had spent the previous night at the Athenaeum, where he had that morning had a nervous experience in the bath imagining an unexpected violent barrage and his having to 'cascad[e] naked in a torrent of soap suds down the grand staircase'. Lehmann was there to supervise their excavation of the basement, contending with removal men who had 'been at work without pause and probably with little or no sleep ever since the raids started, ignoring sirens and bombs and making as much haste as they could through cordoned-off roads that changed every day'. 'They had the trance-like expression of utter exhaustion as they went mechanically through the movements of packing and loading,' he wrote. At one point, Virginia stepped out to visit the bakery. Some kind of tea was, obviously, going to be attempted in the 'untouched' back rooms, for Lehmann and the rest of the workforce. It was while she was there that the bomb which had lain dormant in Brunswick Square suddenly blew. Virginia 'comforted the agitated worn women'.

On 17 September, Leonard and Virginia received the news that Tavistock Square was no more. It was relayed to them by Lehmann, who, residing more consistently in Mecklenburgh Square, would either have heard the impact as it happened a few streets away, or come upon the bombsite while en route into Fitzrovia the following day. Virginia was jubilant. 'Our private luck has turned,' she wrote in her diary. After the initial damage sustained in Mecklenburgh Square, where they had been living for just over a year, Virginia had cursed their decision to commit financially to a new property, believing that 'for the first time' she and Leonard had been 'rash and foolish'. Now, however, she 'need no longer wake in the night thinking the Wolves' luck has taken a downward turn'. It was with a 'sigh of relief', the following weekend, that Virginia went to test the veracity of Lehmann's report and entered Tavistock Square to see, where their house should have been, a 'heap of ruins'. 'Three houses, I should say gone,' she described: 'Basement all rubble. Only relics an old basket chair (bought in the Fitzroy Square days) and Penman's board "To Let". Otherwise bricks and wood splinters hanging. One glass in the next-door house hanging. I could just see a piece of my studio wall standing . . .'

She could pinpoint the exact spot where she had written so many books - the perfect arc of critical success, from *Mrs Dalloway*, through *The Waves*, down to *The Years* - which now was mere rubble. To give a sense of the destruction, Virginia's studio, which was now partially visible, had been way at the back of the house, occupying the space where a garden would have been. It had been a remarkably large room, originally meant for billiards, with a skylight which made it, when combined with a gas fire and an old armchair, ideal for Virginia's matutinal writing sessions. The rooms where they had 'sat so many nights, gave so many parties' were now 'open air' – or, as Virginia told her niece, Angelica Bell, 'Where I used to dandle you on my knee, there's God's sky: and nothing left but one wicker chair and a piece of drugget.' In that part of the house, the walls had been painted with frescoes by Vanessa and Duncan Grant. The 'cold and draughty and ramshackle' basement that had contained the Hogarth office and printing machine was now an unreachable catacomb. The hotel, next door to number 52, was untouched.

Less happily, 37 Mecklenburgh Square had in the interim since Lehmann's letter suffered its worst damage yet. Leonard, in a letter to Margaret Llewelyn Davies, described the unlucky sequence of events thus: 'First the house in Mecklenburgh Square was rather wrecked by bombs falling in the square, that is to say the windows were blown out and many of the ceilings down. We had just had it patched up when another large bomb fell in the street at the back of the square and fairly well wrecked us again.' They were now, he wrote, 'completely bombed out of London'. Despite 'miles and miles of Hyde Park, Oxford and Cambridge Terrace, and Queen's Gate [being] untouched', the damage that Virginia observed across Bloomsbury was 'considerable'. It seemed almost to have been meant for Virginia personally. Vanessa's studio in Fitzroy Street – where Julian and Angelica had played host to second-generation Bloomsbury – had been completely destroyed by an incendiary bomb. Thirty-seven, when they got to it after visiting Tavistock Square, showed an exaggerated version of the dilapidation they had encountered on their previous trip. 'All again litter, glass, black soft dust, plaster powder,' Virginia wrote. They had met, outside, a Miss Talbot and Miss Edwards, clerks at Dollman & Pritchard, the solicitors' office below the Woolfs' flat, who wore trousers, overalls and turbans and were sweeping. Virginia noticed how Miss Talbot's hands were shaking. The two women apologised to the writer for not getting a postcard to her in time, that she might be saved the shock of coming upon her home in this state.

'It's awful,' Virginia reflected. Miss Perkins, too, was entirely shaken up, despite her demeanour being of course 'friendly and hospitable in the extreme. Jaunty jerky talk. Repetitions.' Upstairs they had to lift a fallen bookcase which was blocking their passage. In Virginia's sitting room, window glass was sprinkled everywhere, including over the little cabinet she had bought for £3.15 at a sale of goods by her friend Ethel Smyth's financially ruined sister. Wind was blowing through the room, and around the house. Virginia's thoughts turned to what could be salvaged in 'this little car', its skeleton now exposed to the elements. Top priority was the multiple decades' worth of diaries – perhaps every entry written in London – which would have to be hunted down. They contained so much of her real and mental life; were, though she tried to paint her musings as 'writ[ing] off [her] aimlessness', the embodiment of that desire in her always to grapple with complex feelings and experiences and make them solid and understandable. They might one day make up a book; otherwise they, in their simplicity and consistency, and as a catalogue of memories, were there to soothe her when she had a headache. She was hoping also to find her fur coat, which, she thought, might have been buried under some of the debris. And then there was her father's signed, personally gifted edition of *The Origin of Species*, likely also his correspondence with Darwin and a copy of *The Voyage of the Beagle*. In 1879, Leslie Stephen, a high-profile commentator, had come out to place his faith in the great naturalist, then in the midst of a public controversy and the focus of the ire of Samuel Butler. 'Your note is one of the kindest which I have ever received,' Darwin wrote to Stephen, 'and your advice shall be strictly followed.' These artefacts had trickled down to Virginia after Leslie's death in 1904. Finally, all surviving silver, glass and china would have to be moved to safety; in the kitchen, Virginia packed away plates decorated by Vanessa and drinking glasses by Duncan Grant. And then there was a visitor, Mabel Selwood, governess of the Bells, who found Virginia on her chair, hunting for her possessions. Later, as Mabel was on her way out, she had paused at the door and said to Virginia - her typically 'discreet and matronly' demeanour now 'rather finer and sadder' - 'You hear them whistling round you, you wonder is it our turn next?'

Despite everything, the end of 1940 was a pleasant stretch of Virginia's life. On one day, Saturday, 12 October, she characterises her present life as 'almost too - I won't say happy: but amenable'. It was so pleasant, in fact, that she was beginning to neglect her reading and writing. 'But it's all so heavenly free and easy - Leonard and I alone.' Leonard could only agree: 'In Rodmell in those last months of 1940 we had suddenly entered into the silent, motionless centre of the hurricane of war,' he wrote. Virginia was, as Quentin Bell has written, 'torn between the cosmic disasters of war and the little *ennuis* of private life'. Thursday, 17 October, was 'a perfect day - a red admiral feasting on an apple day', and though most of the English public had felt bitter towards the long, cloudless, balmy season now drawing to a close, for it made them easier targets for bombers, Virginia was resolute in her belief that 'our Indian summer was deserved'. In *Between the Acts* she had one character announce, 'That's one good the war brought us - longer days.' But these were embarrassing thoughts which could not be broadcast. To describe a day in wartime as even amenable was, she knew, a 'treasonable' thought, and at other times she had almost to force herself to acknowledge the gravity of the wartime predicaments of others. 'The most - what? - impressive, no, that's not it - sight in London on Friday was the queue, mostly children with suitcases, outside Warren Street tube,' she wrote:

This was about 11.30. We thought they were evacuees, waiting for a bus. But there they were, in a much longer line, with women, men, more bags and blankets, sitting still at 3. Lining up for the shelter in

the night's raid - which came, of course. Thus, if they left the tube
at 6 (a bad raid on Thursday) they were back again at 11.

Virginia's instinct - the instinct her present mood dictated - was
to look upon such desperate scenes with the eyes of the artist
inspired, rather than as a fellow human being whose situation
might easily devolve into one comparably wretched. What she saw
was 'impressive' - but no, she was being too effusive. Her mind
always seemed to run in a different direction to others', but why
fight it, if she felt happy and contented?

There was a sense that the war had given her the upper hand.
She was no stranger to dark mental forebodings, and as Leonard
has written, 'Death, I think, was always very near the surface of
Virginia's mind, the contemplation of death. It was part of the deep
imbalance of her mind. She was "half in love with easeful Death".'
He, conversely, had some years ago taught himself not to think
about it. Quentin Bell contributes to this discussion the idea that
Virginia, in the manner of one who had suffered immense private,
internal conflict, was in fact relieved to have a problem to share
with others.

9

The Grey Light of Morning

The day that Lehmann had met with the Woolfs at the Russell Hotel, they had cobbled together a satisfactory plan for the evacuation of the Press and then - the Woolfs knowing their plans to spend the afternoon in Mecklenburgh Square were now impossible - settled in to hear Lehmann's account of the past few days in Bloomsbury. He told them that the night of Sunday, 8 September, had been his 'first intimate contact with war', and the beginning of the destruction of their peaceful square. He described the way that bombs whistled, if they fell nearby. He had heard two or three whistles that night, like 'ripping noises in the air, as if directly overhead, getting closer, and each time violent concussions followed by the sound of tinkling glass'. After the first couple of these scares he had believed the sound of the planes to be getting fainter, and had gone over to his window to look at the square. As he pulled the black curtains apart he realised that some of his panes had been smashed. He saw, too, incendiary bombs burning in the square garden and an enormous blaze emanating from the grounds of the

Foundling Hospital opposite Spender's flat in Coram's Fields. His first thought had been, 'How curious and almost incredible it was that this should have happened so near me.'

Lehmann had made his way downstairs after that, presumably to immerse himself in the hubbub of the neighbourhood after such a shocking and unprecedented collective experience. As Virginia had realised, one knew so little about one's neighbours, and yet in these circumstances they were the only people - not your friends, not your family - who shared in one's fate, or, if you were lucky, salvation. Lehmann spoke to a man from No. 46, who had just pulled up in his car and was letting himself in to his building. The man said that he thought the searchlight in the square garden had been destroyed. Lehmann then shouted down to his landlord in the basement shelter; he called something back sleepily, perhaps in fear, and Lehmann left him alone. It was then that he remembered the fire he had seen next to Spender's flat. He went to the door and from there heard the shouts of the men who were tackling the inferno, which, on second inspection, was alarmingly close to where Spender was. 'Well, poor old Stephen's the first to go,' was the 'odd, sad, resigned thought' that went through his head.* The presence of death and murder was, he said, very vivid in those moments. It was strange, he reflected, that the war could now actually be perceived behind all the stories they had been hearing. It had existed in newsprint and on the wireless, and now in the burning wreckages of nearby buildings and the 'enormous bellying cloud of grey dust advancing down the road'.

Lehmann was still standing by the bottom of the stairs when the

---

* In fact the only damage to 6 Lansdowne Terrace was Connolly's favourite window. But the unexploded bomb planted in the square would delay business for over two weeks, and in October *Horizon*'s printers, the Curwen Press, took a bad enough hit for two thousand copies of one issue to be wasted. 'Our office has been bombed and we have been without telephone for the three weeks, but we are carrying on', wrote Peter Watson to his friend Cecil Beaton.

next bomb struck. 'There was another tremendous explosion,' he recalled, 'the house seemed to clench itself like a fist for a moment, then silence.' He went to the door again. Strange, inexplicable sights, including a man in pyjamas walking through the dust cloud to his flat. Lehmann decided that it 'might be as well now to go to a shelter'. The trouble, he soon found, was that the little shelter put up by Irish labourers in the square garden not fifty yards from his flat seemed actually to be repelling people, rather than drawing them to its secure embrace. The man from No. 46 was now moving about the cul-de-sac in an ARP tin helmet, in the process of evacuating the shelter which, he told Lehmann, was perilously close to an unexploded time-bomb. The moment when the house had seemed to clench itself, that had been real – walls and ceilings and the roof testing the tensile strength of the building's wooden skeleton. Under the impact of bombs, Lehmann later found, buildings could actually sway, as if on a pivot, so that those inside felt themselves to be on a boat in a bad crossing. Each of the houses in the row, right down to Virginia and Leonard's, had 'rocked badly'. Not too many hours ago Lehmann had been in his 'shuttered bedroom', dining on chocolate biscuits and a bottle of wine and reading a novel, and now he was outside, by all intents and purposes alone, wondering where he was meant to be. The sounds – planes still circling overhead, the guns attempting to scare them off, the sirens pointing out the obvious fact of danger, the clamouring of firemen perhaps then attempting to pull Spender from the wreckage – melted together in a way that made them easier to ignore. A tree seemed to be growing out of the roof of Byron Court, adjacent to the Hogarth office – in fact the tree was exactly where it had always been, behind the building, and the building itself was completely gone.

A few minutes later Lehmann was sat on a step, 'scarcely under shelter', and talking in a desultory way with a young Auxiliary Territorial Service (ATS) woman in her green blazer and skirt uniform.

He looked across at girls lying asleep against their young husbands, a huddle of young men whose hair was powdered grey with rubble dust, and various women and children. 'Someone produced a Dostoevsky novel,' he noted. The lavatory door banged open and closed. More bombs whistled by. He counted down the hours until dawn, and the retreat of the German planes. 'At last, in the grey light of morning, the all-clear went.'

Virginia and Leonard said goodbye to Lehmann that afternoon to the sound of guns starting up again in the distance. As they headed off to find their car, Lehmann made his way back to Paddington, where he would catch his train on to Bourne End and his mother. He wrote in his diary two days later that Leonard had been 'rather agitated with the confusion of everything, also in a mood of rather unhelpful bravado that slightly annoyed me when we were discussing plans'. Virginia, he thought, had been 'very smiling and apparently collected'. Her worries were normal worries – 'Leo,' she had said to her husband at one moment, touching him on the arm, 'there are aeroplanes overhead, don't you think we'd better take cover?' This was the day that the Germans bombed Buckingham Palace. En route to Paddington, in a taxi, Lehmann was thrust back into that world of danger which he had described for the Woolfs. On Charlotte Street, by his sister Beatrix's flat, three screeches from above and bombs exploding no more than twenty-five yards away, bursting windows and causing traffic to pile up.* Lehmann's taxi swung violently from side to side and was finally stopped in a side-street where residents peered out of their doors to see what was going on. There had been no alarm. A cloud of dense black smoke was seen rising up from Howland Street.

---

* Beatrix, fortuitously, had been out shopping at the time. She had, however, had an equally nasty experience at the same moment in the Euston Road, where likewise no air-raid warning was triggered until after the fact.

CONFLICTS OF INTEREST

Lehmann had been warned about working with the Woolfs. It was not that they were explicitly cruel or unpleasant - there were enough of those types filling managers' chairs around the capital that the possibility, at the very least, had to be considered - but rather that they appeared completely unsuited for this kind of business, and tended to run their Press as though it were a much smaller concern than it really was. As far as anyone could tell, Leonard was in charge, but then the company's *raison d'être* seemed to be Virginia's novels. They presented as much a pair as any married couple could, their names of equal weight on the letterhead, and all was pulled together under that rather forbidding emblem of the wolf's head, shown in profile like the king on a half crown, and, it follows, strangely human. Perhaps the confusion stemmed from the proximity of the office to the Woolfs' own living quarters - upstairs in the same building, meaning that one could finish one's work and within a moment be in a sort of afternoon tea or dinner party atmosphere, looking at murals by Vanessa Bell and Duncan Grant. It was Julian Bell, Lehmann's close friend at Cambridge, where both were finishing in 1930, who was the most anxious that his friend should not enter unwittingly into any agreement with 'Aunt Virginia' and her husband, particularly seeing that Lehmann was such an admirer of their work and should not like to have any preconceptions shattered, and was also happy to remind everyone of the numerous young men who had taken similar roles at the Hogarth and left soon after calling Leonard an impossible manager and Virginia away on another planet. Nothing, however, could dull the radiance, for the twenty-three-year-old Lehmann, of the 'legendary Leonard and Virginia'.

Number 52 Tavistock Square was exactly as he had imagined it. It was the same place where, three years earlier, the illustrator Richard

Kennedy had grown used to the sight of people like Desmond MacCarthy standing on the opposite side of a high schoolmaster's desk used as a counter while they waited for Virginia to finish her writing. All of this took place in a basement which, when the house was used for its intended purpose, had been the kitchen and the servants' quarters. Kennedy, in his memoir *A Boy at the Hogarth Press*, sketched a crude map of the subterranean workshop which shows two windowless rooms connected by a dark, cramped corridor, with space in the first for three secretaries, and, in the room furthest back from the square, Virginia 'composing' at her work-desk - she could also occasionally be glimpsed setting the type for small books of poetry, Lehmann remembered - next to an old printing machine. The nook allotted to Lehmann was a former pantry and cupboard room, imagined by Kennedy to be used 'for the torture of Victorian skivvies', caught between the territories of Leonard, dictating to the secretaries, and Virginia, in the back, doing her own thing. 'It was badly in need of redecorating,' Lehmann wrote. There was a small window, destined to be jammed for the rest of eternity, which looked out onto the 'gloomy wall' of an outside passage, as well as a pitiful relic of a gas fire where employees would try in vain to warm their hands. Large bales of books lay all around, soaking up the damp from the stone floor, and the cupboards were 'piled high with the dusty files of the activities of the Press ever since it had started in 1917'. All of this apparent chaos yet represented to Lehmann a kind of 'sacred ground', particularly that room at the back:

> I would slip in, with carefully controlled eagerness and as silently as possible, to hunt out some books that were suddenly needed on the packing table in the front room, feeling that I was entering the holiest part of the house, the inmost ark of its presiding deity. I was even allowed, later, to work at the desk when they were both away.

Despite his unfading admiration for both of his employers, however, this deference would not last long. In May 1932, Virginia
was making the first reports in her diary of a falling-out between
Lehmann and Leonard. Lehmann had apparently complained to
Vanessa Bell of 'the irascible Leonard and the hard work and the
underpay', asking her to intervene. Virginia was pushed reluctantly
towards diplomacy, though she spoke of Lehmann as of a precious,
mollycoddled child: 'Today we have to discuss with him his "feelings" – I'm not especially sympathetic, thinking of all the time we've
spent.' In that moment, she had regretted the existence of the Press
entirely – what a fuss it all was, so many personalities, and a drain
on their time. She had a headache from all the time they had spent
going round the subject – about ten hours, she thought.

It was agreed – through gritted teeth, presumably, on Virginia's
part – that she was to help John more, and not to sit there 'with
a red cross on [her] door, so that [he] daren't come in'. By 'sitting
there', it was meant that she was apt to wander off and become
engrossed in her own writing. For the battle that raged eternally
in Lehmann's mind of writer versus editor had barely registered in Virginia's; she was, by quite a clear margin, a writer. By
September of that year, Lehmann had walked away from the
Press for the first time to live in Austria. Virginia, in her diary,
was indignant:

> What a blessing! That egotistical young man with all his jealousies
> and vanities and ambitions, his weakness and changeableness is no
> loss. But we – or Leonard, has lost an infinity of time. I suppose
> the severity with which Leonard was speaking to him on Friday
> when I came in to say Tea's ready upset his trembling apple cart:
> his vanity could no longer endure: so he threw up the sponge, but
> I must say with the least possible good manners or consideration.
> On the whole though what a mercy. Now I can roam about the
> basement unperturbed. And, coming from him, with this crashing

folly, one can take the line of least resistance - needn't attempt the amicable go between - needn't ask him to dinner.

Lehmann, unsurprisingly, had a totally different perspective on the breakdown of the relationship. He suspected the famously hot-headed Leonard to be antagonistic to the last, even later suggesting that Virginia's rant could not be trusted to be entirely genuine 'because one must remember that Leonard always had the right to read [her diary]'.

Lehmann had been introduced to the Woolfs by Julian Bell as something of a coming man; they also, of course, knew his famous sister, Rosamond, a writer of 'Greater Bloomsbury' and a favour-ite of Virginia's, who was six years older. On his part, Lehmann envisaged 'hard work, but congenial'. He would be bringing to the Hogarth various 'hubristic schemes to make the Press the centre of literary publishing for my generation', quite the zeal and direction the Woolfs had been feeling they required. They were struggling enormously with their current workload, balancing their lives as writers and publishers. Besides that, there was a risk, they felt - and were at times sure to already be the case - of stagnation. They were yet to properly get to grips with the younger writers, and relied heavily for their income on older 'cash cow' writers, of which Virginia herself was the principal. Virginia was already personally acquainted with Stephen Spender, but was yet to read any of Auden or Cecil Day-Lewis (despite having published his *Transitional Poem* as Hogarth Living Poets No. 8). She promised Lehmann that the work of both men, as well as his own first collection, would now be given due attention, and 'lie beneath the scrutiny of [her] aged eyes'. She must, she wrote, 'go into the question of poetry', though warning Lehmann that doing so might result in unearthing more of her controversial opinions. Virginia possibly only knew the names of these poets through her connection with T. S. Eliot, who had just published Auden's *Poems* at Faber. Starting his job, Lehmann was unconvinced by most of the titles then under contract at the Press, which the Woolfs had accepted before his arrival. What had they been thinking of, he wondered, when they paid for child-flapper-poet Joan Easdale's *A Collection of Poems*?

To make an example of Easdale, it has since been suggested that as a poet she was much closer to Virginia's tastes than any of the male names that soon fixed the gaze of the Press. Easdale's collection was number nineteen in the Hogarth Living Poets series, and was - this fact was told rather triumphantly to Hugh Walpole - Virginia's discovery. 'She sent me piles of dirty copy books written in a scrawl without any spelling; but I was taken aback to find, as I thought, some real merit.' The poems were well received among major critics of the day. She was compared to Edith Sitwell, and was 'reminiscent of the elliptical genius of Emily Dickinson'.* Lehmann, it is suggested, had arrived at the Hogarth Press with the intention of making a moribund British poetry scene fiery and political. The 'strange poems' (Virginia) of the teenage Easdale did not fit that mould, and so Lehmann had commandeered the Hogarth ship for his own schemes. 'Lehmann had enlisted Virginia Woolf in his mission,' Mark Hussey writes - a mission, as we have seen, she did not really understand or share. Indeed, Virginia recognised part of Lehmann's personality that 'craves influence and authority, to publish the books of his friends'. Nonetheless, he had an energy for publishing that neither she nor her husband were at that time able to muster. After all, they could not expect to make him manager without the Press being to some extent transformed in his image. Virginia understood that the progress of art was an

---

* I am relying heavily here on Mark Hussey's essay 'W. H. Day Spender Had a Sister: Joan Adeney Easdale', in *Leonard and Virginia Woolf, The Hogarth Press and the Networks of Modernism*, edited by Helen Southworth. See Hussey's piece for a fascinating retelling of the friendship between Woolf and Easdale. This particular quotation, included in Hussey's article, comes from a review in *The Spectator* by Richard Church.

independent force, unconcerned with the feelings of individual writers.

It was around this time that Virginia had written - at Lehmann's request - *A Letter to a Young Poet* for the Hogarth Letters series. Lehmann was eager for a glimpse inside Virginia's reticent, 'doubtful approval' of the young poets, and she, having just finished *The Waves*, her most avant-garde work ('not . . . poetical,' she explained, 'but purebred prose'), was in the mood to debate this less conventional form. It was an amusing, and friendly, project which they embarked on together. Virginia began her 'letter' by responding to a claim of John's that 'it has never been so hard to write poetry as it is today'. 'Never think yourself singular, never think your own case much harder than other people's,' was her advice. She discusses, somewhat teasingly, the necessity of a writer possessing a sense of humour in regard to their position as a 'leader'; to take oneself too seriously would benefit no one. 'For the first time in history,' Virginia wrote, 'there are readers - a large body of people, occupied in business, in sport, in nursing their grandfathers, in tying up parcels behind counters - they all read now.' These readers must be appealed to, she felt, conceding perhaps to a keep-your-head-down-and-do-your-job understanding of the writer's place in society. By the same logic, politics was no-go for writers not because it wasn't important but because it was not their territory. You could not merely react to something with your intellect and will, but, as Virginia once told Stephen Spender, 'have to be beaten and broken by things before you can write about them'. It was this, one suspects, that T. S. Eliot had meant when he told her 'the young don't take art or politics seriously enough'. It was not that they didn't care enough, but rather that they believed they could jump in and out of things which, to the actual parties involved, represented something very real and permanent.

It should not be assumed that to sympathise with someone's experience was to know it. Virginia questions whether the mundanity of the modern poetic subject, which was, after all, intended to appeal to a wide audience, actually represented a true 'colloquial'. There was that line of Auden's, for instance - 'walking . . . to ease the bowels'. It was jarring, Virginia felt, as if she had stubbed her toe on the corner of the wardrobe. Quoting from Lehmann's 'To penetrate that room', she finds the poet to be withdrawing to his own reflection. 'It is apparently easier to write a poem about oneself than about any other subject,' she wrote. These poems would not be easy for the young woman nursing her grandfather or the man working behind a shop counter to understand, and, in this way, surely their authors were failing in most of their objectives? 'The poet is trying honestly and exactly to describe a world that has perhaps no existence except for one person at one particular moment.' Auden's colloquial meant nothing to 'Mrs Gape' or 'Miss Curtis'; he was simply clogging the poetic machine with 'raw fact', sketching objects and events as they flashed by but failing to capture them. Both Auden and Lehmann, she felt, suffered from their impatience with genuine inspiration and insight. 'For heaven's sake, publish nothing before you are thirty,' was Virginia's final piece of advice.

Lehmann did not believe that the foregrounding of the group Hussey calls 'W. H. Day Spender' had been his idea. If the idea of promoting those voices as somehow essential to their modern age must be attributed to one person alone, then Lehmann could think of none better qualified than the editor of the *Listener*, Janet Adam Smith, who was 'keenly interested in the work of all of us, and a most useful patron for young poets at a period in their career when every guinea counted'. Later, an anthology of the poetry she had selected would show 'how sensitive and intelligent her taste was'. It is clear from Virginia's first letters to Lehmann that, in her mind, at least the names Auden and Day-Lewis were already inextricably linked. Auden and Day-Lewis had been at Oxford together; they made up, along with Stephen Spender, what was colloquially known as the 'Auden Group', or less commonly the 'Oxford Poets'.

They were originally differentiated from the 'Cambridge Poets', at which university separate intellectual projects – the *Experiment* magazine project, part-edited by William Empson, stands out – were under way.

They were bracketed together partly as a natural result of being friends and collaborators, but also because of a desire, in the older section of intellectual society, to put a name to the thing which threatened them. In August 1927, the *Spectator* had published a bad-tempered article by the author St John Greer Ervine which responded to reports of 'young gentlemen now at Oxford and Cambridge' who 'go about informing their friends that their lives have been wrecked and ruined by the old'. He goes on: 'They, it seems, are the victims of the war, although none of them are old enough to have served in it, and they accuse those who did serve in it of having caused its outbreak for the sole purpose of annoying and frustrating them!' Though sounding fantastical, this was, he wrote, 'a fair account of the attitude of mind of the contemporary intellectual youth towards his elders'. One can appreciate the indignation of those of the older generations who, like Ervine, had been conscripted to fight in the first war and now found themselves lumped in with the condemned decision-making figures of their epoch. Though no specific Oxford or Cambridge gentleman is mentioned in the article, in the years that followed, and Auden and his peers rose to fame, they would have been seen as – and saw themselves as – the embodiment of such a mindset. It was a culture war.

Lehmann claims that the idea to extend the perimeter of the anti-establishment 1920s Auden Group came from a man, previously unknown to him, called Michael Roberts. Michael Roberts had ideas about modern poetry that had probably not yet occurred to even its most central practising figures. Up to this point, some of Lehmann's closest Cambridge compeers, most vehemently Julian Bell, had seen themselves in direct opposition to their Oxford counterparts. Julian's personal ambitions for poetry – oddly, a revitalisation of the eighteenth-century rhyming couplet – seemed as singular as any could be, and the *Experiment* movement modelled itself on T. S. Eliot and the French surrealists. Auden, Day-Lewis and Spender 'roused Julian's bristling suspicion'; he disliked their esoteric jokes and found their poetry immature, rather than public and masculine in his own ideal. Roberts, however, had read all of Lehmann's contemporaries and believed that they belonged together more closely than anyone had yet detected. He believed the young men named to be the ones to finally write about modern life in a manner befitting its intense politicisation and intimidating complexity. The writer must in a sense remain in awe of modern life, and thus neither oblique nor omnipotent. Even Eliot was too esoteric. The ideal modern poet was 'abreast of his own times, honest with himself, and uses a technique sufficiently flexible to express precisely those subtleties of thought and feeling in which he differs from his predecessors'.

Virginia's frequent comparisons of the modern poets to Wordsworth (all unfavourable), and as wannabe politicians versus the true poet was a criticism Roberts had pre-empted. Modern imitation of canonical voices was unavailing, he believed; it came off as insincere. Instead, 'new knowledge and new circumstances have compelled us to think and feel in ways not expressible in the old language at all.' John Lehmann called this language 'the old poetic tinsel' – 'Christmas-tree baubles that so many young poets began to drag out again during the war (and were applauded for hanging on their dead branches).' The new poets did not recognise Wordsworth's landscapes. The sky, as seen from the city, by most of the population, was no longer starry; factories had sprung up at the feet of those lonely hills. How much more alive, and true, was the new paraphernalia of dynamos and trains and tractors?

Roberts' ideas would later provide the theoretical framework to the anthology *New Signatures Poets*, number twenty-four in the Living Poets series, which Roberts edited and which was

Lehmann's first independent publishing contribution to the Press. The poets chosen to make English poetry once again a 'popular, elegant and contemporary art' were Auden, Julian Bell, Day-Lewis, Richard Eberhart, William Empson, Lehmann, William Plomer, Spender and A. S. J. Tessimond. Lehmann, though sceptical at first, having been influenced too much by Bell's theory of an Oxford-Cambridge schism, had soon begun to feel flattered 'at the thought of belonging to a revolutionary movement in the arts'. Such lofty praise, where it applied to Lehmann, was perhaps undeserved. His first collection, *A Garden Revisited*, had failed to make a splash. It was a quiet offering, almost prim in its natural imagery and strait-jacket control of cadence, movement, mood and tone. Reading the book, Stephen Spender was befuddled; why, he wondered, did Lehmann seem to play it so safe, shirking the real in favour of the dreamlike? Why did he pretend to be heterosexual? Lehmann had not, like Auden, created a new kind of dramatic imagery and imbued it with a 'distinctive rhythmic life and tone of voice'. So far, his greatest recommendation was the Hogarth wolf emblem on the frontispiece of the book, bestowed by two middle-aged authors out of their depth in modern poetry.

The idea of a 'revolutionary movement' appealed to Lehmann not for self-promotional reasons but because literature, in the collective sense, was to him both dramatic and political, and was the arena where he permitted his passions to be expressed. It was the publishing side of his brain that now took over. The New Signatures venture had about it something of the marketing ploy, though one of honourable motives; Lehmann's 'fresh publishing ardour was inflamed by the possibility . . . of presenting us in some way as a *front*, so that the public, notoriously sluggish in its appreciation of individual poets, should be obliged to sit up and take notes.' And they did. As Lehmann noted, 'Several of the poets were already known individually; but the little book was like a search-light suddenly switched on to reveal that, without anyone noticing it, a group of skirmishers had been creeping up in a concerted movement of attack.' Leonard was approving; he saw the book as a manifesto of its generation. In the success of *New Signatures Poets* Lehmann had put his mark on literature; the poets included in its pages were now the 'New Signatures Poets'. It also, he felt, made up the debt to Virginia and Leonard for the 'rather soggy reception' of *A Garden Revisited*. He had become indispensable to the Press, and to English literature more generally.

As he travelled up to Letchworth that day in the autumn of 1940, all the necessary Hogarth files in the back of the van, it must have been quite clear to Lehmann how fundamental his role now was. Quite miraculously, the publishing world was now 'rapidly recovering from the sharp frost of the previous September', and questions of book-production presented themselves as a distraction from the fear and languor of war. Within the operation of the Press, it was Lehmann who was tasked with keeping pace with these surges.

The Garden City Press had made space for the Hogarth in a couple of rooms at the top of the works. As inconvenient as it would be, going to and from London, there was tremendous peace of mind in having the actual production of the books under the same roof as John and Leonard's publishing work: giving instructions to the printers, getting estimates and keeping careful watch over the making of the books were now seamless tasks, involving merely a walk across the factory. They had, in a sense, cut the war out of the business cycle. But for Virginia, who visited Letchworth in February 1941, there was a sense of having sold out, or given up on the original dream of the Hogarth Press. A world away from their hands-on little studio, where great minds fussed over small details, the Garden City Press seemed merely another cog in the grey and humourless machine of war. Its impersonality was reflected in the surrounding area, where there was 'no country to look at'. What Virginia saw were 'slaves chained to their typewriters, and their drawn set faces, and the machines - the incessant more and more competent machines, folding, pressing, gluing and issuing perfect books'. She had never wanted to make perfect books, never wanted to make life easier by 'stamp[ing] cloth to imitate leather'. She finishes her description with the symbolic image of the original Farringdon Road press now redundant and 'up in a glass case'.

Letchworth was close enough to London that it was considered to be of the same catchment area for raids on the city. That first week, after reassembling the office from Mecklenburgh Square at the Garden City Press, Lehmann had been staying in the family home of the works' manager. Out here, in the green belt, people were less desensitised to the bombing, and he spent most of his first night away from London under a dining room table, side by side with his host's entire family and feeling quite ridiculous. Though he did not say it, for fear of causing offence, Lehmann found the table to be 'ludicrously insufficient protection'. At intervals between the All Clear and the next warning he would go out into the garden to stretch his legs and watch as, thirty-five miles away, 'barrage shells burst like coloured rockets in a Fourth of June display in the clear sky, and the great lateral flashes of bombs exploding flickered like electricity'. And yet, from here, all was silent; he had been cast out from the action of his city, just as he had from Vienna. He was, for the time being, in another world: 'I resisted the impulse to put on a bravado act, and tell my friend that, having experienced the real thing, I preferred sleeping in my own bed until the swish of bombs approached - if it ever did.'

It must have seemed strangely contradictory, coming away here on business while all of that was going on. And there were other reasons why it was strange to be away. Not only had Lehmann recently fallen in love, with the Lithuanian-born ballerina Alexis Rassine, but he had finally found, on home shores, the life of sexual adventure he constantly craved. Isherwood's prophecy had come true, of excitement and fun in the blackout; one night

Lehmann had been dared, by John Banting, to join him on a trip to a 'secret . . . dive' that he knew of. They felt their way down into a darkly lit billiard hall where Lehmann found himself discussing the plight of conscription with a melancholy man from the Gold Coast. Perhaps they spotted each other by one of the coded gestures of the blackout - 'the telling poise of a cigarette', Adrian Wright gives as an example - 'as unvarying as the steps of a well-trained ballet corps'. Sex happened in hotel rooms, or, on at least one occasion, in a friend's abandoned flat with its collapsed ceiling and furniture covered with dust-cloths.

It was a strange time to be doing anything, because everything was now different. A sense of disorientation, unfamiliarity and isolation coloured everything. The glimpses of 1940 captured by Lehmann in his diary are 'images of phantasmagoria': the centre of London on New Year's Eve; pubs either empty or overtaken with foreign soldiers singing the songs of their homelands; a great congregation of Canadians at Piccadilly Circus; two sailors looming up out of the fog and darkness. Nights in the theatre, a barnstorming performance by Beatrix Lehmann, and the return of the ballet reminding one of 'a world of pure art that still, incredibly, can exist in spite of the war'; the first meeting with Rassine. There were *New Writing* parties in Lehmann's front room looking out over the Square, featuring new faces, like George Orwell ('full of friendliness and stimulating talk'), knots of young men in battledress, and Lehmann holding forth, partly to reassure himself, about poetry as 'the conqueror of all the demons that clustered in the air around us'. One day he had gone over to Isherwood's mother's home in Kensington to carry out some instructions regarding her son's library. Kathleen had pushed open the door to Christopher's room to reveal dust sheets covering everything, closed windows and drawn blinds.

Lehmann, like the Woolfs, had been pushed out of London by the attack on Mecklenburgh Square. The last time he had seen his flat, a chalk cross on the door designated it to be unsafe. It was now the territory of the war, a crime scene behind a police cordon or one of a million pieces of evidence that humanity had gone off on a murderous rampage against itself. The damage was mainly superficial, but then it did not take much, in terms of hidden glass shards and windows permanently opened to the elements, to make a home uninhabitable. It was sad. On a summer's day, slightly warped but radiant through the windowpanes, the square had seemed to hum, and London had a weight to it, held down by feet on pavements and figures in repose among the trees. It had been, he thought, a happy life there.

The lease on the flat was almost up, so, cutting his losses, Lehmann had all his books and furniture sent back to his family home in Buckinghamshire. He was now spending most of the week there. The way the war had reorganised his life, leaving a pocket of free time at the weekend, meant that he was now able to take part in the local Home Guard. It was a strange training, involving 'concept' weaponry like the 'fantastic' spigot mortar, or Blacker Bombard, which never quite graduated from these hypothetical scenarios. Lehmann's responsibilities 'consisted in little more than parading on Sunday mornings', or hanging around at HQ, a converted shop sandwiched between a Lloyds Bank and the cinema. There, he would forget about the book of poems or novel carried aspirationally in his pocket and, as he lay wrapped up in an army blanket on the floor, the electric fire blazing, listen instead to the rumours of 'violent passions' going on behind the 'humdrum respectable façade of the neighbourhood'. The case of the Home Guard is one of the more puzzling oversights of British military leadership, for despite being an essential part of the delaying tactics envisaged in the instance of invasion, every person involved was quite painfully aware of the inadequacy of their equipment and the comedic hopelessness of gun emplacements disguised as pigsties and disoriented road signs. 'There would be precious few survivors if the

Nazi armour were to thrust up from the west,' Lehmann reflected.

In his early twenties, he had been - as he called it - 'thrown to the Woolfs'. He was now thirty-three, and every bit his own man, but the separation had not been an easy one. If Lehmann was, in Spender's words, the 'Vesuvius of Mecklenburgh Square', then he found his match for stubbornness and perfectionism in the commanding figure of Leonard. Leonard, even now, approaching sixty, still possessed a formidable energy. There were two Leonards: one who, in disasters and emergencies, often surprised those around him with stoic calm and resignation, but a second who was easily pushed into 'a towering rage' by small errors in the petty cash, or oversights in the day-to-day accounts. An 'over-developed meticulousness' regarding details such as punctuality struck Lehmann as 'quite unworthy of the Cambridge Apostle'. Despite the various exogenous factors named by Lehmann in the phasing-out of the original *New Writing*, behind the scenes the project had faced a resistance which would have been totally unknown to Connolly with his 'Bank of Watson'. Even once Lehmann had bought into the company as partner, taking Virginia's place at considerable personal expense, it had remained 'a bone of contention'. As he wrote, 'Leonard, it soon became clear, did not like *New Writing* and wanted to clip its wings, on the ground that though the reviews were still very good it was not making money.'

Increasingly, as we have seen, Lehmann had his own doubts about the project. His nerve had been shaken by the Molotov–Ribbentrop Pact, and there was a feeling that his band of dependable contributors had become distracted, diffuse. If New Signatures was a 'revolutionary movement', then must it go the same way that all revolutions now seemed to be going? As D. J. Taylor has written, '[unlike Cyril Connolly] Lehmann made a virtue out of his staying power, and yet there lurks a suspicion that his great days belong to that overpopulated corner of the 1930s in which homosexuality and a belief in the unstoppable rise of proletarian socialism sat side by side'. Lehmann now saw that there were faults in the machinery of his vision; the parts were not working together to make a whole. As laudable as his attempts at unification were, in reality his provincial contributors, or those positioned outside of literary society, were periodically falling out of contact, pushed into military service or deterred by scanty literary incomes. Lehmann's most substantial critical work of the period, *New Writing in Europe*, is an impressive demonstration of a ubiquitous eye which kept all of the British Isles in view. It describes a new kind of voice, what Lehmann called 'the man in the street'. Orwell was a perfect example, as was George Garrett, a seaman from Liverpool, whose descriptions were 'more robust' than Orwell's and who was less emotional, and B. L. Coombes, an underground ambulance man in a South Wales colliery. Orwell was writing far more effective essays than, for example, Lytton Strachey ever had:

> Read a page of one of Lytton Strachey's essays and then a page of Orwell. In the former you will find elaborately built sentences (and very skilfully built too), full of Latinate words and allusive descriptions. In Orwell, on the other hand, the sentences are mostly short and as simplified as possible, the words are as near ordinary speech as he can make them without crippling his effects, and his descriptions downright and stinging as a box on the ear . . .

Summarised like this, Orwell, Garrett and Coombes seem to fall neatly into a group. But Orwell was symbolic of a general scepticism which, in the sense that literary culture depended on shared ideologies, was anti-literary, and anti-group. He was the sworn enemy of herdlike 1930s zealotry, and 'attacks parties, personalities and pet beliefs of the Left with indiscriminate violence, butting his head down and charging in all directions'. The only unity suggested by these new writers was the fact that so many of them 'had been moved by the slogans of passion and idealism of the 'thirties, and now found them inadequate'. Since the early years of *New Writing*, George Garrett had stopped submitting work entirely. The man in the street, it seemed, was a man who walked alone. Then there was the problem of Auden and Isherwood, who despite reassurances to the contrary were now unquestionably doing their own thing.

One reviewer of *New Writing in Europe* - in fact Hugh Walpole, who had a large and committed audience at the *Daily Sketch* - had gone out of his way to challenge Lehmann on his unquestioning commitment to his 1930s cohort. 'The harsh fact is,' Walpole wrote, 'the leaders of John Lehmann's *New Writing* are no longer new at all . . . The fact is that this war has, at one stroke, deprived most of Lehmann's 'New Writers' of their contemporaneity.' Walpole could not blame Lehmann for this, but undoubtedly, he felt, Auden and Isherwood's exit to America had '*killed* their influence here'. Grand sentiments of international artistic and political brotherhood aside, it was difficult to escape the feeling that the war was dividing the world in two, between those who had witnessed firsthand its impact and those who had not. Lehmann had dismissed the criticism as a jealous rant about 'the famous imaginary "flight" to America', but Walpole was willing to argue his point. 'Your whole group,' he said, 'are *pre* this war in spirit'. Their war was the Spanish war. They had had their vision of the world, and though it was a powerful one it was also very specific. To be born when they were, and come of age during the First World War furious with those in authority for what seemed a carefree approach to young life; to have ridden high on the wave of paradigm-shifting left-wing politics then felt the crushing agonies of its defeat - this was no normal experience. What Walpole saw as 'lugubrious articles' and 'miserable little realist stories about boys who clout their mothers, kick their fathers and steal from the baker's shop' could never appeal to the general readership. Julian Symons goes further - these writers were embarrassed, he felt, for having been the high-profile advocates of a cause which had led to Stalin. 'After Spain,

and indeed before the end came in Spain,' he felt, 'there was little left of the thirties movement but a feeling of resignation and a
sense of guilt.'

Then, in a different category, there was Henry Green, who the
year before had approached Lehmann at the Hogarth with his novel
Party Going. Green had now turned his attentions to writing about
the war, seen from the perspective of the Auxiliary Fire Service.
Lehmann's sister, Rosamond, had made up her mind to treat the
whole situation of the war as a challenge to her creative powers,
and as a consequence had written what Lehmann saw as the most
beautiful elegy of the war so far, in her story *The Red-Haired Miss
Daintreys*. But neither writer could be fitted into Lehmann's idealistic view of literature. They were free and roaming where Lehmann
had the tendency towards single-mindedness. He would have liked
to be able to say, about this second war period, something as succinct as 'The English poetry of the First World War can, roughly,
be divided into two periods.' Perhaps Rosamond belonged to a
pre-Dunkirk elegiac group, and Orwell to those bent on action and
retaliation, their gazes fixed firmly on the road ahead. But it could
not be done. Virginia Woolf would have - and had - told him off
for his insistence on groupings. It was here that Connolly, as an
editor, was positioned to break away from the pack; his curation,
while less deliberately inclusive, was more open-minded. He cared
less to separate young from old, man from woman, metropolis
from provinces, blue-collar from white.

Such reflections are even more extraordinary when we consider
Lehmann's access to the best-regarded writers of the day. On Friday, 14 March 1941, Lehmann was having lunch with Virginia and
Leonard Woolf at St Stephen's Tavern on Bridge Street.* It was a day
of brilliant sunshine, and from their table on the second floor, by

---

* A typical wartime pub lunch meal was something like the 'poor soup and
oxtail' which Virginia notes as having eaten on Friday, 7 February, at the White
Hart in Holborn.

the window, they could see the wreckage of the Commons Chamber, and across to Big Ben. The usual tensions hung in the air, as they ate and talked. Lehmann had recently sent them a collection of poems - Terence Tiller's first - which he thought more than worthy of publication, but Leonard was now throwing them back in his face. Why, he begged, did the poet insist on such inscrutability? He took pages at random and thrust them at Lehmann, saying, 'But parse this poem, John, *parse* it!' Virginia contributed her opinion that there was music and imagination in the poetry rare for a first book; Leonard was being much too logical. In the end, the decision went Virginia's way.

But they had not gathered at St Stephen's Tavern to discuss Tiller. There was a more important matter at hand; as they built up to it, Lehmann noticed 'a state of unusual nervous tension' about Virginia, 'her hand shaking slightly now and then'. It was more than that, he later reflected; 'agitation' was a more appropriate description. 'Then Leonard revealed the secret: she had written a new novel, which had been given the tentative title of *Between the Acts*.' She had begun writing it, in secret, while the all-too-public curation of *Roger Fry* still ground on. Where that book was constricting, *Between the Acts* was abstract and free-roaming; all forms were welcomed - prose, poetry, drama. 'Let it be random and tentative,' she had told herself, 'don't . . . force my tired and diffident brain to embrace another whole - all parts contributing - not yet awhile.' But if it had begun as a playful and unreal exercise, an escape or protest against the normal writing process, it had now become the same as any other. It was no longer just hers, like the stories she had scribbled as a girl in St Ives, but would have to be given to the world. Leonard and his wife could now not come to an agreement regarding its worthiness, the author herself crippled by doubts. Lehmann was to read it, and would have the final say on whether or not it should be published.

The manuscript arrived from Rodmell on one of the days when

Lehmann was scheduled to be at Home Guard HQ. He had to read it quickly, before setting off for the high street with rifle and tin hat, a task made a great deal more difficult by Virginia's aberrant typing. Nothing, however, could obscure the fact of the book's brilliance. Lehmann was 'amazed and deeply moved by its poetry - in fact it's more a poem than prose. More so than *To the Lighthouse*, she has pushed prose to the furthest inch at the frontier - into no man's land.'

10

The Wave Lapping Blue to the Shore

Leonard Woolf had met the enchanting Virginia Stephen only three times when, in 1911, it was suggested that he move into the house she shared with John Maynard Keynes, Duncan Grant and her brother Adrian Stephen at 38 Brunswick Square. During the seven years he had spent in the jungles of Ceylon, as part of an eminently promising Civil Service career, Leonard had remembered Virginia often, particularly the occasion in the spring of 1903, at Thoby Stephen's rooms at Trinity, when the appearance of Virginia and Vanessa had revealed to him a beauty which 'literally took one's breath away . . . as it does when in a picture gallery you suddenly come face to face with a great Rembrandt or Velasquez'. But that was abstract, homesick, self-pitying love. It wasn't until his return to England in 1911, initially only on leave, that Leonard's fantasies of having Virginia as his wife were rearranged into anything genuine.

But it was frightening, being in love with Virginia Stephen. The day before he visited the house at Brunswick Square Leonard had confided in Lytton Strachey his powerful and conflicting feelings. He had just seen Virginia, and had realised that, though there was little question of him not moving in with her, it would be 'the beginning of hopelessness'. 'To be in love with her - isn't that a danger?' Leonard asked Lytton. 'Isn't it always a danger which is never really worth the risk?'

Thirty years later, he had his answers to those questions. On the morning of 28 March 1941, exactly two weeks after the Woolfs had revealed the existence of a new manuscript to Lehmann - a Friday, about 11.30 - Virginia had set off for a walk to the river, wearing a long fur coat (the same that had been buried in the damage at Mecklenburgh Square?) and carrying the stick which she now used because, as Frances Partridge noted, the traditional effects of ageing on movement had already begun in her. Leonard had last seen her writing in the little studio-shed at the foot of the garden that she had claimed as her own. They had walked back into the house together, with Virginia saying that she planned to do some housework before taking a walk. Leonard did not protest, but suggested that she make time to lie down for half an hour. Back in the house, Virginia asked the housekeeper, Louie Mayer, for a spare feather duster, that she might pitch in with the cleaning. This was an entirely unusual turn of events, but hardly incriminating; it perhaps had something to do with Leonard's advice that she keep herself occupied with non-strenuous activities. But before long, Virginia had made her way back to her studio. Then she came briefly back to the house to, as witnessed by Louie, make herself ready for her walk.

Nothing could have been less unusual than Virginia taking herself off in this way. Walking was as much a part of her writing process as sitting at her desk. It was, moreover, a perfectly bright, cold, clear day. These facts allowed her to pass by some of their neighbours - Bert Skinner, and the farm labourer John Hubbard, who was cleaning out ditches by an osier bed - without causing any alarm. Leonard, who had been working in his upstairs study while Virginia dusted and left for her walk, then returned to what he had been doing in the garden, from where, after a while, he assumed that Virginia had come back in through the front gate and was somewhere within the house. It wasn't until one o'clock that he wandered back inside, for lunch, and discovered the note she had left for him on the sitting room mantelpiece, as well as one for Vanessa. The two letters confirmed the same hideous fact. Leonard shouted to Louie - 'I think something has happened to Mrs Woolf!' - before rushing out to search the house and garden. Louie also rushed out; she ran to a neighbour, Percy Bartholomew, who then went for PC Wilfred Collins at the Rodmell police station. Leonard had traced a familiar route towards the river, where he thought he might be just in time to prevent what was going to happen. Almost immediately he saw her walking-stick lying on the bank, with no body to be seen. It was here, about a mile north of Southease bridge, that Leonard and the other men linked up. Then others arrived. PC Collins was diving for the body while ropes and grabs were brought out from sheds and garages to assist in dragging the river. Leonard went up to the Downs, and then back, searching the meadows and riverbanks. Still, all they had was her stick.

It was with characteristic composure that later that day - the search to continue in the morning - Leonard sat down to write a letter to Vita Sackville-West. The note was perfectly succinct and objective, though one can imagine the shock it would have delivered its recipient.

'My dear Vita,' it began: 'I do not want you to see in the paper or hear possibly on the wireless the terrible thing that has happened to Virginia.' But this was a difficult letter to write. Vita knew Virginia too well to be satisfied with any of the platitudes which would lessen this violent and unaccountable shock. 'The strain of war', which Leonard prefaced with 'I suppose', was the obvious and possibly most satisfying explanation, but in fact, within a few days, he would be furiously contesting this notion with the editor of the *Sunday Times*. She had 'like everyone else ... felt the general strain of the war', but in Virginia's case there had been multiple pre-war precedents. Thirty years later, Leonard was still asking himself 'What was the real state of her mind and her health in the autumn and early winter of 1940?' There had been no 'warning symptoms' like the occasion in 1915, preceding a long mental breakdown, when Virginia, taking breakfast in bed, had suddenly become 'violently excited' and began talking as if her deceased mother was in the room. There were no headaches, just a sudden and all-encompassing 'trough of despair'. One thing Leonard could say for sure was that Virginia had feared going mad more than she was, in actuality, succumbing to that infliction. Judging from his autobiography, Leonard was leaning towards an explanation which centred on Virginia's final book, *Between the Acts* – not the writing, which had initially raised her spirits, but the revising. Only at that stage did the 'black cloud' begin to gather over her. 'She has been through hell these last days,' Leonard finished by saying.

A letter sent to John Lehmann the day before demonstrates the extent to which, as Alix Strachey has said, Leonard 'completely arranged his life and hers so that she would have the minimum of mental strain'. He writes that he is forwarding a letter from Virginia – 'I'll send that to John for you,' he must have said – but that his accompanying note was *not* to be answered. 'I will come up to town and discuss the whole thing with you when I can,' he explained, thinking of how, less than twenty-four hours before, he had had to take his wife to a doctor entirely against her will. And then he told John what to put in his reply to Virginia's letter, the contents of which were related to the difficulty she was finding in readying *Between the Acts* for publication. In it, she apologises repeatedly. She was profoundly sorry for troubling him, but as it

stood the novel was 'too silly and trivial'. 'The fact is it was written in the intervals of doing Roger with my brain half asleep,' she
writes. 'I didn't realise how bad it was till I read it over.' Back to
Leonard's appended note: Lehmann should say that he was very
sorry that they would not be able to publish in the spring, but that
they would hope for the autumn. The issue was that Lehmann had
already announced the book as forthcoming in the *New Statesman*,
had in fact done so in a dismissive gesture of confidence, in defiance of Virginia's wishes. 'I am sorry for your and the Press' sake,'
Leonard went on to say. 'There seems some fate against you in the
publishing world.' The following day Lehmann received a second
letter, in an even more businesslike tone than the one received by
Vita. Lehmann was asked not to tell the news to anyone else until
the body was found. He had not even had time to complete Leonard's request - 'it was all over'.

Then the responses started coming in. Over the weeks that
followed, Leonard would receive over two hundred letters, but
at this point there was only him and a few others moving below
the radar. There was one from Octavia Wilberforce, a pioneering
doctor, whom he had also notified, who had been at Virginia's
bedside - confidante to both husband and wife - through some
of those 'most terrible and agonizing days' of Leonard's life. Since
the outbreak of war, Octavia had been one of Virginia and Leonard's closest friends. She had, for instance, been in the audience for
Virginia's lecture on 'The Leaning Tower', where her 'clinical eye
was again troubled by [the speaker's] thinness'. Octavia had been
introduced to the Woolfs by the actress and Hogarth Press author
Elizabeth Robins, who had kept Octavia up to date on Virginia's
latest releases. Thus did Octavia hear of the 'queer book' *Roger
Fry*, which was 'product of a loyalty and a self-suppression rarely
equalled I should think'. 'Virginia is immensely handicapped by the
fact of Fry's living relatives and what they would expect,' Elizabeth
explained. 'No wonder she called the thing "a difficult biography".

The life of such a genius was worth writing, whether at Virginia's expenditure, who am I to say.'

Octavia had spent part of the 1920s working as a locum assistant to the medical superintendent of Graylingwell Mental Hospital, in Chichester. Her work with the patients had often made her feel 'wretched' - 'the waste, the pity', she thought - because so many were so nearly sane. Virginia was, of course, quite a different case. But the prevailing logic of the time revolved around the effects of dietary health on the brain - 'Half the patients need reducing to make 'em better or well - the other half want building up,' Octavia had written while at Graylingwell - an issue of course that had been amplified by wartime food shortages. Here, Virginia was no exception. By January 1941 she seemed 'a thoroughly frail creature', 'thinner and thinner', who was also in her personality becoming 'vaguer, less expressive'. 'I wish we could do something to binge her up', Octavia wrote to Elizabeth, explaining that the great writer was now unable even to work at long stretches, and never after dinner. Octavia made the ten-mile trip up from her home in Brighton ostensibly to endow Virginia and Leonard with the milk and cream which came from the herd of Jersey cows she kept at Henfield. The extra sustenance, she explained, would protect the Woolfs from the influenza which was prevalent at the time. When Virginia protested, Octavia explained that it would only be 'a small return for the pleasure she had given me by her books'. The milk would also - she and Leonard knew this - be as beneficial as anything for Virginia's mental constitution. For doctors of mental health patients at this time, milk enjoyed the same status as a 'wonder food' that it had for governments and those caring for children during the Great Depression. Virginia had previously been one of these patients, and had been 'overfed' on a diet of four or five pints a day. More than anything else, however, Virginia and Octavia had a brilliant rapport. In the doctor's company, Virginia spoke freely on the most personal of subjects. She asked Octavia once whether

she had also experienced 'dark and depressing times', which sad-
dened the former with thoughts of 'poor Virginia - thirteen when
her mother died - her half-sister, Stella, died at twenty-five and
both were irreparable blows'.

Gradually, however, the conversations had become more urgent.
Where they had explored Octavia's hearty childhood in the large
country seat of the Wilberforces - Virginia was even thinking of
recreating these scenes in a new novel - they now bumped and
chafed against Virginia's unspoken, or only hinted at, private fears.
The idea that the past would recur, that she would be unable to
work again, was upmost in her mind. Octavia had done her best
to counter these thoughts. 'Because you'd had trouble and come
through it - shouldn't this be a reassurance to you that if you take
things easy now . . .?' she implored. 'If you have an appendix operation it leaves a scar on your body but that's all and you forget it - if
you have a mental illness it leaves a scar on your memory perhaps
but that's all.'

Privately, Leonard had explained to Octavia that he thought Virginia was on the verge of danger. Her thoughts, they both saw,
were now racing beyond her control. She was terrified of madness,
and an attempt at suicide was imminent. Though both Leonard
and Octavia knew that the only thing that could save Virginia was
the 'drastic regime' of hospitalisation, they felt even more keenly
that a single wrong word which forced her to confront the reality
of her derangement would kill her. He was thinking of the time
just before the first war when a simple interview with the doctor
Henry Head - an executive decision made by Leonard himself -
had been the necessary though mistaken step which had resulted
in Virginia's overdose of sleeping pills. Leonard's new plan was for
her to visit Octavia in Brighton, but in the knowledge that this time
she was being evaluated in an official capacity by a doctor, rather
than counselled by a friend. Virginia had agreed, though there was
little doubt that everything that happened from now on would be

against her will. She was, therefore, in an irritable mood, arguing all the time that it was '*quite* unnecessary to have come', and bargaining with Octavia that, if she played along and had a full medical check-up, it would be promised that she would not be sent away for a rest cure. It was a strange day; the tension in the house was such that no one, including the 'sleepwalking' Virginia, had taken notice when a bombing raid started at the other end of the street. All things considered, the meeting with Octavia had gone well, but the course of action discussed out of the patient's earshot that day – not to force the issue and put Virginia under the perpetual surveillance of nurses – would turn out, at least on paper, to be the wrong one. Octavia would not see Virginia again.

To Leonard, in her letter, Octavia had a lot that she wanted to say. She wanted, first and foremost, to comfort him, and assure him, as Virginia had assured her, that he as a husband had done everything he possibly could to protect his wife. But still Octavia found herself thinking 'If I'm like this then what is Leonard going through?' She went over to see him, and they talked, in Leonard's upstairs study, about the history of Virginia's illness. 'After a night of absorption of facts,' Octavia wrote the following day, 'I am now sure that, as long as the war was on, I don't think it would have been possible to hold Virginia's mind.' She thought over her final conversations with Virginia, how the writer would sit close to and hug the fire,

> behind her that large window which overlooks the wide expanse of field and valley, flat and green, through which runs that evil river, which a week later was to clutch that free spirit . . . and which now is being dragged and won't give up its jealously held treasure.

Octavia thought how lucky she was to have known that brilliant mind even as briefly, and in such extenuating circumstances, as she had. The next to reply was Vita Sackville-West, who said that she was stunned, and unable to express how she was feeling. 'For you I feel a really overwhelming sorrow, and for myself a loss which can never diminish,' she ended by saying.

Four days after Virginia's disappearance, her body still nowhere to be found, Leonard decided that it would be preferable if he were able to some extent to control the narrative around his wife's death. He wrote to Geoffrey Dawson, editor at *The Times*, explaining the situation much as he had to Vita and Lehmann, but this time needing also to give the basic facts of her illness, for the uninitiated. All her life, he said, Virginia had suffered from neurasthenia. This was a popular though vague diagnosis of the late nineteenth century – the supposed affliction of Marcel Proust – but a diagnosis that disappeared around 1930. It had also, more importantly, been the diagnosis given to Virginia's cousin, James 'Jim' Stephen, whose madness would routinely reach an 'exalted stage', and who was eventually taken to an asylum after being arrested for running naked through Cambridge. During the First World War, neurasthenia was frequently the recorded diagnosis given to victims of 'shell shock'. If it is an accurate description of what Virginia suffered, then it is only by merit of being so broadly defined, taking in, as it did, aspects of post-traumatic stress disorder, anxiety and melancholia. As it had fallen out of medical parlance, it is unlikely to reflect the judgement of Octavia Wilberforce, and in all probability was a term that Leonard had landed on himself. The public, he knew, would have to be satisfied in their desire for a cause-and-effect explanation.

Leonard seemed to be holding it together. Virginia's friends were more concerned about Vanessa. They 'dreaded some such physical collapse as befell her after Julian was killed'. Vanessa had been called to the scene by the Woolfs' gardener, Mr Bartholomew, while Leonard and the other men from the village were carrying out their search of the river. Her husband, Clive Bell, must have been out at the time, for Vanessa arrived at Monk's House alone. She had everything explained to her by Leonard, who then drove her the eleven miles back to her Charleston house, near Lewes, where he thought it best for her to be. The news had to be broken to Duncan Grant, who was living at Charleston and sharing Vanessa's studio space. He was returning from a trip to London that evening, and found out what had happened – they were standing in the kitchen – from Vanessa and Angelica Garnett, Vanessa and the homosexual Grant's now grown-up illegitimate daughter. All three held each other 'in a rare moment of physical and emotional intimacy'. Next to find out would be Clive. During Virginia's life, Clive had been one of the few people who could be depended on to calm her down. She was 'at her best' with him, a friend observed. He would, they remembered, 'act as midwife to her verbal fantasies with a gentle "Ye-e-*e-es*, Virginia?"'

Evidently, Clive at some point had gone over to Rodmell to assist in the search. He reported back to Frances Partridge that Leonard's state of mind remained as calm and sensible as his friends would expect, as well as how, for some days, the search party had 'hoped against hope that she had wandered crazily away and might be discovered in a barn or a village shop.' Such hopes, in the way they refused likelier realities, were a precursor to a more persistent symptom experienced by Leonard, that of looking out in its direction despite knowing that Virginia would not come across the garden from her studio, or listening for her to come in at the door despite knowing she was drowned. In such a mental state, it would have been strange for him to open up *The Times* on 3 April and read, on its main news page, 'It must now be presumed that Mrs Leonard Woolf (Virginia Woolf, the novelist and essayist), who has been missing since last Friday, has been drowned in the Sussex Ouse at Rodmell, near Lewes.' E. M. Forster read this note and was 'unable to think of anyone but [himself]'. 'I can't write any more now,' he told Leonard, after fumbling through two or three sentences, 'only send my deepest love and sadness'. A similar message went out on the BBC that evening.

That March, 5,489 miles away, Christopher Isherwood was grappling with an unfinished screenplay in his office at Metro-Goldwyn-Mayer studios, a sprawling art deco complex pinned down by the resolute California sun. At some point, a roving movie columnist, typically in and out of offices on the trail of stories, poked his head round the door to ask if he might use Isherwood's telephone to call his office and get his messages. Assenting, Isherwood remained sat over his typewriter but permitted an ear to explore the man's conversation. The short intervals of silence in the room represented the voice of an assistant at the other end of the line. Suddenly the man piped up: 'No - *no*, you dope - the name's Woolf - W-O-O-L-F - sure, I'm sure - sure, I've heard of her, you ignorant bastard - she was a great writer - British . . .'

It was three weeks before Virginia's body was found. A group of teenagers had gone out on a cycling trip. They stopped for lunch near the river at Asheham and there saw it floating downstream; at first glance the fur coat, where it billowed up, had resembled a wide log. 'The horrible business of the identification and inquest took place in the Newhaven mortuary on April 18 and 19,' explained Leonard. He went alone to the cremation, which took place in Brighton the following Monday. He had wanted to ask the Dean whether they could play the cavatina from the B flat quartet, op. 130, of Beethoven:

> There is a moment at cremations when the doors of the crematorium open and the coffin slides slowly in, and there is a moment in the middle of the cavatina when for a few bars the music, of incredible beauty, seems to hesitate with a gentle forward pulsing motion - if played at that moment it might seem to be gently propelling the dead into an eternity of oblivion.

In the end he could not bring himself to do so. The horror of the previous weeks had produced in him 'a kind of inert anaesthesia'. Instead, as the doors opened and the coffin was swallowed up, it was to the tune of the 'Blessed Spirits' from Gluck's *Orfeo ed Euridice*. Another beautiful piece of music. At home, that evening, Leonard played himself the cavatina.

EMPTY ROOMS

There is an extraordinary passage in *Between the Acts*, as good as any she wrote, when Virginia seems to imagine a world beyond herself as a writer, a world that she and those hindering 'personal feelings' had been written out of: a purer world in which was achieved the total objectivity and harmony she had always striven for. It was as Leonard said, Virginia 'always wrote objectively, but she lived her life too subjectively. She had, as I often told her, too egocentric a mind.' In *Between the Acts*, the 'camera' of the narration, which has been following the matriarch Lucy Swithin, suddenly looses itself and is alone in an empty room. Candish, the gardener, enters the dining room to rearrange the flowers and then leaves again. We remain where we are.

> Two pictures hung opposite the window. In real life they had never met, the long lady and the man holding his horse by the rein. The lady was a picture, bought by Oliver because he liked the picture; the man was an ancestor. He had a name. He held the rein in his hand. He had said to the painter:
> 'If you want my likeness, dang it sir, take it when the leaves are on the trees.' There were leaves on the trees. He had said: 'Ain't there room for Colin as well as Buster?' Colin was his famous hound. But there was only room for Buster . . .

The paintings seem to gossip between themselves. Then this dies down, and the room is left 'Empty, empty, empty; silent, silent, silent.'

The room was a shell, singing of what was before time was; a vase stood in the heart of the house, alabaster, smooth, cold, holding the still, distilled essence of emptiness, silence.

Virginia's conception of a world from which the ego was extracted was built upon her fascination with rooms. Rooms were an extension, or hive, of the self. They were private, symbolic, as in *A Room of One's Own*. But these were emergent properties. In actuality, rooms existed separately from their occupants; they framed the human drama but took no interest in it. Like the planet itself, they live on when we are gone, though continuing to hold the remnants of us. In *To the Lighthouse*, we observe the rooms of a house interacting with the light and wind from outside while its inhabitants sleep. We feel those walls, floorboards and furnishings, too, not as the trappings of modern life but as the primordial and eternal shelter, more akin to the trees outside the window than to the sentient, mortal beings within. We see the same house decay, like a tree shedding its leaves in autumn, and then be brought to life again. It lives on without its greatest custodian, the late Mrs Ramsey, but seems to hold her memory, her touch and footfall and trail. So Mrs McNab, the local woman who looks after the house, finds that the dressing-table drawers are still full of things like handkerchiefs and bits of ribbon and, in that moment, can see Mrs Ramsey as she comes up the drive with the washing. Virginia, visiting her final London address, 37 Mecklenburgh Square, for the first time, had found herself asking, 'Which of these rooms shall I die in?'

Coming full circle, Virginia's friends were now using the phrases she had created to describe rooms in order to make sense of a world without her in it. It was as if, in death, she had retreated to the same private, sequestered place of her imagination where, during her lifetime, she had produced her masterpieces. Talking with Leonard some months after Virginia's death, Octavia Wilberforce noticed he was still using 'we' and talking in the present tense of the plans he and his wife had made for the publication of various of her books. Telling the story of the origins of the Hogarth Press, he had said, 'We thought we'd publish *Monday or Tuesday*, leaving out one story which she thinks, and I agree, is bad.' Octavia was struck by this. 'His use of the present tense gave me the feeling that he was conscious of Virginia's presence,' she wrote, 'as if she'd just gone into a Room of her Own.'

There was a sense, for a while, that even though it had been a long time since Virginia had had Bloomsbury as a permanent residence, the district was now like a house from which its owner, whose personality the objects and furnishings so embodied, was absent. Despite their former cattiness towards each other, Cyril Connolly was deeply affected by the incident of Virginia's death. He perhaps recognised in Woolf more similarities with himself than he would care to admit. 'I would have given anything to have been fully approved of by her,' he admitted. Summarising her influence on British literature, he described how 'not for the first time the country was never happier than when governed by a queen.' T. S. Eliot had a similar idea. He wanted to point out that 'Virginia Woolf was the centre not merely of an esoteric group, but of the literary life of London.' On how her death had changed the world, he wrote:

> It is what someone, I forget who, must have meant when he wandered about simply saying: 'Coleridge is dead.' I mean that it is neither regret that an author's work has come to an end nor desolation at the loss of a friend, for the former emotion can be expressed, and the latter one keeps to oneself; but the loss of something both more profound and more extensive, a change to the world which is also a damage to oneself.

Louie Mayer had stayed working at Monk's House for many years afterwards, but found it, too, to have become a sad place.

She remembered how, after Virginia had finished making the final touches to *The Years*, she had been so delighted that she had said, 'Now we are going to spend some money and have the kitchen painted and a lot of new things put in for you.' They had spent the rest of that afternoon making plans for the kitchen. Now, however, Louie listened jumpily for a knock at the door, someone coming to tell her something else she did not want to hear. She observed from afar as Leonard filled his days to the brim with writing his books, working on the garden, and going to and from London on business.

Horizon went ahead with a memorial issue, remembering Virginia and her work. It was a strange and wistful volume, featuring Sonia Brownell's introduction to four sombre new paintings from the Euston Road Group, among them Victor Pasmore's *Interior with Lamplight 1941*, perhaps the greatest, and most psychological, blackout painting. That work was reproduced opposite a new photograph by Cecil Beaton, part of a series 'History Under Fire', which showed the view of the western towers of St Paul's Cathedral through a crumbling archway and haze of brick dust. Connolly's 'Comment' was equally depressed in tone. 'It is sad on a spring evening to walk through the bombed streets of Chelsea,' it began. In Chelsea, 'the church where Henry James was buried [was] a pile of red rubble' and 'tall eighteenth-century houses gape[d] with their insides blown out, like ruined triumphal arches'. The lives ruined there had been lives of some consequence; this was Connolly's world, the realm of the 'cultivated *haute bourgeoisie*' where, he felt, books and pictures were actually appreciated, the world Virginia had sneered at. The realm of large swathes of *Horizon*'s readership. Connolly then evoked Virginia's original home, the district of Kensington, which, like neighbouring Bayswater, 'seem[ed] to have been created for destruction, where squares and terraces for half a century have invited dilapidation.' He went on, becoming increasingly more angry and bitter: 'Behind the stucco porches and the lace curtains the half-life of decaying Victorian families guttered like marsh-gas. One has no pity for the fate of such houses.' Virginia herself went unmentioned in the foreword. The actual tributes, filling the first section of the issue, came from Eliot, Rose Macaulay, Vita Sackville-West and William Plomer.

Then there was the question of Virginia's literary afterlife. As John Lehmann explained, Leonard was already beginning to feel the intimidating scale of the work for him to do as Virginia's literary executor. She had – this was not necessarily news to him – 'scarcely ever stopped writing'. There were essays, articles, short stories, anonymous periodical works – not to mention all of her diaries and voluminous correspondence. In her suicide note to Leonard, she had asked that he destroy all of her papers. It was obvious that this could not happen. The over twenty-five years' worth of diary entries salvaged from the 'little car' of Mecklenburgh Square, which for a long time had been sitting in boxes and taking up space at Monk's House, were the first item on the agenda. Virginia had on more than one occasion recorded her intention of – *eventually* – making use of the journals as a resource, but it is uncertain what form she envisaged this would take. Much of the material dealt with only the quotidian aspects of her social or home life; it would not have been deemed fit for publication by a writer as wary of scrutiny as she. Then there were all of the people mentioned in their pages. Writing about John Evelyn for the *Times Literary Supplement*, Virginia had defined two types of diarists:

> There can be no doubt that the good diarists are those who write either for themselves or for a posterity so distant that it can safely hear every secret and justly weigh every motive. For such an audience there is no need either of affection or of restraint. But a diary written to be published in the author's lifetime is no better than

a private version of the newspaper, and often worse. The good opinion of our contemporaries means so much to us that it is well worth while to tell them lies.

Like Evelyn, Virginia had written her diaries for herself – for her mental fixity and because putting feelings and impressions carefully into words was for her to take command of those emotions. But unlike Evelyn, Virginia was not 'neither introspective nor vindictive'. Neither had she been, like Evelyn, the happy and ignorant type; she had revealed the secrets of her heart.

Octavia Wilberforce was privy to some of Leonard's broodings regarding this matter. She visited him in August of that year and told him that both she and Elizabeth Robins were very anxious that he should publish the diaries. Such a window into Virginia's mind and processes would be invaluable to a new generation of writers, they felt. Leonard, however, was 'reluctant because there was too much about living people and because he felt it would give the wrong impression of her as a hypersensitive and moody person tormented by fears'. He would not like this to happen because, as those closest to Virginia knew, she had, for the most part, been 'an especially happy, gay, carefree person'. It was what had happened to Katherine Mansfield, who had been the only person Leonard had known who in conversation had the ability to make tears run down his cheeks with laughter. Her journals 'had given an entirely different and false impression'. Could he not edit all of that moodiness out? Octavia asked. Leonard replied that to do so would not be honest. 'He felt they should be published fifty years hence and leave judgement to posterity.'

And then the question of *Between the Acts*, likely the main artefact Virginia wished to resign to the hypothetical bonfire. Quite possibly the book which had killed her. But though she found this 'so-called novel' 'too slight and sketchy', Leonard thought it, on the contrary, 'a very remarkable book'. 'I had expected from what she had said and feared to find a loss of vigour,' Leonard wrote to John Lehmann: 'I may be wrong, but it seemed to me the opposite, to be more vigorous and pulled together than most of her other books, to have more depth and to be very moving. I also thought that the strange symbolism gave it an almost terrifying profundity and beauty.'

Running constantly behind the action of the book is a sound like a clock's ticking - a piece of machinery trundling away somewhere in the field beyond the garden where the villagers are putting on a play. As the revue skips between the different epochs of English history, the audience nervously awaits the section titled 'The present time. Ourselves', the upshot of which is disorder, confusion, all meaning having broken down. Between acts, there is a desperate scramble for each to find companionship. And though the war is a universal threat, one which will threaten the sanctity of the home, the greatest pains in life remain the private anguishes. One character, Isa, thinks in a language that only one other - a man, not her husband - can understand, and so her feelings remain wedged inside her head. 'O that my life could here have ending,' she thinks, while taking care not to move her lips.

But there was a problem. Leonard felt uncertain regarding the book's current ending. In fact, as he later wrote to Angus Wilson, he was 'uneasy that there is no end, not because artistically and cosmologically there isn't an end but because perhaps the writer missed it'. By 23 June, however, advance copies of the book were being sent out to friends. *Between the Acts* was published by the Hogarth Press on 17 July. It was published in America by Harcourt, Brace and Company on 2 October. That edition was accompanied by a note from Leonard:

The MS. of this book had been completed, but had not been finally revised for the printer, at the time of Virginia Woolf's death. She would not, I believe, have made any large or material alterations in it, though she would probably have made a good many small corrections or revisions before passing the final proofs.

And thus the book retained its original ending. In that final chapter, Virginia seems to evoke certain aspects of her experiences during the final years of her life. The prehistoric darkness of London's streets during blackout hours echoes through the description, as the sun sets on the action of the day, of '[a] night before roads were made, or houses', a night 'that dwellers in caves had watched from some high place among rocks'. Her period of isolation in the countryside, after the destruction of 37 Mecklenburgh Square, was the period of evening when 'you could see more' because 'nothing interrupted, when there was no fish to order, no telephone to answer'. The morning paper is described as 'the paper that obliterated the day before'.

As always when reading Virginia Woolf, one feels an - often guilty - urge to scrutinise, as with X-ray goggles, each character in the book, looking for the soul of the author herself within them. This reader cannot help but return to the only writer in the story, the elusive and isolated Miss La Trobe. Her play ended, and the audience dispersed, Miss La Trobe lingers to reflect on the garden setting and thinks, 'It was here that she had suffered triumph, humiliation, ecstasy, despair - for nothing.' Her spirit is, at its most fundamental, a rebellious one; it lashes out when she begins to feel taken for granted, or otherwise misunderstood and reduced. Such frustrations are inextricable from the injustices of being a middle-aged woman at that moment in history. 'One of these days she would break - which of the village laws? Sobriety? Chastity? Or take something that did not properly belong to her?' She sees herself as 'an outcast', an outsider, but knows, ultimately, that she is the slave of her audience. In the end, Duncan Grant wrote of Virginia, 'the world must accept her on her own terms or not at all.'

Isherwood's Dream, 17 July 1941, Santa Monica

Dream: Returning to London. The houses were smashed, but only the top floors. Thought of John Lehmann, with his top-floor flat in Mecklenburgh Square. Looking from Piccadilly Circus in the direction of Leicester Square there were so many ruins you could see a hill in the distance. Went out to Pembroke Gardens on a bus. Described Los Angeles to the family with great enthusiasm. Tried to get a job through an agent. In the newspaper, an advertisement in fake Elizabethan language for seats in a fighter plane to take part in an air raid. Woke with enormous relief that I'm still here.

PART 2

DESKS, BOILER SUITS AND BUNKS

(1943-45)

11

A New Kind of Warfare

Sir Archibald Clark Kerr wore double-breasted, pinstriped suits, and moved with an avuncular carefulness, a fractional hesitation, which seemed somehow at odds with his sociable, suntanned face. He had soft, hooded eyes, whose pupils seemed to gravitate to the waggish sideways or upwards glance, a fleshy, kinked nose, and a thin, laugh-suppressing mouth. His hair, a light-catching grey, was freshly, carefully cropped - would have been so regardless of climate or activity. He smoked a short pipe, which he would look down his nose at while bringing match to tobacco, his expressiveness in those moments outsourced to the outward creases of his eyes. It was an appearance that patiently took in the world, could listen happily to another talking for hours, and saw far beyond the immediate proximity to a wider, more diverse and exciting human experience, the antithesis of the 'stuffed-shirt diplomatist' the world had been used to before the war. What was John Lehmann thinking when they greeted each other for the first time, this man who had just flown in from Moscow and was open about his determination to get into direct, man-to-man relations with Stalin? It was hard not to be charmed by this man. The betrayal of the international fellow-travelling community by the Molotov-Ribbentrop Pact was still clearly remembered and deeply felt. But Russia, officially, was a friend again, a gigantic ally and war machine capable of replicating the ruthlessness of the Wehrmacht. Was this a conflict of interest? Did conflicts of interest still exist in wartime?

Clark Kerr had known Auden and Isherwood in China, where, as British Ambassador, he had been trying to placate a nervous nationalist leadership who were expecting international aid. He was also, as chance had it, a long-term reader of *New Writing*; a copy of *New Writing in Europe* had been the one book deemed most essential while he was hurriedly packing for his new posting in Moscow. Somewhere within the Russian bureaucratic behemoth Lehmann's name had come up, and now he and Clark Kerr were meeting together in London for a journey deep into the British literary mind. The ambassador explained his intention of returning to the Motherland with as big a collection as possible of the works of young English writers and books about new trends in modern literature. He would need Lehmann's guidance in making his choices, he said. And there was a lot that he wanted to know. Off the record, Clark Kerr expressed his belief – no doubt appealing to Lehmann – that the typical British political types had become out of date, and that if Britain were to 'ride high on the wave of the future' there would need to be a 'silent revolution' supported by intellectuals. To what extent were the novelists and critics of Lehmann's generation interested in politics? That was a difficult question. In return, Lehmann wanted to hear Clark Kerr's opinion on Churchill. Churchill he admired, but not the 'yes-men' who surrounded him.

One evening, there was an 'unusual kind of gathering' held in Lehmann's new flat at Carrington House in Mayfair, in the little warren of streets around Shepherd's Market. Since it was Mayfair, the architects had made a cursory attempt at grandeur in the narrow concrete and stone tile balconies and large glass doors, surrounded by additional casement windows, which opened on to them. Single steps up or down separated the living areas in that art deco style. If anything, the flat resembled Lehmann's former pied-à-terre in Vienna. But he had not been asking for much: 'It seemed as good a place as any in which to face mutilation – or death – though definitely not in the official shelter, which was in the deep basement, amid a formidable tangle of huge hot-water pipes next to the oil-fired boiler.' The place took on new life that evening as it filled up with poets, some arriving from their day jobs and others soon to depart for Home Guard duties. Then there was Clark Kerr, who stood out among the grey wool suits and less demonstrative countenances of the writers. There was the formidable-looking Louis MacNeice with his puckered and lined mouth, and Cecil Day-Lewis of the perpetual frown. Gangly Stephen Spender gave the group a more genial edge, and was quick to sit down on the carpet with long legs outstretched when Clark Kerr settled into an expressive monologue on 'Russian war problems and the Russian attitude to writing in wartime'. This man addressing them could now be said to be their closest link to what was going on in Russia – because he addressed them in person, he could not be censored or smothered – and as a result he felt the full focus of their curiosity. It was an unusual gathering because, as the poets watched Clark Kerr, he began not to seem like a diplomat at all, but rather something new. He struck them as playing a bigger game, urging these writers to step up into the shoes of politicians – a game which was prescient of the Cold War.

Allied relations was an inexact, tentative science, and every avenue had to be explored. Now, literature was being considered as the thing which might bridge the gap. Lehmann was at his new job at the Ministry of Information when a telegram came through from an old pre-war acquaintance Timofei Rokotov, who was editor of

Internationalnaya Literatura in Moscow. 'TAKE OPPORTUNITY GREET LONGSTANDING FRIEND COMRADE IN ARMS AGAINST NAZI TYRANNY,' the message read. And what a different message it would have been only two years before. This man in Russia, who, it later transpired, was already on doubtful terms with the Soviet administration, wanted constant updates on the wartime activities of British writers, including reviews of books as they came out, and copies of the main critical publications. A subsequent message ordered 'DETAILED CHARACTERIZATIONS OF WORK OF MANY WRITERS MENTIONED UNFAMILIAR TO US HENRY GREEN NORMAN CAMERON LAURIE LEE WALTER ALLEN EVELYN WAUGH ELIZABETH BOWEN WILLIAM PLOMER'. Lehmann had assumed that the information he had been asked to provide was to have a more oblique, symbolic purpose, indulged only by the relatively small, highbrow audience of Rokotov's magazine. But soon - this information was told to him in a phone call from a higher-up at the ministry - the men in charge wanted a slice of the action. From now on Lehmann's answers to Rokotov's questions - 5,000 words' free cabling for every article - would be sent direct to Moscow. This was, he supposed, an example of literature, and writers, having the capacity for genuine political influence. It would have been a pipedream once, but now seemed something of a mixed blessing. It had caught the British literary scene at a strange time, a crossroad as such, and the source of the questions was perhaps the last place they felt they had to explain themselves to.

The work was fun to do, Lehmann reflected, but the frequent difficulties it presented were indicative of the wider, more foundational difficulties posed by Anglo-Soviet relations. Lehmann would be nagged to give information on 'MOVEMENT AMONGST ENGLISH INTELLECTUALS FOR QUICKER OPENING SECOND FRONT', a question which to him revealed 'the entirely different conceptions of the role of imaginative writers and artists in war-time which existed in Churchillian Britain and Stalinist Russia'. The concept of a Second Front, which would require all available resources from both the British and American armies in attacking the Wehrmacht while it was preoccupied in the East, was a constant subject of debate, though one that few, if any, British writers felt they had any place in. Was it not the job of generals and the war cabinet to make that case? Perhaps this was what it meant to be a true political writer – to deal not only in questions of ideology but also in the practicalities of war strategy. In actual fact, it was even less romantic than that; until recently, writers in Russia had been sent on assignment to large-scale construction projects or collective farms, with the aim of mythologising Stalin's Five-Year Plan to industrialise the Soviet Union.

It was a strange time, Lehmann reflected – had been a strange time ever since the morning of 11 April 1941 when the All Clear had last rung out across the city. Westminster, that morning, was filled with the smell of burning wood, and the air was poisonous with the fine grit of demolished buildings. As William Sansom wrote, 'many landmarks had gone, many historic buildings would grace the city no longer.' From that morning on, the war began its retreat from the horizon back to the map. The heavy raid that was expected to come at the beginning of June never arrived, and then on the twenty-second of that month Germany broke the Non-Aggression Pact by invading the Soviet Union. Britain was no longer its primary focus, and this meant that the Luftwaffe was moved from French airfields to ones in Prussia and Poland. For weeks the public had stayed on high alert, whispers of 'a third of the Luftwaffe still in France' and 'new, giant planes specially built for England' blowing through London; but night after night the skies were silent, and empty but for that glittering firmament. Life still existed; one could get on with one's work or book a table at the Ivy for lunch. 'One was almost lulled into thinking that, as far as our own little islands were concerned, the Four Horsemen had ceased to ride,' Lehmann wrote. It was in this atmosphere that he had received Rokotov's urgent appeals and been wrong-footed by the expectation from Russia for greater political impetus among the British writers. This seemed a blatant failure of communication; the Russians obviously were not aware of the effect their own decisions had had in depoliticising the British literary world.

It was not only Lehmann's work at the Ministry of Information that seemed to become more complicated as the war progressed. At the Hogarth Press, where his duties during the war were 'hardly more than a kind of holding operation', a brutal embargo with whomever was in charge of the paper supply had made it so that Lehmann now had to rank his authors in terms of importance and continue only with those titles whose value was deemed indisput-able. Top of the list were Virginia Woolf's unpublished works and works which necessitated constant reprinting, as well as books written with Virginia as the subject. Happily, even in death, the well of Virginia Woolf was showing no signs of drying up. Leh-mann's feeling during visits to Leonard at Rodmell, that of being 'haunted all the time by the feeling of her presence in the house', was not completely far-fetched. Unpublished works, stashed away in various nooks and crannies, seemed to nose their way to the surface, demanding new attention. Lehmann was 'absolutely stag-gered' at the amount of material which sat in reserve. But again, as with the debate surrounding the ending of *Between the Acts*, the question of knowing Virginia's mind. One typescript of her last essay on Mrs Thrale would be unearthed, and not much later Leh-mann and Leonard would be surrounded by half a dozen variants, each similarly typed and apparently complete. In her death, as in her life, Virginia represented the bulk of the Press's sales and income. Sigmund Freud's work - published by the Hogarth as part of the International Psycho-Analytical Library - would also be kept in print. At least in the case of the Hogarth Press, paper rationing had forced publishing away from present and future writers and back into its archives. This was not publishing, as Lehmann had always characterised it, and the implication for the British wartime literary product was grave. There seemed to be no other alternative.

The next most important writer – Lehmann was quite emphatic about this – was Henry Green, top of Rokotov's list of apparently significant writers requiring a precis. Green had come over to the Hogarth Press in 1938 after his novel *Party Going*, eight years in the making, had been rejected by his publishers, Dent. They had doubts whether it could be anything more than a *succès d'estime*, and so the book had gone back to Green's desk drawer to gather dust. It had been the idea of his friend, Goronwy Rees, to approach the Woolfs. Lehmann, as we have seen, was mesmerised. He sent a copy of the manuscript to Isherwood, who was then in Brussels with Auden, explaining, in a separate note, 'I believe I've found a really first-class novel. I long for you to read it,' and then 'I'm longing to hear what you have to say about Henry Green's MS, which I have just sent you. I – and many others – think it is an amazing bit of work.' In Lehmann's mind, Green was the future; he was soon, too, a close friend, 'vivacious and endlessly witty and amusing'.

Leonard had been slow to give his approval for *Party Going*, but eventually assented. The novel received an early batch of enthusiastic reviews and began to sell fast. Luckily, Lehmann wrote (because otherwise they would have had to choose between them), Christopher Isherwood produced nothing for the Press after the sections which made up *Goodbye to Berlin*. That hope had begun to fade as Isherwood, in Hollywood, became more deeply involved in the Yoga movement. When Lehmann pressed him for new material, he would become vague, mentioning a handful of projects that were under way ('Well, before the sudden call to the movie-swamp'), and again dangling the promise of a complete

volume of Berlin stories. 'I was beginning a study of Berthold*
working at Gaumont British, which I intend to call *Prater Violets*,'
he wrote. 'I want to do the story of Heinz. And, after that, a somewhat modified version of *Paul is Alone*.' The war was over by the
time Lehmann got a glimpse of *Prater Violet*, 'and neither of the
other two stories was ever completed'. The trouble with Isherwood was that all of his stories had to be written from experience
– an experience which was altogether too marvellous to tolerate
extended breaks for writing. Really, Auden told Spender in 1955,
'the truth of the matter is that what Christopher likes is lying in
the sun in California and being surrounded by boys also lying
in the sun'.

If possible, Lehmann was even more enraptured by Green's new
manuscript, *Caught*. It was *the* novel of the war so far, no question,
and further evidence of a curious phenomenon wherein 'the Auxiliary Fire Service should become a centre of literary and artistic
creation'. While other writers lay dormant, Green had been writing specifically about the war for over three years, sending 'several
short sketches or individual episodes', including 'The Rescue' and
'Mr Jonas', to *New Writing*. Green was enchanted by the new circumstances of his life, telling a friend 'The behaviour of my AFS
unit gets more and more fascinating.' It is perhaps only because
he could see a positive value in the war – the unlikely characters
it brought into close contact – that he was able to put pen to paper
so soon. Even the back-and-forth bureaucracy and jobsworthy
superiors became humorous in this light. *Caught* is a book which
forgets to mention politics, and, as Jeremy Treglown has written,
'part of its distinctiveness lies in the extent to which it isn't about
the war at all, but about people conducting their muddled lives in
much the same way as at any other time.' It was in this way that

---

* Berthold Viertal, with whom Isherwood in the early thirties had worked on
the British Gaumont feature *Little Friend* (1934).

it resonated; as Lehmann had said, the war was background. You still had work to do, and you could still take a date to a restaurant. Green inscribed the last page, 'London, June 1940 - Christmas 1942', as if to say that this was the most immediate novelistic account of the war that any reader was going to get. It was a remarkable feat, Lehmann wrote, as if Green 'had had all the peaceful leisure in the world to work at it'.

Green himself, however, confessed to some circumstantial difficulties, and a feeling that the novel could have been better. His was a unique style, an ornate rococo in which one can imagine the writer fussing over syntactical and formal detail, yet with the ultimate aim of representing the muddledness of life. It was a kind of anti-style, one which was worked at so that it should be free to unravel, like a machine designed to come apart. It is best compared to the writing of Virginia Woolf in the way that it works from back to front, beginning with the subtle inflexion of sense or impression and building outwards to context. It relied on specific patterns of language, like spiralling repetition, and even, in instances, would create a language of its own. Green had, he said, intended to create 'a series of pictures rising one out of the other, the next out of the last, with the gaps in between the silences, to mark the passage of time'. But, he said, 'what one tries to do and what one brings off are two very different things, particularly when under the disabilities of the blitz and the difficult sort of life I make for myself'.

In Richard Roe, Green had found the perfect protagonist for the times. Roe comes crashing through the division of Ivory Tower and modern, working Britain and finds himself just as much at home where he has ended up. He embodies the new homogeneity of wartime Britain, as well as its impossibility and the extent to which it was a performative endeavour. He is a protagonist without any sense of purpose, ideological or otherwise. The narration, moreover, is omniscient only so far as it is able to follow characters into their private lives. But it is too closely tethered, too distracted by detail, to attempt any more general summing-up. *Caught* is perhaps the novel which best exemplifies Orwell's concept of being 'inside the whale', that is being 'in the dark, cushioned space that exactly fits you, with yards of blubber between yourself and reality, able to keep up an attitude of the completest indifference, no matter *what* happens'. The writer who is inside the whale is 'not only individualistic but completely passive . . . a man who believes the world-process to be outside his control'. Orwell means this as a compliment, though we can deduce his intention to be reactionary. Green - or Henry Miller, in Orwell's case - was doing entirely the opposite of the left-wing writers who set a standard by ideological seriousness, and were yet to acknowledge that 'progress and reaction have both turned out to be swindles'.

There is another comparison to be drawn between Green and Miller's work. Green's realistic dialogue was *too* realistic. The Press's printers at Letchworth had begun to object to certain words and phrases in the chatter of the firemen, but only after they had already set up the type. The wartime bureaucracy, as we have seen, was 'only just tolerating the freedom of publishers and editors to print what they liked', and Lehmann thought it possible that *Caught* 'could be viewed by narrow minds as a thoroughly anti-heroic book'. Green, free of any charge of indecency, could yet be punished simply for being inside the whale - for having thrown his hands up and said 'What's the use?' It was one thing for Miller to be 'innocent of public-spiritedness', but now that word 'morale', typed thousands of times each day by government employees, loomed like the guillotine's blade. It was a war, like many others, between nuance and caution; the book was not anti-heroic, but rather represented a 'heroism that showed itself in spite of an extreme distaste for and distrust of heroics'. Lehmann was able to convince Green to alter the handful of sentences earmarked by the printers as overstepping the mark; Hogarth needed the Garden

City Press if they were to continue to operate in wartime. It was a tricky situation. Green, in his way, had created something delicate and unique that the heavy hands of red-tape-entangled third parties could easily destroy. Green, Lehmann recorded, 'was co-operative, but as indignant as I was and said he was not going to change one word more, and couldn't "tolerate any further mucking about with *Caught*". A compromise was reached, Green's 'rare and marvellous gift' preserved.

There was a wide dissonance, then, in the picture Lehmann was regularly being pushed to paint as a critic and the daily, on-the-ground realities of the British literary industry. There is little question that he found this difficult. If he could put up with the Hogarth Press being a 'holding operation' for the time being, he would never completely be able to suppress his belief that it deserved more, and better. Things between Leonard and Lehmann 'went on for the most part pretty smoothly', but there were two or three 'rather violent disagreements' which could not be circumvented. The 'kernel' of these disagreements was that Lehmann wished to expand and Leonard did not. Increasingly, over the next few years, Lehmann 'realised that it would be essential to run the Hogarth Press in a different way: to expand in order to carry a proper staff; to have the opportunity to train managers who could take as much as possible of the complex and time-wasting detail off my hands'. This was not the case for Leonard, who had accepted his Press to be one of the small ones. To attempt anything resembling expansion right now would require an injection of external capital, and the small publisher who accepted this package, who agreed to take a large office more central than Bloomsbury, and to take a large staff, would no longer control his own business. As Leonard put it, 'those who have supplied the capital are now master in his house'. Expansion, Leonard thought, was a euphemism for the final ceding of influence, the termination of the original vision.

LOVE AND RUSSIA

Lehmann had suffered, between 1941 and 1943, a 'severe emotional and spiritual crisis', emanating from various sources but amounting to a doubt in his own value, or his value to others. Lehmann, one suspects, found the revolving-door aspect of war - the constant farewells, the fleeting reunions - almost impossible to bear. Thus separate love-affairs would overlap and become tangled together, beginning to resemble each other in the constant tears and quarrels. None seemed to stick, and moments of joy were as fleeting as the images of one of Virginia's modern poets. As in his friendship with Isherwood, Lehmann expected more from his younger lovers than they could give. He wanted them to have a clear sense of purpose in their work, but, more importantly, in him. Soon it had become impossible to tell whether lovers were leaving because of their war duties or because they wished to.

There was the saga with the ballet dancer Alexis Rassine, dying from the moment of its commencement, and despite flashes of lucidity ('Alexis laughing on the bed and devouring sausages happily in my dressing-gown') the relationship soon constricted and was transposed to a Leicester Square café where, in irregular meetings, they were unable to recover any of that ease, and talked as if they barely knew each other. Lehmann was sleeping badly and, as is quite clear, exhausting himself through overwork. A second lover, Adrian Hart, is euphemised by Lehmann as the 'younger friend who had gone to sea in a state . . . of despair'. Hart was often away on naval postings, but the sense of distance, and danger, was more than circumstantial. Both lay at the core of the relationship; the despair was love's despair. 'The partings of lovers during the war were especially hard to bear, because of the danger which lurked everywhere and the fear that every goodbye embrace would be the last,' Lehmann wrote in *I Am My Brother*. But would his emotions have been any different if the lover were going to spend time ('the danger . . . lurked everywhere') around other young men in London? Lehmann had entered a deep, earth-shattering depression, one he compared to 'open[ing] a trap-door to a shaft of blackness that stretched down beyond knowing'. Seeing him, his friends immediately became aware that something was wrong. William Plomer invited him to walk in Hyde Park. They sat by the Serpentine, and Plomer was happy to listen while Lehmann explained everything that had been going through his mind.

In the war, life had revealed its cruellest trick, its ultimate betrayal. This was the ubiquity of undiscriminating death, that 'intimate contact' with the bombs, which, as they screeched down above the moonlit rooftops of London, seemed undecided on their choice of victim until the final moment. It was a lottery, and millions braced for their share of the impact. Death had become as much the civilian's lot as the soldier's. The life Lehmann had built for himself over thirty-four years seemed 'a thinly constructed door against a great tornado of nothingness'; it was all a self-deception, without certainty or proof. Somewhere nestled inside that deception was the assumption, natural enough amid the fullness of life, that one's life was deep and significant in a way which one could not see. An afterlife, perhaps, awaited, or one would survive immortalised in the associations of one's friends. Poetry was founded on these inferences. Lehmann could imagine now, though, 'the total destruction of a civilisation' – what he called in a poem of that time 'the whole monument of love and history', things which, by sheer accumulation, had justified their importance. 'Come back,' he begs. 'There were dreams, there was faith. We must build. Come back . . .'

Even then, within the greater suffering, was private sorrow. Within the communal pain was the individual, isolating, searching pain. Lehmann, though no longer imagining himself to be as much a poet as an editor, had gone to poetry to try to understand what he was feeling. He found himself writing prose poems, 'because I felt that the argument I was embarking upon was complex and difficult, that I would not know its outcome until I came to the end of writing the poems, and that it was absolutely essential not to falsify even the smallest detail in the interests of musical harmony, rhyme or metrical balance'. In all probability, it was all he could muster. But it was a significant moment for Lehmann, one who had looked at literature always with a sense of purpose, and as an editor admitted to always knowing exactly the effect he wanted to achieve. His rejection by the Russian communist project had made him aware of everything he did not, and could not, know.

The results were remarkable; despite the concession to ignorance, in 'Vigils' Lehmann had achieved his most forceful poetic voice yet. It is, quite extraordinarily, a war poem set entirely indoors, in a domestic setting. It opens with the speaker - presumably not having slept - hearing 'the throb' of British bombers returning home from a raid. The speaker goes to the window, where, pulling back the curtains, he watches 'the noiseless fire of sunrise'. They think about the day ahead, scrutinise the morning papers, search 'among the letters by the coffee-cup for one that still delays'. They wonder whether the stories of resistance and uprising in the news have anything to do with 'the promised revolution that will atone for all'. At the second post, they search again for the awaited letter. The war seems to encroach on the room; the wind, 'blowing from the centre' ('the effect of the war on weather,' Virginia Woolf had written, off-hand, in her diary), buffets the comforting fire down to its embers. A church bell chimes the hour. The bombers head back out again.

And so on. The anxiety of the poem is its physical confinement, the sense of movement being frustrated by an all-pervasive fear. It slips easily between immediate and unconscious states, as a doctor would, at various points, discover a fever-addled patient. At their lowest moment the speaker calls out to someone, 'Listen, sailor:

can you hear me out there, in that black, heaving desert of the sea?' It is a desperate attempt at telepathic communication, which seems – in a war of codes, telephones, telegrams, radio broad-casts, newsreels – to ask no answer but a nod or parched rattle or single blip of Morse code. It is a challenge to poetry itself, to the 'writers of comforting epitaphs' who, the speaker realises, can know nothing of death. This seems to include Lehmann's pre-war self. If 'Vigils' has a predecessor, it is Louis MacNeice's *Autumn Journal*, which shares similar narrative properties and builds its sense of isolation through physical setting and the description of routine:

> And I come back here to my flat and wonder whether
> From now on I need take
> The trouble to go out choosing stuff for curtains

It was the modern poem that had most perplexed Virginia Woolf, eschewing, as it did, unconscious reality for surface reality. This unequivocal war, which, like the burst river at Rodmell, came right to one's doorstep, seemed to hold one on the surface. The war could, after all, be seen from the window.

Lehmann's pre-war poetry typically takes one of a few forms. *A Garden Revisited*, we have seen, was antiquatedly bucolic. One poem begins 'After the supper picnic they returned,/Leaving the weedy creeks, the water voles'; another, 'Sharply the spire beyond the meadow-gate/Points in the morning light immaculate.' It is love which here frustrates, both immediate and as packaged in memory; the physical world can take no blame, for it is infinite and perfect. With the failure of love, so the failure of speech and expression, and the earth itself is left to express everything which the lover cannot. Human contact is always one-to-one. Physical setting is characterised in terms of meetings and departures (two of the poems submitted by Lehmann for *New Signatures Poets* are titled 'To Penetrate that Room' and 'After the Final Shutting of a Door') and is largely uncoloured by the mundane. Otherwise, the poems are anonymous and obscurely contemplative in exactly the way that was so irksome to readers of 1930s poetry. This category comprises mostly the political poetry, the egoless speaker being an enthusiastic model for a new identity of the masses, superseding the individual one. These poems in particular suffer by formal constraint. Their desire to be stirring and quotable places undue emphasis on final lines, just as the necessity of rhyme has, as Lehmann admits, a falsifying effect. He was fascinated by the poetry of the First World War, and in his reading of Rupert Brooke's final poems - especially 'Fragment', written on a troopship taking him to the Aegean where he would meet his death - had identified 'a change in his mood and thinking' signified by a shift away from the rhetoric of his earlier poems. It was a shift, like Lehmann's, away from certainty but towards 'a firmer grasp . . . of the true human implications of the war'.

It was work which eventually had dragged Lehmann out of this submerged state of grief and back to 'the ordinary dry-shore life . . . with its smiling reassurances and solidity'. Lehmann was now so busy that it was becoming almost impossible to get over to Bourne End at the weekends for his Home Guard service, and though he missed the warm bond of local allegiance, he had also a renewed sense of purpose which had London as its focus. Despite what seemed its sealed fate, *New Writing* had eventually received validation of the highest order when it was scouted by the great Allen Lane. It came at just the right time, when the tediously shapeshifting *New Writing*, which had already been through two different publishers and been hacked down to its 'lean war substitute', seemed in danger of losing its identity. Lane had read, and liked, Lehmann's pamphlet *New Writing in England*, and was now prepared to throw the vast resources of Penguin Books behind it. This was, most notably, its generous paper quota.

Business with Lane moved fast. As a publisher he was 'quick and decisive in giving a new project his full support, and, while keeping an eye on the financial and business implications, happy to let his chosen editor get on with the job with the minimum of interference'. Soon after they had opened their correspondence, Lane was visiting Lehmann in his flat. A book comprising the 'best of' *New Writing* was worked out, and shortly after a contract for six numbers of a monthly *Penguin New Writing*. Penguin, of course, was riding high on the wave of the increased book sales of wartime, and it was because of this that, considering the various difficulties of the period, business could move ahead with 'incredible speed'. The increased income also benefited the publisher in another way. Lane had sensed in the restless, impotent undertones of the time that 'war brought with it a hunger for culture', and now, mobilising the techniques he had developed with the sixpenny Penguins, he was working to deliver that culture to the public on an unprecedented scale. According to Jeremy Lewis, the acquisition of *New Writing* was just another example of 'Lane's readiness to subsidize worthwhile ventures from profits made elsewhere'.

Penguin had been the final great revelation in the conception of the new world – great literature obtained as easily as a packet of cigarettes. Kingsley Amis has recalled the 'great revolution' which came, for him, at about the age of fourteen, when Penguin Books appeared and 'for the price of a ham roll you could get a whole novel'. It seemed purpose-built for wartime. With a monopoly on culture perhaps only comparable to the BBC or a major Hollywood studio, Penguin was deemed to have a deeper spiritual and political purpose in the life of the nation and thus was under the wing of the government. It was also set up to be able to mobilise quickly at a time when those who didn't move quickly often found that avenues had been cut off for them by some slight wind change in the war. If Lehmann minded the competition, he could have pointed to the fact that the first edition of *Penguin New Writing* had sold 80,000 copies, whereas *Horizon*, for instance, never sold more than a tenth as many. Lehmann had been able to bring Stephen Spender over from *Horizon*, and with that affiliation, as well as his famous sister Rosamond's, he could boast that 'the three of us could produce a magazine to beat anything of the sort in England'. Though his hubris would soon be found out by the realities of wartime - Penguin's paper quota was reduced from 42 per cent to 37.5 per cent and the magazine was cooked down to a quarterly - having Lane as a benefactor had managed to steady the ship, allowing Lehmann in turn to play the role of benefactor to his writers.

It was Lehmann's job at the Ministry of Information that now took up the most mental space. All seemed to lead back to the question of Russia. As Orwell had written, the political writers of the 1930s had gone down a 'blind alley' in their unquestioned allegiance to 'official Marxism'. They had found themselves 'mixed up in the dishonesties of power politics'. Orwell was sympathetic: 'Literature had to be political,' he wrote, 'because anything else would have entailed mental dishonesty.' But now these writers had been left 'rather in the air'; as much as anything else, they could not continue to risk their intellectual integrity on a political creed. Stephen Spender could see now the overwhelming similarities between communist totalitarianism and Nazi ruthlessness - they were only separated, he thought, by one being masked in the ideology of social justice. But - he excused himself - 'everything I say about Russia is largely conjecture'. 'People whose intelligence and sincerity I trust tell me entirely contradictory facts about Russia, which has become so much an object of propaganda and counter-propaganda that it resembles a vast modern statistical myth.' It had always been conjecture.

After Stalingrad, however, there was a new reason to support Russia, one which required far less intellectual reasoning and

appealed instead to the desire of every person in Britain to be safe
and to win the war. The British public was in awe of the resilience
and 'capacity to suffer' of their new ally. Few, watching newsreel
footage of the Red Army soldiers fighting in the deep snow in their
hooded white coats, could fail to be moved by what seemed then
an unprecedented heroism in the most brutal of conditions. There
was an enormous sense of catharsis in, after so many years, finally
being on the winning side, and the result, as shown by surveys
made at the time, was a new reverential attitude towards the Russians which quickly spread across the nation. Spender admits to
not having been immune himself.

But, Lehmann felt, the news was not entirely good. So far, British writers had been successful in protecting their industry from
regimentation and censorship – as he said, not a single book had
been kept from publication by way of government intervention.
As this 'perfectly reasonable and justified boosting of Russian
achievements proceeded', however, 'some of us began to feel a
little nervous lest our own bureaucracy grow jealous of the firm
control under which the Soviets appeared to keep their writers.'
Indeed, Stalin had latched on to the writers of the Soviet Union in
a way that made most not a little anxious, calling them 'engineers
of human souls'. They were expected to write in whatever genre
his advisers felt would best serve the interests of the state, by this
point a box-ticking kind of 'socialist realism' which was concerned
not with 'objective reality' but rather reality 'in its revolutionary
development'.

Lehmann's work at the Ministry of Information had completely
re-envisioned his role in the British literary scene, making him,
in a sense, its guardian or protector. The battle against censorship
was never finally concluded in favour of the artists, and so 'sentries
had to be posted in continual vigilance'. One evening, at Senate
House, he had been invited to dine with two officials from the Russian department. 'It was an infuriating and entertaining occasion,'

he wrote. As they ate, the conversation came on to the subject of British writers, with Lehmann clearly in the position of interrogatee. In particular, the officials were concerned by the remnants of mordant anti-Soviet feeling which now lingered in the literary world. Lehmann's fellow diners 'showed clearly enough that they thought a good deal more control should be exercised over our writers'.

Lehmann had landed at the Ministry of Information at a time when it was still a target of publicans' jokes. From outside, it was quite inconceivable that the writers and other dishevelled types clocking in each day, who wouldn't have lasted two weeks in a peacetime office, were able to navigate any of the urgent problems of war. Even in Wales, Dylan Thomas could see that 'all the shysters in London are grovelling about the Ministry of Information, all the half-poets, the boiled newspapermen, submen from the islands of crabs, dismissed advertisers, old mercuries, mass-snoopers'. There was a growing debate, as the war progressed, about the need to professionalise the activities of Senate House. Britain, as yet, had no more substantial ally to model itself on in the areas where it was felt it had less natural prowess. As Adam Piette has written, 'It was really only after Russia came into the war as an ally that the word "propaganda" became acceptable to government officials.' The Soviet Union had long been imagining and reinventing itself through propaganda; they could challenge the Nazis in this respect, where Britain could not. Besides the need to perpetuate this unlikely amity with the Russians, there was also a new agenda, sent from higher up down to the Ministry of Information, based around selling an idea of Britain to America. Now, as Lehmann mingled with men with roles both above and symmetrical to his in Russia, there was for the first time a sense - albeit unstated and unwritten - of needing to fall in line with the wider propaganda effort. Lehmann could feel the presence of that 'vast modern statistical myth' as it leered at him in the room. Why, for example, had Moscow radio produced no historical feature? The answer was simple, he was told: the Russians simply wouldn't stand for propaganda.

12

I Am Only Myself in the Dark

On 28 August 1941, a twenty-six-year-old Dylan Thomas wrote to his best friend Vernon Watkins to explain how he should be contacted now that he was in London. He gave the address 'c/o Horizon, 6 Selwyn House, Lansdowne Terrace, WC1', joking 'It's only a forwarding address, I haven't moved into the editor's chair.' The *Horizon* office, appended to Stephen Spender's flat, was the closest thing Thomas had at that time to a home in the city. Spender himself claimed to have been the one who had discovered the young prodigy, and since its formation the magazine had been making a lot of room for Thomas in its pages. But the Welshman was an expensive charge; he enjoyed an unprecedented intimacy with the *Horizon* editors in the sense that all publisher–author etiquette was broken down. If Thomas offered a poem, it was an opportunity too good to pass up, but it had to be paid for on the spot, like a packet of cocaine, regardless of his intentions for the money. He had been the first author on *Horizon*'s books to be offered a stipend, from the proceeds of the 'Begging Bowl', a sort of proto-crowdfunding scheme, just to keep pen on paper. But

even that money Thomas had got through with quite spectacular efficiency, and he was soon asking Watson for more. Later in life, Spender reflected that Thomas was 'singularly unscrupulous about money'. And so a whole team of people came together to try and keep him on track, including his wife Caitlin who, Spender observed, 'struggled to keep Dylan at work – get him to the country, keep him from distractions, make him fulfil obligations'.

In his letter to Watkins, Thomas explained that he and his wife had arrived in London without any money. Thomas had, to his name, 'a deckchair with a hole in it, half a dozen books, a few toys, and an old iron'. They were having an awful time, he said, and he had felt like killing himself. 'We sit in our bedroom and think with hate of the people who can go to restaurants,' he wrote, referring to the bedsit on Manresa Road in Chelsea where they were currently stopping, and to himself and his wife only, their two-year-old son, Llewelyn, having been left to stay with his mother- and sister-in-law in Blashford, Hampshire. As an anecdote, ditching Llewelyn to head to London has all the usual brazenness one expects from stories of the Thomases, but in this case, as Caitlin has written, it was 'very traumatic, quite the most painful thing that ever happened to me'. She could not shake the memory of 'poor Llewelyn gazing out of the window to see us go'. The Thomases were coming off the back of a tumultuous summer, the main factors of which had been (of course) money – pubs and shops in Laugharne finally seeking repayment of generous credit – and Dylan's absolute horror of war. The period had ended with Caitlin going to Cardiff for three nights to have an affair with a man, William Glock, whom she had fallen in love with. It was the first time she had 'calculated an infidelity', though evidently she was not fastidious enough because Dylan (who 'was always going off to London and having affairs') soon found out and was 'very upset'. 'Dylan threw a knife at me (which missed me by miles), and for a long time after that he wouldn't come near me,' Caitlin explained.

The consequence of everything that had happened that summer ('We were on the brink,' Caitlin wrote) was that, when Dylan
realised he would need to move to London for work, Caitlin soon
came to feel that if she did not go with him she would lose him.
'I felt that if I didn't do it Dylan would drift back into that pub life
that he had before he met me, and would soon forget all about me.'
The pub, for Dylan, was an activity which could consume multiple
days, each binge pre-empting the next as rows of light ales were
required in the morning to get over the hangover. Soon another day
would be written off. On the way down to her mother's, boarding
the train to Bristol from Cardiff station, Caitlin had found herself
caught with the luggage in a swarm of commuters on the platform
while the train departed with Llewelyn inside. She used the phone
at the desk to ring up all of the stations en route, but it was not
until she arrived in Bristol herself, four hours later, that she heard
shouts of 'Anybody lost a two-year-old baby?' Llewelyn was found
'black from head to foot in the arms of a woman porter'.

It was in London where Dylan and Caitlin had first met, at the
Wheatsheaf on Rathbone Place in Fitzrovia, a pub about which it
was said that 'everyone or almost everyone came sooner or later'.
Recently established, it was done in mock-Tudor, and the saloon
bar was reduced to half its possible width because of a bay, like that
found on a coaching inn, on the left-hand side. This passage now led
to a warehouse yard, piled high with cardboard boxes. The narrow-
ness of the bar, however, had its advantages; patrons were pushed
together practically on top of one another, and the whole place felt
bright and cheerful. It was an ideal setting for Dylan, who liked to
crawl around on the floor and climb into people's laps, much to the
dismay of one regular, the elderly Mrs Stewart, who came in to do
her crosswords and couldn't stand him at any price. Caitlin was sat
that evening with her family friend, the painter Augustus John, and
in less engaging moments of conversation couldn't help noticing the
thoroughly dishevelled young man across the room who looked, she

said, 'like the parody of a poet'. It was 1936, and, Caitlin reflected, 'we were both so different then, so innocent'; within a moment of catching each other's eyes, Dylan had sidled up to her, began his 'endless jabber' and, just like that, entered her world. He had real charm, Caitlin testified: 'he could get round anybody, chiefly when he was doing this little-boy-lost act; he was so pathetic . . . and sweet.'

He told her he loved her the first night they met. But despite auspicious beginnings, London had become symbolic in the decline of the happiness of their relationship. London was the place Dylan had always gone to 'make a few pounds'. He would return home to Laugharne, unannounced, after a few weeks, claiming he had had the worst time imaginable – in bed with the flu or disgusted by everyone around him. 'I'm not going to London again for years,' he would say, calling it 'the city of the restless dead'. Caitlin had heard it all before. But where was the money he had suffered so much to earn? Without exception, Dylan would come back penniless and 'completely laid out with booze', and there was no doubt in Caitlin's mind that he had been 'flopping into bed with any woman'. During these lost weeks, Caitlin, of course, had been looking after the house and their newborn baby. This was why she could not let him go and live there alone, so easy would it be for drink and play to take her place. And she was protecting him, too. Dylan was a different person in London; he could not work there, and what was he if he wasn't working?

Thomas mentions none of his marital problems in his letter to Watkins, except by allusion to his general malaise. Instead, the blame is all on 'stinking, friendless London'. Away from the financial pressures of the capital, life in Laugharne had, he gives the impression, been perfectly easy. In Chelsea he was forced to sit and watch, from the window by his temporary desk, the 'millionaires' going to and fro on buses. Thomas couldn't even manage to write 'Poem' at the top of a clean page; London was much too pleased with itself. One suspects he was thinking more about his financial predicament than the universal awfulness of wartime when he wrote to Watkins, of the moment they were living in, 'We are prisoners now in a live melodrama and all the long villains with three halfpence are grinning in at us through the bars.' The hunger, anger, boredom, hate and unhappiness of the time seemed to concentrate itself inside that rented room. In London, 'the grey gets in your eyes so that a bit of green nearly blinds you and the thought of the sea makes you giddy as you cross the road like a bloody beetle'. As an afterthought, how was Watkins? Had he been packed off to the army yet?

So for a time Thomas would receive letters from rival editors – John Lehmann, for one – sent care of *Horizon*. If the *Horizon* editors and secretaries had their work cut out with Thomas then they were not the only ones. Lehmann had been on his tail for over a year now, having been promised new stories to be published in *Penguin New Writing* to follow on from that brilliant diversion into prose *Portrait of the Artist as a Young Dog*. 'I had been an eager admirer of Dylan Thomas's early poems,' Lehmann wrote, 'but rather less so of those (with certain outstanding exceptions) which had followed them.' The writing had become, in this second stage of his career, perhaps even too esoteric for this exotic, provincial figure whose esotericism had been his unique appeal. It seemed rather a risk for one who at this stage was still largely unknown, and the war certainly had the ability to kill promising careers. Thomas's last collection, *The Map of Love*, was published just ten days before the declaration of war, and by the beginning of the next year Dent had sold only 280 copies. Lehmann gives the inaccurate impression that *Portrait of the Artist as a Young Dog* was Thomas's first attempt at writing short stories; in fact, the point of *The Map of Love* had been the amalgamation of poetry with that shorter prose form. But it had not been successful. 'I hated *The Map of Love*,' Caitlin wrote, 'and told Dylan so . . . he got so muddled up with surrealism and pornography – I didn't like it at all.'

Of his poems, Caitlin was in broad agreement with Lehmann that they 'had become much too complicated'. She goes on: 'I liked his short, passionate poems like "And Death Shall Have No Dominion" or "The Force That Through the Green Fuse Drives the Flower"; those real, pounding poems.' At times, Caitlin thought, Dylan would make his poems inscrutable on purpose, almost to assert his authority. 'He'd joke afterwards that he couldn't understand them himself,' she recollected. But he did not care what people thought of him. Spending time with Thomas in 1941, Vernon Watkins got much the same impression. Despite the commercial and critical failure of *The Map of Love*, he suggests that by this point there had been 'a casting-off of those habiliments which his newly baptised genius no longer needed'. This was where a more committed editor like Lehmann was needed to intervene, and rein Thomas in. But Thomas, to Lehmann's disappointment, didn't regard his prose as being important. Understandably, 'he looked upon [*Portrait of the Artist*] as a lesser work than the poetry.'

'In many ways,' Caitlin thought, 'Dylan was like a big baby. He was used to being waited on, and never thought of doing anything for himself. Much of his life was an act, like pretending to be sick.' Visitors to the apartment on Manresa Road recall a total contrast between the times when Caitlin was present, her trademark vegetable stew bubbling on the stove, and the 'squalor' when she was not. When she was not in London, Dylan had various advocates and benefactors whom he could call on for help. There were mediators, like Dick Church, with whom Lehmann often found himself debating different courses of action in regard to the unruly son. But still the requests for new material were bounced back with apologies ('I'm afraid I haven't got anything much of it done'), and details on the practical aspects of Thomas's life which had prevented him from working. On one occasion, before he had made the move to London, Thomas explains that he is 'still looking for somewhere to live on extremely little - do you know of anywhere? - and have been so homeless and penniless and uncertain lately that I've only been able to write little bits of the story . . .'

It was a good thing, then, to have him in the city, where his editors could check in on him more easily. Lehmann eventually, 'after a good deal of coaxing', managed to persuade Thomas to let him see the first sections of the 'long story about London' that he had been teasing, to be titled *Adventures in the Skin Trade* – 'a semi-autobiographical continuation of *Portrait of the Artist as a Young Dog*,' Thomas explained. Both were in west London at the time, so would meet once a week in a pub in Shepherd's Market to discuss. All business with Thomas was done 'to the accompaniment of drinks, general gaiety and many vivid descriptions of how the work was progressing', and, to add even greater mystery to this new publisher-author dynamic, the poet would generally bring with him to the pub 'a silent, good-looking young man in a London Irish kilt who seemed to be assuming the office of personal bodyguard'. Lehmann, nonetheless, was very pleased with the sections of the story that had so far been handed over, and had already decided to publish them in *Penguin New Writing*. *Adventures in the Skin Trade* was shaping up to be an amusing and individual account of modern-day London; it was a relief, for Lehmann, to be reading this, and taking a break from the earnest 'reports on war experience' that had recently been filling his in-tray. It promised a 'unique mixture of humour and fantasy, and a strong vein of Dylanesque poetry running through it'.* Lehmann was so eager for Thomas to get the

---

* Interestingly, Dent shared none of Lehmann's enthusiasm. One of the publisher's editors felt that Thomas needed to be warned about the declining quality of his work: 'It seems to us that Dylan Thomas has reached a crucial point in his literary career. He made a flying start, and there has been no lack of recognition of his uncommon talent . . . In our view, however, he has not maintained the position which he gained by his early work.' He could not, they thought, 'build a literary career merely on the miniature furore created by his early work . . . Unless he pulls himself together he is going to fizzle out as an author most ignominiously . . .'

book finished that he decided to answer the author's sullen protests
of helplessness in poverty and agreed to pay him a few pounds
every week. He would not be bailing the poet out with a windfall
like Spender and Watson had done, but a few quid, over a hundred
pounds in today's money, would be a generous sum for a literary
magazine to be doling out at the best of times.

Lehmann's plan, however, did not come off; the work did not
progress. 'I began to realise [Lehmann wrote] that Dylan was treating all of my cajolings and homilies as a huge joke (to which I was
privy), and that while he was getting more deeply involved in war
work or scripts for documentary films, the writing of *Adventures
in the Skin Trade* was running down like a clockwork toy.' He wondered whether, now that Dylan was in London permanently and
had seen what it had been reduced to, he had lost heart in his innocent, pre-war vision of the city described in the unfinished book.
Perhaps only Caitlin knew the truth: outside of the office, Dylan
was not working at all. Despite also being Thomas's editor, Stephen Spender was surprised, later on, to find out that, privately,
the Welshman had written next to nothing during the war. The
saga around *Adventures in the Skin Trade* effectively killed the poet's
association with *Penguin New Writing*, not because Lehmann no
longer wanted to take the risk of working with Dylan, but because
all of the unmet deadlines and unanswered letters had 'put a spoke
of embarrassment into [their] relationship'. Lehmann regretted
this deeply.

Thomas had got a taste of the bombing, tentatively, on trips
down to London during the Blitz. He had heard the Hyde Park guns
booming, seen the guns on the roof of Selfridges and witnessed
a plane brought down in Tottenham Court Road. Otherwise, the
planes had largely missed them. Dylan had had letters from his
mother detailing the extensive raids on Swansea, and from Watkins
too. 'I can't imagine Gower bombed. High explosives at Pennard.
Flaming onions over Pwlldu. And Union Street ashen,' he had

replied. From the home of John Davenport at Marshfield in Wilt-
shire, about a hundred miles from London, where the Thomases
had been staying throughout the summer of 1940, they had heard
war planes every now and then. Even here, the war seemed very
far away, but on those nights with the errant planes Dylan became
terrified and would bury his head under the covers down at the
bottom of the bed while Caitlin sat up reading. He would remain
there, 'whimpering', until it was all over.

All of this considered, the blackout could not possibly have
meant the same to Thomas as it did for Spender, Lehmann, Connolly and Orwell in London. One suspects it would have been
emphasised in his letters if, during one of those trips to London
in 1940, he had had to go down into an air-raid shelter or brace for
impact. The period when the Thomases moved to London, in the
second half of 1941, was a quiet one for Britain; Germany would be
tied up with invading the Soviet Union until November. Shortly
afterwards, America would enter the war, and help to steady the
ship. Though temporarily off the menu, however, death by bombing was clearly something Thomas had visualised intensely. Like
Virginia's scrunching and scrambling and crushing, the Blitz world
of Thomas's *Deaths and Entrances* (1946) is a world of flames and
bones which, specifically, takes you at your most defenceless –
perhaps in bed. In the title poem, published in *Horizon* in January
of 1941, Thomas imagines the German pilots as being able to pick
out their victims. The speaker might be fumbling with his keys in
the dark outside his flat when his 'luminous' heart is targeted. 'Are
you frightened these nights?' Thomas asked Watkins, in Swansea.
'When I wake up out of burning birdman dreams – they were frying aviators one night in a huge frying pan; it sounds whimsical
now, it was appalling then – and hear the sound of bombs and gun-
fire only a little way away, I'm so relieved I could laugh or cry.'

If Thomas was to be considered in the newly established category of 'civilian war poets' it was with the codicil that the poet was

blind to any greater, collective endeavour and always did entirely his own thing. Thomas, clearly, was at home with the war's over-riding apocalyptic theme, and related to the cornucopia of fear and despair therein, but it is hard to imagine anyone being as successful as he at avoiding the war in all its forms. By the time of the 'Little Blitz' at the beginning of 1944, Thomas was gone again, moving with Caitlin and the children to a cottage at Bosham on the Sussex coast. After 'Deaths and Entrances', his next poem, 'Ballad of the Long-Legged Bait', made not a single reference to the war; it was a long, sardonic joke 'about a man who fished with a woman for bait and caught a horrible collection'. To judge from the long tussle with Connolly over its publication – the poem ran to 216 lines and threatened to overstrain *Horizon*'s meagre paper ration – Thomas seems to have forgotten there was a war on entirely.

A LACKADAISICAL OFFICE

Dylan, Caitlin tells us, 'drank himself silly' the night before his army medical to give himself a hangover. Despite an early train to Llandeilo, about thirty miles inland from Laugharne, he was at the bar at Brown's Hotel for several hours, mixing beer with sherry, wine and gin. 'The next morning he came out in spots,' Caitlin writes, 'and was shaking and coughing his guts up. At one stage, he even fainted. They classified him C3, right down at the bottom of the list.' Returning, jubilant, to Laugharne, he had gone back to the bar to celebrate his achievements. 'I've done it; I've done it; I've got away with it,' he kept saying. Some of Dylan's friends wanted to know *how* he had done it, thinking that perhaps they could bor-row his technique. Hearing the details, however, it became clear that this was not something that just anyone could do. Previously, Dylan had been using Caitlin's connection with Augustus John to try and reach the ever-busy Kenneth Clark, head of the War Artists'

Advisory Committee at the Ministry of Information. Augustus had told Dylan that Clark knew some of his writing, and might be able to help him with a job. In his letter to Clark, Thomas explained that the date was fast approaching when he would have to officially declare himself a conscientious objector. 'I don't want to do that,' he wrote, 'because, though I will not fight, I am perfectly willing to do some kind of work.' 'My great horror's killing,' he explained. In response, Thomas had had a letter from Clark's wife, offering an introduction to their friend at Parliament, Captain Victor Cazalet, who was organising his own unit of anti-aircraft gunners (as Caitlin said, 'a way of joining the army without having to leave the country'). Cazalet's battery, as they were called, could not have sounded less like Dylan's kind of people. They were 'the monstrous regiment of gentlemen,' as one of Evelyn Waugh's friends called them.

It is unclear when exactly Thomas began his work in the wartime film industry. He was doing short radio scripts for the BBC through 1940, often on heroic imperial figures such as the Duke of Caxias and Christopher Columbus, to be broadcast overseas. At one point, he contacted one of the BBC's producers to try and gain some clarity regarding 'what's wanted' in terms of overall message, or propaganda. He follows these inquiries, humorously, by asking, 'Could I have a script to do without battles, d'you think? Or perhaps with only 20 or 30?' In Thomas's letter to Vernon Watkins, quoted earlier in this chapter, he had mentioned that he was looking for a (more regular and lucrative) job in films.

Now, in 1943, two men were standing in a lift together, in the building of Strand Films at 1 Golden Square. It was a typical Soho corner building, with the black entrance door facing the street at a diagonal, and rose about seven storeys to match the impressive height of the rest of the square, with a Parisian-style roof sloping down toward a narrow balcony. Though clearly heading to the same place, neither of these men had any idea who the other was, and they stood in silence. The shorter, and younger, wore a green pork-pie hat pulled down level with his slightly bulging eyes. His full lips were set low in a round full face, a moribund fag-end stuck to, and drooping from, the lower one. His nose was bulbous and shiny. Where it protruded from a soiled and wrinkled raincoat, his left arm could be seen to be in a sling. As the other was, of course, incapable of knowing, this young man was finding life miserable in London, and currently missing his wife, who had left, as she frequently did, to visit their son. She would receive letters, on Strand Film Co. headed paper, saying 'I love you. I love you', and begging for declarations of love, or assurances of amiability, in return. The letters would complain of the 'horrible' places in the capital, like the Gargoyle Club, where her husband was forced to drink – a plea for sympathy, or forgiveness, made even more pathetic in light of the testimony of one patron of the club who recalled seeing the man 'immensely drunk and wildly jovial, gulping the wine he had snatched off a stranger's table from his own dilapidated shoe'.

The other man in the lift sported a silver-tipped Malacca cane, buffed to a similar sheen to the shorter man's nose, and wore a white corduroy jacket. It was his first day in the office. As the old, capricious lift went about its jerky ascent of the building, this man noticed the other taking quick glances at his outfit and accessories. When this happened, the taller man would become self-conscious and peer down to ensure that his flies were buttoned. When, finally, the lift emitted its groan of exhaustion and clanked to its destination by the double doors marked 'STRAND', the shorter man immediately threw back the gates and disappeared into the office and down the corridor. 'Dylan Thomas in 1943 did not greatly resemble that much-produced early photograph known to him as the Fucking Cherub,' Julian Maclaren-Ross reflected later. 'Certainly I failed to recognize him from it on the morning we first met.'

Left alone, Maclaren-Ross pushed through the still-swinging doors and approached a switchboard desk, presided over by a red-haired secretary. Before he was able to introduce himself, a speaker buzzed somewhere on the desk and produced the 'disembodied voice' of Donald Taylor, the firm's manager, asking whether Mr Maclaren-Ross had arrived yet. He was shown through to an office on the right-hand side of the building where Taylor was waiting for him, as well as the young man from the lift.

Now, without his hat and raincoat, Dylan cut quite a different figure altogether. There was a convergence, in his dress, of weathered bohemianism - the soiled sling was now on full display - and a rather hopeless attempt at conformity in the poorly fitted but 'respectable' blue suit. Dylan could fit in, more so than Maclaren-Ross, in an office, and yet had the air of 'a young provincial tradesman or perhaps a farmer up in London for the day on business'. He wore a bow-tie over a celluloid collar which pinched on his stout neck and, it was clear, was 'beginning to put on a bit of a pot'. His full cheeks were carefully shaven, as if, against all odds, that one morning ritual was engrained deeply enough to have survived in an otherwise chaotic routine.

Taylor introduced the two men, explaining that they would have to get to know each other as they were going to be working together. 'At this Dylan visibly recoiled,' Maclaren-Ross writes, explaining that his 'general get-up' was clearly visibly embarrassing to the poet. Taylor went on: 'You can share that office through there, Dylan show him where it is, I'm sure you can sort out between you the best method of working.' Maclaren-Ross asked what they were going to be working on. 'The Home Guard script,' was the reply. 'Feature length. Dylan will explain. I expect it to be the most fruitful collaboration.'

With that, the two writers left the room and walked across to the office that had been assigned to them. 'Dylan and I stood uneasy and shamed-faced,' Maclaren-Ross wrote, 'like two strange children sent off to play alone by a benevolent adult, in the belief that because they are contemporaries they're bound to get on well.' From the single window in their new office, Thomas and Maclaren-Ross could see across the rooftops to the site of St Anne's church in Dean Street. St Anne's had been bombed twice during the autumn of 1940, once with high-explosive bombs and then, a couple of weeks later, with incendiaries. All but the church tower, with its golden, glinting weathervane, had been completely razed, and on those days when the air-raid sirens were still projected, falsely, across the West End, it was a blunt reminder of how close the bombs had tended to fall. Now, Thomas and Maclaren-Ross seemed to see only the neat, flat lawn of stone and dirt, denoting the efficacy of the civic workers, where once had been a sea of rubble. 'Have you been in the Home Guard?' Maclaren-Ross asked. 'Never,' Thomas replied. 'Neither have I.'

Maclaren-Ross had instead been in the infantry, though not for long. Roughly six weeks after the evacuation of Dunkirk, he had been summoned for his medical examination. He faced it head on, unlike Dylan, and in spite of the effects of years of poverty and heavy smoking on his physique was delivered an inauspicious A-1 grading, meaning fit for front-line service. From there he had gone on to the muddy barrack huts of ITC training on the Devon coast. In the army he was the unostentatious 'Private Ross'; being a writer published by *Horizon*, his superiors were quick to point out, meant very little there. Training began shockingly early, at six o'clock sharp, and otherwise the atmosphere of close monitoring and pernickety discipline seemed to resemble most closely his days at school. In military exercises, the trainees used broomsticks as props, since – as Orwell had been declaiming – rifles were in short supply. Maclaren-Ross's days as a prospective front-line soldier finished with him being reclassified with a temperamental knee, and from then on it was a string of unimportant jobs in various 'undisclosed destinations'.

A strange paradox of the British literary industry in the Second World War is that the prose writers who flourished during this time tended to be the ones in physical occupations. These writers benefited, it seems, from Henry Green's 'lulls'; they benefited from boredom. As Maclaren-Ross's biographer has written, the army 'gave him time in which to work. It simplified his life. It freed him from employment worries. It forced him to concentrate on fulfilling his ambitions. And, above all, it presented him with a plethora of "excellent material for satire".' The same could be said for Henry Green, Evelyn Waugh, and many others. In October 1942 Maclaren-Ross had sent John Lehmann a few lines of biography to accompany one of his stories in the magazine, explaining that he was an 'orderly room clerk' who 'works ten hours a day and writes stories in spare time'. But just because manual work suited these writers does not mean that they suited it. To give a sense of how eventful Maclaren-Ross's life was, in a subsequent letter to Lehmann, sent in May of 1943, the writer was proposing two new stories, one 'based on my experiences as a prisoner in the Regimental Gaol' and the other 'a report of life in this hospital, which is a psychiatric hospital for neurosis cases'. Maclaren-Ross's 'desertion' – really an extended trip to London during which he had made appeals to various acquaintances for better wartime work – was actually the protest of 'an intelligent man of 31, travelled, educated abroad, sophisticated and an anti-fascist, a writer who can write over 17 stories in spare time and get them published', and who 'cannot be utilised, owing to his medical category, in any better capacity than an office boy in an orderly room.' When finally he returned to the West End, for the first time since early 1940, Maclaren-Ross was immediately branded as 'a Soho non-blitzer'.

Thomas had been with Strand Films for two years by the time Maclaren-Ross joined. So far, he had had a role in at least half a dozen productions. Far from the glorified, turgid histories of his radio days, screenwriter Dylan was increasingly tasked with making propaganda of a staider and less excitable sort. *New Towns for Old* (1942) was his first 'war film' and seemed to reflect the shifting interests of the Ministry of Information after Stalingrad towards a bolder national identity. The short film showed the efforts of councillors in the fictional settlement of Smokedale (really Sheffield) to make the city more liveable for the post-war world. Thomas's job had been to outline all of the efforts of slum clearance and suburban expansion in as few words as possible - leaving plenty of time for montage shots of clever engineers remapping the city - while giving the language an authentic South Yorkshire slant. 'We began to build a new Smokedale,' explains a councillor dressed in trilby hat and tweed jacket, 'new flats, new homes away from t' smoke, over here [in the green belt] where they should be ... new schools, new hospitals, new roads, new life.' But, inquires a credulous visitor, what if the war brings a stop to all of this? Then they would have to work even harder, once the war is won, to make this utopian dream a reality. And how could they ensure these plans would be seen through? The councillor turns to face the camera: the plans will come true because the hardworking people of Britain will make sure they do. Nineteen forty-two was the aspirational year of the Beveridge Report, which provided a blueprint for a new welfare state for post-war Britain.

But the MO was constantly changing, and it was not long before some in government - including Churchill himself - began to worry that films like *New Towns for Old* were encouraging a 'rising feeling of suspicion and disquiet' among the populace. As Richard Taylor has written, 'the efforts of the MOI, Strand Films and Dylan Thomas were already somewhat ahead of their time and raised for a number of diehards the spectre of some kind of endorsement of socialism'. Such was the fine line that all of the writers now subsumed in the world of propaganda were forced to tread. It could not have been less like the writing they were used to. Scripts would be bounced back by the various councils and boards involved until all initial inspiration or originality had been safely rendered out. Much more popular with the higher-ups were films like *Balloon*

Site 568, also 1942, which, though taking some liberties with its enigmatic title, was really a straight-down-the-line advertisement for female recruits.

In reality, the rather artless Dylan Thomas with his 'pub style' presented little in the way of a subversive or visionary force, and Strand Films was more likely to go the way of oblivion by drink than political mutiny. According to another writer, the American Ivan Moffat, their floor at 1 Golden Square was 'a lackadaisical office, with much sitting about and playing cards'. Dylan was often seen scribbling on the backs of envelopes, in all probability keeping his best ideas – meaning what he actually felt about the state of the country – for himself. As Paul Ferris has written, facile though the scripts may have seemed to a writer like Thomas, 'The work suited him. He was a poet, going through a period of uncertainty about his own writing, who had transplanted himself to a job that required facility with language and little else.'

It was Dylan's aforementioned politeness that ensured he maintained a generic sense of decorum while in the office. Maclaren-Ross remembers a morning after a particularly heavy night in the Wheatsheaf. They had spent the evening arguing: 'Fucking dandy. Flourishing that stick,' Dylan had said to him, 'Why don't you try to look more sordid? Sordidness, boy, that's the thing.' Now each was feeling rather sheepish. When Maclaren-Ross walked into the office, he was surprised to find Thomas already present, 'hunched up over the desk as if he'd been stabbed at it'. He was trying to insert a pencil into a rotary dial so that he could ring up for the time, but failing as he could not stop his hands from trembling. Thomas needed to know whether the pubs were open yet. 'They're not,' Maclaren-Ross told him. 'It's only half-past ten.' Dylan was experiencing one of his famous remorseful hangovers. He apologised to his colleague for being rude about his teddy-bear coat, and was anxious to know whether his cane had survived the evening. Then he began to convulse with powerful sneezing. 'It's the drink coming out,' he explained, and again expressed his impatience for eleven thirty and the Back Bar of the Café Royal just next door. But when Maclaren-Ross suggested they pick up a bottle of whisky to 'guard against these hangovers in future', Dylan was 'absolutely appalled'. *'In the office?'* he asked. Clearly there were *some* boundaries that Thomas set for his behaviour. In the end, they made it to the appointed hour, and a double Irish, as well as pint of bitter with spaghetti bolognese at Fava's in Frith Street for lunch, was enough to set the poet right again, and enable them both to work that afternoon.

The Home Guard script was now moving along, though likely in quite a different direction to what Donald Taylor and his 'fruitful collaboration' had anticipated. The two writers assigned each other characters and dictated alternate lines of dialogue while Dylan transcribed. The script, however, was already taking on a distinctly Dylan- or Julianesque tone. Clearly, both were itching to break out of the imaginative constraints imposed by the industry's brand of 'safe' writing.

> Neither of us having served in the Home Guard [Maclaren-Ross wrote] we'd had to invent our own, like Kafka's *Amerika*; and what we concocted was a lively comedy-thriller set in a village 'somewhere in England', stuffed full of eccentrics and containing also a fifth column group, a delayed-action bomb, and a German parachutist who'd been in civvy street a music hall Master of Disguise.

Dylan was also eager to represent the group of the Free Japanese who kept their headquarters on the floor below, a move which they debated in their 'afternoon drinking place', the Horseshoe Club on Wardour Street. Maclaren-Ross's main concern was with which of them could possibly write the Japanese dialogue.

A curious fact of the wartime film industry is what constituted a 'documentary'. Settings could be entirely fabricated as long as they

met the criteria of 'somewhere in England', and even the more lyrical scripts, which were Dylan's forte, were accepted to stand in
for normal speech and sentiment in espousing the British values of
adaptability and perseverance in wartime. But it was features that
Thomas and Maclaren-Ross really wanted to be doing – that they
spent all day discussing. 'Have you seen *The Cat Creeps?*' one would
ask. 'No, but I've seen *The Crimson Claw*.' The possibility of writing features was dangled over them like a carrot, the boss Donald
Taylor saying 'You boys sit tight. We'll be making features soon.'
As an outlet for their excitement, they had begun to work, off the
record, on a script to be titled *The Whispering Gallery* or *The Dis-
torting Mirror*, a film containing a scene where the villain's sex was
changed by an operation halfway through. They spoke proudly of
the 'H' certificate – meaning most mature – it would garner. They
also wanted to create an entirely new form of literature characterised by an elaborate film script that could be experienced as a film,
with an 'absolute visual impression', when only being read.

Eventually Maclaren-Ross had got to meet Caitlin, who, amid
all of the grapevine-tales of his womanising (such as having a
girl in his sleeping bag on the roof at Golden Square during fire-
watching), Dylan still insisted was the only woman he ever really
cared about. With Dylan in full-time office work, Caitlin was now
spending a lot of her time with friends in the village of Talsarn, in
Cardiganshire, or back in Laugharne, where she now had another
baby, Aeronwy, known as Aeron, to look after. Caitlin disapproved
of Dylan's film work, seeing it as a poor use of his time, but also as
the anchor that was holding him to London. Since both the job and
London amounted to a distraction from poetry, Caitlin saw Dylan's
persistence in these regards as deliberately undermining her efforts
to 'save him from himself'. If Dylan's opinion of London had been
improved by a regular income and a genial work placement, Caitlin still only saw the worst of it. Manresa Road seemed to become
even more dilapidated with each of her absences. The roof now

leaked, and Aeron had to sleep in a cradle with an umbrella over it. The smell of cat faeces wafted up from a neglected apartment below. On cold nights, the Thomases had to use an old, dirty rug as an extra layer of bedding. The list of hardships goes on.

Dylan had told Maclaren-Ross that he 'managed to marry the prettiest girl I knew', adding 'Can a bloke do more?' 'Caitlin was indeed pretty,' Maclaren-Ross concurred, 'pink-cheeked with brilliant blue eyes and a few blonde strands always straggling loose from an otherwise neat hair-do.' He met her only a few times, but remembered two public quarrels that broke out between her and her husband. Caitlin had every right to be angry with him. In her memoir, she explains that 'This was the first time in our lives that we had ever had a regular income, and with our rent at Manresa Road only £1 a week we should have been able to manage quite comfortably, but we never did: whenever Dylan had money he drank it, and always wanted more.' Regarding what Caitlin thought of Maclaren-Ross himself, there is no mention. London was still the pleasure city for Thomas, and Maclaren-Ross, with his props and general ostentatious garb, would have seemed exactly the kind of eccentric that her husband would choose as a co-conspirator. On the other hand, it is possible that she barely registered him at all. The inherent sadness of the Thomases' relationship was beginning to rise to the surface, all very publicly. On one occasion, after Dylan's death, Maclaren-Ross had found himself alone with Caitlin for the first time. They were at the Mandrake Club, and Caitlin was too drunk even for him to keep up. That night ended with her being carried by Louis MacNeice, kicking and screaming, to Broadcasting House, where *Under Milk Wood* was to be broadcast for the first time.

13

Epitaphs

The Orwells were the modern wartime couple. Both were now working full-time in their respective offices, with jobs of roughly equivalent importance. Orwell was at the BBC, broadcasting to India, and Eileen, having left the Ministry of Information, was now at the Ministry of Food, broadcasting to the housewives of Britain. With these new, well-paying jobs, it was agreed between them that they could now finally afford an apartment with a bit more space. They settled on 10A Mortimer Crescent, which comprised the lower two storeys of a Victorian villa, in the classic pale-brick-with-white-trim London style. Here, unlike at their previous London addresses, they had a decent-sized garden at their disposal. Anthony Powell was largely alone in the capital at the time, his wife being often away with their young child, and as a result had formed a close relationship with the Orwells. He visited 10A on at least one occasion, and even he could see that the Orwells were coming up in the world. The sitting room boasted 'a general background of furniture dating from more prosperous generations of bygone Blairs' and even, rather grandly, several eighteenth-century family portraits hanging on the walls. Powell had recently met Orwell for lunch at a Greek restaurant in Soho and was surprised to discover his companion had preordered a bottle of wine, when that resource seemed most difficult to procure. So it was not as if Orwell was any 'confirmed enemy of good living'. 'I'd say just a touch of elegance,' David Astor, publisher of the *Observer*, remembered later of 10A. It was, undoubtedly, a step up from Wallington with its outdoor toilet. Friends who came for dinner during wartime often found it more convenient to stay on for the night, and then tackle the disrupted transport networks the following day. Orwell delighted in being able to offer these guests hot baths, but as at least one guest testified, the flat, in the 'gypsy' way of life the Orwells seemed to enjoy living, was still 'desperately cold and draughty'.

The Orwells' nephew, Henry Dakin, felt that deep displays of affection were not really part of Orwell and Eileen's relationship. They clearly, however, cared a great deal for one another, and friends of Eileen were frequently incredulous at her insistence on putting Orwell's health above anything else. One gets a picture of the kind of couple they were – resourceful, independent, united by purpose – from reading *Homage to Catalonia*, where Eileen is frequently alluded to as being in Barcelona (she was working with the Independent Labour Party (ILP)) and sending treats for Orwell at the front. She had followed her husband out to Spain, and was just as eager to witness and be involved with everything that was going on. Eileen had been popular with the other Brits out in Spain and here, a few years into the war, still cut much the same kindly but absorbing figure. She could dress up and be 'quite dazzling', but was celebrated more for her laid-back temperament when in repose. 'Eileen was one of the nicest and least dressy women that I have ever known,' Henry Dakin remembered. 'A great deal of the time she wore her black overcoat . . . and chain-smoked cigarettes,

letting the ash fall off the end of her cigarette and down her coat.'
Eileen joked around this time that if she and George didn't smoke
so much they'd be able to afford a better flat, but what did that matter when they could name T. S. Eliot among their recent guests?
The war, however, had not been kind to Eileen. No doubt over-
worked at the Ministry of Food, she was also still mourning her
treasured older brother. That spring of 1940, with BEF casualties
rising to around 68,000, Eileen had been convinced that her brother's silence meant the worst. 'I'm sure Eric is dead,' she had said to
a friend, pacing up and down the room and smoking with an even
greater appetite than usual, 'I just don't know what we shall do
with Mother.'

The newspapers reported a heroic death, treating wounded soldiers on the beach, though no body had been recovered. In actual
fact – Sylvia Topp clarifies that Eileen would never have heard this
side of the story – Eric had been killed when a café he was sitting in took a direct hit from a bomb. He had, strangely, refused to
take cover in the cellar below, and so 'caused his own death by his
stubbornness'. Topp suggests that Eric might have felt repulsed by
the claustrophobic prospect of being trapped beneath a collapsed
building, but of course this cannot be known. All kinds of strange
decisions were made in the heat of battle.

Friends recorded that Eileen had become almost mute with grief.
She was, Sylvia Topp has written, 'profoundly depressed for well
over a year', and inconsolable. 'You know how it is,' Orwell confided
to a friend's wife at the time, 'the seeming uselessness of trying to
offer any consolation when somebody is dead.' But the war did not
stop for grief. In May of 1941, the Blitz had seemed to be coming
closer for the Orwells. One bomb had fallen near enough to their
Marylebone flat to set fire to the communal garage; a second had
shattered the windows where they were having an evening meal at
the home of friends. During that latter incident, as the blast lifted
them all out of their seats, Eileen had begun to scream 'No, no – not

again!' as if, mentally, she had been transported back to some earlier, more fragile stage of her grief. Remarkably, she kept up her 'daily work of inconceivable dullness' at the Ministry of Information right through until July 1941. It was only when she quit the job, on Orwell's recommendation, that she began to feel slightly better. A friend who met the Orwells in the pub after Eileen had quit her job was 'glad to see her recovered from the blow of her brother's death, outwardly anyway'.

THE LIARS' SCHOOL

Labour politician Sir Stafford Cripps had the accolade, not uncommon during the years of disharmonious National Government, of being disliked by both sides of the house. In 1942, this put him up in the public's estimation. He had been ambassador to Russia from 1940 and despite eventually - serendipitously - achieving his aim of bringing about an alliance with the Soviet Union, he had been as unpalatable to Stalin as he was for most of his domestic adversaries. Cripps's well-publicised Marxist sympathies had not extended to the Soviet administration, which he found appropriately sinister. Nonetheless, he stepped off the plane onto British soil on 23 January as something of a national hero, certainly given more credit for the new alliance than he deserved, but also, as Roy Jenkins writes, 'thought to have imbibed the secret of how to wage total war'. He was seen as clever and rather enigmatic, and being away in Russia for two years had allowed him to distance himself from a government whose popularity in that period had taken a downward turn.

There were various competing influences in Britain at this time, but the public paid little notice to this, instead shunning factional politics in favour of a few fairly simple tenets which seemed almost universal at the time. One of these was that the war should be fought more aggressively. Cripps managed to capture this mood with a radio broadcast given for a substantial Sunday evening prime-time audience at the beginning of February, in which he had highlighted a disappointing new complacency in the war leadership. 'There seems to be a lack of urgency in the atmosphere of the country,' he argued; 'It is almost as if we were spectators rather than partici-pants.' It was at this point that Orwell reopened his wartime diary, after a six-month hiatus during which he had become 'definitely an employee of the BBC', broadcasting to India with the Eastern Service. It was Cripps that he wanted to talk about.

Like Churchill, Cripps was from an aristocratic family. He was the archetypal 'gifted man', Orwell wrote, who gets into a commanding position because of his background, and even then 'only gets there in moments of disaster when others don't want to take responsi-bility'. As with Churchill, Cripps's personality had been impressive enough to keep him in politics, but also sufficiently abrasive to keep him – as they called it in the war – 'being arsed about' between jobs. Even Orwell, so clear on most things, found him inscrutable; 'I can't yet give you a worthwhile opinion as to whether Cripps is the man the big public think him, or are half-inclined to think him,' he wrote in May 1942. That was not so important right now. Really, Orwell felt, Cripps was a symbol. Orwell's wish that the war would precipitate unprecedented social change in Britain was, if not artic-ulated, then undoubtedly felt by a large portion of the population. 'The basic fact,' he wrote, 'is that people are now fed up and as ready for a radical policy as they were at the time of Dunkirk.' The difference now was that 'they . . . have, or are inclined to think they have, a potential leader in Stafford Cripps'. At the same time, Churchill's popularity after the fall of Singapore had 'slumped heavily' and his position was shaky. Orwell goes on: 'I don't mean that people in significant numbers are crying out for the introduc-tion of Socialism, merely that the mass of the nation wants certain things that aren't obtainable under a capitalist economy.' The war had uncovered for many people the class nature of their society. It had not been, as it was thought it might be during the Blitz, 'the great leveller'; one only had to put one's nose inside an expensive hotel to see that wealth disparity was still as egregious as ever. As in Barcelona, once the dust had settled on the first upheaval, the rich were now finding ways to carry on with their pre-war dissipation, which chiefly meant evading food rationing. There was even a new wealth division caused by the disparity in wages between the underpaid armed forces and better-compensated munitions workers. The speeches of Churchill, rousing and all-encompassing though they were, could not mask the obvious truth that 'the old gang stays in power and nothing really alters'.

As Orwell reopened his diary, the war was entering a new phase. Now that the previous goal of getting America into the war had been fulfilled by Japan's attack on Pearl Harbor, the attention of the British government had turned to the quickly developing situation in India, where Mahatma Gandhi had been urging Indians not to support the war effort of their oppressors, and other groups in the Indian National Congress were agitating for the country to rescind its commitment in favour of the Germans and Japanese. India's value to the British Empire had many facets, but at this point seemed most pertinent in the context of recent British defeats in Malaya and Burma. The two million Indian troops fighting with Britain would therefore need to be reassured before they continued to fight at the best of their ability, but they were also seen as fair game for German propaganda. The same was true for its leadership; certain high-profile figures, namely Subhas Chandra Bose, had already defected to Berlin. Suddenly, in the midst of war, the British Empire seemed about to lose the jewel in its crown. It had been a long-drawn-out saga, dividing the British leadership along lines of stubbornness and imperial prejudice and essentially resigning the truculent Churchill to the backbenches for the duration of the 1930s. But still the British government was refusing to loosen its grip on India. Cripps had arrived home at just the moment when pressure was mounting on Churchill to revise his war cabinet. Cripps, who had long held strong views on how a settlement with India might be reached, was invited to become a senior minister, and at once began to assert himself regarding the India dilemma. To Orwell, this was a mistake on Cripps's part. Considering the 'blaze of undeserved glory' that had accompanied him on his return from Russia, it might have been possible for him to appeal directly to the public and 'then and there have forced a more radical policy on the government, particularly in the direction of a generous settlement with India'. The debate around Cripps was only going to become more central to Orwell's life in the weeks to come.

William Empson had met Orwell on the first day of a six-week training course for the BBC, at a location – Bedford College, University of London – which was known colloquially as 'the Liars' School'. The sobriquet is misleading, suggesting, as it does, aggressive tactics and long-sighted aims within the organisation. In fact, the BBC at that time did not really know what it needed to be, and was instead taking orders from the Ministry of Information, an arrangement which quickly descended into farce 'due to the fact that many different persons of differing ranks at the Ministry were giving instructions to BBC staff'. Part of the difficulty was that Churchill himself had never had much time for the BBC; it was well-meaning, certainly, but the idea that it represented British public opinion by default was entirely arbitrary. Churchill had taken his grievances to his newly appointed Minister of Information, Duff Cooper, with the suggestion that the latter should find a way of 'establishing more effective control over the BBC'. Like the Ministry of Information, a major effort was going on at the BBC to professionalise and get a grip on the workings of propaganda. The Liars' School, as Empson remembered it, was really more like a crash course in the various impressive but wicked modes of Nazi deceit.

One example that stuck in Empson's memory was of a doctored recording of one of Churchill's speeches where all of the negatives had been taken out so that it ended with 'we will . . . surrender'.

At this point, the *Road to Wigan Pier* author would certainly have been Eric Blair to his superiors, but to Empson he introduced himself as George Orwell. This was typical. As W. J. West has written, '[Orwell's] own rule at first seems to have been to use his real name when writing formally . . . and "George Orwell" when writing informally or to close friends.' But at the BBC - Orwell's first regular job since serving with the Imperial Police in Burma - the distinction not only had administrative consequences but was central to his conception of his new, more public identity. The gradual morphing of his identity under the bright lights of public view, though often thought of as lost years, in fact represents a clear turning point in his fictional output, preceding his first attempt, in *Animal Farm*, 'to fuse political purpose and artistic purpose into one whole'. As Eric Blair, he could shelter in a greater anonymity, whereas George Orwell would be held to a higher standard of honesty and outspokenness.

A year later, the question of the author's name would be raised inside the offices of these superiors as a Mr Brander spotted an opportunity to '"cash in" on the popularity of "George Orwell" in India' (or rather, the notoriety; Orwell's *Burmese Days* (1935) had been banned in the country). The issue was whether the man behind the weekly news commentary for India would come forward and speak under his own name. Orwell himself was hesitant. Did he really want his image as a political thinker to be associated with the BBC's various propaganda obligations? 'I am not thinking about my personal reputation, but clearly we should defeat our own object in these broadcasts if I could not preserve my position as an independent and more or less "against the government" commentator,' he explained to Rushbrook Williams, director of the Eastern Service. Reading this letter, one can sense Orwell's panic at both wanting to fulfil the duties he had been delegated in the war effort and avoid making the world worse off by becoming a mouthpiece for the British state's posturing. It would be better, he optimistically suggested, if he could take an anti-fascist line, rather than a pro-imperialist one.

Later in life, Empson, like many others, found himself wondering why Orwell was there. Empson would have read Orwell's most recent published work, the pamphlet *The Lion and the Unicorn*, and found expressed in no uncertain terms the author's belief that British imperialism in India was an exercise in fascism which must now be stopped if the British administration was to be believed to be anti-fascist. 'For at least eighty years England has artificially prevented the development of India, partly from fear of trade competition if Indian industries were too highly developed, partly because backward peoples are more easily governed than civilized ones,' he had written. Britain must now 'tell the Indians that they are free to secede, if they want to.' A bigger question was how or why Orwell had been hired, but he appears, in his interview, to have made a clear statement 'accept[ing] absolutely the need for propaganda to be directed by the Government, and stressed his view that in war-time discipline in the execution of government policy is essential'. This view would later be brought into question as Orwell became less and less impressed with the government's decision-making; suddenly, in March 1942, he had begun to feel that perhaps the BBC was not for him. '[I] shall remain in it if the political changes I foresee come off,' he had written in his diary, likely referring to India, 'otherwise probably not.'

Orwell, Empson unquestioningly assumed, had carefully weighed up reasons for being where he was. But what were they? The novelist had recently given a sympathetic view of the BBC for his reading audience in America, saying that 'in spite of the stupidity of its foreign propaganda and the unbearable voices of its announcers' it just about remained truthful on most subjects. But this was hardly fulsome support. Empson considered the position of his wife, Hetta, who had also been at the Liars' School, but had felt justified in working directly for the government - as opposed to driving lorries or ambulances through the Blitz - once Hitler had invaded Russia. 'Orwell,' Empson reflects, 'was the only student who jeered at those who expressed pleasure at having recently acquired the powerful ally.' But perhaps the answer was a simple one. Orwell wanted Britain and its allies to win the war, and that would not happen if Hitler broke through Russia to the Persian Gulf and India joined up with Japan. Whatever war meant to Orwell, it certainly meant picking a side and doing *something*. And it should feel like war, not, as a friend had joked to him in Spain, like 'a comic opera with an occasional death'. Orwell's great bugbear of this time was in fact pacifism, which made a philosophy of doing nothing even while one's opponent was doing something. More than anything else, doing nothing frustrated Orwell's romantic conception of political life. He had felt at a loose end for the duration of the war so far, admitting to John Lehmann that 'What is so terrible about this kind of situation is to be able to do nothing. The government won't use me in any capacity, not even a clerk, and I have failed to get into the Army because of my lungs. It is a terrible thing to feel oneself useless and at the same time on every side to see half-wits and pro-fascists filling important jobs.' Even doing something badly was preferable, for that in its own way appealed to another of his beliefs: pessimism.

Prior to the Liars' School, Orwell's relationship with the BBC had been as a freelancer, doing occasional talks on literary, rather than political, matters. These essays for radio, like 'Proletarian Literature' and 'What's Wrong with the Modern Short Story?', introduced Orwell to a much wider audience, and in exactly the form - as proved by *Horizon* - where his clear, persuasive voice resonated most. Here, he was constantly being told to be less political, and to focus on the literary matters at hand. In 1942, as a full-time employee, he was given the chance to expand and develop these literary features. The freedom of movement Orwell enjoyed in that work, compared with the tight leash of political or current affairs broadcasting, is remarkable. He was permitted to scour London for diverse and interesting contributors, first recruiting the Indian novelist Mulk Raj Anand who had, in fact, been the first person to be approached for the role which Orwell now filled. Anand had been wary of attaching himself to the Eastern Service owing to the 'invidious' position of Indians living in Britain; he felt himself caught between the two countries, disappointed by the dubious new pacifism of the Indian Congress but also angry at how Britain, through negligence, had allowed India to become a 'blind spot'. But Anand knew Orwell from his time fighting in Spain, and clearly felt that by helping out on these literary talks he would not be crossing any lines in the eyes of his countrymen.

Next, Orwell wrote to the Chinese novelist Hsiao Ch'ien, who was commissioned to give a talk on contemporary Chinese litera-ture, and then to Arthur Calder-Marshall. What Orwell eventually came up with was *Voice*, quite literally a magazine - including an editor's note and contents page - for the airwaves. It was a first for British radio and in other ways, too, a novelty for the histori-cally dour BBC who, it is said, 'regarded the phrase "living poet" as a contradiction in terms'. Hunched over a microphone, Orwell opened the first issue by explaining - much as Connolly had in January 1940 - that 'this is the worst possible moment to be starting a magazine'. He goes on:

While we sit here talking in a more or less highbrow manner - talking about art and literature and whatnot - tens of thousands of tanks are racing across the steppes of the Don and battleships upside down are searching for one another in the wastes of the Pacific. I suppose during every second that we sit here at least one human being will be dying a violent death.

Orwell asks his 'readers' to try to imagine the magazine in front of them. 'It's only a small volume,' he explained, 'about twenty pages.' They should open it up to the table of contents, and as they do so acknowledge the fine paper quality, 'pre-war paper – you don't see paper like that in other magazines nowadays – and nice wide margins'.

One cannot look at the pictures of Orwell leaning against the wall of a recording booth with a dog-eared script and marker pen in his hands, his tie askew and a handkerchief stuffed into his jacket pocket, beside him a smiling Empson and a curious Mulk Raj Anand – or piled around a microphone with, among others, the *Poetry London* editor J. M. Tambimuttu, novelist Venu Chitale and T. S. Eliot – without feeling that he was very much in his element in these virtual salons. The air-raid alerts had started up again around this time in 1942 and Orwell admitted to being 'inwardly rather frightened', but the atmosphere in the studio during those sessions, with a dense fog of cigarette smoke and the buzz of chatter, had the timeless quality of a Connolly house party. Indeed, many of Connolly's house guests, including Stephen Spender as well as Connolly himself, had crossed over, the atmosphere of the Bedford Square soirée so much intact that during one broadcast Connolly had excitedly disclaimed his former co-editor's talents, calling him 'an indifferent poet', and later tried to excuse himself by saying the remarks made were 'only for India'. Still safely within the world of literary deliberation, Orwell, giving these talks, would have noticed the invisible presence of the censors only by the stamps which came back on the scripts he had devised. He might have assumed these represented the wagging finger of one of his BBC higher-ups, like his direct superior Desmond Hawkins, but in fact they came from across London, in Senate House, perhaps even from a fellow writer. So why was Orwell not happy? During the weeks when he had been preparing the first issue of *Voice* he had come home from the office and begun a rant in his diary. 'I am doing nothing that is not futility and have less and less to show for the time I waste,' he wrote. He was 'just footling round doing imbecile things . . . things which in fact don't help or in any way affect the war effort, but are considered necessary by the huge bureaucratic machine in which we are all caught up'.

Orwell wanted to get things done, even if that meant becoming more 'propaganda-minded' and sinking further into the mire of 'filth'. He was sick of 'stupid propaganda', meaning that which was petty and superficial, and wished just once to get away with 'a successful piece of scoundrelism'. So Eric Blair arrived at 200 Oxford Street - a former department store - each day not as the expansive, all-encompassing 'Orwell' of his writing, but as a regular employee, with the same restrictions as anyone else. Some days, he was there as early as 6 a.m., commuting in from St John's Wood by the Bakerloo line from Maida Vale or by a longish walk around Regent's Park. On those days, he would be at his desk behind a lath-and-plaster partition by the time the 'huge army' of charwomen began to assemble in the reception hall and overhear the 'wonderful choruses' they sang together as they swept the passages. From that moment on the building would be filled with the tumultuous vibrations of work. 'We worked against a background noise of conversation, dictation, clattering typewriters and, owing to the shortage of studios, even the rehearsal of talks and features in various oriental languages,' Orwell's colleague, John Morris, wrote. Empson, who sat on the other side of a partition to Orwell and had by now become his 'most and perhaps his only intimate friend in the department', could hear the novelist interviewing Indian propagandists whom he was vetting or briefing.

On arrival, Orwell would be handed transcriptions prepared by the BBC Monitoring Service - 'a substantial book in itself', W. J. West has written - of the recent radio broadcasts of a dozen Axis stations, such as the 'Germany Calling' announcements of the bogeyman Anglo-Irish defector 'Lord Haw-Haw' and the

Nazi-controlled 'Workers' Challenge', which purported to be run
by a group of socialist British workers disaffected by the way the
capitalist bosses and the establishment were directing the war.
There were also the speeches of Hitler, Goebbels and other Axis
leaders to work through. Almost certainly with one of his pungent
roll-up cigarettes between his lips, Orwell would begin to pen his
newsletters and commentaries directly responding to, and trying
to undo the damage of, the false or harmful information that had
been disseminated overnight. These rebuttals would then be trans-
lated and read out over the airwaves by natives of the recipient
countries, that way sounding like accounts of the war literally as
seen 'through eastern eyes', rather than the view of some omniscient British narrator. In his other capacity, as a literary critic,
Orwell's words could come from his own mouth, but he was not
a charismatic voice actor. 'His weekly broadcast talks were beautifully written,' John Morris remembered, 'but he delivered them in
a dull and monotonous voice. I was often with him in the studio
and it was painful to hear such good material wasted.'

As a writer at the BBC he was in a crowded field, and there were
names which loomed much larger than 'Orwell' in the corridors of
the organisation. On certain evenings, a squat, rotund man wearing a raincoat and trilby would swing into the building and make
a beeline for the elevator. Upstairs, in the recording studio, a team
of men would be making preparations for his arrival, setting up
headphones to relay the sound from the microphone and putting
out a glass of water. They would take his hat and coat as he entered
and then shuffle off behind the observation window to begin the
soundcheck. The man would take a sip of his water and then lean
in: 'Hello, recording. J. B. Priestley and *Britain Speaks*!'

Priestley's rise to household fame during the war years had been
one of the defining moments of the period. It was said that of all
the figures then in the public eye, Priestley was next in popularity
to Churchill. He had begun his 'Postscripts', as they were called,

just after Dunkirk, and had presided over this prime-time Sunday evening slot 'during those blazing summer weeks when France collapsed and we were threatened with imminent invasion'. Despite his obvious and universal popularity, Orwell was following the newspapers in October 1940 when Priestley was suddenly 'shoved off the air', presumably as a result of Tory party pressure. This was the perfect example of how the corporation was having to bend over backwards in wartime; much in the same vein as Orwell, Priestley had been advocating for the country to become more democratic and egalitarian, but as factional politics came into play – in this case 'the Margesson crew' – he was shut down. Priestley's Sunday-night broadcasts 'were by implication socialist propaganda', Orwell wrote.

As the months went on, Orwell grew more and more assured of the powerlessness of his India broadcasts in affecting the course of events. Every day he was subjected to interminable departmental meetings, where the massive weight of bureaucracy which bore down on them was made startlingly apparent. In the BBC's previous offices, at 55 Portland Place, where Orwell started out, the location of these meetings had been a room 101, suggesting, what becomes abundantly clear the more one reads of Orwell, that his greatest fear was this political impotence. Empson has expressed his belief that, from the interviews that were conducted at the next desk, Orwell too often 'found himself having to allow broadcasts to go out to India, from speakers too important to offend, which he thought likely to do more harm than good'.

Adding to his frustration, the country, then going through one of its most unstable periods of the war so far, seemed to be entirely without direction. Orwell had given a broadcast at the time of the fall of Singapore in February which foreshadowed a difficult year ahead. As well as having been a Crown Colony since 1858, Singapore was the major British military base in the south-west Pacific. Eighty thousand British troops had been captured as prisoners of war. Feeling equally gloomy that evening was Winston Churchill, who confided to Violet Bonham Carter, his closest female friend, his fear that 'our soldiers are not as good fighters as their fathers were. In 1915 our men fought on even when they had only one shell left and were under a fierce barrage. Now they cannot resist dive-bombers. We have so many men in Singapore, so many men - they should have done better.' By the time of the second major British surrender of that year, to Rommel's forces at Tobruk at the end of June, Churchill was facing a motion of no confidence. His army still had only a handful of land victories to show for what was now thirty-two months of war, and the sentiment in the House of Commons - as expressed by Aneurin Bevan - was that 'the Prime Minister wins debate after debate and loses battle after battle'.

It was the middle of March when Stafford Cripps set off for India on what was to become known as the 'Cripps mission'. He carried with him a proposal for a more generous renegotiation of terms with the Indian Congress. The British public saw its global dominance hanging in the balance, and was gripped. Orwell could barely think about anything else. As Empson had written, Orwell 'felt Hitler's war would be worthwhile if it spelt the end of the British Raj', but India's move to independence had to occur in amicable circumstances, with the assurance that no wartime adversary would be benefiting from the divorce. Orwell had been instructed to 'give Cripps a build-up', but also to portray him as something of a political maverick, presumably so that the government's back would be covered in the likely event of his failure. As a consequence, the statement issued by the Eastern Service on 21 March, once it had come back from the Ministry of Information, was cloying and jejune in all the ways that Orwell was not, full of good wishes for the Indians and praise for the British cabinet's enormous political wisdom in choosing Cripps for the job. Not being able to show his true feelings on this subject was taken by Orwell as a personal failure, rather than a reality of wartime. Two weeks later, when the Cripps mission was deemed to have failed, Orwell gave his most damning verdict yet on his contribution to the war. It was around the same time that Connolly was due to make a contribution for *Voice,* and he had asked Orwell if he might be able to quote a passage from *Homage to Catalonia.* It got Orwell thinking about the book, and as he opened up his personal copy his eye fell on a passage which he had forgotten:

> One of the most horrible features of war is that all the war-propaganda, all the screaming and lies and hatred, comes invariably from people who are not fighting . . . It is the same in all wars; the soldiers do the fighting, the journalists do the shouting, and no true patriot ever gets near a frontline trench, except on the briefest of propaganda tours. Sometimes it is a comfort to me to think that the aeroplane is altering the conditions of war. Perhaps when the next great war comes we may see that sight unprecedented in all history, a jingo with a bullet-hole in him.

'Here I am in the BBC, less than 5 years after writing that,' he added, as a footnote, in his diary. 'I suppose sooner or later we all write our epitaphs.'

At the end of April, Orwell paid a visit to the viewing gallery of the Commons, whose members, after the bomb damage to their own House, now sat in the House of Lords. It was the India debate, and there was a moderate but not overwhelming attendance. On his part, Cripps was excellent; Orwell remained impressed by his honesty, and indeed the two would meet on a few future occasions, initially with Orwell waiting in a reception room at the Lords, hoping to catch a glimpse. On the second occasion, a pre-arranged meeting, Orwell took Empson with him, as well as Guy Burgess, who was also on the BBC's books. Otherwise, it was a poor show. At the India debate, looking around, Orwell felt that 'everything had a somewhat mangy look. Red rexine cushions on the benches – I could swear they used to be red plush at one time.' His comments recall Winston Smith's reflections on a much-degraded London in *Nineteen Eighty-Four*:

> He tried to squeeze out some childhood memory that should tell him whether London had always been quite like this. Were there always these vistas of rotting nineteenth-century houses, their sides shored up with baulks of timber, their windows patched with cardboard and their roofs with corrugated iron, their crazy garden walls sagging in all directions? And the bombed sites where the plaster dust swirled in the air and the willowherb straggled over the heaps of rubble . . .

Here, at the present time, Britain still had to face its long descent from pre-eminence. Orwell could have been giving an assessment of his own contributions at the BBC when he wrote, 'This is the twilight of Parliamentary democracy and these creatures are simply ghosts gibbering in some corner while the real events happen elsewhere.'

14

Cocktails, and the Greatest Evil Ever Committed

The pre-war tradition of gathering in the evening was still kept up where cocktails could be cobbled together. Often, now, they migrated out of disproportionately bomb-damaged Bloomsbury, and a short journey was required to get to Mayfair from Senate House. Or it was another night at Connolly's in Bedford Square, where literary dinner parties still manifested of a quality astonishing for wartime.

Going through the doorway at Bedford Square, or other, pokier residences around the city, one would encounter strange and random assortments of friends old and new. The connecting thread was often who had contributed to a certain publication that month, hence the presence of visitors from the country, or soldiers, sailors or airmen fortuitously on leave. Well-represented within these walls are 'the various swollen departments of the bureaucracy', such as Graham Greene, who had just published his first novel in three years, written between shifts searching cargo ships and keeping track of the Vichy forces in French Guinea with MI6. Cecil Day-Lewis is there, and with Greene begins to regale the audience with screwball tales of inefficient officialdom. Day-Lewis has been working as a publications editor at the Ministry of Information; he has just published arguably his greatest collection, *World All Over*. His philosophy of the war is an intriguing one. It is, he believes, 'a delirium of nations – a fever of which I had already felt premonitory symptoms working in my own blood, as in the blood of many millions, to be endured and if possible recovered from . . .'

At Senate House, he feels he has gone through the looking-glass. It was 'a land of wild make-believe at the Ministry of Information', Evelyn Waugh observed, 'where the only problem of the war is to decide precisely what sort of government shall be set up in Germany, immediately, bloodlessly.' If Day-Lewis has read Greene's latest book, *The Ministry of Fear*, he will have found his uncanny vision of wartime London to be corroborated. In the book, the Blitz serves as the watershed between a quaint, flags-and-bunting London and another situation both phantasmagorical and malign, because 'blast often did odd things'. In the opening chapter, a nominal attempt at recreating a pre-war fête in a Bloomsbury square seems especially incongruous against 'the untidy gaps between the . . . houses – a flat fireplace half-way up a wall, like the painted fireplace in a cheap dolls' house, and lots of mirrors and green wallpapers'. Round the corner, in Holborn, the 'shops were reduced to a stone ground-plan like those of Pompeii'. The protagonist, Arthur Rowe, keen to try each of the handful of attractions, pays to have his fortune told, but instead of getting that information is told a weight to submit for the cake-guessing game on another stall. He does what he is told, and wins the cake, but his good fortune sets in motion an inexplicable and maddening chain of events. It is a world, and a time, in which much is inexplicable. Who, awaking with no memory of the past decade, the narrator asks, could have believed that 'a man who had been considered too brilliant and too reckless ever to be trusted with major office was the leader of his country'? Greene put in a letter to his sister that the book had 'sold 15,000 before reprinting' – 'momentarily satisfactory', he added, suspicious of wartime book sales. Showing in Oxford at that time was the first stage production of *Brighton Rock*, starring Richard Attenborough and Hermione Baddeley; it seemed that, in these 'mediaeval cit[ies] of darkness and brigandage', as Stephen Spender had put it, the lure of Greeneland was its relevance. Greene himself could see this, suggesting, of the different genres he worked in, 'the thrillers are like life'. John Lehmann thought it the best of Greene's novels, finding great truth in the descriptions of 'a ceaseless murderous struggle for power . . . a struggle which uses the individual with utter ruthlessness'.

A certain class of detective and spy stories was becoming more important as literature because of their applicability to modern life. Day-Lewis's theory of delirium explains another noteworthy novel of the war so far – as noirish and nihilistic as Greene's – Patrick Hamilton's *Hangover Square*. In that book, the extent of the post-Munich delirium is such that actual war is seen as the last hope in purging the world of its sickness. 'What if a war was what he was waiting for?' the narrator, George Harvey Bone, wonders of himself. 'They might get him – he might be conscripted away from drinks, and smokes, and Netta.' Hamilton was living in Henley-on-Thames during the war. Unlike much of literary London – a milieu with whom he had little interaction – Hamilton's Marxism had survived the Molotov-Ribbentrop Pact intact; he saw the fighting on the Eastern Front as 'the bloody birth and climax of history'.

Standing at the window is Laurie Lee, who will soon join Day-Lewis in the publications department but for now is making documentary films with the Crown Film Unit. He has recently returned from the Scottish Highlands where they have been filming *Before the Raid*, based on Lee's script; the village of Portmahomack is chosen to resemble a Norwegian fishing village, where the action is supposed to have taken place. Lee is pressed by John Lehmann to write more poems for *New Writing* (he is considered one of the great poetic revelations of the war so far) but grins evasively.

William Plomer is somewhere milling within the two dozen guests. He spends his days in 'the bomb-proof depths' of the Admiralty, where a colleague is Ian Fleming. There is Sonia Brownell, now working at *Horizon* in her evenings and on weekends while spending her days at the Ministry of War Transport, 'full of dark intimations about the future of our supplies of spam and pilchards from overseas, as she shakes her head of pageboy gold', and elsewhere George Orwell, the man she will marry after the death of Eileen in 1945 from cardiac arrest during a hysterectomy. It was at an occasion just like this – a dinner party given by Connolly – that they had first met. Sonia had just finished reading *Burmese Days* when the opportunity arose for her to meet its author. Her initial impression, however, was not good. 'His first few sentences were quite off-putting,' she would confess, many years later. 'He said that one should never write anything the working classes don't understand. He then said one shouldn't use adjectives and Cecil Day-Lewis said, "What about Shakespeare?"' On this later occasion, he is similarly inscrutable, the keen eyes suggesting more a kind of fanatical melancholy than humour, and the deeply etched lines round his mouth only rarely stretching to a smile. He wishes to talk with John Lehmann about a feature he is working on in his new capacity as producer for the BBC Eastern Service; would Lehmann be interested in doing a broadcast on twentieth-century English poetry? Later, he is overheard holding forth on Stalin as a war leader and Soviet diplomacy. Louis MacNeice, also from the BBC, is in the corner discussing poetry with Henry Reed.

Spending his days among the men of the AFS, Henry Green has developed an appetite for social life. In particular, he has a fascination with wartime pub life. 'It was not only that he liked to drink, which he often did to excess,' his son later reflected, 'but he loved to eavesdrop on and to chat and mingle with the pub regulars. Later, in the fifties, he could spend up to four hours a day in two different pubs.' For now he is still literary London's most valuable asset, and has just contributed a story, 'The Lull', to *Penguin New Writing*. His story seems to fill in the gaps left by Greene's Buchanesque caper; between the capricious nights are long daytime stretches of boredom and restlessness, and getting on one another's nerves. At the party, there is a sizeable contingent from the literary machine of the fire service. Stephen Spender is there, 'looking taller than ever and quite impossible in his uniform, full of eager information about the organization of discussion groups in the AFS, which he claims as a great discovery in democratic education'. Spender, who joined up after the first Blitz, could categorise most of his time with the fire service as 'the lull', but he had quickly found another use for his time, becoming a discussion group leader in an education scheme for the London firemen. 'We simply went from station to station, opening discussions on Russia, China, the law, history, art, and many other subjects,' he remembered.

There are writers there whom one would not immediately associate with this modern Bloomsbury set, but whose talent is such that they will be esteemed under any vanguard. Though based at the rich and magnificent Clarence Terrace in Marylebone, Elizabeth Bowen had been in Bloomsbury a few times during the war to meet Virginia Woolf, who described their wonderful and effortless intimacy: 'On top of bus, we talked again - a good idea; talking in many changing scenes: it changes topics and moods, battling among the Billingsgate porters with their shelly fishy hats; then stopping: crossing: running up bus steps.' Bowen had gone to visit Virginia Woolf at Rodmell shortly before her suicide, when they had discussed Bowen's recent dramatic mission to Ireland for the Ministry of Information, and the various issues Virginia was running into in the writing of *Between the Acts* ('For six weeks I have been trying to get the characters from the dining-room into the drawing-room and they are still in the dining-room,' Virginia said). Otherwise, Bowen, an air-raid warden, tends to keep her distance from literary social life: 'I am firmly and increasingly convinced that artists were intended to be an ornament to society,' she wrote; 'As a society in themselves they are unthinkable.' As a society they were also dwindling.

AN EDITOR'S RESPONSIBILITIES

The host, Connolly, was struggling at this time. Parties like this one were how he liked to spend his time, and since his move to Bloomsbury they had been taking up a lot of it. Connolly dinners were famed around London. Evelyn Waugh, for instance, records being served 'truffles and lobsters', a fantastical menu for wartime. Such ostentation did not sit well in unobtrusive, bohemian Bloomsbury. Connolly, as one observer noted, was '*grands crus* and truffles', while the rest of the neighbourhood subsisted on '*vin ordinaire* and sandwiches'. To E. M. Forster, Connolly 'discredited pleasure'. But though his guests would have appreciated the changed circumstances that allowed them to become reacquainted with these pre-war pleasures, there was also a new line of jokes which satirised Connolly's grandiose sense of importance. All of the powerful declarations made in *Horizon* at the beginning of the war seemed really to have devolved into something rather superficial. The war had got rather boring, Evelyn Waugh wrote to Nancy Mitford, but it would pick up when some of the soldiers had been killed off and 'you and me and Connolly are left to defend culture without interference'. The great Connolly wartime project was running into the ground, and it was taking with it any sense that he was ever going to deliver on his promise.

Although much of the practical work was now being done by Lys Lubbock, Sonia Brownell and Peter Watson, *Horizon* had always, unmistakably, been a Cyril Connolly enterprise. Justifying his decision to leave *Horizon* to work with Lehmann at *Penguin New Writing*, Spender had described how it was the Connolly personality alone that gave *Horizon* its idiosyncratic character. It also gave it its complacency, and the two editors had frequently clashed because Spender was perceived as working too hard 'and trying to steal an advantage over him'. Connolly saw his own personality so much in the magazine that he had grown to dislike it. All editors, he explained, nurtured a desire to sabotage what they had created. At fifty issues, he told subscribers, *Horizon* would disappear forever. It might 'commit suicide' by publishing one number 'in which everybody said what they really thought, and then be suppressed'. 'Suppression,' he wrote, 'is the deep unconscious goal of every magazine . . . and a magazine, to be good, should never quite be respectable.' One day the police would kick down the door at Bedford Square and pull all copies of *Horizon* down from the shelves of bookstalls around London. Its editors would be 'charged with Individualism'. Perhaps as a way of inviting the demise of *Horizon*, Connolly had actually taken a second job, as literary editor for the *Observer*. He managed about eleven months until differences with the paper's owner, David Astor, were deemed to be irreconcilable. '[Connolly] expects to be directed down the mines soon,' Evelyn Waugh told his wife.

An editor begins with a vision, and within a short time that vision is shown to be realistic or not. Connolly had initially thought that there might be a way to shift the emphasis of wartime towards creative production. He had been right to assume that a population unable to travel abroad and boarding themselves up in their homes every evening would be constantly hungry for new reading material. But a war is first and foremost a practical rather than spiritual encumbrance. Boredom breeds languor, rather than its opposite, and an obstacle like paper rationing is an insurmountable obstacle. *Horizon* came out on more or less the same date every month and each time was an identical seventy-two pages. In a pinch, Connolly would forgo his 'Comment' for the month to fit another poem or article, and on a few occasions the magazine's printers - now the Curwen Press - were forced to set letters or the final paragraphs of stories on the cardboard inside back cover. How much of an editor's job in wartime was trying to fit a decent range of contributions into a constricting amount of space? 'There was rather a problem over the make-up of the February issue,' Lys wrote to an absent Connolly at one point, 'we couldn't get the Sitwell story (36½ pages) and Douglas Cooper's (17½) in at the same time. Miss Temkin tried every combination, but it just couldn't be done.' This was a monthly occurrence. Though, superficially, all was well, there was something impossibly deflating in the realisation that 'however good a magazine one edits were to be, not a single extra copy could be sold, and that, however bad, not a single extra copy would be wasted.' The wartime public was so desperate for anything resembling new reading material that Connolly could have printed bad Georgian poetry upside down and still dispose of every copy, 'and yet were we to offer the first presentation of "In Memoriam" . . . we would be lucky to get one review.'

Heaped cruelly on top of this was the constant brain drain of young talent to the armed forces or Civil Service, talent which could have brought those seventy-two pages to life. 'It is only among young writers that movements exist,' Connolly lamented, 'and only movements can hold together a magazine and prevent it from becoming a shapeless miscellany.'

With Jean in America and largely out of contact, and Diana working as a secretary at *Horizon* but released from his personal life, Connolly was now living as an unofficial married couple with Lys. Diana, though originally meant for painting, had turned out to be a proficient poet and short-story writer. This development was, she always claimed, thanks to Connolly, but it had also allowed her to extricate herself from him. 'Of course I am only mature now because you have matured me,' she had written, from Oxford, in a parting letter. But she could not stand being compared to other women for any longer. Jean, as she constantly heard, was more sexually forthcoming, and made Connolly feel a man; Lys was 'very domestic' and loved cooking for him. Diana could offer him neither of those things – she had cooked for him plenty before but had not enjoyed it, and at night she liked to wear 'anti-aphrodisiac bedsocks'. 'You must count me out really this time,' she ended the letter by saying, 'I will not be faithful, I want love too.' Diana had advised in that letter that Connolly should try and 'set up properly' with Lys, and that is what he did. They started at a studio maisonette in Drayton Gardens, South Kensington, in the spring of 1941.

It was at Drayton Gardens that Stephen Spender had chosen to hold the reception for his second marriage, to Natasha Litvin, the reason for which probably had a lot to do with Lys's powers as a hostess. Natasha was a young pianist who, with Lys and Diana, had been one of what Connolly called 'the Oxford Girls', enjoying a microcosmic reconstruction of London society away from the bombs (and where Natasha deemed it safe to store her Bechstein piano). They congregated around the Randolph Hotel, and, as Lys wrote, 'everybody drinks much too much beer'. Lys was actually in Oxford to support her then husband Ian Lubbock, an actor who was doing a stint in *Uncle Vanya* at the Oxford Playhouse. Natasha was giving small concerts at the time ('very good', Diana noted) and it was likely at one of these that she met the Lubbocks, who later invited her back to London with them. She met Spender at a party at 6 Lansdowne Terrace – where they were introduced by Tony Hyndman, the ex-boyfriend, of all people – and they were married shortly after. The union was approved by most, though there was a feeling, among Spender's older, homosexual friends, Lehmann included, that Natasha was 'rather too innocent for the situation' and Spender, denying his sexuality once again, was 'mad'.

This was the period, for Connolly, of denial – the denial which his detractors had always felt was at the bottom of his puffed-up sentiments about the war. With Lys – and pooled ration-book allowances – he had finally achieved 'something permanent in the flux', but it was a private equanimity, which came at the price of his altruism. Connolly was now conspicuously well-off, living – as was common knowledge – on his ex-wife's payroll as well as Peter Watson's. He was coasting in his job, and the editorship of *Horizon* remained a reserved occupation. None of this was at all represent-ative for this period of the war. The average writer's journal from 1942 or 43 is a much bloodier affair and testifies to a 'make or break' nature of the moment. Erik de Mauny, for instance, was in Egypt as Rommel's forces drove through to Alexandria; there, German bombardment was a present reality. De Mauny was beginning to experience strange nervous symptoms around his time, including 'a sudden fainting sensation, a hideous feeling of being terribly ill'. 'You can't evade war,' he wrote, 'it seeps into everything.' Scottish poet G. S. Fraser characterised Egypt in 1942 as like 'something sick and dying; an old beggar, propped against a wall, too palsied to raise a hand or to supplicate alms'. The poet Alan Ross was on a ship navigating ice and German U-boats in the Arctic. He described how 'snow lay crusted on the decks, on the life-lines run fore and aft, on the rails, the guns wore coats of it, were trained every half-hour, so that they did not freeze'. In the course of the diary entry Ross's convoy is attacked by enemy destroyers. By evening, he is lying face to face with a dying comrade, blood from the man's wound trickling through his outstretched fingers, growing sticky and congealed.

Peter Quennell was living as a lodger at the house at Drayton Gardens, and then followed the 'Connollys' to 49 Bedford Square. There, he occupied a couple of rooms in the attic. Quennell's was a transitory existence. He had been bombed out of the Chelsea flat he kept for the first stretch of the war, and since then his most consistent base had been in his 'immense but overcrowded room' at Senate House, where during the Blitz he had often had to sleep. When Quennell entered the Ministry, he saw himself being fast-tracked as a 'master-propagandist, whose diatribes, scattered across Europe, made Dr. Goebbels wince with fury'. No such promotion had ever fallen his way. In fact, all of the secret stuff was organised out of a secluded Bedfordshire country house, where Quennell was never invited. To alleviate the mundanity of this bog-standard war job, he had devised a way of keeping reference books among the papers on his desk and thus continuing his biography of Byron during interminable working hours. With his colleagues, he would then have dinner at a little Italian place down the street ('enormous portions of pasta and flasks of rather rough chianti'), and drinks at the Ministry's own bar, 'a crowded, hot and noisy place'.

At night, he would frequent the various clubs in Soho. Institutions like the 400, Jamboree, the Nut House and the Gargoyle Club had sprung up and were doing excellent business all over the city. All wings of the armed services were represented behind their blacked-out doors, as well as all of the Allied Powers. 'They were invariably crowded and hot,' Quennell wrote, 'and the atmosphere was dim and dense – so dense that, towards the end of the night, one felt that it was becoming semi-solid; and the entertainments they offered were strikingly monotonous.' Most famous amongst these pleasure spots was the Gargoyle, the clientele of which was 'part suburban, part outrageously bohemian'. It was here that Quennell had seen Dylan Thomas 'not enjoying London'. The Gargoyle was a level above its neighbours; founded before the war by David Tennant, 'a rich and restless dilettante', it had a fountain on the dance floor and two bold and brilliant Matisses at the entrance and above the bar which, according to Anthony Powell, 'lent an air of go-ahead culture to the club'. In the morning, after these nights, it was a trip to a specific chemist's in Piccadilly for their 'powerful morning pick-me-ups, some reputed to possess not only nerve-steadying but strongly aphrodisiac properties', a portion of which were probably opium-based.

Quennell seldom saw Connolly while they were living together, so much were they operating on different schedules. Connolly woke late, took long baths and would often not arrive at the *Horizon* office until midday. His rooms at 49 Bedford Square 'had a pleasantly occupied look and, thanks to his acolytes' patient help, numerous domestic comforts', while the bedroom Quennell scrambled out of each morning to get to Senate House 'afforded a drab spectacle of bohemian laissez-faire', with furniture piled up and pictures still in boxes from the evacuation of his Chelsea flat. Putting together the few fleeting glimpses he got, Quennell's picture of Connolly at this time was of a man growing reluctantly towards middle age but probably experiencing the happiest period of his life so far. In his letters, Connolly referred to number 49 as his 'mansion', clearly feeling he had landed on somewhere he could hunker down in his trademark slovenly fashion. Continuing the tradition of bestial adornment he had begun with Jean, Connolly now kept a white cockatoo stationed behind his chair in the living room – 'a ferocious bird', Quennell writes – trained to 'descend like a snow-white thunderbolt . . . on any newcomer who crossed the threshold'. Most fascinating of all was the way his new lifestyle could sequester itself from outside events. 'About his own existence he drew a magic circle,' Quennell reflected, a circle which was guarded by Connolly's 'native power of charming'. When it came to Connolly's turn in the fortnightly fire-watching rota for men living and working in the area, Quennell would see him head cheerily out 'carrying a case of cigars, a hot-water bottle and a heavy tartan rug'. No other person Quennell knew possessed the same ability to imagine the war away.

Perhaps all of these behaviours – Quennell's nocturnal gallivanting included – were really distraction techniques. According to Stephen Spender, 'the values of pleasure, personal relations, the flesh' at this time were really 'a refusal to be privately miserable about public tragedy'. Every single person bore within them a sense of 'the desolation of the world'. So the tone of Connolly's 'Comments' had become increasingly flippant, as if he no longer saw the use in sincerity.

Literature was adapting to the historical moment, as it always did, but it seemed to be moving somewhere out of Connolly's reach. Though now with much less gusto, he was still pursuing his idiosyncratic schemes to get writers recognised as potentially valuable contributors to the war effort. He persevered in his one-man campaign for the instatement of 'war writers' to carry out parallel duties to the celebrated war artists, attempting another appeal in February 1943 despite it being '*Horizon*'s most lost of lost causes', received with 'total indifference'. A more recent innovation suggested a path to greater Anglo-American unity by way of guided tours of England for US writers. 'There should be many houses open to them,' Connolly wrote, 'and a variety of tours, for example a visit to the Georgian architecture of Bath, Clifton, and Cheltenham, as well as to Plymouth and Bristol, to the haunts of Tennyson, James, or Coleridge, as well as to Dover.' But Connolly knew it was useless. Literature was in fact becoming more democratic but less important; it was a nice recreational activity but had no pulling power. For instance, he had quietly been following a strange side effect of the paper shortage, which was that more and more people were turning to poetry to express their innermost feelings, taking advantage of the brevity of the form. He was now receiving poems 'not only by professional poets, or even amateur ones, but in many cases by people who have never written a poem before'. They came scrawled on regimental notepaper 'or on the shoddy white foolscap of our suave bureaucracy'. 'We have had poems sent from schools and prisons, and even from large country houses,' Connolly explained.

That was how things stood. All of the professional writers had slipped quietly off to America or the Civil Service and no one would ever write a novel again. This was understandable. As Connolly reassured his *Horizon* readers, 'we must remember that the life many of us are now leading is inimical to the appreciation of literature; we are living history, which means we are living from hand to mouth and reading innumerable editions of the evening paper.' Little more could be said. Connolly even went as far as declaring a 'moratorium on art' until the war was over.

A wartime editor, however, had always to live at least theoretically in the war. Every now and again, the twisted realities of the historical moment were dragged garishly into view. There was an episode in 1943, for example, which demanded Connolly's complete editorial attention. Living also with the Connollys at Drayton Gardens was the Hungarian novelist Arthur Koestler, who, in the words of Jeremy Lewis, was 'a veteran of Nazi Germany, Soviet Russia and the Spanish Civil War'. He was also a veteran political prisoner, arrested by Franco's troops in Malaga in 1937 and then, in 1940, making his way to England via a brief incarceration in the South of France as well as a spell in a Vichy internment camp. Even the British authorities, upon Koestler's arrival, had seen fit to lock him up in Pentonville prison, before releasing him to dig trenches. As a consequence, he had a first-hand perspective on a cross-section of European political extremes shared by possibly only a handful of other people. He had been making himself a nuisance right across the continent and made no exception for Connolly, who 'endure[d] him out of loyalty to literature'. 'Like everyone who talks of ethics all day long one could not trust him half an hour with one's wife, one's best friend, one's manuscripts or one's wine merchant,' Connolly ranted, 'he'd lose them all'. But there was - this fact he admitted begrudgingly - little question of his importance to literature. One cannot read about the protagonist of Koestler's *Darkness at Noon*, Rubashov, without thinking of Orwell's Winston Smith. Rubashov, imprisoned in the 1938

Moscow Show Trials, finds himself one day asking what would be better, 'two decades of dreams on a paillasse in a dark cell or two weeks' reality in the light of day'. For Orwell, who met Koestler through Connolly, *Darkness at Noon* was the first book to address the reality of life in the Soviet Union. In his review of the book, he stated that 'What was frightening about these trials was not the fact that they happened . . . but the eagerness of Western intellectuals to justify them.'

Koestler could give a similar insight into the realities of life under Nazi domination. The information he had – obtained from a contact in Poland named Karsky – represented a truth that many would find difficult to accept. He tried it out on the *Horizon* set, with whom he was starting to feel at home, despite being for them 'a strange bird on the periphery', and though initially hesitant they had come wholeheartedly to believe him. The issue was that the Ministry of Information had been refusing to use in their campaigns stories of the worst German atrocities, a fact attributable either to anti-Semitism among government officials or a concern with the way the public might be influenced by Nazi 'racialism', with the consequence that (as Koestler wrote) 'for an educated Englishman it is almost easier to imagine conditions of life under King Canute in this island than conditions of life in, say, contemporary Poland'. But Connolly was all ears. For the October 1943 issue of *Horizon* he went ahead and published an extract from Koestler's upcoming novel *Arrivals and Departures* which turned out to be seriously controversial. The segment was titled 'The Mixed Transport', and Connolly felt the need to give it an introduction, as if preparing his audience. If Hitler is unique in any way, he wrote in his 'Comment', 'it is that he has contributed more pain to humanity than any other figure in the world's history'. The twentieth century, moreover, would one day be known as the 'century of fear'.

'There are trains which are scheduled on no timetable,' Koestler's story began, 'but they run all over Europe':

> Ten to twenty closed cattle-trucks, locked from outside, pulled by an old-fashioned locomotive. Few people see them because they start and arrive at night. I have travelled in one.
>
> I have never spoken of it before. They call them Mixed Transports because they contain various categories of freight. Ours started with seventeen carriages.

As the train sets off, Koestler's narrator, a political prisoner, hears a sound rise up from the seven carriages at the rear 'like the Muezzin's call from a minaret'. It is a prayer and, as he later learns, these are the carriages filled with Jews – 'that is to say, two loads of Useful Jews who were being taken to dig fortifications, and five loads of Useless Jews, old and sickly ones, who were taken to be killed.' The rest of the story gives an account of the Nazis' use of mobile gas chambers in the killing of 152,000 Jews at Chelmno in Poland in late 1941. Some of its details, like the prisoners watching from stationary carriages as the part of the train with the engine is detached, and later elderly 'useless Jews' having to climb up ladders to get into the parked vans with doors 'like a safe's', are almost unbearable.

The story confronted the atmosphere of denial which had been allowed to settle like an opaque fog over England. *Horizon* immediately began to receive letters from its subscribers which were both incredulous and fearful. They demanded to know whether the account was true, or if it was meant to be speculative. The poet Osbert Sitwell was one. He suspected Connolly for having played a 'very wicked' trick on his readers. 'Is this rigmarole of Koestler's intended as fact or fiction?' he asked. Either way, Koestler was 'ill-advised' and 'blatantly impertinent'. Sitwell had fought in the First World War and found then that many of the worst accounts of the activities of German troops circulated back home bore no relation to what was actually going on. Surely it was the same this time around? Sitwell went as far as betting Connolly £5 that 'if you are alive ten years after the war has ended, you will truthfully and willingly admit that you have been hoodwinked and nose-led'. Koestler was furious. He wanted to fire off a reply to Sitwell calling him an apologist for German atrocities, but Connolly directed him to the letters section of *Horizon*, where he addressed Sitwell and further swathes of suspicious readers as one. 'In your letter of . . . October you asked me the idiotic question whether the events described in "The Mixed Transport" - viz. the massacre of Jews - are "based on fact" or "artistic fiction",' he began. His letter ends with a wake-up call to middle-class England:

> If you tell me that you don't read newspapers, white-books, documentary pamphlets obtainable at W. H. Smith bookstalls - why on earth do you read *Horizon* and call yourself a member of the intelligentsia? I can't even say that I am sorry to be rude. There is no excuse for you - for it is your duty to know and to be haunted by your knowledge. As long as you don't feel, against reason and independently of reason, ashamed to be alive while others are put to death and guilty, sick, humiliated, because you were spared, you will remain what you are: an accomplice by omission.

This cold bucket of water was meant for everyone, Connolly included, who hitherto had been enjoying what Orwell called 'the deep, deep sleep of England'.

15

Men at Arms

It was around the time of Connolly's fortieth birthday in September 1943 that Evelyn Waugh realised he was done with the war. 'I have got so bored with everything military that I can no longer remember the simplest details,' he confided to his diary:

> I dislike the Army. I want to get to work again. I do not want any more experiences in life. I have quite enough bottled and carefully laid in the cellar, some still ripening, most ready for drinking, a little beginning to lose its body. I wrote to Frank [Pakenham] very early in the war to say that its chief use would be to cure artists of the illusion that they were men of action. It has worked its cure with me. I have succeeded, too, in dissociating myself very largely with the rest of the world. I am not impatient of its manifest follies and don't want to influence opinions or events, or expose humbug or anything of that kind. I don't want to be of service to anyone or anything. I simply want to do my work as an artist.

Waugh was currently stationed out at Windsor with the Royal Horse Guards, a glorified but inauspicious appointment which meant he had missed out on the recent Allied victories in North Africa, and felt both exasperated and embarrassed at his own idleness during this time. To his diary: 'It will be difficult for our descendants reading of the titanic war effort of 1943 to realise that this is how active and fully-trained officers, yearning to get to the front, are obliged to spend their time.' Many of his postings seemed more decorative than functional, and there was a lurking suspicion - looking around at his senior and well-to-do comrades - that they had been invented to 'gratify ambitions'. 'I think we are the only mess in Europe which constantly drinks claret, port and brandy at dinner,' he reflected at one point. But his war seemed destined to be frittered away in sumptuous purgatory. England, Waugh thought, was probably the only country in the world where people were resorting to bribery to get into the war.

Returning to London, as he did on increasingly frequent leaves, Waugh was dismayed by how it, too, seemed to have lost its sense of purpose. It was shabbier and shoddier than he had ever seen it. The crowds were uglier and more aimless. Soldiers sprawled along the edges of streets with cigarettes hanging in their mouths, their uniforms open to the sun and their caps 'off at extravagant angles'. Young women in trousers and high heels and film-star coiffures hung around them. These images further compounded Waugh's sense of alienation from everything that was going on. A war is a busy, bustling thing; among this noise and these crowds, recollections of writing in peacetime seemed almost the definition of tranquillity.

Waugh could not write with his wife around, let alone an entire company of soldiers. The declaration of war in 1939 had forced him to abandon 'a major work', an extract of which he eventually sold to *Horizon* as 'Work Suspended'. He had initially joined the Royal Marines, and by the beginning of 1940 was being sent to various

backwaters of the country for training and menial postings. Each of
these locations was in some way prohibitive to writing. In Marine
barracks at Hawick in Scotland, his hut was too dark and cold to sit
in. In the mess, the wireless played ceaselessly and the soldiers –
despite none having a sense of humour – never stopped laughing.
A requisitioned Victorian villa at Kingsdown in Kent was severely
overcrowded, one bath being shared between sixty men and, in
Waugh's bedroom, five men without a single coat peg. All activity
at the villa was amplified to a headache-inducing volume owing
to the lack of carpeting, and in the main recreational area a ping-
pong table was the enemy of peaceful contemplation. At Matlock
in Derbyshire, where he was later dispatched, there was nowhere
at all to sit and write. Even if there were, Waugh wrote, 'by the end
of the day my eyes are so dazzled by scrutinising photographs that
all I have in mind to do is sit in the twilight drinking beer.' In 1941,
Waugh sailed with his division to the Middle East, where they took
part in a night raid on the German-controlled coastline of Libya.

Still, in a few months of 1941 Waugh had been able to cobble
together *Put Out More Flags*, the first of his wartime satires. The
idea had come to him after reading Henry Green's 1940 memoir *Pack My Bag*, which recalled the author's upper-middle-class
upbringing ('I was born a mouthbreather with a silver spoon') and
schooldays, no doubt reminding Waugh of some of his *Vile Bodies*
personalities, many of whom reappeared in the new novel as his
'assortment of Georgian left-overs'. But Green's 'self-portrait' was
most notable at the time for its pessimism. In the opening passage
he had explained his motivation for putting his life story on paper
at the age of thirty-five as a desire to do so 'before one is killed'.
'Surely it would be asking much to pretend one had a chance to
live,' he wrote. 'If we have no time to chew another book over we
must turn to what comes first to mind and that must be how one
changed from boy to man, how one lived, things and people and
one's attitude.' Waugh seems to have taken this up as a challenge,

and *Put Out More Flags*, though a fully-fledged war novel, is also a statement of the continuance of humour and silliness. It is nostalgic, as Green's memoir was, but also captures a once insular and carefree society at a moment of enormous social upheaval. Waugh admitted in a letter to his father that the novel had been 'dashed off to occupy a tedious voyage', which is probably not too far from the truth; he tended to write one or two thousand words at each day's sitting, and so would have achieved these fifty thousand in no more than a few months. But this was 'a minor work', as he explained, the best one could aspire to in wartime, or so he thought.

The possibility for heroic personal reinvention in wartime quickly dissipated as middle age touched him dully on the shoulder and returned him to the back of the queue. At least in this one respect - and one respect was quite enough - the world was saying that it no longer needed him. It was the barrenness implied by that epiphany that eventually led Waugh to his 'magnum opus'. At the end of 1943 he was 'fighting the Great Boredom', and in the New Year reports had inquired with his colonel for three months' leave to write a book. '[I] am going to the Ministry of Information this afternoon to try and enlist their support,' he added, without mentioning any of the friends in high places he would be leaning on for help. Almost no other writer (and even Graham Greene could not claim to be best friends with the prime minister's son) could have expected such a special dispensation for a book which, as Waugh openly admitted, had zero propaganda value - indeed, a large part of the book would actually be about 'how much I hate the army'. But it worked. As he explained to his wife, this book would be different to *Put Out More Flags* in that it would require complete isolation and focus. It was going to be 'very high quality'. Wistful for her company though he was, he would never be able to maintain the 'fervent preoccupation which is absolutely necessary to composition' if she were at close quarters with him. He planned to take a room at the Easton Court Hotel in Dartmoor, where he hoped the military would not pester him, and in fact began writing at his club, White's, in London. There, he was permitted to use an entire lounge as a private sitting room. He bought 'a very expensive concoction' which he hoped would restore his vitality after the inertia of military life and, by ten o'clock on the first morning – less than a week after his initial request for leave – had started work on *Brideshead Revisited.*

A BUSTLED AND BULLIED LIFE

The substation at Cricklewood comprised four army huts which contained, separately, a recreation room, a bunkhouse for sleeping, a kitchen and mess room, and a washroom and lavatory. The men, all new recruits of the London branch of the Auxiliary Fire Service, wore blue dungarees 'like rompers'. These, Stephen Spender wrote, had the effect of 'smooth[ing] out the excrescences of middle age, reducing all our bodies to a childish-looking uniformity'. It was not possible to tell who were the poets and who the taxi drivers, bricklayers or builders. There were certainly going to be no special dispensations granted here.

The daily routine at Cricklewood involved getting up at 7.30, breakfasting at 8, cleaning out the huts from 8.30 to 9.35, going on parade until 10 and then doing drills from 10.15 to 11. Afterwards, there was more cleaning to do, an activity the men would drag out until lunchtime. For the remainder of the day, they were on standby. Spender estimated that around forty-eight out of every seventy-two hours were spent waiting for an order or to go to mess or bed. The problem was that, since April 1941, there had been no fires to put out. In these long, empty hours spent in the recreation room, Spender got used to the sound of the BBC Light Programme on the wireless and the clicking of snooker balls. He, too, had come up against the Great Boredom, though without any cigars or claret to alleviate the futility. It was not 'done' to sit in the corner of the room and read Proust, and writing was pretty well impossible, so he played darts and listened to dirty stories instead. 'My life seems completely wasted at present,' Spender told William Plomer, '[but] it gives some sort of satisfaction to the British Lion, I suppose.'

Though externally a sprightlier individual, Spender had (quite dramatically) failed his army medical, where Waugh had not. As summarised by John Sutherland, 'colitis, poor eyesight, varicose veins, lingering organic weakness from his childhood illnesses and the 1934 tapeworm rendered him totally unfit'; he was branded with a pitiful 'C' grading, just edging a semi-conscious, hung-over Dylan Thomas and the same as George Orwell, excluding him even from the fire service. Spender could have accepted the judgement of fate and retreated into his literary activities, but as with lots of writers there was a genuine desire to contribute. By the time he had haggled his way up to a 'B' grading, making him eligible to put out the nation's fires, the Blitz had ended. So the transition was made from a busy working life to a static uniformed one. Surely, Sutherland asks, Spender had more to offer? Among other things, he spoke German fluently and had an intimate knowledge of enemy country; he was, moreover, only thirty years old at the declaration of war. In the great reshuffle of wartime, Spender seems to have landed in that blind spot which was familiar to lots of the nation's intellectuals. That is, unless there was something more sinister going on. George Orwell, for one, believed that there was a 'backwash' of reaction against those whom the government saw as instigators in the more revolutionary moments in the country's recent history. The war in Spain cast a long shadow, and as Orwell wrote, 'the government have more or less frankly gone on the principle of "keeping the Reds out of it"' (certainly MI5 had been keeping files on both Orwell and Spender since the mid-1930s). Writing for the American readers of *Partisan Review*, Spender attempted to explain why he had 'been spending [his] time chiefly in the company of unskilled workmen, ex-clerks, and the like'. The reason, he purported, was quite simple: 'creative writers in war-time England have no status at all'.

The whole experience in the fire service felt like a test of character. Privately, much of the work - specifically cleaning toilet bowls and wiping spittle off duckboards - seemed insulting in how it demeaned his abilities. The humiliation, Spender reflected, 'was more a feeling that this was the only use they could put poetry to'. It was shocking, after the Spanish war, 'a left-wing war in which poets and novelists could be important figures' (Orwell), to see how far the poet had fallen in the world's estimation. There was also the culture shock of living in such close quarters with men whose idea of time well spent was so different to his own. 'We listen to jazz all day,' Spender noted, in an irritable mood. 'If any good music at all comes on the wireless, someone turns it off at once.' But in general he was fond of his comrades, and was frequently impressed by their warmth, good nature and humour, which stood in humbling contrast to his own humiliation at his lowered circumstances. Spender seems to have quite liked the egalitarian constitution of the fire service, where protocol was largely brushed off and one did not have to salute for superiors. He had, finally, got to mix with the working classes - one of the original reasons for associating himself with the communist movement.

At roughly the midpoint of the war, Spender published an article in *Horizon* summarising the failures of the poetic medium up to that point in the conflict, particularly in the case of young writers. His tone is for the most part sympathetic. Most writers then were leading a 'bustled and bullied' life, and as Spender knew from recent experience, 'it is not enough to have inspiration, one must also have a few hours every day alone, sitting in a room, *without the wireless on*, in order to develop, to think over, to explore, inspiration.' But there were deeper problems to be faced. The most significant was that no poet who was currently involved in the war seemed to be able to offer any real insight into what was going on. There were lots of interesting and capable poets at work, but 'the war has only made . . . [a] superficial impression on them'. 'One is aware of barrage balloons in the sky, the boredom of fatigues, home-sickness, a few bombed ruins, but certainly not of Dunkirk and Libya; still less of what the war is about.' Instead the war was seen from outside. Again, this was not something for which any individual could be blamed. In comparison to the First World War, which seemed always to have a clear focal point running up from France to Belgium, this modern conflict was broken up into numerous storylines which played out simultaneously. 'So far from feeling at the centre of the war the members of the Forces feel shut off from life before and after it, and even from the war itself,' Spender wrote. Modern weaponry, furthermore, denoted a style of fighting which was less tactile and more impersonal. What seemed to be most lacking, though, was any kind of political interpretation. To express either 'any positive faith in the democracy for which we are fighting' or 'any effective statement against war' seemed to be beneath these new poets. Spender had to remind himself that they did not have the same frame of reference as his own generation, and were in fact the 'war's victims', having graduated into the conflict without ever knowing a world at peace.

Spender's comments in this article drew an immediate response from the younger poets, who agreed with much of what he was saying but wished to emphasise just how hopeless their position was. In a letter to *Horizon*, Alex Comfort, then twenty-two, admitted that there was indeed 'an attitude of passivity'. As he saw it, this war was not seen as a 'struggle' in the way that Spain was a struggle, meaning that he was not fighting for something he wholeheartedly believed but rather to suppress some evil aberration. This war poetry 'was written within the circle of the war which the individual fighting man sees, a circle in which there are no general principles and no objective except the next point to be occupied or abandoned':

> Because of this smallness of scope - limited for the civilian to the crater in his street, and for the soldier to his immediate and rapidly varying field of operations - our best chance of making an imaginative use of events is to confine ourselves . . . to the small, which we can comprehend, and which we can handle out of our experience - the capture of a small village, the lines seen from a night watch post.

According to Comfort, there was much that Spender was unable to grasp. This war was not a struggle because it was a 'degenerative' rather than a revolutionary process. It aimed simply to get the world back to where it had been before Hitler, grasping again at the transient spectre of peace, with one side of the human race trying to clear up the mess created by the other. They might succeed in doing so, but perhaps humanity's destination had already been determined. The hole sinks and is filled in again, tediously, repetitively. 'That is why so many writers "disclaim all responsibility" for the war,' Comfort writes. 'It is not that they are either intellectually lazy or intellectually incompetent - like the rest of the nation, at heart, they are just unutterably weary.'

Comfort is correct in his observation that even Spender's poetry was moving away from 'events' and towards the 'romantic or fantastic interpretation of the state of mind of humanity'. That year, Spender had come out with a new collection, *Ruins and Visions,* which, in the words of Michael Brett, 'depicts the coalescence of private and public histories'. This was a new way of thinking for Spender, whom Orwell had called a 'public-spirited' poet, because in this instant the public world is recognised as a threat to the private one, and it is the private life which must come to the rescue of man's purpose and contentment. The collection is split up into four sections, 'A Separation', 'Ironies of War', 'Deaths', and 'Visions'. Taken as a sequence, there is a clear narrative arc leading from public and private catastrophe towards questioning and, finally, resolution, which takes place in 'a space beyond words'. The experiences of a lifetime are compacted between the two eclipsing incidents of war. Spender, at the age of just thirty-three, had already lived through two world wars, and in *Ruins and Visions* that fact has started to hit home. Reviewing the collection in *Horizon*, Kathleen Raine began by addressing Spender's fame, which exposed him to 'attack and ridicule'. Over his career, Spender, she says, has been the kind of poet who is 'a teacher of the world, rather than a learner from it'. This is a dangerous game, for this poet creates a standard for himself to always be able to accurately interpret what is going on. Spender, Raine thought, 'sometimes . . . sees right into the heart of the matter, but more often he misses the point altogether. His mind acts like a searchlight - it sometimes finds the aeroplane, and is always looking for it; but it has not the power of seeing all round.' Raine suggests that Spender's mission, going forwards, should be to embrace complexity, rather than being lured, by the 'tidy pattern of the words', towards a quick solution.

Part of the culture shock of being in the fire service was in the politics of the men. Orwell, during his time with the Local Defence Volunteers in St John's Wood before joining the BBC, had envisioned a future for himself and his colleagues 'as a kind of people's army that might play a pivotal role in domestic consciousness-raising'. They could, he thought, be 'a popular militia, armed and politically conscious', an idea which appealed because, as Spender wrote, Orwell was constantly imagining society as like 'a pendulum swinging between extremes'. None of that was evident in Spender's section of the fire service, which was not seething with revolutionary ardour but instead patient and resigned to its task. It was a steady society founded on values of human courage and sympathy, which Spender saw as natural to the working classes.

These qualities were the by-product of a lifetime of 'vulnerability, closeness to unkind realities, and physical proximity to each other'.

Spender's colleagues' perception of their role, or place, in the war shed some light on the mentality of the "new writers" since 1937'. He characterised this insouciance for the *Partisan Review*. During his training, Spender himself had begun to experience panic attacks when thinking about what lay ahead of him. This was because he took a dramatic view of the war. After one lecture on identifying the different types of gases ('those which smelt like pear-drops, carnations and sickly-scented hay') he had hidden for half an hour in a telephone box, 'overwhelmed by the vision of human beings asphyxiating one another in poisonous over-sweet scents'. None of this, however, seemed to come as a surprise to his colleagues. The assumption generally was that, rather than turning up for parade each day as representatives for certain values or a way of life, they were merely reporting for a 'day's work'. 'They do not think of it as their war,' Spender explained – not because it was the 'bosses' war' but rather 'because it is too large and vast and horrible for them'. The average man considered himself to be much smaller and saner than it, and few even acknowledged that they were involved in a major historical event. What held the men together, Spender thought, was the completely serious acceptance of the necessity of their work. At the back of their minds at all times was a fixed image of future air raids and fires which they would need to put out. The idea that buildings would be knocked down was as familiar and even normal to them as that they should be put up. On top of this, the men imagined their enemies to have a roughly similar understanding. The German conscript, too, was 'on the job'. 'That's his job' was their attitude to a Nazi dropping an incendiary bomb; 'and this is ours' as they put it out. The effect of this, Spender wrote, was to make the war seem no longer a conflict between Germany and Britain but instead 'an inter-relationship of jobs within a system'. One day Spender was approached by a fellow fireman, who had a question for him: 'You've been to Germany, haven't you? What are they like?'

For reasons which had to do with his divorce from Inez, Spender was required to keep the flat at Lansdowne Terrace until 1942. But besides contributing a poem or article every couple of months, he no longer had anything to do with *Horizon*, and it was strange to have all his stuff right next to where Connolly, Watson, Lys and Sonia were doing their work. Natasha tended to swing by the office around five o'clock to pick Spender up for dinner, and often found the editorial discussion still to be in full flow. Her impression was that Watson, as time went on, was gaining more influence, asserting himself when Connolly was inclined to 'dig his heels in and sulk'. Spender was seemingly quite happy to be extricating himself from this triumvirate, particularly after Connolly's comments on Orwell's India broadcast. Connolly, it now seemed clear, would only ever be happy as a 'soloist'. But Spender could not move in with Natasha right away; for the time being, her base was still in Oxford, and as he correctly surmised, it would be better not to do things in too much of a hurry 'so that people get used to the idea of our marrying'.

The opportunity for cohabitation arose at the end of that year, when the now twenty-year-old Lucian Freud had informed the poet of a space that had become available in a house owned by his father in Hampstead. Spender had done a similar favour for Freud, who had tended to make use of the Lansdowne Terrace flat on the frequent occasions when Spender was not. This was too good an opportunity to turn down: Spender could transfer to the substation at Maresfield Gardens, a few hundred yards from the property, and that way increase his time spent with Natasha and with his writing. Lucian's father, Ernst, was an architect whose houses were starting to pop up around London and the Home Counties, and during the bombing in 1940 he had decided to put his skills to use in reinforcing the house's ground floor to 'pillbox durability'. Were he to find himself on duty when the next raid came, then, Spender would know that Natasha was safe. In return for the entrée, Stephen and Natasha would simply have to allow Lucian use of one of the rooms as a studio.

The problem – as Spender must have anticipated – was the relationship between Freud and Natasha. Despite Spender seeming rather committed to this great wartime romance, Natasha, to the youngest generation of Freuds and his friends, seemed oddly parochial and protective of her relationship in a way which seemed anomalous to modern, semi-bohemian society. She was hung up, Freud remembered, on Spender's Jewishness, and would say to him things like 'Stop that silly Schuster nonsense', meaning the name – Spender's grandmother's – by which Freud used to refer to him. She saw their Jewishness as a pact, particularly where their shared heritage was alluded to in a 'private language' they had developed together on the Christmas trip to Wales. Freud could recall at least one occasion when Natasha had been more openly anti-Semitic. She believed, he claimed, that every sad-looking Jewish man or woman spotted on public transport was a spy, and had even, at times, gone as far as reporting them. 'They were just refugees,' Freud said. What is unclear is when this prejudice had developed; certainly, Freud felt, it fed off her paranoia regarding her husband's past. Natasha had spoken at length with Stephen about Tony but still felt the first thirty-one years of his life to be something impenetrable, a party she had not been invited to. 'She thought I was an awful little squirt,' Freud reflected. 'She assumed – wrongly – I had been, or was, a boyfriend of Stephen.' Freud was merely 'one of a number of people Stephen made amorous propositions to.' The atmosphere in the house was tense to say the least.

It was at the Maresfield Gardens substation – a converted girls' school – that Spender had begun to daydream about a scheme for workers' education as a way to overcome the tedium of the lulls. He was a teacher of the world, as Kathleen Raine had said.

By chance, others, elsewhere in the AFS, had had the same idea. Already a 'group of ordinary firemen' were spreading the gospel of progressive education, planning and war aims, and wanted to bring Spender in as a discussion group leader to broaden their horizons into the arts. It became a second full-time job for Spender, and, like Orwell at the BBC, he was able to call on his art-world friends to create a really professional programme. Even Kenneth Clark was brought in to speak. The success of the scheme further testified to a maturing of the national consciousness during the Second World War; it had outgrown its former constitution, and even if not revolutionary per se, was going to insist on substantial changes to British society.

There was rain and low cloud through most of the summer of 1944, and the British public joked that it was the result of a new German secret weapon which could control the weather. Behind the jokes, though, the nerves of the average Londoner ran higher than at any previous point in the war. January 1944 had seen the return of bombing to the capital, and almost nightly the chorus of anti-aircraft guns made its tremendous noise. 'Here was the same experience to be faced all over again,' William Sansom wrote of this period. It was depressing. After several years of exhaustive work and short rations the nation, mentally, was at the end of its tether. When, if ever, was this going to end? How much more could a human being take? Morale, if temporarily rekindled by the need to co-ordinate on a larger scale, was being stretched thinner and thinner. The army fought on, but the civilian seemed ready to give up. After four years under siege, the country was tatty and soiled. Leaving his flat each day, Cyril Connolly found nothing remotely uplifting in 'the contraceptives in the squares, the puddles of urine in the telephone boxes, the sulphurous wines and goat stew in the restaurants, the bored, pale, ferrety people milling around the streets'. Like real ferrets, the population of London was again required to move under ground. This was the 'Little Blitz'.

There was a feeling people got sometimes when the bombs were raining down on them, one which they had never had before and would never have again. It was not a lurch or a frisson, but rather a deceleration, or stabilising, of impressions, as if previously disparate elements had suddenly found each other and could now click into place. It was the subtle and momentary will to death, a kind of epiphany of the natural birth-to-death process of life in which, at this most concentrated point, there was no past and no future and nothing mattered outside of the comedy of this fundamental experience. Peter Watson had felt it in 1940 on nights when, eschewing the option of an air-raid shelter, he had remained glued to his bed in his flat in west London. For Cyril Connolly, it had been around the same time. One night he had been walking home from the pub with Peter Quennell when bombs began to light up the neighbourhood. Quennell had been afraid, diving into a doorway, but Connolly had merely turned to his friend, smiled, and said, 'Be calm. Really, you know, we've all had interesting lives.'

In these moments, the order in life was revealed to be in its fragmentation, its justice in its irony. So Connolly had stood on that rooftop with Orwell and both, in the vision of destruction, saw a judgement on themselves and everything the world had become. This once-energised, political generation, Spender admitted, had regarded the war 'almost with relief, as a fulfilment of their prophecies'. As Louis MacNeice had written in 'Brother Fire', each secretly craved the decimation of the world they had failed and which had failed them. They echoed the fire's thoughts of 'Destroy! Destroy!' because it was what they deserved. A new generation was here now who could share none of the blame, who would emerge from all of this clean. Would poetry matter to them?

For Spender, the epiphany eluded him until these early months of 1944. It was strange. For the first time in a long time he had felt really contented. He was much more excited about his new marriage than he had been about being with Inez. Now, nothing was

hidden from the other, and long talks with Natasha had had a 'revolutionary effect' on Spender's personality. Stephen explained that
he had been thinking about Tony and the lives destroyed by the
Spanish Civil War. He talked about his early years in Hamburg and
Berlin with Christopher Isherwood. He admitted that he blamed
himself for the break-up of his marriage with Inez, that he had
spent too much time working. They discussed the feelings of guilt
that each was experiencing, in particular relating to the First World
War and the sadness and privation that thereafter had hung over
their parents' lives. 'From now on there is no question of blame,'
Natasha had said. 'There is only us.'

The Spenders were in their flat at Maresfield Gardens one night
when a bomb had fallen on a house across the road. Spender had
always been able to comfort himself during raids by picturing the
vast scale of the city which ensconced him, and the invisible speck
he represented within it. The man in the plane with his thumb
poised over a button was a symbolic, rather than actual, problem.
Now, however, his attacker seemed to insist on his own reality. As
it fell, the bomb had made a noise like that of a train emerging from
a tunnel. 'One felt oneself to be tied to the rails,' Spender remembered. He and his wife were sat on the fortified ground floor when
it came, but still the room rocked. From upstairs, where their
bedroom was, came the sound of things collapsing and the tinkling of falling glass. The ceiling of the first floor had come down
completely and lay 'like a blanket of lath and plaster' over their
bed. In that brief interval between first detecting the sound of the
bomb and then its scattering impact, a thought had entered Spender's head: 'This is something I have all my life been waiting for.' It
seemed the end of the world.

In the aftermath, he looked out of the window of the decapitated bedroom at the sight of London lying below, 'black and calm,
with a few isolated fires rising from scattered areas, like tongues of
flame fallen from the heavens upon a darkening view of Florence,

in some late morbid visioning of Botticelli'. During the Little Blitz, Spender had got to see his first bit of action as a fireman - 'a relief', he told Edith Sitwell, after years of waiting. He claimed that being amid the flames had had a calming effect, and it was perhaps for this reason - some latent primordial craving - that he decided to go out and find the site of one of the blasts, wanting to see 'some tangible result of the raid', as if to check it had been real. Once outside, he was immediately engulfed in the great cloud of dust caused by the explosion, and could see nothing. When he began to climb down the hill, he soon became lost in a maze of streets, and was surrounded by darkened houses. It was in that moment, however, that he felt the comforting sense 'of the sure, dark immensity of London like a warren, containing a scattered, breeding life concealed in the burrows of the ragged, dilapidated streets of Kilburn and Maida Vale. They could be destroyed at one place, but then - the wound sealed off - would flow through other channels and streets and tunnels.'

16

Flying Bombs

The 'flying bombs' had begun, like most things during the war, as a rumour. It was a rumour Leonard Woolf had heard one day from an editor at the *New Statesman*, Aylmer Vallance, who was also a colonel on the General Staff at the War Office. Vallance had recently been interrogating captured German officers and had been able to glean from those men the plan that, despite the direction of play, Germany would eventually be able to win the war through the unprecedented might of some 'secret weapon'. To Leonard, Vallance gave a detailed picture of what this contraption would look like, and how it would work. Such prophecies were not uncommon. They were a natural consequence of the abrupt transition from nightly bombardment to safety, and the beginning of a respite which seemed so implausible that it was almost more rational to talk of 'new, giant planes specially built for England'. As Orwell observed, the first, false air-raid siren in London in 1942 - after a year without one - had set the population on edge like none before it.

It had to do with the planned Allied invasion of Europe, which had been anticipated ever since American soldiers had started to appear on the streets of British towns and cities. Every time the possibility of a 'second front' came up in conversation it was appended – in a lower tone – with each person's fear of an escalation of German raids. What seemed certain was that Germany would lash out with raids made in revenge and desperation and perhaps of a kind that London had not yet known. These could be gas attacks, or high-saturation attacks of the kind the British had inflicted on Cologne and Hamburg. Anything was possible once order had broken down and the war was mutating into its final, truest form.

It was 6 June 1944 when General Eisenhower's message finally came through. Allied forces had landed in Normandy. William Sansom has recalled the feeling of disquietude which spread through the streets of the capital in that moment, of being caught between the impulses to feel relieved, wave flags, and to hunker down and await with solemnity the next piece of news. As Londoners passed the corners of shopping streets, they lingered momentarily to strain their eyes at the far-off news placards, before shuffling quietly on. Landlords used the interval to clean their empty pubs. Everyone waited, feeling the contribution of their own silence to the city's unusual hush. 'Now again they looked warily at the silent skies,' Sansom wrote. No one took the Germans lightly.

Cyril Connolly's 'Comment' in that month's *Horizon* picks up this image of Londoners stopping and waiting for news of the landings. 'This number of *Horizon* appears during one of the decisive battles of the world's history,' he wrote. 'It is a moment when every civilian forgets the past months of anxiety, impatience and boredom and can think only of the present operations and of the men who are risking their lives in them.' This was issue number fifty of the magazine, the point at which Connolly said it would commit self-sabotage. But he could not have known that it would fall on such an important date. The editor's excitement is palpable, and it is a wonder that they were able to get an issue together at that time:

> At last the mists are going to lift, the ten-year nightmare finish, Himmler's fat handshake, Hitler's putty face 'like a dirty plate' will survive only in waxworks; once again, as at Salamis, the peoples who value liberty are about to bring down ruin on those who have despised it: we shall return to Europe to draw strength from the continent we have set free until the full tide of our Western civilization flows back over the scattered dried-up rockpools that every nation has become, to set them all breathing and moving again in the cool element of which they have so long been deprived.

With all of this to look forward to, how could anyone have focused long enough to read Edward Sackville-West's ten-page essay 'Music: Some Aspects of the Contemporary Problem', or Enid Starkie on the eccentrics of the 1830s? But there were short poems by Mac-Neice and Spender which could be skimmed and forcibly reread as one paced the room with the wireless playing in the background.

On 13 June the first flying bomb, or V1, landed in London – in Bethnal Green. It was thought at first to have been a German fighter-bomber with its tail alight, caught by the heavy gunfire that had preceded it, and then sputtering down to earth as its engine stopped. Spectators had even cheered the sight. Three days later, however, a report was compiled by the Chief Warden which explained the reality of this mysterious aircraft. His conclusion was that it had been a pilotless aircraft and that the area of blast damage caused was as large as 200 yards. It was on the same day that the attack started in earnest, with these 'doodlebugs', as they would soon be known, arriving constantly by day and by night. This first, suffocating evening under the V1s is immortalised in Graham Greene's *The End of the Affair*. Maurice Bendrix is in bed with his married lover Sarah Miles when they hear what they imagine to be planes, breaking through the night defences. One after another, they begin to come down over Clapham Common with their tails burning, and it is only through the repetition of this that it begins to dawn on the narrator that these could not be planes, being picked off like clay pigeons, but rather something new. 'Robots,' he calls them.

Where the bombs struck would be left giant plumes of dust that rose above the rooftops, demonstrating the force with which they descended. Sansom calculated that while in the original Blitz the average number of people killed by each bomb was 0.71, in the case of the V1s it was 9.2. Moreover, being unmanned, they did not discriminate in their targets; family homes, women and children were as much in the firing line as docklands and government offices. Moving quickly through the low, dark cloud of that summer, they could no more be anticipated than nullified. A hurried blast of an air horn was all that Londoners would get as a warning to cover themselves from flying glass. 'At night they pulled bedclothes over their faces and waited,' Sansom wrote, 'one . . . two . . . three . . . four seconds, and either the windows came flying in or they didn't.'

Rather than diving for cover, John Lehmann explains, people used to freeze. The fact that the doodlebugs were coming over at all hours of the day meant that not only sleep but also work, meetings and parties were now constantly being interrupted. Lehmann was having lunch at the Savoy with Kenneth Clark one afternoon, engaged in stimulating conversation, when the 'disagreeable splutter' became audible in the distance. 'As it grew louder,' he wrote, 'we all became a little more thoughtful; conversation faltered, dried up here and there for some seconds though the thread was never entirely lost; gestures were inhibited, not a fork was lifted to a mouth for the brief span of time that seemed an eternity.' Even more so than with the bombs that were dropped from planes, one strained to interpret the direction of travel of the missile by the depth and tone of its inhuman moans. There were two outcomes in those moments: either one heard the splutter fade away into the distance, taking another life in another part of the city, or the sound grew louder until it seemed directly overhead. Muscles would tense and faces wince, each praying they would not hear the engine cut out. On another occasion the three Sitwells - the fifty-six-year-old Edith and her two younger brothers Osbert and Sacheverell - were giving a poetry reading at the Church-ill Club on Bond Street. It was a major event. The Sitwells were literary royalty, and having them all on the same bill represented an unmissable opportunity especially for those American soldiers who had been following their work from afar. The room quickly filled up. It was while Edith was reading, incidentally, a poem about the first Blitz, that a rattle from the sky 'grew to ominous proportions' and seemed to be aimed at the exact spot where she was standing. Only once, between a line or stanza break, did her eyes lift to the ceiling, before continuing to read at a greater volume. 'It was a magnificent performance,' Lehmann wrote, 'worthy of a British Admiral coolly dictating orders from the bridge in the middle of a fierce naval engagement.' The implication, as everyone in the audience felt at the time, was that poetry was more important than all the terrors that Hitler could launch against them.

Things had turned properly sour between the directors of the Hogarth Press by this point, and it is possible to read Lehmann's admission of how the new bombs affected people's attitudes as somehow connected to his treatment of Leonard. Despite his claims of a lively community spirit which made London during this period the most exciting of his life, the truth was that the war had made Lehmann bitter. 'One grew hard about other people's misfortunes,' he said, of life under bombardment. He had also grown hard in his business affairs, and as a consequence the famous Press was breaking up, eventually to be handed, by Leonard, to Chatto & Windus. 'Your attitude and language to me during the last 12 months or so are absolutely inexplicable to me,' Leonard had written to say. 'In no other of my many business relations am I consistently told that I am senile, out of touch, irrelevant, and petulant.'

Leonard had briefly moved back into 37 Mecklenburgh Square until the beginning of the Little Blitz. When he first returned, in April 1942, 'there were no windows and no ceilings, and nothing in the house, from roof to the water pipes, was quite sound'. He had three of the rooms patched up and lived in those until he could bear it no longer.

One of the bombs hit the gardens outside Connolly's flat in Bedford Square, a shock which convinced him of the necessity of taking cover in air-raid shelters. Peter Quennell had been watching from one of the windows and recorded afterwards that 'it just goes bowling thro' the sky, explodes and there you are.' It also convinced Connolly, in June 1944, a week after the first V1 in London, to compose his will. He discussed the matter with Lys, who was 'exceedingly buzz-bomb conscious', and they sat down together to give these statements 'by my own hand'. Lys wrote on *Horizon*-branded letter paper, and Connolly on an even more austere scrap torn from a notebook. Lys promised all of her money to Connolly, her share of a family house at Maidstone to her brother, and all of her 'wearing apparrell' [*sic*] to her sister. Connolly's bequests were more complicated, but all his goods and chattels, royalties on books published and unpublished, money in the bank, books, pictures, furniture, clothes, motorcar and any other valuables were to go to his 'great friend and companion' Lys. The two Peters, Watson and Quennell, would be remembered in any form they saw fit, as well as Sonia Brownell, Elizabeth Bowen and, surprisingly, Diana Witherby. Jean, then living in New York, could have any papers or paintings which she might ask for. Peter Quennell would act as literary executor, with the help of both Lys and Sonia.

Connolly's friends, through the first Blitz, had been impressed at how much he continued to be himself. Something about the flying bombs, however, gave them an added touch of existential menace. 'I know one is not supposed to say so,' Connolly wrote in *Horizon*, 'but I don't care for flying bombs: to all guilty people (and by now

all civilians are guilty) they are the final appointment in the den-
tist's chair.' Casualties apart - Connolly and Lys are said to have
been out walking one day when a woman was blown up in front of
their eyes - the V1s had made London 'more dirty, more unsocia-
ble, more plague-stricken than ever'. All niceties - manners, casual
conversation - were forgotten as 'hunted' civilians sought to protect themselves. 'Never in the whole war has the lot of the civilian
been more abject, or his status so low,' Connolly reflected. It all
seemed a new method of torture designed to engender insanity
in the shortest time possible. Without the daytime respite, there
was nowhere to hide, and one felt increasingly cornered. In rather
a desperate attempt at wartime innovation, Connolly and Lys had
adapted the cupboard under their stairs to serve as a home air-raid
shelter, though notably one which did not involve stepping out
into potential wind and downpour. In the scramble which now
followed the sputtering on the horizon, Lys, with her dainty frame,
found she could climb inside 'as neatly as a maggot into a pea-pod',
while for the rotund Connolly it was a far more visceral challenge.
One can imagine him with his neck bent under the diagonal of
the stairs, cursing this 'grey little fey little island' of ration books
and blackouts. Not only was it wrong for humans to live and work
in cities, it was especially cruel to confine them to England. *Horizon* was at this point running a light-hearted series entitled 'Where
Shall John Go Now?', in which writers took turns to recollect the
destinations they would be visiting first when the war was over.
The images in Connolly's dreams were all of France. 'Streets of
Paris, pray for me,' he wrote around this time, 'beaches in the sun,
pray for me . . . summer rain on quays of Toulon, wash me away.'

Another person who had become sick of the war and of London
was Peter Watson. He took a pragmatic approach to life, declaring once - with the art collector's sense of risk management - that
'The emotions have so little to do with what is suitable', and in this
case the sensible thing to do was remove himself from the capital.

Since he could afford it, he decided to rent a house in the country, and settled on one which had long been known to the *Horizon* set as owned by the painter Dick Wyndham. A short journey from London, Tickerage Mill in Uckfield, Sussex, was a wonderful, maze-like house of honeyed brick situated by a tranquil lakeside. It was where Connolly had first laid eyes on Diana, and thereafter he would think of it as a sanctuary – 'the red lane through the Spanish chestnut wood . . . the geese on the pond . . . the wood-fire crackling in the low bedroom . . . what could be more womb-like or reassuring?' Watson spent the best part of the spring moving Wyndham's 'old-fashioned, cluttered, ramshackle furnishings' out and into storage, and giving the whole place a Bauhaus high finish. At Tickerage Mill, as others testified, the mind was able to dream again. Watson would take the guests down to the cellar and allow them to peruse the Wyndham family's collection of vintage wines, and afterwards they would invent menus and wine pairings that they would be enjoying if they could.

Everything changed with the arrival of the V1s in June. Though they were programmed to land on London, many, it seemed, were falling just short over Kent and Sussex – 'Bomb Alley', as it was being called. Watson, like everyone else, hated the rockets, finding they produced an unusual whimpering fear in him that the incendiaries and high explosives had not. On nights when the rockets fell and Watson was all alone in that big house – for there could not always be guests around – he would lie on the ground and bite down on the carpet until the ordeal was over. 'The doodles are so bad for the stomach,' he remarked to a friend.

KICKING WHILE THEY'RE DOWN

It was in June that Natasha Spender became pregnant for the first time, and by the time the baby was due to arrive the country was under siege from a new weapon, the noiseless V2. As was now a familiar story, there had been a brief period of a couple of weeks at the end of July and beginning of September when Londoners had thought themselves free again. The army was overrunning the missile launching sites and Germany, it seemed, was all but defeated. William Sansom describes what happened next:

> On 8 September, with no warning, a shattering explosion punctuated the afternoon. It was a curious explosion, a double thunder-clap, followed by the noise of a remote and aerial express train. The streets speculated. No warning? No news in the paper? Then perhaps an arms factory exploded? A gasholder? Sabotage on some military road?

But news spread quickly through the city in wartime, from person to person. It was, people heard, the first long-range rocket. They also heard, wrongly, that the crater was a quarter of a mile across, that each warhead packed in twenty-five tons of explosives – that a new 'freezing explosive' had been introduced to the fight. The seeds of these rumours had been laid by German radio.

According to John Lehmann, these were 'much worse than the doodle-bugs'. It was their 'unpredictable imminence' which made them so awful, the fact that, because there was no warning, one could sit for hours contemplating a sudden death and bracing constantly for impact. 'It was uncomfortable to feel that one might at any moment, perhaps without even a second's warning, be hurled in fragments into eternity,' Lehmann wrote. The attacks from the V2s were the first to completely prevent him from working. During this period of his wife's pregnancy, when explosions could be heard throughout London, Spender would be 'conscious of the angels of death outside, riding the night skies, and the child in the womb'.

The V2 attacks reached their peak in March 1945, the same month that Natasha went into labour, at a hospital in Hammersmith.

Then, for the final time, things began to wind down. In his book *Citizens in War - and After,* Spender described the spectacle of the city waking up again after the final air raid: 'Light trickles drop by drop like water into the great tank of fire and smoke and broken glass and rubble which is a city. Gradually the whole sky fills with pale watery light . . . People who have not slept turn over and sleep for an hour.'

As peace and freedom came within touching distance, Londoners who had survived multiple periods of bombardment feared that they would be taken, cruelly, in the final moments. A new neurosis flourished, the anxiety against being killed by 'the last bullet'. But Germany was done; 'one after the other,' Lehmann wrote, 'the walls of Hitler's empire were breached, and the Allied troops poured into their victorious meeting among the ruins.' Christopher Isherwood wrote a letter to Lehmann from California which ended 'Dare one begin to say "Till we meet"?'

An entry in Isherwood's diary written in the weeks after the final V1s and before the V2s shows that he was feeling tremendous guilt about the contrast in his own and his friends' situations. 'What have I done today, to express my solidarity with such people?' he asked himself, 'Nothing':

> Only one hour of meditation. And only an hour and a half yesterday.
> I ought to be ashamed of myself. Or rather, I ought to *do* something.
> Just being ashamed is worthless, is even bad, because negative.
> Aren't I reverting to the masochistic self-flagellation of my twenties?

Isherwood was still hung up on the events of 1939 in a way that Auden was not. He remained introspective and embarrassed about the decisions and fallout of the 'Auden-Isherwood affair'. But, really, he had not known the half of it. Isherwood had only recently been able to get his hands on a copy of Connolly's broadcast for India on 'Literature of the Nineteen Thirties' (containing his criticism of Spender's poetry); it had been lent to him by some friends. Almost three years on, he was finding out the jury's verdict on his charges: by Connolly's reckoning, he and Auden, as artists, had been 'perfectly free to go and live where they liked . . . though as leaders of a literary-political movement they have done untold harm to their cause by remaining there'. Isherwood felt that Connolly's talk handled the subject 'fairly and intelligently'. He wrote Connolly a long response – assuming he could still remember what he had said – which attempted to explain how the situation of his leaving had been just as confusing for himself as for his friends watching on. Isherwood's mantra in the 1930s had been 'never stop moving', but the assurance it afforded him was similarly transient. Beyond that was a world of conflicting responsibilities – the awareness of different personal relationships pulling in opposite directions – which daunted by its terrific scale and sense of possibility. Once he was in America, and the war had begun, that inability to say just what it was he wanted from life – always his safety mechanism – had begun to protect him in a different way. For the first time, the way to shirk his responsibilities was to stay put, rather than to flee. 'There was cowardice,' Isherwood wrote to Connolly, not about the air raids but about the need, were he to return to England, to justify himself – to say who Isherwood was and what he stood for. There would be no option, back home in the thick of things, to be a pacifist and hide behind the tenacity of others. Then the 'press attacks' had come, which only hardened his cowardice and defiance. At one point there was a fifty-fifty chance whether he would remain in America or return to his country of origin; 'I delayed,' Isherwood explained, 'because that is always easiest.'

Isherwood's vocal sense of regret went a long way to placating his friends at home. They were also pleased to hear that he did intend to write again. He would not have, he said, if he had not been introduced to Hindu philosophy. But with radical changes in Christopher's life came a radical new perspective on the London literary scene which would have been shocking to those who had never left it: 'As for the "literary-political movement" to which you say I have done "untold harm",' he wrote to Connolly, 'thank God I have.' They had advertised themselves and convinced everyone they represented a movement; as Isherwood wrote, 'a certain childishness in myself . . . enjoyed the fuss and helped it develop.' Now they would all sink or swim on their own.

And then, suddenly, Auden was in town. He was on his way to Germany to assist in a survey which judged the effects of Allied bombing on German morale, and knocked on the door of Lehmann's flat one Sunday morning in full American officer's uniform. Auden had arrived in much too upbeat a mood for a native population that was still stupefied from the bombs. And how many actually wanted to see him? As Lehmann wrote, 'he had torn up his English roots and replanted himself in America without, it seemed, a lingering glance of regret.' How much was he aware that he was now a controversial figure here? Auden's demeanour on that first visit assumed a level of intimacy, both with his old friends and their country, that most felt was now impossible. Lehmann had forgotten how egotistical he could be. 'I'm the first major poet to fly the Atlantic,' Auden declared, as if they had not just been through half a decade of war. Also, he bragged, the American Navy had ordered 1,100 copies of his collected poems. All came flooding back as Lehmann sat and listened to this 'Uncle Sam Auden' declaring the death of Britain and the superiority of American civilisation. It was the last thing anyone needed to hear.

17

City of Lights

Paris reminded Connolly of Jean, whom, for the rest of his life, he would never really get over. Though love came again in different forms, it was she who had defined it for him, and it was the period in the 1930s - much of which was spent in France - which had defined his life. Paris was 'the quiet of hotel bedroom and of empty lounge; the bed covered with clothes and magazines', laziness reciprocated by one's surroundings, the same way that, only with Jean, Connolly had found a harmony of hedonism, a symbiosis of squandering. Love demanded innocence and naivety, and Paris, in the early thirties, was as airily content as they came; it lived cheaply and knew everything and was completely free.

'We love but once,' Connolly wrote in *The Unquiet Grave*, 'for once only are we perfectly equipped for loving.' Once only do we get to be naive, and then we fall from innocence, and everything thereafter, however much it might try to force the matter, remains a parody of the thing that came first. So from June 1940 to August 1944, Paris, like the lover, had been chewed up and spat back out again. Connolly had spent the past few years daydreaming about everything he would do once the drawbridge was let down on the city, most of which involved picking up where he had left off, but if love could not happen twice then could Paris? The problem with all these 'Where Shall John Go?' submissions was that they assumed the world would still be there when they returned to it.

For a while now, *Horizon* had been depending on dispatches from British and American troops – as well as the occasional Resistance writer – to get a picture of the French capital. One of the first *Horizon* contributors to make it to France after the liberation, the future Labour politician Woodrow Wyatt who had been involved in the second wave of beach landings, had to field a long list of questions. And then, more gloatingly, there was Philip Toynbee, who teased that he was composing his article in the Café Flore while waiting to meet Sartre. Though providing an insightful survey of French literary activity in the four lost years of occupation, Toynbee inflamed the British inferiority complex by making hasty and unneeded comparisons between each country's recent output in different forms. 'I know that praise of France at the expense of England is a greatly hated activity,' Toynbee boasted, 'but after sixteen days in this astonishing Paris of September 1944, it is an activity which cannot honestly be avoided. In the literature of these four years France has been incomparably and undeniably superior.' The comparisons did not stop with literature. London, he wrote, was still an 'unliberated' city; in Paris, 'the galleries are opening, the bookshops are anything but bare, the people are a thousand times more alive than London people.' Sure, there had been changes – the price of wine had gone up to 20 francs a glass, for one – but these were superficial. Toynbee's assessment, Jeremy Lewis writes, was probably 'music in Connolly's ears', confirming his doctrine (a convenient one for covering his own back) that writing was impossible in England yet flourished across the Channel.

John Lehmann was less pleased. He had worked harder than anyone during the war to keep the British literary machine working, and now penned a response to Toynbee urging a less excitable judgement of British writing. 'It is gratifying . . . to know that the hopes we have entertained that France's literary traditions were too strong to be withered by the defeat of 1940 have been so amply justified in the event,' Lehmann began. But this achievement did not have to come at the expense of Britain's own. Toynbee wrote that he had been in Paris for only sixteen days – was it even possible, Lehmann wondered, for him to have read all the works that he was now wielding over their British counterparts? He could give a long list of British titles which would stand up in any comparison, like, for instance, T. S. Eliot's *Four Quartets*, published by Faber between 1940 and 1942. The point, however, was that it shouldn't be a comparison. Arthur Koestler had been observing this almost hysterical level of Francophilia through the duration of the war; 'a single word like *"bouillabaisse"*, *"crève-coeur"*, *"patrie"* or *"midinette"*,' he joked, 'is enough to produce the most violent spasms.'

The long German occupation of France had ended with a final struggle in August 1944, and in January of the next year Connolly stepped off a plane in Paris to an icy chill and a thick layer of snow on the ground. As interested as he was in everything that had been, and was, going on in Paris, he had been impatient to start his life again. He confided in Lys that the plan was to 'live intensely for the next ten years, accepting every pleasure and new experience that comes [my] way'. All questions of writing were to be deferred to the 'best' years of his life – say, between fifty-six and seventy-six. It was a risky plan, and Connolly knew it was the wrong one. In *The Unquiet Grave*, published at the end of 1944, he had been upfront about his own failures as a writer, and admitted that, in his life, only producing a masterpiece would be of any value. 'No other task is of any consequence,' he wrote. For now those thoughts could be pushed to the back of his mind. Connolly was the first writer in London to be given permission to visit France on grounds of journalism, despite the fact that war was still being waged only 150 miles away in the Ardennes.

The heavy snow transformed Paris into a northern city, and Connolly imagined himself on the Eastern rather than the Western Front of the war's shrinking radius. It was deserted, as if something big was coming or had only recently left, and, in a sense, that was true. The presence of the Germans could still be felt all over the city, the same way their planes would still haunt the skies of London after they had been withdrawn. No nostalgia was triggered when he walked on Paris's fabled streets; it was as if the pavements and buildings had been retrained to answer to the footfall of the German officer's boot, rather than the sounds of civic exultation. This was particularly true of the Rue des Saussaies, Rue du Cherche-Midi and Rue Lauriston where the Gestapo had had their headquarters. They would have to be reclaimed. When one sat in a café chair one felt the pressure on the wicker of past occupants who crossed their legs in billowing grey jodhpurs rather than corduroys, and whose eyes trained the street for other reasons than simple pleasure. With business this slow, waiters could easily be pulled aside and their stories of occupation drawn out. There were even people who wanted the Nazis back. 'And yet,' Connolly wrote, 'the visit made me indescribably happy.'

To the outside observer in 1945, Paris seemed to have got the better end of the bargain than London. It was still largely as Connolly had left it - the buildings were white or golden as they were meant to be rather than stained black, and the streets had kept all of their teeth. Any setbacks seemed temporary, as if at any moment residents might begin to stick their heads out of doorways and realise with relief that everything was as it should be. This initial impression did not survive long under scrutiny. Below the surface, Paris was on its knees. Severe shortages of food and fuel had quelled the city's energy, meaning this uncharacteristically sharp winter weather could not have come at a worse time. Cafés could offer neither milk nor coffee, and went without electricity through the daylight hours. Of public transport, only an irregular Métro service ground on. All of this came after four years of being bullied and suppressed. 'One must first of all imagine every petty restriction under which we have chafed,' Connolly wrote in *Horizon*; 'rationing, call-ups, identity cards, black-out offences, form-filling, etc., as being imposed not by our Government but by our conquerors, with a curfew and a continuous parade of enemy uniforms thrown in.' It was Connolly's nightmare. Not once during the past five years of war had the British government stopped him from doing what he wanted to do.

But still Paris seemed like it could be reborn, in a way that London, at that time, did not. From abroad, 'London seemed utterly remote - a grey, sick wilderness on another planet.' It was exhausted, crippled by 'irritable lassitude, brain-fatigue, apathy and humdrummery'. Partly this was because the war had not yet ended there; V2s were still playing their mind games with the populace. But in Paris, the civilian virtues - personal relations, adult-minded seriousness, aliveness, love of the arts - still reigned. The values of the Resistance movement, which Connolly saw as an example of pure humanism, still set the tone, bringing the cafés to life even when there was no coffee. At the Café de Flore on the Left Bank, for instance, one could drink beer instead and find at a fixed location in the room Simone de Beauvoir. In Sartre's absence, de Beauvoir had shown Connolly a copy of her companion's manifesto for *Les Temps Modernes*, allowing him to take it back to England as a scoop for *Horizon*. The document seemed to represent some greater truth about Paris, and Connolly rejoiced at being around people who still thought there were debates to settle, questions to answer, and new places for literature to go. His exhilaration was partly at 'returning to a world of ideas'. 'For the English literary world,' he wrote, 'is not a world of ideas but of personalities, a world of clubs and honours and ancestor-worship and engagement books.' As for the French, in everything but ideas they travelled light. If you wished to meet one of their writers, you would find him among his fellow writers - a welcome change from London where 'personalities' had to be hunted for several weeks and 'finally corralled at bay under some formidable mantelpiece'.

The message from young, poor, brave Paris, as Connolly interpreted it, was that 'everything you love is still here': 'The ideas, buildings, books and pictures, the wine, the people, the trees. And they won't run away. Art and life are beginning again. The European orchestra is tuning up . . .' So that was that. All of Connolly's worries had been for nothing.

Back in London, Lys was covering for Connolly in his absence. *The Unquiet Grave* had been out for almost a month and was being sold as a limited paper-bound edition directly from the *Horizon* office on Lansdowne Terrace. They sold out quickly, with Sonia buying the last three copies for friends. *Horizon's* new printers at the Curwen Press were also taking orders for unbound 'wartime' copies, which came in thick and fast after the book was reviewed not just in the typical literary supplements but also in publications with universal appeal such as *Vogue* and the Australian men's magazine *Cavalcade*. There was a buzz around Connolly at this time which had followed him to Paris; as his hosts in the French capital, Duff and Diana Cooper, observed, the critic was 'fêted as tho' he were Voltaire returned'. Cecil Beaton had got in contact wanting to take Connolly's portrait again for the first time since 1942. The reason was clear: *The Unquiet Grave* had been published under the pseudonym of 'Palinurus', the mythical helmsman of Aeneas's ship who successfully steers his vessel past Scylla and Charybdis and other ocean perils, but who one night falls asleep at his post and is tossed overboard, and so there was a new Connolly identity for Beaton to capture. In Connolly's recasting of the Palinurus myth, however, he is engineer of his own fate, quitting because he does not want to succeed and resigning from 'the struggle'. That earlier picture, showing the *Horizon* editor reclining against a modernist desk with a spotlight shining through a glass ball of roughly the same proportions as his head, had suggested, simultaneously, the burdensome weight of the writer's brain and (in almost a pastiche of the *Armada Portrait* of Elizabeth I) the civic responsibility of the editor. How would Palinurus be cast? Connolly took the cessation of the bombs on London as absolving him of any surviving sense of national duty. However he had justified the trip to Paris to the wartime authorities, he found those promises easy to discard. After the first trip to Paris came another one, and then he and Peter Watson were off to Switzerland. Connolly bought an extravagant new dressing gown, and boasted of his brilliant tan. Lys stayed at home in Bedford Square through this time and she and Sonia redecorated the house and spent the evening entertaining writers. If they needed any help with *Horizon* they would write; otherwise, they got on with it themselves.

The most remarkable thing about *The Unquiet Grave* is the extent to which Connolly was aware of his faults. Everything he did, he claimed, was a struggle against his own personality: 'sometimes at night,' he wrote, 'I get a feeling of claustrophobia; of being smothered by my own personality, of choking through being in the world'. Connolly knew as well as the most mature, level-headed person how he needed to be and what he needed to do, but also that he would never be able to be or do those things. Lys was okay with him putting off his writing for a later stage of his life, but she could not allow him to give up on it altogether. 'The only time in eight years I have seen you completely happy was when you were writing and re-arranging *The Unquiet Grave*,' she implored him. Even in the case of *The Unquiet Grave*, the book almost did not happen. Connolly had been keeping a journal in three notebooks provided to him by the manager of the Curwen Press, though in a desultory way, and it was going to require a Herculean effort to

get the entries into any kind of order. It seems fairly likely that
he would not have bothered to do this himself. The manuscript
was typed out twice by Lys and Sonia and then the whole book
had to be reset: '*The Unquiet Grave* by now consisted of thirty long
galley proofs scissored into little pieces like a string of clown's
black sausages, covered with insertions and deletions and spread
out on the floor to be arranged and rearranged into a mosaic.' It
was a collaborative effort of the remaining *Horizon* employees. Lys
wrote to Connolly in France whenever an acquaintance - including elderly relatives and family friends - complimented Palinurus's
writing, but always neglected to mention her own contribution to
the book.

John Lehmann had felt twitches of envy watching Connolly go
off to Paris so soon after it opened up. His own travel permit had to
be worked much harder for, but eventually came through in September, a few months after the VE day celebrations in London.
Quite how Connolly had made such a frictionless exit in January
was a mystery to him. Lehmann's journey was more difficult in
every way. Instead of being delivered by plane, he faced a long and
slow passage by boat which ended with a long delay waiting for
the right tide to float them into the makeshift French port facilities.

The discomfort of his journey was forgotten as the first recog-
nisable landmarks appeared from the window of the train. It was
incredible, he briefly thought, not only that Paris had survived 'as
mistress of itself' but also that he was alive to see it. Those six years
of war had felt more like sixty, and the thing about a six-year-long
war was that as well as being a protracted period of hardship it
was also a sizeable portion of a lifetime. A lot had happened, both
relating to the war and in its own right. Lehmann had been with
Stephen Spender in his flat at Carrington House when Churchill's
voice came over the radio at three o'clock in the afternoon on Tuesday, 8 May. It was after Auden had come and gone, and Spender
admitted that his own meetings with the famous poet - one of his

oldest friends - had culminated in a 'violent row'. Auden had given him a similar lecture to the one Lehmann had received:

> He launched into a long lecture, quoting detailed statistics of pig-iron production and the industrial man-power graph, on the world power position after the war. Great Britain, her Dominions and Empire had apparently been liquidated, while the two giants, the USA and the USSR, towered over the world. Britain, in fact, was lucky to have survived the war at all . . . The second part of the lecture consisted of an exposé of the superiority of American culture.

Both agreed that there was, of course, some truth in Auden's prognosis of the post-war situation. But that did not stop it feeling 'like a jab from a blunt hypodermic needle'; naturally, both were hyper-sensitive at that time to any hint of superiority. So as Churchill's closing statement drifted up from the wireless - 'Advance, Britannia! Long live the cause of freedom! God save the King!' - Lehmann and Spender sat together, as they had six years ago when the news announced Germany's invasion of Poland, discussing the betrayals by their closest friends.

That evening, though carrying a suitcase and destined for a late train from Paddington, Lehmann had taken a detour through Hyde Park to see the crowds on the Mall. They were more dazed than excited, he thought, and awkward about celebrating. They gathered and moved in a slow groundswell as if the city were revolving beneath their feet. Though Churchill had warned of further struggles lying ahead in the restoration of the country, no one was thinking about that. A final All Clear droned from the sirens and then died away forever. All that Lehmann felt confident in guessing for the future was that 'the two great Anglo-Saxon leaders, who had conducted us to victory with such skill and staunchness, should write the peace that would inaugurate the new age their inspiration promised us.'

It was late when Lehmann got to Paris. He was exhausted from his journey but wanted, before going to bed in his hotel, to take a quick walk down past the Madeleine to see the Place de la Concorde and the Champs Élysées again. 'I could not wait till the morning for that,' he remembered. The blackout in London had ended on 23 April, just after the liberation of the Bergen-Belsen camp and Richard Dimbleby's unforgettable BBC broadcast, but still Lehmann found himself drawn to lights which shone in the dark. A few lamps still burned along the Champs Élysées and seemed to usher him forwards. In the warm halo of their glow, he could just make out that the chestnut trees, standing in their obedient single file, were already shedding their leaves, and new, spring-green buds were beginning to sprout. Lehmann had forgotten that they did this, here.

He had business to get on with in Paris, and was kept busy going to and from the offices of magazines who wanted to acquire the translation rights to *New Writing*'s best stories and essays from the past six years. French publishers were also keen to scoop the rights for Christopher Isherwood's, Bill Sansom's and Henry Green's Hogarth books. One thing Lehmann did not get to see, which Connolly did, was the shooting gallery at Issy-les-Moulineaux, one of the Nazis' worst torture chambers near Paris. It was a closed asbestos shed in a field, and when Connolly went inside he was confronted with one of the most confounding sights of his life. Thousands of hand marks were printed deep in the material of the walls, creating an effect like an exaggerated pebbledash of peaks and slopes. Not one survivor had been found to explain the meaning of these impressions, Connolly noted. Nor was there an explanation for the 'huge furnace for blowing in hot air'. 'Only the bullet-torn posts at the end with their blood-stained rags attached to them told a clear story.' What the handprints seemed to say was 'We were here'.

The revelations from across the strata of Nazi internment camps continued to drive home the nightmarish unfathomability of the last six years. Lehmann saw that these evils had been able to assert themselves because other, vital principles had been neglected, such as 'the death or murder of the imagination, the atrophy of the faculty of considering others as oneself'. It was only that which held communities together – 'the deep instinctive belief, for it can never be proved by reason, that another man is as good as yourself' – and its grip was always feeble. The societies that managed to keep hold remained open and were perpetually renewed; those that let go became hierarchical and closed. Perhaps it was easier to let go.

In the meantime, while Connolly and Lehmann were rediscovering Paris, Spender had left the fire service (the various ailments which had threatened to keep him out in the first place were now presenting an unmanageable pain and difficulty) and moved to an intelligence branch of the Foreign Office. At the end of the war, he volunteered to join the occupying forces in the British zone of Germany.

Spender filed for his special travel permit giving his occupation as 'poet and journalist', no doubt seeing his future role in Germany as serving some more abstract ideological purpose. When the document came back to him, however, it had been over-stamped with the impersonal handle of 'government official'. It seemed to symbolise something. In the war, British writers had had to sell themselves as bureaucrats to be recognised as having any value whatsoever. Spender, until recently, had not even been able to do that. He travelled through Paris, where he was due to give a lecture on 'The Crisis of Symbols in Poetry', and, despite a lifelong dislike of France, felt for the first time the magnetism that had a hold on his friends. 'Paris springs at one and away from one with all its converging and radiating avenues, like an impulse of the mind,' he wrote. As John Sutherland has written, 'Coming as he did from bomb-torn London, with the "corpse cities" of Germany in prospect, [Spender] was entranced by the unruined beauty.' His

observations of Paris at this time are less superficial than Connolly's, and go further in explaining why it was that hope had
survived here and not in London. The French people, he thought,
were ashamed of their country. Collaboration had killed any sense
of national civic virtue, and it was common to hear the French
comparing themselves unfavourably to the British. The British,
they kept saying, had been able to bring their finest qualities of
self-sacrifice and mutual co-operation steadily to bear against the
pressure of the war. 'We, on the other hand, developed the worst
as well as the best qualities. It became a virtue to cheat, be dishonest and extravagant under the Germans.' Spender's French contacts
expressed their hope that England would apply its 'sane moderate way of life' to 'lead Europe out of a second abyss'. The French
economy was shot through with inflated German money and now
played second fiddle to the black market. There was genuine concern about whether France would be able to compete in a new era
of 'power politics'. The French were, however, able to see themselves as starting at 'year zero', and there was 'a strong urge to reach
towards a core of actuality'. Their disgrace would fuel their rebirth.

Spender found it difficult to explain to his French friends
everything that had happened in England. He told them about his
own work, about Auden and Isherwood having gone to America
- 'but I had the sense of something irreparable having happened.
Everything had been altered.' And it would go on altering. The
invisible barrier which Spender could feel, which kept the words
from forming in his brain, was the awareness of triviality, of
impermanency. The problem was not, simply, that societies could
be made to forget the rule 'that another man is as good as yourself',
but that all life, however hard one fought to mask this fact, was
'harnessed to inexorable laws of destruction and to the perversity
of human nature'. Everything that was good could, with further
alteration, be gone. As Spender put it, 'the Nazis had taught a whole
generation of people in the world that they were no longer young

and that they could not foster the hopes that young people have.'

When the Nazis arrived in power in 1933, Spender had been one of the country's most exciting new poets. Now, twelve years later, he was something of a veteran in this world. In his youth, he had chased always an ideal version of himself, and expected others - indeed, human life as a whole - to correspond to his idealised version of them. 'I imagined that there were people,' he wrote, 'who, through purity and innocence, or through self-discipline and asceticism, or through identifying themselves with a public cause, attained perfection.' Perhaps that could have been true, if they had lived in a vacuum, but 'since we live in time we are never complete'. He held friends to unattainably high standards. Auden and Isherwood's departure had, he said at the time, 'helped discredit the movement of the 1930s'. Really, it was the world which had done that. The movement - a rallying of the hopeful young - had been made bankrupt by world events.

Germany looked even worse than Spender had imagined. This had been his favoured country in the thirties, as Austria had been Lehmann's and France had been Connolly's. As he rode the train into Cologne there seemed to be not a single house left. Walls stood like thin masks 'in front of the damp, hollow, stinking emptiness of gutted interiors'. It took 'a real effort of the imagination' to conjure the city as he had known it well ten years before. Everything was gone.

Part of Spender's duties in Germany involved talking to as many people as he could. One conversation in particular stood out for him. He went to visit the rector of Bonn University, a Dr Konen, who lived in a house on a hill above the Rhine. In the course of their conversation, Spender brought up the supposition of everyone in England that, in Germany, 'the minds of the young were poisoned by Nazi teaching'. Dr Konen responded that it was more complicated than that: 'He said that the young were confused, spiritually starved but not poisoned in the simple and direct way that we imagined.' Those young people who had perceived an affinity between the Nazi truculence and their own disposition had immediately committed themselves, while most were reluctant to surrender their lives to endless duties and fatigues. Their families, too, had not wanted to see them disappear, body and soul, into the machine, with the loyalties of blood broken up. 'During the war many of my students have visited me,' Dr Konen explained, 'I can assure you that most of them have wanted nothing more from the future than a wife, a home and a job.'

It was the same story, everywhere, of young lives thrown off course, subsumed and eventually rubbed out. As Spender went to leave, Dr Konen stopped him at the door. 'I have every confidence that if I am asked to teach my students again, I shall be able to do so,' he said. Human beings would always be driven by intellectual need. A university, like the work of a poet, represented a certain benefit to the community.

The objective of Spender's mission to post-war Germany was, in a word, de-Nazification. Part of this, as some inspired civil servant had been astute enough to recognise, would involve reopening the public libraries. Spender was working at a particular library one day when the librarian, whom he was directing in this substantial task, summed up in a sentence what it was they had to do. 'I understand exactly what you want, Herr Spender,' she said, compliantly. 'I must take all the books by Nazis off the shelves and put them in the cellars, and bring up from the cellars all the books by Jews and put them on the shelves.' There was plenty of work to be done.

18

'Where are the war poets?'

Deep with the first dead lies London's daughter,
Robed in the long friends,
The grains beyond age, the dark veins of her mother,
Secret by the unmourning water
Of the riding Thames.
After the first death, there is no other.

'A Refusal to Mourn the Death, by Fire, of a Child in London',

Dylan Thomas

With the long-drawn-out conclusion of the war, the gradual opening up of the world. Cities further afield than Paris - Athens, Prague, Warsaw, New York. These pockets and promontories, cut off for over five years, now wanted to know what had been going on elsewhere. It fell to editors like Lehmann, Spender and Connolly to fill them in; invitations to speak at international conferences flew in from every direction, with the same hungry demand for 'British wartime literature'.

If you had been editing literary magazines during the war, as these three had, you were used to this question. Your job had been to bring out the best in British wartime literature, to compensate for its deficiencies; whether you felt you had been successful in doing so was another question. Lehmann, for one, intended to give the international audience a picture of formidable achievement. It was an argument he knew by heart, and thus had ready whenever he felt the 'bellicose and polemical impulses' begin to stir in him. The names rolled easily from his tongue: George Orwell, Henry Green, Rosamond Lehmann, Elizabeth Bowen, Edith Sitwell, Alun Lewis, Roy Fuller, Louis MacNeice . . . 'Don't forget that T. S. Eliot completed his great sequence of meditations on the meaning of time, art and God, the *Four Quartets*, during those years,' he would say. The stickier debates were always around poetry, which, Lehmann writes, became an obsession of 'the nostalgic elderly schoolmasters and the vulgarians of what is now called The Establishment, whose cry in 1939 had been "Where are the war poets?"'

The problem wasn't the lack of names, however, but that these names had to be listed in the first place. Every person he addressed at these lectures, were they asked to name a war poet or poem, would likely have relapsed to the First World War. Perhaps they would have landed on Rupert Brooke's 'The Soldier':

If I should die, think only this of me:
That there's some corner of a foreign field
That is forever England.

Or Laurence Binyon's 'For the Fallen'. Lehmann himself - like Auden and Spender - had been obsessed with Wilfred Owen. As might surprise some, Owen, in this scenario, was an exception. He was not a 'First World War poet' in the sense that his poems had defined the war for contemporary readers. The majority of Owen's poetry had been published posthumously, from 1920 onwards, following his death on the Sambre-Oise Canal a week before Armistice Day. Their greatest effect, therefore, was on readers such as the aforementioned. These were Lehmann and Auden and Spender's formative years, and as a teenager Owen's angry expressionism had been a worldview in itself. Poems like 'Dulce Et Decorum Est' were political and confrontational but with that level of control that makes some lines a shout and others an undertone through gritted teeth. More so, perhaps, than that, they were clear and persuasive in their arguments. For readers now they are graphic, visceral and immediate enough to actually *be* the First World War. Wilfred Owen was a later poet than, for example, Brooke, in that his limited oeuvre begins in 1916, and covers the period of the Battle - or battles - of the Somme. He is a poet, then, of the gruesome war of attrition which came to define the conflict, when, as Lehmann writes, 'fighting men were treated simply as numbers to be expended'. Those poems will never cease to be shocking to readers.

'The Soldier' and 'For the Fallen' were both written in 1914. Brooke was working on his *1914 Sonnets* - what Lehmann calls 'his only true war poems' - actually while in training. These were 'undeniably skilful and mellifluous,' Lehmann wrote, but also 'hit exactly the right note'; up until that moment, the country had been seeking its youthful and idealistic hero who in all aspects - his stoicism, his beauty, his artistic flair - seemed to embody its dreams 'of a just war against ruthless enemies'.

Even at the time, Brooke's eagerness to fill that role had struck his fellow poets as disingenuous. He had, they observed, taken charge of his own image. According to Charles Hamilton Sorley, he was 'far too obsessed with his own sacrifice, regarding the going to war of himself (and others) as a highly intense, remarkable and sacrificial exploit, whereas it is merely the conduct demanded of him . . . by the turn of circumstances'. Brooke had other things working to his advantage besides his strange willingness for martyrdom. He was, Lehmann wrote, 'preternaturally good-looking', and could be, therefore, not only an emotional touchpoint for the conflict but also a physical symbol of British virtue. And Brooke had friends in high places; in 1912, following a falling-out with much of the Bloomsbury Group, most notably Lytton Strachey, he had begun to move in more influential, 'public' circles. This would come into play later on. Brooke's fame was fast-tracked when the *Times Literary Supplement* ran 'The Soldier' alongside another of his sonnets, 'The Dead', in their March 1915 issue, and then the first of those poems was picked by the Dean of St Paul's, William Ralph Inge, to feature in his Easter sermon. He had, he said, 'just read a very beautiful little poem' on the subject of the posterity of those men lying in 'hastily made graves in a foreign land' - a sonnet by a young writer 'who will, I venture to think, take rank with our first poets'. 'So potent is a time of trouble to evoke genius which might otherwise have slumbered,' Inge added, as an aside.

Less than three weeks later, Brooke was dead. He had developed pneumococcal sepsis from an infected mosquito bite while at sea with the British Mediterranean Expeditionary Force and passed away on a French hospital ship moored off the Greek island of Skyros. Winston Churchill, then First Lord of the Admiralty and one of Brooke's 'friends in high places', was put in charge of the obituary in *The Times*. 'He expected to die,' Churchill wrote, 'he was willing to die for the dear England whose beauty and majesty he knew.' Churchill's description of Brooke's mindset in his final moments was developed from the blueprint provided by 'The Soldier' - he died, it was told, in 'perfect serenity, with absolute conviction of the rightness of his country's cause'. Nonetheless, a life 'ha[d] closed at the moment when it seemed to have reached its springtime'.

It is difficult to judge the effect of premature death on literary legacy, and would be crude to suggest it is any kind of guarantee of public or critical attentiveness. In the case of Alun Lewis, perhaps the soldier-poet of the Second World War most in the vein of a Wilfred Owen or Siegfried Sassoon, the sentiment, upon his suicide in Burma in March 1944, was that here was a career that had not been allowed to reach its full potential. All of the newspapers said the same thing: 'We have lost a young writer of exceptional promise' (*Western Mail*); 'a poet of considerable promise' (*Liverpool Echo*). This was despite almost every newspaper reporting his death as 'on the battlefield'. It was also widely reported that Lewis, for his short-story collection *The Last Inspection*, had been posthumously awarded the John Llewellyn Rhys prize for 'best book of the year'. But this was not enough; still the myth-making concoction was lacking vital ingredients. Lewis was not to be branded one of the country's 'noblest sons', as Churchill said of Brooke.

Laurence Binyon's 'For the Fallen', perhaps the most famous war poem ever written, is an interesting study. Binyon was a 'survivor'; he lived through the Great War and went on to contribute to *Horizon* before his death after an operation in 1943. Though already in his mid-forties in 1914, Binyon had, in 1916, gone out to the Western Front as a Red Cross orderly. As with Brooke, however, his celebrated war writing had actually begun well in advance of any battlefield experience. 'For the Fallen' was a poem of 1914, written during a visit to the north Cornwall coast; it was a reaction to reports in the newspapers of escalating casualties on the continent. Binyon would go on to write with the same craft and cool-headedness about his actual, first-hand experiences with the Red Cross - so why 'For the Fallen' and not 'Fetching the Wounded'? We can see now that there was a brief window at the beginning of the conflict when the nation was thirsting after poetry which reflected back its own image - and its image of the war - in the most complimentary light; by 1916, the realities of the war had become difficult to stomach, and reading contemporary poetry was as depressing as reading the newspaper.

It is one of the poems Binyon published in *Horizon*, in 1942, titled 'The Burning of the Leaves' and collected as 'The Ruins', that is now considered to be his true masterpiece. But 'The Burning of the Leaves' is nothing at all like 'For the Fallen'. It is a meditation on both physical and spiritual solitude, describing, in falling cadences, a private depression which supersedes public or national grief. Binyon was seventy-four by this point, and represents himself with a 'stooping and feeble . . . old man' haunted by 'memory's golden land' in a present which seems to be disassembling everything worthwhile that humanity has built. The final line of the poem is 'The world that was ours is a world that is ours no more.' Less than seven months after its publication in *Horizon*, Connolly was writing Binyon's obituary alongside those of the younger dead, like Rollo Woolley, whose plane had been shot down in Tunisia (Woolley had had one short story, 'The Pupil', published in the magazine, and was found after his death to have filled a page in his journal with the words, in large capital letters, 'MY STORY PUBLISHED IN HORIZON'). Binyon's poem had been universally cherished by *Horizon* readers (indeed Connolly thought it was the best they had printed) and received similar glowing tributes from critics at other publications, including the reviewer in the *New Statesman* who judged that he had now written the finest poems of both wars. The disparity in the fates of two poems here becomes pitifully rudimentary: 'For the Fallen' had been published in *The Times* newspaper and thus reached the entire nation; 'The Burning of the Leaves' travelled only in a literary magazine.

In September 1944, Dylan Thomas had been hunkering down at the Thomas family's new 'house' in New Quay - a little wood-and-asbestos 'pagoda' conjuring images of the American frontiers - while the flying bombs were driving a further one million people out of London. Donald Taylor, at Strand Films, had said that if Thomas felt he were able then he had no objection to him working on his scripts from outside of London. So occasionally Thomas would check back in for news, asking Taylor, on the nineteenth of that month, for example, 'Has V2 really arrived? Here there are rumours.'

But there is something more remarkable going on in Thomas's letters of this time. He was filling them with poems – some light-hearted, poking fun at his neighbours in Wales or the high-mindedness of London, others teasing and nostalgic. There was one to the hard-drinking Welsh art critic Tommy Earp which ended 'Is there a chance of one I never see/Coming up, also? Write me: Ever . . . D.', but which otherwise contained all the complex symbolism, dark imagery and linguistic smashing and juggling of a Thomas poem (what he called 'good old 3-adjectives-a-penny belly-churning Thomas'). So he was back in Wales and the poetic part of his brain, now uncorked, was pouring generously again. Caitlin had been exactly right in her analysis of London and the home country's contrasting effects on Thomas's writing. Earlier that year, Thomas had written 'Ceremony After a Fire Raid'. Now, in quick succession, came 'Holy Spring' and 'Vision and Prayer', the latter written in twelve stanzas shaped either like diamonds or hourglasses. Then 'Poem in October'. He continued at this pace, working 'among cries and clatters like a venomous beaver in a parrot house', right into 1945.

On 28 March of that year, his best friend, Vernon Watkins, received a strange letter. It described what is now a central anecdote in Dylan Thomas lore. Three weeks earlier, Thomas had been out at the Black Lion pub with film-writing colleagues from London when intermittent verbal confrontations with a local man, William Killick, on leave from a commando station in Greece, escalated into a punch-up. Paul Ferris supplies the context for the tension brilliantly: '[Killick] had spent a year living in caves with a gun in his hand. Now the clever people were laughing among themselves, showing no respect for a fighting man.' One of those 'clever people' was Killick's wife, Vera, described by Thomas as 'a girl who lives on cocoa and books on third-century brass', whom

Killick suspected of being in some kind of clandestine pact with the Thomases. Thomas had left the Black Lion that evening knowing full well he had come off second best in the fight, but anticipating no further trouble. It was not until he and his friends had settled back in at the pagoda house, to have a drink with Caitlin, that they realised the extent of the commando's paranoia and pent-up aggression. Thomas and his guests were caught – 'innocently,' he told Watkins – 'in a Case of Attempted Murder, Caitlin, I, and three others being the attempted murderees'. All of a sudden, volleys of bullets from a Sten gun had begun to puncture the 'paper-thin walls', missing the adults 'by inches' and Aeronwy, the Thomas's infant daughter then asleep in a cot, 'by feet'. It was Killick, stumbling around the property blind drunk in sunglasses and hoping to give the occupants a scare. He had then burst inside, waving both his gun and a grenade, and declared Thomas and his entourage to be 'nothing but a lot of egoists'. The murder attempt had fizzled out once all of Killick's ammunition had been sent through the room's asbestos shell and out into the New Quay night. It was like the final flick of the tail – a sting experienced vicariously through Killick's erratic mental state – of a war that Thomas had always managed to avoid. 'At debts' and death's door I now stand with a revolving stomach, waiting for V1000 and the Bubonic Plague,' Thomas wrote to Watkins.

That letter to Watkins, casually scandal-bearing and classically Dylan though it was, had surprisingly also come packaged with new poems. These were the masterful 'A Winter's Tale', which pre-empted the shadowy omniscience of *Under Milk Wood* with its refrain of 'Listen . . .', 'The Conversation of Prayers', 'This Side of the Truth' and, finally, 'A Refusal to Mourn the Death, by Fire, of a Child in London'. By now Thomas had the best part of a new collection ready to go. More significantly, the poems that he was collecting appeared, one after another, to be filling a similar mould. The war was forcing itself into the limelight of his poetic world.

Evidently it was the bombs that got Thomas going. For this recent flurry he had the flying bombs to thank, those 'things that scream up into the stratosphere . . . and then pour down on to Manresa Road', the flat they still kept in London. In January 1941, 'Deaths and Entrances' – which would provide the title for the coming collection – had represented the more modest fruits of the first Blitz, and then nothing for several years. Of the new crop, 'The Refusal to Mourn the Death, by Fire, of a Child in London' ticked the most boxes as a potentially canonical 'war poem'. Its theme was grief, of the public and shared kind, and it was quotable. What separates a poem like 'The Refusal to Mourn . . .' from, say, 'Deaths and Entrances', is really only its final line. For the latter, Thomas had been unable to resist the urge of mystification that Caitlin saw as his own brand of mischief. Now the game-playing had stopped: Thomas was pushing to make sense of the war, and he wanted to give that knowledge to his readers. The conclusion he settled on was 'After the first death, there is no other.'

He had said, early on, that he 'want[ed] to get something out of the war'. He had felt its pull, specifically the temptation, in the pubs, on Saturday nights

> to want to allow myself to get that fuggy, happy, homosexual feeling and eat, sleep, get drunk, march, suffer, joke, kill and die among men, comrades, brothers, you're my pal, I'm with you son, back to back, only die once, short life, women and children, here's a photograph of my wife, over the bloody, down the bloody, here's to the bloody, shit and blood.

But the man who would hide under the covers whenever he heard planes coming over, and who now, after Killick's attack, went to bed under the bed, was clearly not fit for any 'brothers in arms' scenario. The desire to help in some capacity, however, was genuine, and it was a desire that was shared by nearly all the writers in this book. Thomas's war had begun with a frantic search for work (including his inauspicious attempt to join 'Cazalet's battery') and ended with the fruits of that search, namely a full-time job in which his creative brain was reprogrammed to advertise government schemes and direct public opinion. He had experienced none of Henry Green's 'lulls', which seemed to have a muse-like effect on writing, and which presumably came into play in the inconceivably long and spirit-flattening months spent by Wilfred Owen on the Somme; nor could he, like Waugh, decide to give himself a sabbatical. Within that desire to contribute to the war was contained the belief, sheepishly unexpressed, that perhaps the writer might be able to contribute by writing. Kenneth Clark had been able to bring the painters in, but the writers were left out in the cold. Whether or not this was linked to deep state aims to curtail the leftward ideological drive spearheaded by writers during the Spain years, as Spender and Orwell had discussed, is unclear.

It was suggested, earlier in this book, that any claim Thomas had to being a 'war poet' – even a 'civilian war poet' – had been jeopardised by his absence from London at some of its key moments, and the blasé attitude which seemed to accompany his comings and goings. With this late blaze of poem-writing, however, Thomas seemed to be saying that he had, in fact, been paying attention all along. In the minds of foreign readers, there was little doubt that the young Welshman was a central figure in the reaction of Britain's writers to the war. In 1942, Thomas had begun to correspond with the American poet and anthologist Oscar Williams, regarding some poems recently published in *Horizon*. Williams had then been working with the Connecticut publisher James Laughlin, founder of New Directions Publishing, who wished to reproduce some of Dylan's poetry for American readers for his series 'The Poets of the Year'. By the end of 1944, Williams was writing to Thomas for his own sake. Months before the fighting would stop, he had already embarked on what must be the first anthology of Second World

War poetry. He was asking for contact information for reprinting rights, as well as enticing writers to send him a paragraph or two of their thoughts on 'war and poetry'. Perhaps, again, to the detriment of his 'war poet' legacy, Thomas seemed reluctant to portray himself as serving any higher purpose in his poetry. 'I shan't know until I start writing whether I have any clear ideas on this, or on any other, subject,' he replied. 'I prefer what I think about verse to be *in* the verse.' Williams chose four of Thomas's poems, most of them already discussed, to feature in his anthology; he also chose five by Stephen Spender.

Williams had enough ideas of his own to cover all of his contributors. His introduction to *The War Poets* provides an invaluable insight into the unique mindset of the Second World War writers. He begins by challenging the assumption, by those working in the popular press and a general public 'unfamiliar with the publications in which good modern verse is likely to appear', that the Second World War had not produced fine war poems: 'The trouble is that the popular press is not "where" real poetry is to be found. The general run of periodical editors fears to print anything but sentimental versifying on the premise that good poetry is over the heads of their readers.'

Clearly, there was not going to be any 'sentimental versifying' on this occasion. Where war was concerned, that impulse had died before 1916. Moreover, none of the mutations of the poetic form since that time had had the purpose of simplification. As we have seen, Connolly and many others of his generation had railed against the quaintness and fanciful naivety of Georgian poetry (a typification which certainly denoted Rupert Brooke) - their Milky Way had at its centre *The Waste Land*, and vers libre read in translation. But as Williams acknowledged, it was 'sentimental versifying' that the general public at least thought they wanted, and believed they were missing. Were they to be polled, the average person in the street would say that there was too much technical innovation in modern poetry, and not enough plain language; modern poets wrote in a 'private language' and therefore could not commune with a nation. Williams believed that people could be convinced otherwise:

> The best living poets, far from being more private in language than poetasters, fully use speech-terms and images drawn from daily contemporary life, whereas the poetasters luxuriate in obsolete language (and now pretentious sentiment) copied from the poets of past times, surely much more of a private academic lingo than the normal vocabulary of daily life.

This is true, but perhaps misses the point. The 'private language' that the general public took issue with was not vocabularic but rather the messages which had to be scrutinised to be understood. One wonders how much language really comes into it. As T. S. Eliot said of Kipling's 'Mandalay', a poem which was 'best when read aloud', 'the ear require[d] no training to follow [it] easily'. It could be - and was - repeated by heart in a vague way which made inferences on the specific vocabulary from the bumps and dips of the metre. It did not matter whether every word was correct, because each phrase, taken in isolation, would boil down to the same raw ingredient. The message of the poem is clearly established within the first two, or four, lines and then declines any detours for the duration: Britain has the largest empire of the world - a fact which proves its supremacy - and the British 'character' has its place in all corners of the globe. A poem like Spender's 'Air Raid', published in *Horizon* at the fearful climax of the Blitz, would not only be very difficult to commit to memory, but also, crucially, replaces the emphasis on words. Words, here, are not simply there to reinforce the sentiment of the opening couplet; each new one can cast doubt on or directly contradict the last. The poem constructs a detailed and accurate image, one that almost every person in the country at that time would have recognised, of a family home opened up to the street and a ringing telephone with no one left to answer it, and makes room for the reader's own reflections. Williams is suspicious of Rupert Brooke's approach, which seems to view words as a potential distraction from the message, and in doing so quietly disarms the reader of their right to questioning or a response. A passage like the one quoted earlier in this chapter 'divert[s] the attention of the reader from any mental image of the soldier's mangled body to the concept of the soldier's placid acceptance of being a bit of soil "for ever England".' Was this a kind of 'bad patriotic' manipulation, Williams wonders, or was it a realisation that 'most people do not have the courage to face honestly the facts of others' intense suffering'? 'It is easier to have the attention diverted, conscience soothed, and the guilt of responsibility converted into a conviction that the suffering is justified since it is in a noble cause,' he writes.

One can imagine a parallel universe where Thomas's phrase 'After the first death, there is no other' is quoted as readily and widely as 'They shall not grow old, as we that are left grow old', as a pacifist motto. At the time, however, though it would have given clarity to private mental sensations, there was no use for it to be blown up any larger. Thomas's line is a concluding line both in the poem and for war poetry - for any kind of reflection about war - in general. It attempts to close a long period of deliberation in which the meaning and implications of war were picked over endlessly. War is death, destruction and boredom, nothing else, Thomas says. It is a statement of weariness, and one suspects that this is how it connected with readers, who were then experiencing the same trundling mental and physical exhaustion, bodies on the verge of giving up, as the poet himself. There was little use in continuing to consciously mourn if nothing was going to change.

The poetry of the First World War was poetry of disbelief - disbelief in the circumstances of a war whereby over half a century's industrial, scientific and technical progress had been turned, viciously, on the destruction of human bodies. Siege guns emptying men from waterlogged trenches, poison gas, belt-fed machine guns, planes with synchronised machine guns, armour-plated tanks – all of this was new to the world in 1914-18, and seemed to show the direction of travel in this monstrous twentieth century. There was no committee or sponsorship fund pushing tired pencil to crumpled paper; the phenomenon of the widespread poetic outpouring was organic. The shock at finding oneself each day in worsened circumstances, the constant fear both for oneself and for humanity as a whole, was the stimulus for what we can think of as introspection put on record. The carnage and stalemate of the later battles 'could not fail to have its effect on the minds of the intelligent and articulate soldiers in the field,' wrote Lehmann.

For most of the individuals in this book – Virginia Woolf was right, in her 'Leaning Tower' lecture, to differentiate the experience of those in their thirties and forties from her own – the world seemed to have been waging war on itself almost constantly since their birth. Take Dylan Thomas, for instance, born 27 October 1914, almost four months to the day since the assassination of Archduke Franz Ferdinand. The fighting continued until he was four years old. Three months into his eighteenth year, Hitler was made chancellor of Germany. By the age of thirty he could say that a third of his life had been spent in world war. For George Orwell, our oldest male character, born 25 June 1903, and Cyril Connolly, his schoolmate, the First World War had been a persistent backdrop to their adolescent years, when they were old enough to comprehend its significance. Names of former Etonians only a few years older than themselves were added each year to the dedicatory plaques in the colonnade by the school's main quad. If the conflict was to go on indefinitely, as many feared it would, it would soon have been their names up there.

This is the sentiment of most of the poets who gave statements for Williams' book, that war was an almost permanent state of existence in the twentieth century and, after three decades, there was little more to be said on the subject. As the former *New Verse* editor Geoffrey Grigson put it, simply 'nothing new has happened in this war'. 'Men have been tortured, women have been murdered, explosives have exploded' - the same things that had been going on before. Grigson alludes to a letter by Rainer Maria Rilke 'in which he said that the whole possibility of human suffering has already been, and is always being, experienced'. The editor appends his own thoughts to this: 'It is the quantity, not the quality or depth of suffering, which has been increased by this war.' Williams had been unable to entice Thomas to give his views on poetry's current dilemma but had better luck with Vernon Watkins, an accomplished war poet in his own right and similarly worthy of study. Watkins seemed to feel that poetry was exactly where it needed to be; historically, as their sense of their own importance became inflated, poets tended to veer towards dishonesty. Watkins was obviously thinking about his war-writing antecedents when he proposed that 'the truest statements about war are made under one's breath, and the most false on public platforms. Bad art and false gods motivate war as much as national greed.'

The poets were just as 'unutterably weary' as everyone else, Alex Comfort had told Stephen Spender. He had been right to make his comparison not with the First World War but rather with Spain, a true 'struggle' as he envisaged it. As dire as the circumstances were, Spender had said that the Spanish conflict 'aroused hope all over the world'. The Second World War aroused no hope, just the slow drip of tedious, edging progress and the gritting of teeth until the danger had passed. As good as some of Spender's Second World War poetry is - both of his wartime collections had a section dedicated entirely to the war - one cannot escape the feeling that he had used up much of his analytical energy on the war in Spain.

'Thoughts During an Air Raid', rather confusingly a poem about Spain published at the beginning of the Second World War before the Blitz, opens, unforgettably, in a tone of irony:

> Of course, the entire effort is to put myself
> Outside the ordinary range
> Of what are called statistics. A hundred are killed
> In the outer suburbs. Well, well, I carry on.

A younger poet perhaps feels more confident in their ability to make on-the-spot judgements. A younger Spender would certainly have felt more comfortable putting thoughts to paper in a quick turnaround, compensating for the deficiencies of those thoughts with clever language. Contemporary critics like Kathleen Raine, however, had been pushing him towards a more clearheaded handling of complexity. He seems to have heeded this advice, the same way that, back at university with his mentor W. H. Auden, he had been told to abandon his practice at the time of writing four poems every day and go for one every three weeks. So in 1949 the world was treated to a second wave of Spender war poems, written in a peaceful moment after the dust had settled, comprising some of his most unique and marvellous efforts of a two-decade career. 'Rejoice in the Abyss' collects the lingering impressions of his time at Maresfield substation and of the flying bombs coming down around the Freud house, and describes the dead from all of human history floating above the rooftops of London in the icy night and appearing indifferent to the fates of the lives yet being played out below. Then, in the final stanza of 'Epilogue to a Human Drama', he seems finally to arrive at a conclusion to a decade's worth of thinking about the war. It is a parting word, his last on the subject, which, like Prospero's speech to Ferdinand and Miranda, attempts to summarise all of the various parts played in the saga of wartime - the heroes, maidens, fools, victims and chorus. Now, the victims await the pickaxes of the heroes to break through the rubble that entombs them, bringing sun and water. The chorus assists by providing cups of tea. All, in their way, represent an unshakeable underlying morality.

THE END OF AN ERA

Horizon lasted until Christmas of 1949, exactly a decade after its inception, by which point Connolly seemed quite happy to kill it off. As people settled into their reshuffled post-war positions (with a new Labour government and Germany cut up like a cake and handed around) and the world at least donned the clothes of a new era, Connolly began to feel that the magazine had become too synonymous with the slow dénouement of the conflict, and the potential troubles that would follow it. There was also, it seems strange to say, a curious kind of nostalgia for wartime *Horizon* coming from its readers. 'It is fashionable to exclaim that *Horizon* was much better in the war "when it really stood for something", and that it has gone off since,' Connolly wrote in his penultimate 'Comment'. This was not true, he felt; really, people had been happy to read almost anything during the blacked-out hours, and now they were unable to dedicate the same amount of time to appreciating its contents. But that was all by the by. He did not want to be trapped by the legacy of wartime, and he was starting to see how the role of an editor can become a dishonest one. British short-story writers, poets and essayists had recently all been surpassed by their American counterparts - Connolly blamed the 'decay of hope' - and it shouldn't be the job of an editor to paper over the absence of high-quality new writers. The same familiar hopefuls continued tirelessly with their pursuit of publication, but their pages were rejected 'by texture, smell, paperweave - heartlessly - because within a month they all will be back'. Often the task of sifting through the poetry drawer was delegated to 'a visiting poet who has dropped in for tea' - Connolly didn't care. At the end of the war *Horizon* had become a 'display window' for Sartre and Camus and other French writers, and if it continued it would be doing the same for American ones. In that scenario, Connolly would be getting everything second-hand. 'A decade of our lives is quite enough to devote to a lost cause such as the pursuit and marketing of quality in contemporary writing,' he reflected, with perhaps less bitterness than might be expected. 'In the end, despite all the good will in the world, the public gets the magazines it deserves.' Connolly told subscribers that he would be taking some time to focus on his own writing, but that was not really true: he never published another novel nor attempted a work of criticism as substantial as *Enemies of Promise.*

The 'inscrutable Forties' were over, and what had *Horizon*'s editor learned? He had been mulling this over for the final 'Comment':

> One can perceive the inner trend of the Forties as maintaining this desperate struggle of the modern movement, between man, betrayed by science, bereft of religion, deserted by the pleasant imaginings of humanism against the blind fate of which he is now so expertly conscious . . . 'Nothing dreadful is ever done with, no bad thing gets any better; you can't be too serious.' This is the message of the Forties from which, alas, there seems no escape, for it is closing time in the gardens of the West and from now on an artist will be judged only by the resonance of his solitude or the quality of his despair.

This was a private pessimism not necessarily representative of the humour of an entire nation or continent. Connolly's love life was doing the thing it always did - tangling him up in contradictory promises, pushing him to tears and his companions to psychoanalysts. His private life is carefully disguised in that penultimate

'Comment', where he tells readers that 'we have to quit our premises in Bedford Square at the end of this year and those who have
enjoyed offices in Bedford Square require immense energy to seek
them elsewhere.' He gives the impression that they were being
forced out - perhaps, like the Woolfs in Tavistock Square, the landlord had found a more commercial use for the property - but really
the issues were financial. Lys partly blamed Connolly's beloved
'mansion' for the breakdown in their relationship, writing to him
afterwards that 'If we could only have been a little more ordinary
in our way of life, we should both have been much happier.' She
went on:

> I need the reassurance of bourgeois comfort and am very good at
> supplying it. Little by little, all our values seemed to get wrong and
> we were both unhappy without knowing why. All that extravagant
> entertaining was an attempt - and a successful one - to avoid facing
> the issue, and led to the anxieties and discomforts of living beyond
> one's income.

All of this, in a way, makes the wartime achievements of *Horizon*
more impressive. As was often said at the time, no one in their
right mind would have started a literary magazine in 1939. Connolly, however, was 'the day dreamer . . . the escapist'. If he had
to run a magazine and keep a literary salon on credit then, fine,
so be it. Such practical considerations did not really exist to him,
anyway.

The final month covered by *Horizon*, January 1950, was the
month that George Orwell died. The timing was uncanny. Orwell
had been, along with only a couple of others, *Horizon*'s star turn.
Dedicated readers of the magazine would be able to chart his
progress to literary fame and esteem from the time of his first contribution 'Boys' Weeklies', the essay about which Peter Watson,
adjusting to his new circumstances in a literary rather than artistic

world, had asked Connolly, 'Please tell me who is George Orwell: his article is *splendid*.'

Connolly was now living in a shared house on Sussex Place, just north of Hyde Park near Paddington station, and his visits to his oldest friend at University College Hospital on Euston Road would therefore involve a tube ride or taxi up along the western edge of Bloomsbury, from which vantage point the area, contained within four intersecting roads, seemed surprisingly small, though bigger on the inside. Connolly had been shocked, thirteen years earlier, by the 'ravaged' appearance of his estranged classmate – the classmate who, by his generational genius, had more than repaid all of Connolly's earlier, potentially futile, support. What kind of figure did Connolly see now? Orwell had been under medical supervision, of one kind or the other, since the beginning of January the previous year. At UCH, he occupied room 65, where he tended to be found sitting upright in bed 'wrapped in an old camel-coloured woollen cardigan'. Orwell had the 'London chest'. The effect of this most recent bout of tuberculosis on his breathing and lucidity had rendered him incapable of any writing save for the occasional cursory letter. Connolly had been there on 13 October when a clergyman had come to officiate Orwell's marriage to Sonia Brownell, by which point his friend was said to have a fifty-fifty chance of survival.

In August 1945, two days after V-J Day, Orwell had published *Animal Farm*. He had followed it up, just over three years later, with *Nineteen Eighty-Four*, the book which, after reading it in typescript, Orwell's publisher Fredric Warburg had declared to be 'amongst the most terrifying books I have ever read'. Both novels seemed to be about the war that had passed, with the threat of Nazi invasion and all of the 'filth' Orwell had had to sift through at the BBC, but also the world as it appeared now, in its post-war state – hungry, threadbare, deteriorating, nostalgic for the old kind of paper you wanted to smell and run your finger across. After his death, Orwell would become a key name in the Cold War against his great nemesis Stalin - the real writers' war; the CIA would in 1955 drop copies of *Animal Farm* behind the Iron Curtain. So the figure Connolly looked down at in that hospital bed, who would soon be slipping away from them, who seemed to embody the massive scope of an unprecedented half-century in all of its wars and woe - that was what a war-writer looked like.

Notes and Further Reading

1. Long Goodbye

For Christopher Isherwood's memories of leaving London and travelling on the *Champlain*, see the opening chapter of his *Diaries: Volume One: 1939–1960* (Methuen, 1996) and the final chapter of *Christopher and His Kind* (Magnum Books, 1978). I used Peter Parker's *Isherwood: A Life* (Picador, 2005) for additional archival colour. The description of Isherwood's 'false, hysterical' spell in New York in 1938, as well as his relationship with Auden, can be found in the same place in his diaries. The phrase of Isherwood's, 'convenient ventriloquist's dummy', I found in the 8 March 1939 edition of the *Yorkshire Post*, though its actual source is the preface to *Goodbye to Berlin* (Vintage, 1989), p. viii. Isherwood's memories of the Munich Agreement are found in his unpublished earlier diaries, extracts of which are reprinted in *Down There on a Visit* (NEL Signet, 1968).

Isherwood's memories of his father are found in his first, long entry in the first volume of his published diaries. His remark, 'So utterly self-satisfied', is from p. 114 of *Down There on a Visit*. Auden's comments on the parochialism of his homeland are reproduced in Richard Davenport-Hines' biography *Auden* (Vintage, 1995), which was my go-to text for anything Auden-related in this chapter. Official records of Auden and Isherwood's passage were found on passenger lists on Ancestry.co.uk. Woolf's meeting with T. S. Eliot, at which they discussed Auden and Isherwood's departure, took place on 19 December 1938, and is described in her diary. Anthony Powell's outburst on the death of Auden was reported by Kingsley Amis in his memoirs. John Lehmann's more measured response is given in the second volume of his autobiography, *I Am My Brother* (Longmans, 1960), on p. 31, and at p. 240 of the amalgamated *In My Own Time: Memoirs of a Literary Life* (Little, Brown, 1969).

2. Dishonourable Gentlemen

The official transcripts of all House of Commons sittings can be found at Hansard.parliament.uk. John Lehmann supplies some context for the hostile atmosphere between politicians and writers in *I Am My Brother*. Wyndham Lewis's diatribe was published in the 26 June 1940 issue of the *Bystander*.

3. Two Bloomsburys

'Shaped like the eyes in peacocks' feathers' is a phrase of Virginia Woolf's from *The Years* (Vintage, 2016), p. 4. The writer who recalled the 'consoling' effect of gas lamps is H. V. Morton, in his book *Ghosts of London* (Methuen, 1939), pp. 55–6.

'So with the lamps all put out . . .' – *To the Lighthouse* (Vintage, 2004), pp. 119–20. Woolf's observations of London in wartime occur simultaneously to the events she is describing in her diaries and letters. Leonard Woolf's remark on his wife's acute sense of beauty is from a letter to John Lehmann, dated 3 April 1941. 'It's awfully queer, she thought . . .' – *The Years*, p. 83. 'Am I that, or am I this? . . .' – ibid, p. 128. 'Jealously, hoping that nobody . . .' – *To the Lighthouse*, p. 100. 'The view, which a moment before . . .' – ibid, p. 218. 'What was it made of? . . .' – *The Years*, p. 142.

Lehmann's reflections on Woolf's wartime journal-writing are found in the first section of *I Am My Brother*. His reflections on her process of writing *Roger Fry* are in *Virginia Woolf and Her World* (Thames and Hudson, 1975), p. 104, as well as the note on Fry's death. Woolf's description of Fry as 'a saint who laughed', among other things, is found at p. 297 in the finished book *Roger Fry* (Peregrine Books, 1979).

Leonard Woolf's phrase beginning 'the umbilical cord was severed . . .' is on p. 43 of his autobiographical volume *The Journey Not the Arrival Matters* (Hogarth, 1969). Virginia Woolf's essay on George Eliot is collected in *Genius and Ink: Virginia Woolf on How to Read* (*TLS*, 2019); the quotation beginning 'became one of the butts . . .' is on p. 49.

The descriptions of Virginia Woolf's first years living in Bloomsbury with her sister are all informed by her biographical essay 'Old Bloomsbury', collected with four other essays in *Moments of Being* (Pimlico, 2002). When Fry pops up again, that information is from *Roger Fry*. Stephen Spender's memory of Woolf calling him 'Maida Vale' is relayed in various places, but most notably at p. 152 in his autobiography *World Within World* (Faber, 1977). Alix Strachey wrote about Woolf for the commemorative volume *Recollections of Virginia Woolf by Her Contemporaries* (Peter Owen, 2013), edited by Joan Russell Noble. Christopher Isherwood submitted his reflections for the same volume, though they were originally printed in the magazine *Decision*. Lehmann's 'She was irradiated in my eyes . . .' is in the first volume of his autobiographies, *The Whispering Gallery* (Longmans, 1957), on pp. 168-9. Woolf gives Connolly his baboon sobriquet in *Diaries 1931-35* (Penguin, 1985), 30 April 1934.

Auden's epithet for Lewis, 'that lonely old volcano of the Right', is from his poem 'Letter to Lord Byron', in *Letters from Iceland* (Faber, 2002). 'An isolation full of sublimity' - *Mrs Dalloway* (Penguin Modern Classics, 2000), p. 101.

Woolf's essay on Jane Austen is in *The Common Reader* (Mariner, 2002). John Lehmann talks about Monk's House in *I Am My Brother*, p. 34. 'It was hard . . . to draw out . . .' - *The Whispering Gallery*, p. 170. Lehmann's plans for operating the Hogarth Press in wartime are outlined in his memoir *Thrown to the Woolfs* (Weidenfeld and Nicolson, 1978), p. 80.

Leonard Woolf's memories of his life becoming like a 'terrible nightmare', as well as his meditations on Nazi anti-Semitism and the corruption of Germany and the world, are in the opening pages of *The Journey Not the Arrival Matters*. The anecdote of Julia Strachey's planned makeover is in Frances Partridge's wartime diaries, 22 May 1940. The two letters in *The Times* are quoted in the same diaries on 2 July, the snippet about Raymond Mortimer on 7 June. Leonard's letter to Lytton Strachey from Sri Lanka is dated 21 March 1906.

John Lehmann's observation 'She was a socialist basically because Leonard was a socialist' is in *Virginia Woolf and Her World*, p. 103. Woolf's deliberations about *Three Guineas* and the essay for Phyllis Moir at *The Forum* are concentrated mostly in the diary entries of 14 May and 16 December 1939, and her letters to Lady Shena Simon written between November 1939 and January 1940. The essay written from 'the shadowed half of the world' is 'Thoughts on Peace in an Air Raid', collected in volume 6 of *The Essays of Virginia Woolf* (Hogarth, 2011).

4. Memories

The descriptions of John Lehmann in London in the first weeks of the war are all prompted by the sections beginning on pp. 23 and 39 in *I Am*

My Brother. I found useful information on attitudes to literature in 1939 in Robert Hewison's fantastic book *Imagination at War: British Fiction and Poetry 1939-1945* (Papermac, 1995), recommended for further reading on this subject. The specific quotations by Herbert Read and Geoffrey Faber were found on pp. 8-9. Discussion of *New Writing* in its original, more politicised form are also in *I Am My Brother*, pp. 40-2. 'The contemptuously told-you-so Right' and additional reflection on the fallout of the Molotov-Ribbentrop Pact is located on pp. 26-9 of the same book.

Christopher Isherwood's phrase 'high-cheekboned, Gothic style' is from *Down There on a Visit*, p. 27. I relied heavily on Adrian Wright's biography *John Lehmann: A Pagan Adventure* (Duckworth, 1998) when filling in the background of the editor's life; 'Lehmunn the Hun' is quoted on p. 28. Lehmann writes about his time in Vienna in *The Whispering Gallery* and his autobiographical novel *In the Purely Pagan Sense* (Gay Modern Classics, 1985).

The quotations from Lehmann and Stephen Spender about Spain are, as I have written, from the book *Poems for Spain* (Hogarth, 1939). The descriptions of Senate House are from the same sections of *I Am My Brother* as those describing the early weeks of the war.

Cyril Connolly's description of Spender as 'an inspired simpleton . . .' comes from a short profile, 'Stephen Spender', published in *The Evening Colonnade* (Arts Book Society, 1974). The quotation from *Lions and Shadows* is on p. 173 (Methuen, 1985). Lehmann's phrase 'the most rapidly self-revealing person' is from *The Whispering Gallery*, p. 176. Spender's letters to Isherwood are collected in *Letters to Christopher* (Black Sparrow Press, 1980).

Lehmann covers the Auden-Isherwood affair in pp. 31-2 of *I Am My Brother*. Dean Walter Matthews' letter to the *Spectator* was published in the 21 June 1940 issue. Evelyn Waugh's letter to Lady Diana Cooper is dated 24 December 1939 and collected in *The Letters of Evelyn Waugh* (Weidenfeld and Nicolson, 1980). Lehmann's characterisation of Spender – 'a great maker of legends . . .' – is in *Christopher Isherwood: A Personal Memoir* (Henry Holt, 1987), p. 8. Isherwood identifies Berlin's 'commercial line' in *Christopher and His Kind*, p. 29. The quotation of Spender's beginning 'It dripped with peace . . .' is, again, traceable to many sources, including *World Within World* (p. 264) and a journal entry for 5 September 1939 reproduced in *Stephen Spender: Journals 1939-1983* (Faber, 1985). 'The mortal sickness of Western civilisation . . .' and 'were chained still by guilt . . .' are from *The Whispering Gallery*, p. 176. The passage of Connolly's beginning 'created sick, commanded to be sound . . .' is in *Enemies of Promise* (Penguin Modern Classics, 1979), p. 218.

Lehmann's most sustained attempts at describing Isherwood come, unsurprisingly, in *Christopher Isherwood: A Personal Memoir*. Isherwood's description of Berlin as a 'skeleton which aches in the cold' is in *Goodbye to Berlin* (Vintage, 1989), p. 230. 'Laid out like a patient . . .' – *The Whispering Gallery*, p. 209. 'Rational, easy-going atmosphere . . .' and 'Jew-baiting, sabre-rattling . . .' – ibid, p. 210. Lehmann remembers W. H. Auden's 'long foolscap sheets' in *The Whispering Gallery*, p. 254. 'Prelude to a long maturity . . .' and the quotation beginning '*Mr Norris Changes Trains . . .*' are in *I Am My Brother*, pp. 16–18.

Virginia Woolf's phrase 'the young Brainies' is in her diary entry for 22 October 1937. Lehmann's letter releasing the Woolfs to write 'a steady stream of masterpieces' is reprinted in *Thrown to the Woolfs*, p. 60. The exchanges between Lehmann and Isherwood regarding the Press are recounted in the same book, pp. 74–6.

Spender's memory of Auden and Isherwood as 'a club of two' is found in a diary entry of 7 August 1979. Isherwood's letter to Lehmann beginning 'John, I am so utterly sick . . .' is reprinted in *Christopher Isherwood: A Personal Memoir*, p. 53. The long quotation by Spender beginning 'He wasn't really political . . .' is from a BBC documentary titled *Christopher Isherwood – A Born Foreigner*, as is the later quotation beginning 'It was only if he was there . . .' The exchanges between Lehmann and Spender in the Athenaeum Club are captured in *I Am My Brother*, pp. 32–3. The anecdote of Lehmann and Isherwood on the day of the Munich Agreement is given in *Christopher Isherwood: A Personal Memoir* on p. 48, among other places. The quotation from Adrian Lewis beginning 'there is a longing . . .', as well as the passage from Lehmann's letter to Isherwood beginning 'Don't come back now . . .', were found in *John Lehmann: A Pagan Adventure*, pp. 106–7. Lehmann expresses 'dismay' at Isherwood getting close to Gerald Heard in *Christopher Isherwood: A Personal Memoir*, p. 53.

5. Towards the Fire

For background on Stephen Spender, Inez Pearn and Tony Hyndman I made frequent use of both Hugh David's and John Sutherland's biographies of the poet. Spender's letter to Christopher Isherwood ('He has just made the most terrific scene' and 'I'm just not capable . . .') is in *Letters to Christopher* and dated 22 November 1936. Spender contemplates his own perspective on homosexuality in *World Within World*, where Tony is given the identity 'Jimmy Younger'; all quotations pertaining to the breakdown of their relationship, from 'keep[ing] their friendship static' to 'The strain on my side . . .', are found on pp. 183-4.

'It is not only unhappiness . . .' - *Stephen Spender: Journals 1939-1983*, 26 October 1939. 'In the mood when people . . .' - *World Within World*, p. 175. Spender described his first heterosexual experience in a letter to Isherwood dated 14 September 1934, omitted from *Letters to Christopher* but reproduced as an extract in John Sutherland's biography, *Stephen Spender: A Literary Life* (Viking, 2004). 'Semi-deified' is a phrase of Philip Toynbee's, found on p. 197 of the same book. The quotation by Lucian Freud beginning 'we've got so and so . . .' is from *The Lives of Lucian Freud: Youth* (Bloomsbury, 2019) by William Feaver, p. 64.

Spender's uneasy relationship with the British Communist Party is dissected expertly in Duncan White's *Cold Warriors: Writers Who Waged the Literary Cold War* (Little, Brown, 2019). Virginia Woolf records the rumour about Harry Pollitt in her diary entry of 18 February 1937, the same day that Spender 'came for tea'. The quotation by Hugh David is from p. 191 of his *Stephen Spender: Portrait with Background* (Heinemann, 1992). 'Confronted me with the consequences . . .' - *World Within World*, p. 212.

Charles Madge's 'unforgettable' look is mentioned in Vicky Randall's introduction to *Spanish Portrait* (Clapton Press, 2019) by Elizabeth Lake (Inez's penname). 'Throughout the duration of our marriage . . .' - *World Within World*, p. 258. 'Somewhere I felt that . . .' - ibid, pp. 192-3. Spender's admission 'I know that she cannot bear being with me . . .' is found in the most recent edition of his diaries, *New Selected Journals* (Faber, 2012), in the entry for 3 September 1939. 'I inhabited a mental world . . .' - *World Within World*, p. 209.

'As through a thick pane . . .' - ibid, p. 285. Spender's impressions of London as it appeared at the time of the declaration of war are found in the first entry to his journals, as are the admissions about his mental state. 'My mother still liked him . . .' - *Spanish Portrait*, introduction. The quotation beginning 'Peter asked me specifically . . .' is from Michael Shelden's book about *Horizon*, *Friends of Promise* (Hamish Hamilton, 1989), p. 31. The Geoffrey Grigson anecdote is preserved in Spender's journals, in the entry for 26 October 1939.

'Every day an occasion arises . . .' - Spender journals, 20 October 1939. 'I am not officially connected . . .' - Spender, letter to William Plomer, 19

October 1939. Lehmann's recollections of the consequent 'explosion' are in *I Am My Brother*, p. 43. The quotation from Lehmann's diaries ('natural traitor . . . pathologically eaten up . . .') was found in Adrian Wright's biography, pp. 100-1. 'John gets garrulous after wine . . .' - Virginia Woolf diaries, 29 November 1939. 'His great joints seemed to crack . . .' - ibid, 23 September 1939.

'Wild blue eyes and a bad complexion' - diaries of Harold Nicolson, 22 June 1930, reproduced in Sutherland's biography, p. 105. 'A rattle-headed, bolt-eyed . . .' - Virginia Woolf diaries, 2 November 1932. 'Talks incessantly and will pan out . . .' - Woolf, letter to Quentin Bell, 21 December 1933. 'At a gulp . . .' - Woolf diaries, 20 April 1935. 'Audens and Spenders', ibid, 24 July 1934.

Spender defended Woolf against the Wyndham Lewis onslaught in the 19 October 1934 issue of the *Spectator*. 'The moral of the book . . .' - Spender, letter to Isherwood, 21 October 1934. 'The most delightful book . . .' - Spender, letter to Woolf, 4 July 1934. The David Leeming book mentioned is *Stephen Spender: A Life in Modernism* (Henry Holt, 1999). 'She also talked about the danger . . .' - Spender journals, 20 October 1939.

'To them there was something barbarous . . .' - *World Within World*, p. 141. Spender's warning to Isherwood about becoming 'Hogarth Pressy' is in a letter from winter 1934. 'Like a watered-down aristocracy . . .' - *World Within World*, p. 141. 'He was beautifully elegant . . .' - Spender, letter to Isherwood, 21 October 1934. 'The purpose of art . . .' - *Stephen Spender: A Life in Modernism*, p. 69. 'Was inevitably the exceptionally sensitive person . . .' - *World Within World*, p. 96. 'Bloomsbury was felt to be inadequate' - 'Stephen Spender', *The Evening Colonnade*.

'Areas of sensibility of which . . .' - *World Within World*, p. 96. 'In a trance - unconsciously' - Woolf diaries, 16 March 1935. 'Through the veins of the hand . . .' - *World Within World*, p. 158. The discussion of Eliot's politics comes from the penultimate chapter of Spender's book *Eliot*. Eliot tries to justify his belief in Original Sin in a letter to Spender dated 9 June 1932. Spender recounts his conversation with Eliot in *World Within World*, p. 147. 'Turned outwards from himself . . .' - *World Within World*, pp. 96-7. Woolf quotes Lawrence on 3 May 1931 in her diaries. The proceeding discussion of Henry James and the modernist sensibility takes its quotations from the introduction to Spender's *The Destructive Element* (Jonathan Cape, 1935). 'What a writer writes about . . .', ibid, p. 189.

Herbert Read's review of *Poems* is quoted in Hugh David's biography, p. 159. Spender's letter to Isherwood is dated 23 January 1933. Isherwood's question to Spender about the author of the 'portentous tripe' is quoted in *Christopher and His Kind*, p. 93, along with the rest of his reaction to the collection. Spender considers his own abilities in contrast to Auden's in a letter to Isherwood of 7 March 1935. 'An embarrassment to my friends' luggage . . .' - Spender, introduction to *Collected Poems 1928-1953* (Faber, 1959).

Spender suggests that Isherwood and Heinz move to America in a letter dated 7 March 1935.

6. The Pain Two Lovers Inflict

Description of Cyril Connolly in the *Horizon* office is informed by Stephen Spender in *World Within World*, p. 295, and the first sections of Peter Quennell's *The Wanton Chase* (Collins, 1980).

The quotation beginning 'As a man, he was suffering . . .' is from the first page of Cyril Connolly's introduction to *The Unquiet Grave* (Penguin Modern Classics, 1967). Peter Quennell's concept of the 'lost girls' is outlined on pp. 71-3 of *The Wanton Chase*, and expertly parsed in D. J. Taylor's book *Lost Girls* (Constable, 2019).

'All the gossip is of traffic casualties' - Evelyn Waugh diaries (Weidenfeld and Nicolson, 1976), 17 October 1939.

'An editor frays away his true personality . . .' is from Connolly's 'Comment' for the November 1949 issue of *Horizon*. The quotations 'the two faces' and 'the tyranny of the human face' are from p. 64 of *The Unquiet Grave*. 'Like a worn gramophone record' - ibid, p. 117. Connolly's letter to his mother ('cheering up Peter') is quoted in *Friends of Promise*, p. 30. The quotation 'the best living parodist' comes from an essay-pamphlet by Spender titled, I think, 'Cyril Connolly', as do the proceeding anecdotes.

'The streets look shabbier . . .' - 'Comment', May 1940. 'Green grass, blue sky . . .' - 'Comment', March 1941.

The 'clarion call' of journalism is a phrase from *Enemies of Promise*, p. 97. 'The flat ephemeral pamphlet . . .' - Auden, from the poem 'Spain'. 'Believed in devoting a long life . . .' - 'Comment', January 1943. 'Put them down in the sun . . .' - 'Comment', February 1943. 'The English were once a migrant species . . .' - 'Comment', May 1942. 'An angry protest against the office walls . . .' - ibid. 'A steady humanitarian trend' - October 1943.

The quotations beginning 'the only country in Europe . . .', 'stolid, practical, tolerant . . .' and 'etiolated by official conformity' are all from

Connolly's 'Comment' of January 1943. 'The artist-administrator in the Civil Service . . .' - 'Comment', May 1942. 'The appreciation of art is spreading . . .' - 'Comment', December 1942. 'We are in a world . . .' - *Enemies of Promise*, p. 106. Spender's essay 'Two Landscapes of Novel' is from an issue of *Encounter*. The quotation beginning 'keeping the calendar at 1938' and ensuing discussion about appeasement is from the August 1942 'Comment'.

'Archaic and unreal . . .' - 'Comment', May 1940. 'Negatives every conception of what life is for . . .' - ibid. The extract from Sigmund Freud's *Beyond the Pleasure Principle* is quoted in *The Unquiet Grave*, p. 121. The quotation beginning 'to create something permanent in the flux . . .' is from a letter to Jean Connolly quoted on p. 328 of *Cyril Connolly: A Life* (Random House, 1997) by Jeremy Lewis.

Connolly contemplates the success of the first issue of *Horizon* in his 'Comment' of February 1940. D. J. Taylor discusses the reputation of 'Georgian' writing in *The Prose Factory* (Vintage, 2017), which devotes a chapter to 'The Georgian Twilight'.

Connolly's diary entries from 1927 are reproduced in 'England Not My England', collected in *The Selected Essays of Cyril Connolly* (Peresa Books, 1984), pp. 83–97. He returns to London later in life, and reflects on his favourite iteration of the city, in 'One of My Londons', ibid, pp. 98–108. 'Are run-down, querulous . . .' - *Enemies of Promise*, p. 148. Connolly's description of the 'cycle of the hours' is from p. 96 of *The Unquiet Grave*. His experiences with air-raid shelters are recounted on p. 328 of Jeremy Lewis's biography.

7. England Their England

George Orwell's observations of London in wartime, and commentary on the developments of the war, occur simultaneously with the events he is describing in his diaries. The quotation beginning 'The attack on England must come . . .' is a diary entry for 30 May 1940, reproduced in *I Am My Brother*. Orwell's letter to *Time and Tide* is dated 22 June 1940, and is collected in *A Life in Letters* (Penguin Modern Classics, 2011). 'It is seemingly quite impossible . . .' - Orwell, 'London Letter', *Partisan Review*, Summer 1945 issue.

The long quotation of Connolly's beginning 'He liked these very morbid stories . . .' is from the 1983 BBC *Arena* documentary on his life and works. 'One of those boys who seem . . .' - *Enemies of Promise*, p. 163. For correspondence between Orwell and Connolly, one of the most interesting artefacts is the article 'Some Letters by George Orwell' published in the January 1962 issue of *Encounter*. It is in a footnote in that article that Connolly describes their first meeting in the 1930s and Orwell's 'ravaged' appearance.

The quotation beginning 'Connolly, in his own special way . . .' and the one that follows it are from 'George Orwell: A Memoir' by Anthony Powell in *Atlantic Monthly*, October 1967.

'Tr[ying] to overcome his prejudice . . .' - Connolly, footnote to 'Some Letters by George Orwell'. Orwell's letter to Denys King-Farlow is dated 9 June 1936. 'A sort of poisonous jungle . . .' - *The Road to Wigan Pier* (Penguin Classics, 2001), p. 152. Orwell's review of *The Rock Pool* is found on pp. 254-7 of *The Collected Essays, Journalism and Letters of George Orwell: Volume 1: An Age Like This, 1920-1940* (Penguin, 1970). Connolly's reviews of *Burmese Days* and *Keep the Aspidistra Flying* are quoted in *Cyril Connolly: A Life*, p. 290.

'Much more social than before' - Connolly, letter to Peggy Bainbridge, quoted in *Cyril Connolly: A Life*, p. 288. Connolly's *New Statesman* article was published in the February 1937 issue. 'Could mount a very solid . . .' - *Sunday Times*, 21 January 1973, quoted in *Cyril Connolly: A Life*, p. 289.

Orwell's letter to Nancy Cunard is dated 3-6 August 1937, and quoted in D. J. Taylor's biography, p. 245. 'Quite why Orwell should have . . .' - Taylor, p. 246. Orwell's letters to Spender are also included in 'Some Letters'. Orwell's analysis of communism as the 'patriotism of the deracinated' and of its effect on writing is from 'Inside the Whale', *Inside the Whale and Other Essays* (Penguin, 1962), pp. 36-40.

'Suffered from a typically English form . . .' - 'George Orwell: 2', *The Evening Colonnade*, p. 378. 'I remember this rather drizzly voice . . .' - quoted in *Orwell: The Authorised Biography* (Heinemann, 1991), Michael Shelden, p. 354.

Anthony Powell discusses the quirks of Orwell's personality in *To Keep the Ball Rolling* (Penguin, 1983), pp. 65-76.

The descriptions of specific Luftwaffe raids in this book are based on information found in William Sansom's *The Blitz: Westminster at War* (Oxford University Press, 1947), the value of which book, to my research, could not be overstated. 'Lived in a trance-like condition' - *World Within World*, p. 292. 'The streets would have an unreal air . . .' - *The Blitz: Westminster at War*, p. 38. 'Seen against the silhouetted foreground . . .' -

Spender, *The Thirties and After* (Fontana, 1978), p. 91. 'It recalled Turner's picture . . .' - Peter Quennell, *The Wanton Chase*, p. 19. 'Felt enormously at home in the Blitz . . .' - 'George Orwell: 3', *The Evening Colonnade*, p. 383. Connolly describes Orwell as a 'John the Baptist figure' in the 1983 BBC *Arena* documentary.

'*Horizon* provided Orwell with a . . .' - Taylor, *Orwell: The Life*, p. 276. Orwell's 'London Letter' was published in the March–April 1941 issue of *Partisan Review*. 'Were required to work in shifts . . .' and proceeding quotations - *The Wanton Chase*, pp. 13–17. 'No poet got into trouble . . .' - Lehmann, *I Am My Brother*, p. 29. 'Tower[ing] vast and white . . .' - *Nineteen Eighty-Four* (Penguin Modern Classics, 2003), p. 5.

8. Now We Are in the War

'Was an intellectual in every sense . . .' - Leonard Woolf, *The Journey Not the Arrival Matters*, p. 42. 'There happened to be quite a high tide . . .' - ibid, p. 34.

Frances Partridge remembers Virginia Woolf's attack on Alix Strachey in *Memories* (Phoenix, 2001), pp. 116–17. Woolf's letter to Stephen Spender is dated 16 December 1939. Hermione Lee writes of Woolf's 'uncertain relationship with self-revelation' in *Virginia Woolf* (Vintage, 1997), p. 18. 'Now I am beginning to feel . . .' - Spender, *The Temple* (Faber, 1988), p. 54.

'The supreme flowering of bourgeois society' - Connolly, 'Comment', January 1943. Woolf's 'The Leaning Tower' lecture can be read in full in *The Essays of Virginia Woolf: Volume 6: 1933 to 1941*, pp. 259–78.

Julian Bell's memories of a politicised Cambridge are quoted in *Stalin's Englishman: The Lives of Guy Burgess*, Andrew Lownie (Hodder & Stoughton, 2016), p. 44. The short quotation 'a land fit for heroes to live in' is in the same section.

Isherwood rants about the 'old men who had made the war' in the first entry to his 1939 diaries. The comments of Spender's that I have interspersed within Woolf's lecture are from the chapter 'Background to the Thirties' in *The Thirties and After*.

'The real air war began . . .' - Leonard Woolf, *The Journey Not the Arrival Matters*, p. 32. 'Fell just before eleven o'clock . . .' - Sansom, *The Blitz: Westminster at War*, p. 23. 'It's impossible not to remember . . .' - Francis Partridge diaries, 19 May 1940. 'In many men's troubled, taut minds . . .' - *The Blitz: Westminster at War*, p. 26. Report Centres and other official quarters . . .' - ibid, p. 27. 'The powdered smell of smashed plaster . . .' - ibid.

John Lehmann describes the bombing of Mecklenburgh Square in his diary entry for 11 September 1940, reproduced in *I Am My Brother*, pp. 78-82. 'Cascad[e] naked in a torrent of soap suds . . .' and proceeding quotations - *I Am My Brother*, p. 87.

Leonard Woolf's letter to Margaret Llewelyn Davies is dated 14 November 1940 and is collected in *Letters of Leonard Woolf* (Bloomsbury, 1992). I found the letter from Charles Darwin to Leslie Stephen on the Kotte Autographs auction website.

'That's one good the war brought us . . .' - Woolf, *Between the Acts*, (Vintage, 2000) p. 120. Leonard considers Woolf's attitude to death in *The Journey Not the Arrival Matters*, pp. 73-4.

9. The Grey Light of Morning

'Rather agitated with the confusion . . .' and proceeding quotations - diary entry for 15 September 1940, quoted in *I Am My Brother*, p. 84.

'For the torture of Victorian skivvies . . .' - Richard Kennedy, *A Boy at the Hogarth Press* (Penguin, 1978), p. 40.

John Lehmann describes the offices of the Hogarth Press in *The Whispering Gallery*, pp. 166-77. 'Hard work, but congenial' - Lehmann, *Thrown to the Woolfs*, p. 8. 'Hubristic schemes to make the Press . . .' - *The Whispering Gallery*, p. 202.

Virginia Woolf's letter to Lehmann in which she discusses the younger poets is dated 30 September 1931.

'She sent me piles of dirty copy books . . .' - Woolf to Hugh Walpole, 12 April 1931. I am relying heavily here on Mark Hussey's essay 'W. H. Day Spender Had a Sister: Joan Adeney Easdale', in *Leonard and Virginia Woolf, The Hogarth Press and the Networks of Modernism* (Edinburgh University Press, 2010), edited by Helen Southworth. See Hussey's piece for a fascinating retelling of the friendship between Woolf and Easdale. The quotation beginning 'reminiscent of the elliptical genius . . .', included in Hussey's article, comes from a review in the *Spectator* by Richard Church.

'Not . . . poetical, but purebred prose' - Woolf to Lehmann, 17 September 1931. Woolf's 'Letter to a Young Poet' is collected in *The Essays of Virginia Woolf: Volume 5: 1929-1932* (Hogarth, 2009).

'Keenly interested in the work . . .' and proceeding quotations - *The Whispering Gallery*, p. 179. Sir John Greer Ervine's article for the *Spectator* is, as stated, in the August 1927 edition.

Lehmann discusses the *New Signatures* anthology on p. 173 of *The Whispering Gallery*. 'Abreast of his own times . . .' - Michael Roberts, introduction to Hogarth Living Poets No. 24 *New Signatures* (Hogarth, 1932), p. 8. 'New knowledge and new circumstances . . .' - ibid, p. 7. 'The old poetic tinsel . . .' - *The Whispering Gallery*, p. 176. 'Popular, elegant and contemporary art' - *New Signatures*, p. 20. 'Rather soggy reception' - *The Whispering Gallery*, p. 182.

'Rapidly recovering from the sharp frost . . .' - *I Am My Brother*, p. 55. Lehmann describes his experiences at the Garden City Press in *I Am My Brother*, p. 86. 'Secret . . . dive' - ibid, p. 67. 'The telling poise of a cigarette . . .' - *John Lehmann: A Pagan Adventure*, p. 121. 'Images of phantasmagoria' and 'a world of pure art . . .' - *I Am My Brother*, p. 60. Lehmann describes the parties in his flat on p. 61 of *The Whispering Gallery*. He returns after the bombing on p. 85. He describes his Home Guard activities on p. 89 of the same book.

'Quite unworthy of the Cambridge Apostle' and proceeding quotations - *Thrown to the Woolfs*, p. 67. 'Leonard, it soon became clear . . .' - ibid, p. 73.

'Lehmann made a virtue of . . .' - *The Prose Factory*, p. 217. Lehmann characterises Orwell, Garrett and Coombe's brand of writing in the chapter 'The Man in the Street' in *New Writing in Europe* (Pelican, 1940), pp. 75-91. Hugh Walpole's review of that book is quoted in *I Am My Brother*, p. 103. Lehmann responds to it on the same page.

'The English poetry of the First World . . .' - Lehmann, *The English Poets of the First World War* (Thames and Hudson, 1982), p. 8. Lehmann meets with the Woolfs on p. 112 of *I Am My Brother*. 'Amazed and deeply moved by its poetry . . .' - Lehmann diaries, quoted in *John Lehmann: A Pagan Adventure*, p. 120.

10. The Wave Lapping Blue to the Shore

'Literally took one's breath away . . .' - Leonard Woolf, *Sowing* (Hogarth, 1916), p. 183. Leonard's letter to Lytton Strachey is dated 1 November 1911.

Louie Mayer's memories of Virginia Woolf's suicide are included in the book *Recollections of Virginia Woolf*, pp. 154-63. Leonard's letter to Vita

Sackville-West is dated 28 March 1941, the one to John Lehmann on the same day. Alix Strachey's reflections are also in *Recollections of Virginia Woolf*, pp. 111-18. 'Too silly and trivial' - Woolf, letter to Lehmann, 27 March 1941.

'Most terrible and agonizing days' - Leonard Woolf, *The Journey Not the Arrival Matters*, p. 44. Octavia Wilberforce remembers her close relationship with Woolf, as well as her experiences in psychiatric hospitals, in her fascinating memoir *Autobiography of a Pioneer Woman Doctor* (Cassell, 1989). Her letters to Elizabeth Robins are reproduced there.

'Exalted stage' is a phrase of Woolf's own, from *Moments of Being*, p. 98. 'Dreaded some such physical collapse . . .' - Frances Partridge diaries, 8 April 1941. 'In a rare moment of physical . . .' - Frances Spalding, *Vanessa Bell*, (Ticknor and Fields, 1983), p. 317. 'Act as midwife to her verbal fantasies . . .' - Partridge, *Memories*, p. 80. 'Hoped against hope that she . . .' - Partridge diaries, 8 April 1941. 'Unable to think of anyone . . .' - E. M. Forster, letter to Leonard, 3 April 1941. Leonard remembers Woolf's funeral in *The Journey Not the Arrival Matters*, p. 95.

'Always wrote objectively . . .' - quoted in *Autobiography of a Pioneer Woman Doctor*, p. 187. The passage from *Between the Acts* can be found on pp. 36-7. 'We thought we'd publish *Monday or Tuesday* . . .' - *Autobiography of a Pioneer Woman Doctor*, p. 187. 'I would have given anything . . .' - quoted in *Cyril Connolly: A Life*, p. 251. 'Not for the first time . . .' - ibid, p. 252. T. S. Eliot marks the death of Woolf in *Recollections of Virginia Woolf*, pp. 119-22.

Connolly's 'Comment' describing the bombed streets of Chelsea is in the May 1941 issue. 'Already saw that there would be . . .' and proceeding quotations - *I Am My Brother*, p. 115. Woolf's essay on John Evelyn is collected in *Genius and Ink*, pp. 81-94. 'Reluctant because there was too much . . .' and proceeding quotations - *Autobiography of a Pioneer Woman Doctor*, pp. 186-7.

'So-called novel' is a phrase from Woolf's final letter to Lehmann. 'A very remarkable book . . .' - Leonard, letter to John Lehmann, 3 April 1941. 'Uneasy that there is no end . . .' - Leonard, letter to Angus Wilson, 22 April 1962. 'Night before roads were made . . .' - *Between the Act*, p. 219. 'The paper that obliterated . . .' - ibid, p. 216. 'It was here that she had suffered . . .' and proceeding quotation - ibid, pp. 210-11. 'The world must accept her . . .' - *Recollections of Virginia Woolf*, pp. 18-22.

11. A New Kind of Warfare

John Lehmann describes his interactions with Sir Archibald Clark Kerr in *I Am My Brother*, pp. 148-53. 'It seemed as good a place as any . . .' - ibid, p. 144. Lehmann reproduces the telegrams from Rokotov on p. 146 of the same book.

'The entirely different conceptions of the role . . .' - ibid, p. 147. 'Many landmarks had gone . . .' and proceeding quotations - *The Blitz: Westminster at War*, p. 92. 'One was almost lulled into thinking . . .' - *I Am My Brother*, p. 143. 'Hardly more than a kind of . . .' - ibid, p. 153.

Lehmann's letter to Christopher Isherwood about Henry Green is dated December 1938 and quoted in *The Whispering Gallery*, p. 329. Lehmann discusses Isherwood's feeble attempts at producing a wartime novel in *I Am My Brother*, around p. 153. W. H. Auden's observation beginning 'the truth of the matter . . .' is from Spender's journal entry for 9 June 1955.

'The Auxiliary Fire Service should become . . .' and 'several short sketches or individual episodes' - *Thrown to the Woolfs*, p. 115. 'The behaviour of my AFS unit . . .' - quoted in *Romancing: The Life and Work of Henry Green* (Random House, 2000) by Jeremy Treglown, p. 115. 'Part of its distinctiveness . . .' - Treglown, introduction to *Caught* (Harvill, 2001) by Henry Green. 'Had all the peaceful leisure . . .' - *Thrown to the Woolfs*, p. 115. Green's letter to Lehmann ('a series of pictures rising . . .') is quoted in the same book, p. 117. George Orwell's essay 'Inside the Whale' is found in any good anthology of his non-fiction, in this case *Inside the Whale and Other Essays*, pp. 9-50.

'Only just tolerating the freedom of publishers . . .' and proceeding quotations - *Thrown to the Woolfs*, p. 117.

'Went on for the most part pretty smoothly' and proceeding quotations - *The Journey Not the Arrival Matters*, p. 108. 'Realised that it would be essential . . .' - *I Am My Brother*, p. 311. 'Those who have supplied the capital . . .' - *The Journey Not the Arrival Matters*, p. 109.

Lehmann remembers his 'severe emotional and spiritual crisis' in the short section titled 'The Other Dimension' in *I Am My Brother*. Lehmann's 'Vigils' can be found in his *Collected Poems*, pp. 60-65. *Autumn Journal* by Louis MacNeice is a long poem which can be found in *Louis MacNeice: Collected Poems* (Faber, 2007), pp. 99-164. 'After the supper picnic they returned . . .' - 'Talk on the River', *Collected Poems* (Eyre and Spottiswoode, 1963), pp. 14-15. 'Sharply the spire beyond the meadow-gate . . .' -

'Bathers', ibid, pp. 15-16. 'A change in his mood and thinking' and proceeding quotations - Lehmann, *Rupert Brooke: His Life and His Legend* (Weidenfeld and Nicolson, 1980), p. 169.

'Lean war substitute' - *Thrown to the Woolfs*, p. 85. 'Quick and decisive in giving a new project . . .' - Jeremy Lewis, *Penguin Special: The Life and Times of Allen Lane* (Viking, 2005), p. 176. 'War brought with it a hunger for culture' - ibid, p. 175. Kingsley Amis remembers Penguin Books in his 1986 appearance on BBC Radio 4's *Desert Island Discs*. 'The three of us could produce a magazine . . .' - quoted in *Penguin Special*, p. 176.

Orwell discusses the entanglement of literature in politics in his BBC broadcast 'Frontiers of Art and Propaganda', collected in *Seeing Things as They Are: Selected Journalism and Other Writings* (Penguin Modern Classics, 2016), pp. 144-7. Stephen Spender is quoted ('everything I say about Russia is largely conjecture' and proceeding quotations) in Robert Hewison, *Imagination at War: British Fiction and Poetry, 1939-1945*, p. 147. 'Perfectly reasonable and justified boosting . . .' - *I Am My Brother*, p. 243. I got my information about writing in the Soviet Union from Duncan White's *Cold Warriors*, particularly the first chapter on Isaac Babel.

'Sentries had to be posted in continual vigilance' - *I Am My Brother*, p. 243. Dylan Thomas's letter mentioning the Ministry of Information is dated 14 September 1939. 'It was really only after Russia . . .' - *Imagination at War*, p. 145.

12. I Am Only Myself in the Dark

Dylan Thomas's commentary of his life during wartime occurs simultaneously with the events he is describing in his letters. 'Singularly unscrupulous about money' and proceeding quotation - Stephen Spender journals, 28 April 1958. Caitlin Thomas wrote a hugely entertaining and moving memoir titled *Life with Dylan Thomas* (Henry Holt, 1988). She discusses her and Dylan's affairs and their decision to leave London in pp. 74-6. Caitlin leaves Llewelyn on the train in *Caitlin: The Life of Caitlin Thomas* (Pimlico, 1995), Paul Ferris, p. 90.

Caitlin recalls her first meeting with Dylan on page 1 of her memoir. 'I'm not going to London again . . .' - letter to Vernon Watkins, 20 December 1938. 'Completely laid out with booze' and proceeding quotation - *Life with Dylan Thomas*, p. 60. 'Stinking, friendless London' and proceeding quotations - letter to Watkins, 28 August 1941.

'I had been an eager admirer . . .' - *I Am My Brother*, p. 95. 'I hated *The Map of Love* . . .' and proceeding quotations - *Life with Dylan Thomas*, p. 70. 'A casting-off of those habiliments . . .' - Vernon Watkins, introduction to *Adventures in the Skin Trade* (Aldine, 1965). 'He looked upon [*Portrait of the Artist*] . . .' - *Life with Dylan Thomas*, p. 70.

'Dylan was like a big baby . . .' - ibid, p. 67. Lehmann quotes from Dylan's letters in *I Am My Brother*, p. 96. He describes mentoring Thomas in London pubs on the following page. 'I began to realise that Dylan . . .' and proceeding quotations - ibid, p. 97. 'I can't imagine Gower bombed . . .' and 'Are you frightened these nights? . . .' - letter to Watkins, 1940. 'About a man who fished . . .' - letter to John Davenport, 8 January 1941.

Caitlin describes Dylan's night of drinking before his medical in *Life with Dylan Thomas*, p. 72. 'I don't want to do that . . .' - letter to Sir Kenneth Clark, 25 March 1940. 'A way of joining the army . . .' - *Life with Dylan Thomas*, p. 72. Waugh mentions Cazalet's battery in his diary entry for 18 January 1940.

Julian Maclaren-Ross devotes an entire chapter of his *Memoirs of the Forties* (Cardinal, 1991) to Dylan and Strand Films, pp. 118-34. 'Could I have a script . . .' - letter to Royston Morley, 1940. 'Immensely drunk and wildly jovial . . .' - *The Wanton Chase*, p. 25. 'Gave him time in which to work . . .' - Paul Willetts, *Fear and Loathing in Fitzrovia* (Dewi Lewis, 2013), p. 103. 'Orderly room clerk . . .' - letter to John Lehmann, 25 October 1942. 'Based on my experiences as a prisoner . . .' - letter to Lehmann, 5 May 1943. 'An intelligent man of 31 . . .' - letter to Rupert Hart-Davis, 14 February 1943.

Richard Taylor writes about Dylan's various projects at Strand Films in his informative essay '"False hopes and airy visions?" Dylan Thomas and British film propaganda in the Second World War', published in *Propaganda and Conflict: War, Media and Shaping the Twentieth Century* (Bloomsbury, 2019), pp. 99-113. 'A lackadaisical office . . .' - quoted in Paul Ferris, *Dylan Thomas* (Dial Press, 1977), p. 181. 'The work suited him . . .' - ibid, p. 192.

'This was the first time . . .' - *Life with Dylan Thomas*, p. 80.

13. Epitaphs

I relied heavily on Sylvia Topp's book *Eileen: The Making of George Orwell* (Unbound, 2020) in building an accurate picture of the Orwells' home life. 'A general background of furniture . . .' - 'George Orwell: A Memoir', *Atlantic Monthly*, October 1967, p. 65. 'Confirmed enemy of good living' - ibid, p. 64. 'I'd say just a touch . . .' and 'desperately cold and draughty' - quoted in *Eileen*, p. 327. Henry Dakin recalls his aunt's stylishness on the same page. 'I'm sure Eric is dead' and proceeding quotation - ibid, quoted on p. 290. 'Caused his own death by . . .' - ibid, quoted on p. 291. Eileen Orwell's grief is described on p. 292 of the same book, the bombing incident on p. 311. 'Daily work of inconceivable dullness' - letter to Eileen Myles, March 1941, collected in *George Orwell: A Life in Letters*. 'Was glad to see her recovered . . .' - *Eileen*, p. 312.

'Thought to have imbibed the secret . . .' - Roy Jenkins, *Churchill* (Pan Books, 2001), p. 683. Cripps' radio broadcast is quoted on the same page. 'Definitely an employee of the BBC' - George Orwell diaries, 28 August 1941. Orwell considers Cripps' qualities in his 'London Letter' for the 8 May 1942 issue of *Partisan Review*. For background information on the 'Quit India' movement I read *Churchill, Cripps, and India, 1939-1945* (Clarendon Press, 1979), by R. J. Moore.

William Empson discusses his time at the BBC with Orwell in a chapter of *The World of George Orwell* (Weidenfeld and Nicolson, 1971), edited by Miriam Gross, pp. 93-100. 'Due to the fact that . . .' - quoted in Edward Stourton, *Auntie's War* (Black Swan, 2018), p. 249. 'Establishing more effective control over . . .' - ibid, quoted on p. 9.

'Own rule at first seems . . .' - W. J. West, introduction to *Orwell, the War Broadcasts* (Duckworth, 1985), p. 23. 'To fuse political purpose . . .' - George Orwell, *Why I Write* (Penguin, 2005), p. 10. '"Cash in" on the popularity . . .' - quoted in *Auntie's War*, pp. 317-18. 'I am not thinking about . . .' - ibid, p. 318. 'For at least eighty years . . .' - *The Lion and the Unicorn* (Penguin Modern Classics, 2018), p. 70. 'Tell the Indians that they . . .' - ibid, p. 69. 'Absolutely the need for propaganda . . .' - *Auntie's War*, p. 310. '[I] shall remain in it . . .' - Orwell diaries, 14 March 1942.

'In spite of the stupidity . . .' - Orwell, 'London Letter', *Partisan Review*, 15 April 1941. 'A comic opera with an occasional death' - Orwell, *Homage to Catalonia* (Penguin Modern Classics, 2000), p. 27. 'What is so terrible about this . . .' - quoted in *I Am My Brother*, p. 93. 'Regarded the phrase "living poet" . . .' - *Orwell, the War Broadcasts*, p. 37. Orwell's preface to the first episode of *Voice* is reproduced in *Seeing Things as They Are: Selected Journalism and Other Writings*, pp. 172-3.

'Inwardly rather frightened' - Orwell diaries, 15 March 1942. Cyril Connolly's remarks about Stephen Spender in his broadcast are quoted in John Sutherland's biography, p. 288. 'I am doing nothing . . .' - Orwell diaries, 23 July 1942.

Orwell rants about 'stupid propaganda' in his diary entry for 27 April 1942. 'Huge army . . . wonderful choruses' - ibid, 10 June 1942. 'We worked against a background noise . . .' - John Morris, 'Some Are More Equal than Others', *Penguin New Writing*, September 1950. 'Most and perhaps his only . . .' - ibid. 'A substantial book in itself' - W. J. West, introduction to *Orwell, the War Commentaries* (Duckworth, 1985), p. 13. 'His weekly broadcast talks . . .' - Morris, 'Some Are More Equal than Others'.

The little anecdotes about J. B. Priestley come from an article by Trevor Hill, 'Memories of 200 Oxford Street', abridged from his book *Over the Airwaves* (Book Guild, 2005) and published on the website www.orbem.co.uk.

'Our soldiers are not as good fighters . . .' - quoted in Jenkins, *Churchill*, p. 681. 'The Prime Minister wins debate after debate . . .' - ibid, quoted on p. 697.

Orwell commentates on the progress of the Cripps mission and describes his own meetings with Cripps in his diaries, around the dates mentioned. 'He tried to squeeze out some childhood memory . . .' - *Nineteen Eighty-Four*, p. 5.

14. Cocktails, and the Greatest Evil Ever Committed

John Lehmann describes at length a cocktail evening among literary London in *I Am My Brother*, pp. 169-73. 'A delirium of nations . . .' - Cecil Day-Lewis, *The Buried Day* (Harper, 1960), p. 87. 'A land of wild make-believe . . .' - Evelyn Waugh diaries, 19 January 1940. 'Blast often did odd things' - Graham Greene, *Ministry of Fear* (Random House, 2010), p. 77. 'The untidy gaps between . . .' - ibid, p. 11. 'Shops were reduced . . .' - ibid, p. 40. 'A man who had been . . .' - ibid, p. 143. 'Sold 15,000 before reprinting' - letter to Elisabeth Greene, 18 August 1943. 'The thrillers are like life' and proceeding quotation - *I Am My Brother*, p. 227. 'What if a war was . . .' and proceeding quotation - Patrick Hamilton, *Hangover Square* (Abacus, 2016), p. 22. 'The bloody birth and climax . . .' - quoted in *Through a Glass Darkly: The Life of Patrick Hamilton* (Abacus, 1993), Nigel Jones, p. 250. 'His first few sentences were quite off-putting . . .' - quoted in *Friends of Promise*, Michael Shelden, p. 159.

'It was not only that he liked to drink . . .' - Sebastian Yorke, 'A Memoir', included in *Surviving: The Uncollected Writings of Henry Green* (Chatto and Windus, 1992), pp. 286–302. 'We simply went from station to station . . .' – Stephen Spender, *World Within World*, p. 305. 'I am firmly and increasingly convinced . . .' – quoted in *Elizabeth Bowen* (Avon, 1979), Victoria Glendinning, p. 152.

'Truffles and lobsters' – Evelyn Waugh to Laura Waugh, 19 September 1943. The quotation beginning '*grands crus* and truffles . . .' and Forster's phrase 'discredited pleasure' are found in Spender's essay-pamphlet 'Cyril Connolly'. 'You and me and Connolly . . .' – letter to Nancy Mitford, 31 May 1942.

'And trying to steal an advantage . . .' – *Desert Island Discs*, 2 April 1989. 'Commit suicide . . .' and proceeding quotations – Cyril Connolly, 'Comment', *Horizon*, December 1942. 'Expects to be directed . . .' – letter to Laura Waugh, 19 September 1943. 'Superficially all is well . . .' – 'Comment', October 1942.

'Rather too innocent . . .' – Adrian Wright, *John Lehmann: A Pagan Adventure*, p. 124. Extracts from memoirs by Erik de Mauny, G. S. Fraser and Alan Ross are collected in the anthology *Leaves in the Storm* (Lindsay Drummond, 1947).

'Master-propagandist, whose diatribes . . .' – Peter Quennell, *The Wanton Chase*, p. 14. 'Enormous portions of pasta . . .' and proceeding quotation – ibid, p. 16. 'They were invariably crowded . . .' and proceeding quotations – ibid, pp. 24–5. 'Lent an air of go-ahead culture . . .' – Anthony Powell, quoted in *David Tennant and the Gargoyle Years* (Weidenfeld and Nicolson, 1991), Michael Luke. 'Powerful morning pick-me-ups . . .' – *The Wanton Chase*, p. 25.

'Had a pleasantly occupied look . . .' and proceeding quotation – ibid, p. 25. 'A ferocious bird . . .' – ibid, p. 23. 'About his own existence he drew . . .' and proceeding quotation – ibid, p. 21. 'A refusal to be privately miserable . . .' – Stephen Spender, 'Being Young Poets', *Encounter*, July 1962.

'*Horizon*'s most lost of lost causes' – 'Comment', February 1943. 'There should be many houses . . .' – 'Comment', June 1941. 'Not only by professional poets . . .' and proceeding quotations, 'Comment', June 1940. 'We must remember that the life . . .' – 'Comment', January 1941.

'A veteran of Nazi Germany . . .' – Jeremy Lewis, *Cyril Connolly: A Life*, p. 364. 'Endure[d] him out of loyalty to literature . . .' – quoted in ibid. 'Two decades of dreams . . .' – Arthur Koestler, *Darkness at Noon* (Jonathan Cape, 1985), p. 123. 'What was frightening about these trials . . .' – George

Orwell, *The Collected Non-Fiction* (Penguin Modern Classics, 2017), p. 741. 'A strange bird on the periphery' and 'for an educated Englishman . . .' - quoted in *Cyril Connolly: A Life*, p. 365. The reactions to Koestler's story can be found on the same page. 'It is that he has contributed . . .' and proceeding quotation - 'Comment', October 1943. 'The Mixed Transport' is printed in that issue. Koestler's reaction is found in the 'Correspondence' section of the December 1943 issue. 'The deep, deep sleep of England' - Orwell, *Homage to Catalonia*, p. 196.

15. Men at Arms

'I have got so bored . . .' and 'It will be difficult . . .' - Evelyn Waugh diaries, 29 August 1943. 'Gratify ambitions' - ibid, 13 March 1942. 'I think we are the only mess . . .' - ibid, 28 September 1942. 'Off at extravagant angles' - ibid, 15 May 1943. 'By the end of the day . . .' - letter to Laura Waugh, 20 June 1942.

'I was born a mouthbreather . . .' and further quotations - Henry Green, *Pack My Bag* (Hogarth, 1992), p. 1. 'Assortment of Georgian left-overs' - Peter Quennell, review of *Put Out More Flags*, *Horizon*, May 1942. 'Dashed off to occupy . . .' and proceeding quotation - letter to Arthur Waugh, 5 December 1941.

'Magnum opus' - letter to Laura Waugh, 1 February 1944. 'Giant boredom' - letter to Laura Waugh, 28 September 1943. 'Am going to the Ministry of Information . . .' and 'fervent preoccupation which is absolutely . . .' - letter to Laura Waugh, 25 January 1944. 'How much I hate the army', 'very high quality' and 'a very expensive concoction' - letter to Laura Waugh, 1 February 1944.

Stephen Spender describes the uniforms of Cricklewood substation in *World Within World*, p. 268. 'My life seems completely wasted . . .' - quoted in *Stephen Spender: A Literary Life*, p. 283. 'Colitis, poor eyesight, varicose veins . . .' - ibid, p. 282. 'The government have more or less . . .' - George Orwell, *The Collected Non-Fiction*, p. 740. 'Been spending [his] time chiefly . . .' - 'War and the Writer', *Partisan Review*, January 1942. 'Was more a feeling that . . .' and 'we listen to jazz all day . . .' - quoted in *Stephen Spender: A Literary Life*, p. 285.

Spender's article on poetry in wartime is titled 'Poetry in 1941' and found in the February 1942 issue. Alex Comfort's response is included under 'Correspondence' in the May 1942 issue.

'Depicts the coalescence of private and public histories' - Michael Brett, introduction to *New Collected Poems*. Kathleen Raine reviews Spender's *Ruins and Visions* in the September 1942 edition of *Horizon*.

'As a kind of people's army . . .' - D. J. Taylor, *Orwell: A Life* (Vintage, 2004), p. 285. 'A popular militia, armed and politically conscious' - George Orwell, 'The Home Guard and You', *Tribune*, 20 December 1940. 'A pendulum swinging between extremes' - *The Thirties and After*, p. 98. 'Vulnerability, closeness to unkind realities . . .' - Spender, *Citizens in War, and After*, p. 35. 'Those which smelt like pear-drops . . .' and proceeding quotation - *World Within World*, p. 267. Spender describes his colleagues' attitudes to the war in his *Partisan Review* article of January 1942. The quotations from 'on the job' to 'you've been to Germany . . .' are from *World Within World*, p. 267.

'Dig his heels in and sulk' - quoted in *Stephen Spender: A Literary Life*, p. 277. 'So that people get used to . . .' - ibid, p. 276.

'Pillbox durability' - ibid, p. 287. Lucian Freud recalls living with Spender and Natasha in *The Lives of Lucian Freud: Youth*, William Feaver, pp. 143-5. 'One of a number of . . .' - ibid, p. 98.

Spender describes the fire service education scheme on p. 305 of *World Within World*.

'Here was the same experience . . .' - *The Blitz: Westminster at War*, p. 178. 'The contraceptives in the squares . . .' - Connolly's 'Letter from a Civilian', published in the September 1944 issue of *Horizon*. 'Be calm . . .' - quoted in Michael Shelden, *Friends of Promise*, p. 63. 'Almost with relief . . .' - Spender, 'Modern Poets and Reviewers', *Horizon*, June 1942. Spender talks with Natasha on p. 279 of *World Within World*. Their flat is bombed on pp. 307-9 of the same book.

16. Flying Bombs

'New, giant planes specially built for England' - *The Blitz: Westminster at War*, p. 93. William Sansom recalls the mood on 6 June 1944 on p. 184 of the same book. Cyril Connolly's 'Comment' is, as stated, for the June 1944 issue.

'At night they pulled bedclothes over . . .' - *The Blitz: Westminster at War*, p. 192. 'As it grew louder . . .' - *I Am My Brother*, p. 280. 'It was a magnificent performance . . .' and 'One grew hard about other people's misfortunes' - ibid, p. 281. Leonard Woolf's letter to John Lehmann is dated 23 October 1943. 'There were no windows and no ceilings . . .' - *The Journey Not the Arrival Matters*, p. 150.

'It just goes bowling thro' . . .' and 'exceedingly buzz-bomb conscious' - quoted in *Lost Girls*, D. J. Taylor, pp. 76-7. Connolly and Lys's make-shift shelter is described on the same page. 'But I don't care for flying bombs . . .' and proceeding quotations - 'Letter from a Civilian', *Horizon*, September 1944. 'Grey little fey little island' is a phrase of Connolly's from *The Unquiet Grave*, p. 50. 'Streets of Paris, pray for me . . .' - ibid, p. 62.

'The emotions have so little . . .' - Peter Watson, letter to Waldemar Hansen, 17 March 1952, quoted in *Queer Saint: The Cultured Life of Peter Watson* (John Blake, 2015), Adrian Clark and Jeremy Dronfield (eBook version). 'The red lane through . . .' - *The Unquiet Grave*, p. 96. 'Old-fashioned, cluttered, ramshackle furnishings' - *Queer Saint*. 'The doodles are so bad . . .' - ibid.

'On 8th September, with no warning . . .' - *The Blitz: Westminster at War*, p. 197. 'Much worse than the doodle-bugs' and proceeding quotations - *I Am My Brother*, p. 282. 'Conscious of the angels of death outside . . .' - *The Thirties and After*, p. 97.

'Light trickles drop by drop . . .' - *Citizens in War, and After*, p. 53. 'The walls of Hitler's empire . . .' - *I Am My Brother*, p. 291. 'Dare one begin to say "Till we meet"?' - ibid, quoted on p. 285. Christopher Isherwood's diary entry is dated 3 August 1944. Isherwood quotes from Connolly's India broadcast, and reproduces his response, in a diary entry for 10 September 1944. Lehmann describes the event of W. H. Auden's return to London on p. 288 of *I Am My Brother*.

17. City of Lights

'The quiet of hotel bedroom . . .' - *The Unquiet Grave*, p. 83. 'We love but once . . .' - ibid, p. 11.

Philip Toynbee's article 'Notes on the Literary Situation in France' is found in the November 1944 issue of *Horizon*. 'Music in Connolly's ears' - *Cyril Connolly: A Life*, p. 379. 'It is gratifying . . .' - 'The Battle of the Books', *Horizon*, January 1945. 'A single word like "*bouillabaisse*" . . .' - quoted in *Cyril Connolly: A Life*, p. 378.

'No other task is of any consequence' - *The Unquiet Grave*, p. 1. Connolly describes his visit to Paris in the May 1945 issue of *Horizon*. 'Fêted as tho' he were Voltaire returned' - quoted in *Cyril Connolly: A Life*, p. 391.

'I get a feeling of claustrophobia . . .' - *The Unquiet Grave*, p. 11. '*The Unquiet Grave* by now consisted . . .' - foreword to the Penguin Modern Classics reissue of the book.

John Lehmann describes his own visit to Paris in pp. 301-7 of *I Am My Brother*. W. H. Auden's lecture on the 'superiority of American culture', delivered to Stephen Spender, is described on p. 290. 'Like a jab from a blunt hypodermic needle' - ibid, p. 289. 'The two great Anglo-Saxon leaders . . .' - ibid, p. 293.

Spender's visit to Paris features in his *European Witness* (Right Book Club, 1946), in the section titled 'French Interlude'. The first ninety pages of that book are dedicated to his tour around Germany. The incident with the librarian is described in *The Thirties and After*, pp. 99-100.

18. 'Where are the war poets?'

'Don't forget that T. S. Eliot . . .' - *I Am My Brother*, p. 235. 'The nostalgic elderly schoolmasters . . .' - ibid, p. 238.

'Fighting men were treated simply . . .' - John Lehmann, *The English Poets of the First World War*, p. 37. 'His only true war poems' - ibid, p. 25. 'They hit exactly the right note . . .' - ibid, p. 27. Charles Hamilton Sorley is quoted on pp. 27-8 of the same book. 'Preternaturally good-looking' - ibid, p. 15. I found the transcription of William Ralph Inge's Easter sermon in the 5 April 1915 issue of the *London Standard*. Winston Churchill's obituary for Rupert Brooke is reproduced at https://exhibits.lib.byu.edu/wwi/poets/rbobituary.html.

Lawrence Binyon's 'The Ruins' was published in the October 1942 issue of *Horizon*.

Dylan Thomas's letter to Donald Taylor is, as stated, from 19 September 1944. 'Is there a chance of one . . .' - letter to T. W. Earp, 21 September 1944. 'Good old 3-adjectives-a-penny . . .' - letter to Vernon Watkins, 28 May 1941. 'Among cries and clatters . . .' - letter to Oscar Williams, 28 March 1945.

Paul Ferris describes the incident with William Killick on p. 208 of *Dylan Thomas*. Thomas's letter to Watkins is dated 28 March 1945. 'Things that scream up into the stratosphere . . .' - letter to Watkins, 27 July 1944.

'To want to allow myself . . .' - letter to Desmond Hawkins, 24 September 1939.

'I shan't know until I start . . .' - letter to Oscar Williams, 31 December 1944. William's book *The War Poets* was published in 1945 by the John Day Company.

'Best when read aloud . . .' - T. S. Eliot, *A Choice of Kipling's Verse* (Faber, 1941), p. 11.

'Could not fail to have . . .' - *The English Poets of the First World War*, p. 38.

'It is fashionable to exclaim . . .' and proceeding quotations - Cyril Connolly, 'Comment', *Horizon*, November 1949. 'By texture, smell, paper-weave . . .' - 'Comment', December 1949. 'A decade of our lives is quite enough . . .' - 'Comment', November 1949. 'One can perceive the inner trend . . .' - 'Comment', December 1949.

'Please tell me who is George Orwell . . .' - quoted in *Cyril Connolly: A Literary Life*, p. 350. 'Wrapped in an old camel-coloured woollen cardigan' - D. J. Taylor, *Orwell: The Life*, p. 414. 'Amongst the most terrifying books . . .' - quoted in *Auntie's War*, p. 321.

List of Illustrations

1. W. H. Auden and Christopher Isherwood, 1937 (Alamy)
2. Sir Jocelyn Lucas, 1959 (Getty)
3. Virginia Woolf, 1939 (Bridgeman)
4. John Lehmann, c.1936 (Getty)
5. Stephen Spender, 1945 (Getty)
6. Cyril Connolly, 1942 (National Portrait Gallery, London)
7. Senate House, London, c.1965 (Henry Grant Collection / Museum of London)
8. Virginia Woolf, 1938 (National Portrait Gallery, London)
9. Mecklenburgh Square, London, 1937 (© London Metropolitan Archives, City of London)
10. Leonard Woolf reading Virginia's diaries, 1965 (Gisele Freund / Science Source)
11. John Lehmann and Leonard Woolf, 1944 (Getty)
12. Dylan and Caitlin Thomas, c.1944 (Getty)
13. BBC Oxford Street, 1953 (Getty)
14. Interior of a house in Bedford Square (© London Metropolitan Archives, City of London)
15. Stephen Spender, c.1942 (Getty)
16. Blackout in Bloomsbury, London, 1939 (Alamy)
17. The veiled Eiffel Tower, Paris, 1944 (© Lee Miller Archives, England, 2021. All rights reserved. leemiller.co.uk)
18. Packing books in the blackout, c.1940 (Getty)

Acknowledgements

This was a lockdown book, and also my first attempt at writing a book. I can say without a moment's reflection that, should this project be deemed a success, it would not be so were it not for a large number of people frequently going out of their way to help. Many of those were on Twitter. I would like to apologise to them for being so forthright in my appeals. A frantic 'DM' is not a fair substitute for a drink or lunch and nor should it ever be accepted as one.

Writing non-fiction has shockingly little to do with the person in the chair, in front of the computer screen. To write even these two chapters about Cyril Connolly, a bag of letters had to be transported first from Worcestershire to Norwich and then northbound on to me. I would like to thank Matthew Connolly for being so obliging, and David Taylor for giving enthusiastic support to one who is an ignoramus in all areas where he is an expert. The same can be said for Peter Parker and Adrian Wright. Adrienne Rusinko has been busily gathering and scanning documents at Princeton University Library while I sit comfortably at my desk. For everyone who has previously written on this period (Sylvia Topp, John Sutherland, William Feaver, Richard Davenport-Hines, Duncan White, Hilary Spurling), this book clearly would not exist without its accomplished ancestors.

I would like to thank my editor Maddy Price, who certainly had better things to do with her time than read this book many times over. Victoria Hobbs was the first person in the industry to put their faith in a young, unqualified author. Alan Samson extended a similarly warm welcome. Even further back, Sarah Bakewell on the Oxford University Creative Writing Masters course was kicking opening chapters into shape.

I am thankful to Steve Hunnisett, Darcy Moore, Lesley A. Hall, Francesca Wade (all via Twitter!) and Steve Hancock for valuable titbits of information and important advice.

Finally, I want to say that our collective memory of the Second World War is no accident. It requires lots of people to still be engaged in their own private detective work. Politicians are fond of telling us what they wish the war to have meant. Don't listen to them: the war meant a million different things to a million different people.

Index